THE MODERN LIBRARY
of the World's Best Books

THE COMING STRUGGLE
FOR POWER

>>

The publishers will be pleased to send, upon request, an illustrated folder setting forth the purpose and scope of THE MODERN LIBRARY, *and listing each volume in the series. Every reader of books will find titles he has been looking for, handsomely printed, in unabridged editions, and at an unusually low price.*

>>

THE COMING
STRUGGLE FOR POWER

>>

BY

JOHN STRACHEY

WITH A NEW INTRODUCTION BY THE AUTHOR

>>

BENNETT A. CERF · DONALD S. KLOPFER
THE MODERN LIBRARY
NEW YORK

Manufactured in the United States of America
Bound for THE MODERN LIBRARY *by* H. *Wolff*

CONTENTS

v

PART V

THE POLITICAL STRUGGLE IN BRITAIN

PART VI

COMMUNISM

INTRODUCTION TO THE MODERN LIBRARY EDITION

THE QUESTION OF FORCE AND VIOLENCE

ON March 13th, 1935, in a suburb of Chicago, Illinois, I was arrested by two officers of the Federal Government of the United States. The charge was that I had advocated the overthrow of the United States Government "by force and violence."

Since no statement of mine advocating such action could be produced, the Federal authorities relied upon numerous passages in my books and articles in which I had described myself as a communist. For, they argued, syllogistically, all communists advocate the use of force and violence. Strachey is a communist. Therefore Strachey advocates the use of force and violence. This reasoning on the part of the Federal authorities served to raise a question which, I believe, agitates the mind and conscience of almost every man and woman who is concerned with the present condition of the world.

Do the communists advocate that the establishment of a new social system shall be accomplished by violent means? This question concerns especially those people who are today convinced that much at any rate of the communist case against capitalism is true, and who, therefore, feel that some change in the basic organisation of society is necessary. Such people often feel, however, that they can give no support to the communists if this often repeated charge of favouring violence is justified.

But the communists do not advocate or desire the use of force and violence.

This assertion may well seem incredible to those who are alone familiar with communist views as these views are described by the communists' most bitter opponents. We have all read a thousand times in the capitalist press that the communists favour violence, that this is the chief difference between them and the Socialists, that the communists openly "preach revolution."

None the less, I repeat, the communists do not, nor ever will, advocate or desire the use of force and violence.

It seems, then, that the communists have very different views on this question to those usually ascribed to them. In order to define precisely the communist position on the question of force and violence it will be necessary to raise three issues. First, we must enquire whether it is possible for us to live peacefully under our present social order. Second, we must define the difference between *predicting* that violence unfortunately will occur at certain junctures in human history, and *favouring* or *desiring* the occurrence of such violence. Third, we must deal with the question of whether or not there exists in Britain and America democratic machinery capable of effecting basic social changes by peaceful and constitutional means.

In the first place, then, what are the presuppositions of those who accuse the communists of advocating violence? The assumption which is always made, though usually tacitly, is that we live today in a kind of Eden of peaceful co-operation and social harmony. The one feature, it is implied, which mars the otherwise idyllic scene is the existence of certain criminal lunatics, labelled "the communists" who, for some totally inexplicable reason, are bent on turning an existing Arcadia into a scene of destruction, carnage and rapine.

Now if this assumption were true, who would not condemn such destructive fanatics. If it were true that we could, if we would, live in peace and plenty under capitalism, then, beyond a doubt, almost everybody would be ready to reprobate those who seemed likely to disturb us.

But does this assumption of an existing system of social and economic harmony bear any resemblance to the reality of the present world? To ask such a question is unfortunately to answer it. The world of our epoch is racked by extraordinary, intense and ever recurrent outbreaks of violence, both within and between every capitalist state. No capitalist community is free from social conflicts within itself, from strikes, lockouts, and demonstrations of the unemployed and the underfed. And all these events involve varying degrees of violence, frequently including the loss of life. Dwarfing, however, even these recurrent outbreaks of social violence, the shadow of a new outbreak of the incomparable violence of general war advances upon us. This veritable inferno of existing or impending violence (and no Eden) is the social scene upon which the communists appear. If, then, the communists were so mad as to "advocate violence" they would be undertaking an altogether redundant task. The presuppositions of the accusation against the communists are totally misleading. For that accusation to have weight it must be *possible* for us to live in peace under capitalism. And this is precisely what is impossible.

Shall we, however, be told that the existing violence of our world is merely the result of the baleful activities of the communists themselves, that if only the communists were imprisoned or exterminated life under capitalism would become an idyll? Even in regard to the violence of industrial disputes such a contention is manifestly absurd to everyone who knows anything of modern industrial life. (This allegation of communist responsibility for every industrial dispute is made by the same people who, on other occasions, never tire of telling us of the insignificance, incompetence and impotence of the communists.) But it is impossible even to suggest that the communists are responsible for the far greater violence of past, present and future capitalist wars. Hence there is no doubt that whatever the communists are *preaching,* other people are here and now *practising* a constant use of violent methods for attaining their ends.

What then, must be our surprise when we discover that the people who are, demonstrably, responsible for the extreme violence of our times, are the very people who so loudly arraign the communists as disturbers of the peace? For, after all, so long as capitalism exists, the capitalists and their spokesmen must bear the full responsibility for both the social and the international violence which their system visibly involves. They are quick enough, in all conscience, to claim credit for the achievements of the system. They must carry the burden of its liabilities also. They have the power; they have created the world in their own image. They cannot escape responsibility for what it is like.

These censors of the communists are, then, the very men who are leading our whole civilisation straight upon its destruction in a new world war. They are the capitalist statesmen, who turn aside for a moment from the pressing business of drilling their police or building their tanks, their battleships and their bombers, to raise pious hands in holy horror at the wickedness of the communists who (they say) "advocate violence."

In the hearing before the District Director of Immigration which followed my arrest and which, apparently, resulted in the proceedings against me being dropped, I was asked to summarise my position. I replied as follows:

"I do not believe in or favor force or violence. What is true is that I cannot conceal from myself the fact that force and violence have been used and are now being used by the capitalist class all over the world. I believe that this use of force and violence has happened and I admit that I believe that it may happen again, but that does not mean that I am in favor of it happening again or that I advocate it in any conceivable way.

"On the contrary, I believe that the undeniable fact that an ever-growing use of force and violence hangs over the world to-day is a nightmare to me and to all decent people. As we sit at this hearing to-day the continent of Europe is on the brink of an outbreak of force and violence between the capitalist governments of that continent. First Europe and then the whole world is, in the opinion of every expert adviser, about to be plunged, if not this year, then in some future year, into the inferno of international capitalist war; and I cannot conceal from you, Mr. Inspector, that I consider that for any capitalist government to-day to accuse me of advocating force and violence is an insolent presumption."

So far I have sought to demonstrate two simple propositions. First, that the spokesmen of the capitalists paint a preposterously misleading picture of the world when they accuse the communists of disturbing a peaceful and harmonious scene with the advocacy of violence. Second, that the very men who make this accusation are themselves engaged, not indeed in the advocacy of violence, but in its ceaseless practice.

These facts discredit the particular persons who habitually accuse the communists of advocating violence. But they do not necessarily disprove that accusation itself. It may be that the capitalists have no shred of right to make the accusation; yet the accusation itself may be true. But every responsible communist repudiates the truth of the accusation itself. What in fact then is the nature of communist doctrine on the difficult question of force and violence?

The communist is, and always must be, the champion of civilisation against all and every form of barbarism. He actively works for the banishment of all forms of force and violence from human affairs. He must desire, above everything, the establishment of a form of society in which social and international peace becomes, for the first time, possible. But he knows that such a harmonious society is not possible till the factories, the fields, and the mines, have been taken out of the ownership of a numerically small class and made the common heritage of man. Hence, in working for the abolition of capitalism, he is convinced that he is attempting to achieve the one thing which can make peace possible.

But, we may be asked, if this is so, why do not the communists abjure, utterly and immediately, the use of force and violence? If it is true that a peaceful society is their aim, why do not they set an example of absolute pacifism, quietism and non-resistance now? This sleek, ingenious objection comes readily enough to the lips of the better-informed apologists of capitalism. And, in truth, nothing more convenient to the capitalists can be imagined than that their opponents should take up such a position. "How delightful it would be," the capitalist statesmen wistfully reflect, "if only everyone who cannot agree with us would accept the principles of non-resistance. Then, we should be assured that whatever we did, we should never encounter any inconvenient opposition."

As long ago as 1884, Frederick Engels, one of two co-founders of the modern communist movement, answered them in a letter to Auguste Bebel, a leader of the German working class. The passage is worth quoting, not only in order to show that the communist position on the question of force and violence has always been the same, but also because Engels reminds the capitalists of something which they now often forget; namely, that they too have been in their time great makers of revolutions; that capitalism has not been in existence for ever, but was on the contrary established everywhere by the violent overthrow of feudalism, the social system which preceded it.

Engels speaks of Europe, but his words apply even more directly to the United States, which have an avowed and explicitly revolutionary origin.

"Throughout the whole of Europe the existing political situation is the product of revolutions. The legal basis, historical right, legitimacy, have been everywhere riddled through and through a thousand times or entirely overthrown. But it is in the nature of all parties or classes which have come to power through revolution, to demand that the new basis of right created by the revolution should also be unconditionally recognised and regarded as holy. The right to revolution *did* exist—otherwise the present rulers would not be rightful—but from now onwards it is to exist no more."

What, Engels continues, is the position of those German political parties which will only allow the German worker's party political rights on condition that it renounces all thought of armed resistance in any circumstances?

"What is the position of the parties?" Engels writes.

"In November 1848 the Conservative party broke through the new legal basis created in March 1848 without a tremor. In any case it only recognises the constitutional position as a provisional one and would hail any feudal-absolutist *coup d'état* with delight.

"The Liberal parties of all shades co-operated in the revolution of 1848-1866, nor would they deny themselves the right to-day to counter any forcible overthrow of the constitution by force.

"The Centre recognises the church as the highest power, above the state, a power which might in a given case, therefore, make revolution a *duty*.

"All these are the parties which demand from us that *we, we alone of them all*, should declare that in no circumstances will we resort to force and that we will submit to every oppression, to every act of violence not only as soon as it is merely formally legal, legal according to the judgment of our adversaries—but also when it is directly illegal. Indeed no party has renounced the right to armed resistance, *in certain circumstances,* without lying. None has ever been able to relinquish this ultimate right."

The reader of this introduction who is unfamiliar with communist thought will, I fancy, be feeling a growing sense of bewilderment.

"If all this is what the communists really think, and believe," he will be saying "why do they often talk about revolution, and, if I am not mistaken, about the necessity of revolution?"

These questions of the nature of revolutions and of the likelihood, or inevitability, of their future occurrence, figured prominently in one stage of the dialogue between the U. S. Inspector of Immigration (Mr. Zucker) and myself in Chicago. The Inspector read out a passage from this book, to be found on page 359 of this new edition.

Inspector: I read into the record the following excerpt found on pages 357 and 358:

"The coming of communism can alone render our problems soluble. A working-class dictatorship can alone open the way to communism. A working-class dictatorship can only be successful if the workers as a whole achieve a clear understanding of the historic destiny of their class. And this understanding, in turn, cannot be developed unless the working class succeeds in organising its most conscious and clear-sighted members into that indispensable instrument of the workers' will, a Communist party. The assumption of power by the workers can occur by means of a revolution alone: by means, that is, of an event which takes place over a limited number of years, and of which there may be a critical moment such as the conquest of the existing state apparatus in a capital city which can be 'dated' to a given week of a given month of a given year. The coming of communism itself, however, after the achievement of working-class power, must be a gradual process. And it is only gradually, with the emergence of communism, with the creation—and that, we may be sure, only by Herculean labours and painful sacrifices—of the essential economic basis for a classless society, that the problems which to-day threaten civilisation with eclipse will actually be solved."

Inspector: Have you anything to say?

Strachey: Yes, I would call your attention to the fact that once again I am expressing my view, for what it is worth, of the way in which social and political events take place, whether we like it or not.... Then, I think that I had better explain what the word "revolution" means in the passage cited, as this is not clear without the context. The word "revolution" means the transference of political power from one social class to another. Now there have been instances in history in which such a transference of power has taken place without any violence occurring. Such revolutions have been called peaceful revolutions and the leading historical example is the transference of power from the British aristocracy to the British middle or capitalist class by the "Reform Bill" of 1832.

I further call your attention to the fact that on line 3 of page 358 I state that there may be a critical moment in such revolutions "such as the conquest of the existing State apparatus in a capital city." I do not see how any student of history, whatever his views, could deny that there may, unfortunately, be such moments in the future just as there have been in the past, but this does not mean that he wishes or advocates that such critical moments should occur.

If I might use a simile I might say that when sitting on the seashore, I might take the view that the tide would come up and wet my clothes but this would not mean that I should favor or advocate the coming up of the tide.

I believe that this difference between *predicting* that the abolition of the capitalist system will involve violence, and *advocating* or *desiring* such violence, is a distinction of primary importance. For no one could deny that communists do predict that violence will take place. But such prediction does not mean that they have ever dreamt of advocating or desiring violence. The best demonstration of this vital point was made by R. Palme Dutt in his periodical the *Labour Monthly* in 1926.

Dutt is the leading communist thinker of the English-speaking world and is a responsible member of the Communist International. Hence his words will serve to shew that the repudiation of the accusation of favouring force and violence was not the suddenly evolved casuistry of a communist author under arrest, but is the consistent attitude of all communist spokesmen. Dutt is answering the familiar accusation of favouring force and violence which Mr. James Ramsay MacDonald (at that time the leader of the British Labour Party, but now Lord President of the Council in the British National Government) had just preferred against the communists with particular venom.

Dutt wrote:

"It is a lie to say that the revolutionaries advocate violence and civil war. What the revolutionaries say is that the issue of bourgeois violence confronts the working class, and has got to be faced, and that the workers cannot afford to put their trust in the capitalist law and the capitalist state machine for their protection. And events are daily proving the truth of this.

"Imagine a parallel. Suppose a scientist to declare, as a result of his investigations, that an earthquake will take place in England within ten years, and that all houses, unless reinforced in a certain way, will be shattered. It is reasonable to doubt his conclusion, to discuss his evidence, to examine the facts and see how far they bear him out. But the MacDonald method is different. Mr. MacDonald would say: 'Infamous scientist! He is in favour of earthquakes. He wants to shatter all our houses. Out with him! Earthquakes are all very well for countries like Japan: but we do not want them here. We like to live at peace. We have always lived at peace. Expel this scientist! Vote for me and no earthquakes!' And amid general applause, by an overwhelming majority, a resolution would be carried denouncing the scientist and denouncing all earthquakes. ... Neither the communists, nor any other section of the working-class movement, desire or advocate violence or civil war in any form. Communism stands for the abolition of every form of coercion and every form of violence. Compared with communism, the Quaker opposition to violence is half-hearted and insincere, for the Quakers rest on capitalism and the capitalist apparatus, draw their wealth from it, are mixed up with their financial investments and shares in the whole of imperialism and its daily violent subjection and coercion of the majority of the human race. Communism alone proceeds along the correct method to remove coercion by removing the causes of coercion. But this process involves struggle in the existing world of struggle; and communism teaches that, so long as the working class submits to bourgeois violence, so long they not only do not escape struggle but, by the continuance and expansion of capitalism and imperialism, the sum-total of violence in the world is increased."

Many readers, and in particular those who desire fundamental social change, but who believe that such change will come about gradually and peacefully, will, no doubt, still be feeling dissatisfied with our presentation of the problem. They may maintain that the whole issue has been misstated.

"There is really no question," they may say, "of any passive submission to the will of the capitalists. It *is* demanded of the communists that they should pledge themselves in all circumstances not to use violence. But this will not leave them helpless. On the contrary there exists in Britain and America a well-developed democratic, constitutional procedure by which social changes, no matter how far-reaching, can be effected. The communists have only to convince the majority of the electorate that their case is sound for them to be able forthwith to use the existing state machinery, first for gaining valuable concessions for the working class and ultimately for the expropriation of the capitalists and the organisation of production for use on a socialist basis, and none will say them nay."

The communist answer to this assertion is, quite simply, that neither part of it is true. It is not true that there exists to-day in England and America democratic, constitutional machinery which can be used for the abolition of capitalism and the organisation of socialism. It is not even true that our existing democratic machinery can be used to win significant reforms without it being first paralysed and then abolished altogether by the capitalists.

We are not here concerned with the preposterous disadvantages under which the workers of a capitalist community must suffer if they seek to use the existing democratic machinery for their purposes. I am taking no account of the fact that the wealth of the capitalists gives them a 99.0 per cent monopoly of all our modern and perfected means of influencing and confusing men's minds; that the press, the radio and the cinema are just as much the private property of the capitalists as are the coal mines or the steel mills; that the schools and, to a very great extent, the pulpits, too, can be, and are, used to prevent men from becoming conscious of the possibility of any alternative to capitalism; that democratic electoral machinery responds only when it is approached with hard cash in hand. For it is true that all these enormous difficulties can be, and have been, in some measure overcome by working-class political parties, operating in capitalist democracies. The sheer, intolerable pressure of capitalism upon the workers is so great that working-class political parties of an ostensibly anti-capitalist nature have struggled into existence almost everywhere. And they have in some countries, such as Germany, for example, won sufficient votes to attempt to use the existing machinery of the state to win concessions, and to look forward to using it for the abolition of capitalism itself.

Now, whenever and wherever this situation has developed to a point at which its power has begun to be called into question, the capitalist class has immediately scrapped the democratic and constitutional system and has resorted to rule by what we have come to know as the method of fascist dictatorship.

This point emerged towards the end of my examination in Chicago. The following passage from a book of mine, called *The Menace of Fascism* was read:

"Indeed the conditions of political life in a modern capitalist democracy may well be compared to a game of cards. The capitalists sit playing against the workers. For a number of years the game goes on in a perfectly orderly way. Neither side shows any signs of trying to tamper with the rules (to alter, that is, the framework of the Constitution). And then it becomes apparent that the stakes of the game have gradually been raised until all that either side possesses is now at hazard. (The economic crisis, that is, has grown worse and worse until the inescapable issue has emerged: either slow starvation and ruin for the workers, or the taking of the means of production from the capitalists.)

"Moreover, when this point is reached, another fact also becomes apparent. It becomes apparent that under the existing rules of the game the workers would, sooner or later, (and in spite of all the advantages of the capitalists)—the workers by sheer, overwhelming weight of numbers would, if the democratic system were preserved, acquire a parliamentary majority. Will the capitalists, in these circumstances, scrupulously preserve the rules of the game and meekly hand over their whole property as the forfeit? To ask such a question is surely to answer it. Of course they will cheat; of course they will tear every constitution in the world to shreds rather than allow their property and privileges to be taken from them. Who wouldn't?"

Q. Mr. Strachey, do you have any comment to make on that passage?

A. Yes, this passage does, I think, state as clearly as I have been able to state it anywhere, my view of what is only too likely to happen. I call the Inspector's attention to the fact that it is once more merely a statement of what it seems to me is likely to happen, but it does put my view, which has grown in my mind as a result of my experience in European politics, that it is the capitalists who resort to force and violence, if and when they see their position encroached upon by the workers' use of the democratic and constitutional methods of political change.

I do not see how anyone reflecting upon the history of Europe since the War can possibly deny that everywhere and always the capitalists have unhesitatingly resorted to violence just as soon as they felt their position being encroached upon in any way.

The communists had persistently predicted that this would be so. They had persistently warned the working class that if they relied upon the capitalists paying the forfeit, if they lost the democratic game, they were deluding themselves most tragically, and would find themselves suddenly face to face with an outbreak of capitalist violence and terror with which they would be quite unprepared to deal. The communists, undoubtedly, made themselves unpopular by repeating this truth: those labour leaders who preferred to tell the workers that there was no danger of the capitalists ever breaking the Constitution, that there was no need for the workers to prepare for civil conflict, were able, by this pleasing message, to win great popularity.

Indeed those leaders have in many countries retained their positions at the head of the working-class movement, right up to the moment at which they have been engulfed by that wave of capitalist violence which they had declared to be inconceivable. These labour leaders have not hesitated to join with the capitalist propagandists in twisting the meaning of the communists' warning to the workers to prepare for the use of relentless violence against them, into an advocacy of the use of violence, or even into a criminal appeal for violence for its own sake. The leaders of the British Labour Party in particular make great play with Lenin's well-known warning of heavy civil war in England. R. Palme Dutt, in the article from which we have already quoted, answered them as follows:

"Lenin spoke of heavy civil war in England. But when that quotation is given, it is never given in full. Lenin did not say, 'Let us make civil war in England.' Lenin did not say, 'Hurrah for civil war in England.' Indeed, on another occasion, Lenin declared, as Marx had declared before him, that if the revolution could be carried through peacefully in England, then speed the work. But what Lenin did say was that he was convinced that the revolution could not be carried through peacefully in England. And for this statement he gave sober, matter-of-fact evidence and reasons, which have to be gainsaid before the conclusion can be gainsaid. What Lenin did say was that the English workers must 'prepare for,' *prepare for,* not seek for, aim at, hope for—*prepare for* the necessity of winning their freedom, not through 'easy parliamentary victories' but through 'heavy civil war.' That was a sober estimate of the future by the greatest working-class strategist in history. It was a scientific statement, backed by evidence, representing the outcome of his life's work, study, thinking, and experience of the working of social forces."

Lenin wrote of England. He judged that the British capitalists were sufficiently tough, tenacious and relentless to fight by any and every means to retain their power and privileges. Some Americans may feel, perhaps, that the American capitalists are different; that they are mild, democratically minded men who would certainly obey the dictates of popular assemblies even to the point of dispossessing themselves of all their wealth. The American Communist Party, on the contrary, takes the view that the American capitalists have shewn themselves to be fierce, arbitrary and relentless fighters for their class interests. The American communists believe that there is no possibility of the American capitalists allowing the transition from one social system to the other being effected without violence. They believe that it is the duty of every responsible person to warn the American workers of this fact; they believe that those who prefer the popular course of telling the American workers that they can rely upon the democratic machine to protect them do but delude and betray those workers most cruelly.

This then is the communist view of the use of force and violence. Let us attempt to summarise it.

The communist regards the banishment of force and violence from human affairs as one of his principal objectives. He believes, moreover, that the achievement of social and international peace is possible, after the tormenting coercions of capitalism have been abolished. But this hope and vision of the future does not blind him to the realities of to-day. He sees around him a world in which unending and ever-growing violence is being used. He has analysed the causes which are driving man against man in a deadly and fatal struggle both within and between every capitalist community. He is convinced that outbursts of this violence must become ever more frequent and more frightful until they have drowned civilisation itself in human blood, unless their cause is removed. And the cause of contemporary social and international violence is the private ownership of our fields, factories and mines and their operation for profit.

The communist is further convinced that for the workers to pledge themselves in no circumstances to use force in the struggle to abolish this system would be to make the abolition of capitalism forever impossible. For the capitalists, all experience teaches, do not hesitate to use any degree of violence in order to perpetuate their system. But the perpetuation of capitalism means ever-recurrent outbreaks of world-wide violence on a scale compared to which the violence involved in the abolition of capitalism is infinitesimal. Hence every communist is convinced that his is the only way in which force and violence can be immediately minimised and ultimately abolished.

I believe, then, that those who are held back from acceptance of communism by horror at the violence which, they believe, communism involves, misunderstand the issue. It is not communism which involves violence. It is capitalism which tortures the world with violence. Truly communism cannot claim to be able to abolish this violence by a magic stroke. But communism does shew men the way by which the causes of human violence can be eradicated step by step. I do not, of course, suppose that this summary discussion of a great issue will, in itself, convince the doubtful. But if it succeeds in making its readers observe, and reflect upon, the way in which world events develop during the coming years, it will have served its purpose. For then, I think, these events themselves will infallibly demonstrate the truth of the communist contention.

JOHN STRACHEY

July, 1935.

PREFACE

This book attempts to combine an economic and social analysis of capitalism with a description, based on my experiences in British politics, of the methods by which the system is to-day maintained. For example, the book includes on the one hand discussion of current monetary theories, and on the other an estimate of the respective roles in world affairs of the Conservative and Labour parties of Great Britain. For there can surely be little doubt that an attempt thus to combine an analysis of theory and a description of practice is by far the most fruitful method of discussing the contemporary situation.

In these pages, the reader will find no mention of the part played by their author in the political events which are discussed. But it is perhaps necessary to say a word of comment upon a political career which, though of little interest to anyone except myself, has been devoid neither of incident nor variety. I believe that no excuse is either possible or is, for that matter, necessary, for the mistakes, waverings and contradictions of my political past. For he who supposes that an Englishman of the present day can find his way either to intellectual certainty or political consistency, without doubts, hesitations and errors, shows little appreciation of the gravity or the complexity of the present situation.

Many of these pages contain evidence of the road along which I have travelled. Indeed, the reader will see at once that the argument of this book follows the course of its author's transition from old views to new. And it may well be that any value which it possesses will depend to some extent on precisely this fact. For this method of approach to an intellectual position unfamilar to most Englishmen may prove useful as an introduction to the subject.

For this reason, if there should be any Marxist or communist readers of this book, I should desire to make it clear to them at the outset that it does not profess to be a scientific, still less an authoritative, exposition of communist views. The book is the result of the participation in, and the observation of, British politics during the last ten years, combined with such economic and historical information as I have been able to acquire.

PREFACE TO THE REVISED EDITION

THIS new edition contains a note on the striking events which have taken place in America in the period since February, 1933, the date of the book's first publication.

I have put these observations on the policies now being pursued by the American Administration at the end of the book rather than at the beginning because, being brief, they necessarily assume much which is discussed at length in the body of the book. I fear that a reader who approached this new chapter without having first gone through at any rate the earlier chapters of the original text might consider the present addition to rest upon arbitrary and unproven economic assumptions.

Chapters II to VII, in particular, contain the attempt to establish the economic presuppositions on the basis of which alone the political analysis contained in the new section is legitimate.

J. S.

PART I

THE BIRTH OF CAPITALISM

CHAPTER I

THE STRUGGLE FOR THE MARKET

THE capitalist system could not develop until the market was established.

"Socialism," defines Mr. R. G. Hawtrey of the British Treasury, "is a solution of the economic problem based upon the authority of the State instead of upon the motives of the market." Entirely inadequate in his definition of socialism, the eminent British official is more penetrating in his implied description of capitalism. Thus the converse of his original proposition would be more accurate. We might define capitalism as "a system which attempts a solution of the economic problem by reliance on the motives of the market." This definition is still, however, imperfect. For, although the existence of the market is unquestionably essential to capitalism, it is to-day, as much of this book will be devoted to showing, no longer the most characteristic feature of the system. Nevertheless, the economists are right when they tell us that the free market, the establishment of the principle, that is, that money can buy what it likes, how, when and where it likes, was the essential prerequisite of the capitalist system. And the best proof of this fact is not to be found in any analysis, however refined and subtle, of society as it exists, but in the history of how this society arose.

Men become fully conscious of what they have done only some centuries after they have done it. And only lately has it been realized that what Western man accomplished by some four hundred years of struggle, between the fifteenth and the nineteenth centuries, was the establishment of the free market.

So natural to us is the existence of the market that we find it hard to grasp the fact that there was a time, not so very long ago, when there was no market. We are familiar with the idea of feudalism. Yet we often fail to realize the essential fact about feudalism, the fact that you did not in the Middle Ages (and do not to-day wherever feudalism still exists) live by buying and selling. Again we learn from our historians of the struggle for "freedom." British historians especially regard modern history as nothing less than the story of some great liberation. They do not, however, tell us for what purpose this freedom was won. And yet there is no doubt about it. The freedom for which Henry Tudor broke with Rome, for which Hampden and Cromwell fought, for which Halifax and Churchill betrayed James, which Locke began to make conscious, for the sake of which Jefferson and Washington defeated George III, and for which Grey reformed, was the freedom to buy and to sell. The whole long struggle for Liberty, about which the historians tell us everything except what it accomplished, was a struggle for that freedom of contract, which is the legal expression of the free market.

Undoubtedly, that struggle began long before men were fully conscious that the free market was to be the result of their efforts. Thomas Cromwell did not anticipate Adam Smith. Men do battle for immediate ends. Gradually, however, the consciousness of the object of their struggle dawned upon those who took part in it. If the object of Thomas Cromwell was simply the aggrandisement of his friends, and the destruction of monopoly but a means to that end, his great-great-nephew Oliver had already begun to know better. And by the end of the eighteenth century Jefferson and Paine knew very well for what they fought.

It is at length beginning to be admitted that this struggle and nothing else is what European history since the Reformation has been about. Not that the contest was confined to the economic field. On the contrary, it spread to every aspect of human consciousness. For its object was nothing less than to create a complete new basis for human life. Consequently it had first of all to supplant the extant form of society, on the basis of which men had hitherto existed. We call that previous social system feudalism. Now feudalism was an elaborate system of human relations, which had been in existence for several centuries and possessed a highly developed and elaborate equipment of political, æsthetic and religious institutions and ideas. During long centuries men had learnt just how it was necessary to live (that is, to act, to feel and to think) under the conditions of those times. And these conditions were those of communities in which agricultural production was by far the most important economic activity; in which the possibilities of transport, even for a few miles, were so limited that the importance which the exchange of commodities (the market) could possibly have was very small; in which the methods of production, and of such distribution as there was, were simple handicraft; in which, above all, these methods changed very little.

And yet the methods of production did change. The scholars now inform us that as early as the twelfth century the germs of change can be detected. In fact, of course, feudalism was never completely and perfectly established in practice. Long before any of the numerous systems of society under which man has lived have been fully established, the signs that they will some day themselves be superseded become visible. As the slow centuries of the Middle Ages wore on, the cultivation of the soil became more rational, methods of transport improved, roads grew a little more passable, ships a little more seaworthy. At length (some time about 1400) the possibility, the actual physical possibility, of the exchange of goods on the great scale, the possibility of the market, became considerable.[1] But that did not mean that the modern free market was forthwith established. On the contrary, deep-rooted and formidable institutions, fixed ideas, religious, political and social, all perforce founded on the impossibility of the market, stood flatly in the way. Accordingly they had to be, and were, dynamited out of the way. It took, however, some four centuries to do it. The stormy life of Europe in these latter centuries has been the history of the process. For once it had started, the pace of change quickened decade by decade. No sooner had human institutions been adapted so as to admit of the possibility of a market of a given economic importance, itself made possible by previous technical developments, than these technical developments themselves made another and far longer stride forward, so that almost before they were properly established each new set of human institutions became out of date. For history in an

[1] By an exchange of goods "on the great scale," is implied such things as the existence of whole communities, maintained by means of foodstuffs brought from a distance and exchanged for, say, an important raw material, or for manufactured goods. Isolated examples of such a condition of things may be found in antiquity and in the Middle Ages around the shores of the Mediterranean, because bulk transport by coasting vessels which never went out of sight of land was possible on the waters of that inland sea in even very primitive vessels, and before the principles of navigation were discovered. Elsewhere, as in the great mediæval fairs for example, there were exchanges of goods brought from a distance, but they certainly could not be the basis of life.

epoch of rapid technical and economic change, is no smoothly flowing river.

In modern Europe it has been rather a river of blood. The sword and the sword alone has sufficed to cut through and break up the old social forms and make room for the new. Swords, however, need arms to wield them. The free market did not establish itself. It needed human instruments to fight for it. And these instruments could only be the new men whose lives had come to depend on the existence of the young market. These new men were the merchants, the "middle" men. For why should feudal lord, feudal serf, or established urban guildsman, fight for the market? These new men, however—middle men—half way between lord and serf, who slowly grew in number and in power with the insidiously growing market, they could fight for the market, they could and they did so fight even though at the beginning they did not know for what they fought. They fought it seemed to them merely for the right to live. But their right to live had become dependent upon the maintenance and the growth of the market. Thus when they fought for themselves they could not help fighting for the market. Small wonder then that they grappled desperately with every interest which their instincts told them was hostile to the principle of free exchange.[1]

This book has no direct concern with the early history of the market. Our only concern is to note that the market *has* a history: that it is not a "natural" condition of affairs ordained from heaven, from everlasting to everlasting. On the contrary, the market is an artificial human institution, established by five centuries of embittered and sanguinary struggles on the part of the nascent middle classes of Europe. This vast "war" extending in time over several centuries, and in space over the whole of Christendom, culminated, it is now recognised, in three violent and obdurate engagements. These were the Reformation, which in Germany and England breached the smooth, unscalable wall of Roman Catholicism; the English Rebellion of 1640 and Revolution of 1688, which for the first time gave the middle class political power in a great state; and the French Revolution, which finally broke the back of European feudalism.

[1] Not that the merchants did much of the fighting in person; they used their wealth to get others to fight for them.

The first of these pitched battles for the market occurred on the apparently distant and unrelated field of religious belief. When the clash came, the new "middle" men of the Reformation had already up to a certain point established their markets. The first marked technical revolution had taken place. Navigation had suddenly bounded forward. Agricultural practice (because, it is suggested, of the shortage of labour after the Black Death) had improved. It had been discovered that both food and wool, the two staple products, could be produced and distributed with a smaller expenditure of human labour than formerly. Above all, the improvement in transport by water made the exchange in bulk of these staples for the first time profitable. Up till then the impossibility of bulk transport had confined exchange to luxury articles (such as spices, silks, jewels) with a very high value in proportion to their weight and bulk.[1]

With the improvement in navigation the specialized production of staples at a distance from their market became possible and profitable. There were, then, more goods to exchange and more possibility of exchanging them. But a whole world of social relations stood in the way. And these established social relations found at once their supreme expression and their trusty support in one massive and puissant institution, the Catholic Church. How, for example, could the English peasants be dispossessed and the great sheep runs, which were to produce the wool for the "staple trade," be enclosed, if an unshaken Church held some of the best land itself, and supported actively the maintenance of the old feudal relationships on the rest? How could the quick, shrewd and independent spirit of traders be acquired if a supreme and authoritative Church, with all educational institutions in its hands, taught that happiness in this life and salvation in the next, were not determined at all by individual actions but by a perfect trust in the opinions and instructions of the nearest priest?

It is true that the priests of the Catholic Church taught that salvation was obtainable by works rather than by faith. But "works" did not in the least signify the estimable conduct of the individual, his thrift, his industriousness, and the like. Works meant adequate donations to the Church. It is true that the theological champions

---

[1] Or to such things as salt, which while necessaries, are only necessaries in small quantities, and which are only found at isolated points on the earth's surface, and so *must* be transported.

of the new men of the market, the ecclesiastics of the Reformed Churches, preached that men might be saved by faith alone. But this was essentially an assertion of religious individualism: a reassurance to the Protestants that they could die in the grace of God without having to utilize the costly services of Rome.

For the oldest and greatest monopolist of all, Holy Church herself, the monopolist in God, had to be assailed if the new middle men, the soldiers of the market, were to grow and prosper. Let no one suppose that such a phrase as "the monopolist in God" is some far-fetched flight of fancy. God—the blessings, the forgiveness, the indulgences of God—was in the sixteenth century a commodity, or rather a service. And the provision of God's mercy was an essential service to the men of that time. At that particular stage in the development of the human consciousness, and it is a stage which has occurred before in history and may occur again, some impressive form of religious consolation was urgently necessary to men. Without it they could not bear life. And Holy Church had monopolized, had most effectively "cornered" God's mercy. The Church had succeeded in making men believe that God dealt out His mercy only through an accredited priest. And in a transaction of this special character, when the want to be satisfied was a purely subjective one (though none the less real on that account), if men believed that a thing was so then indeed so it was in fact. Accordingly, as everyone knows, indulgences, sold at good, stiff, monopoly prices, were one of the most important commodities of the epoch. Holy Church sold them, but, as usual, had some difficulty in collecting her receipts. Accordingly the great contemporary European banking house of Fugger was in the habit of discounting them at a quite reasonable price. (It may perhaps be some consolation to those great London banking and acceptance houses of to-day, which are desperately trying to collect loans from Eastern Europe, to remember that their illustrious predecessor, Messrs. Fugger, also burned its fingers very badly in Germany, in the matter of defaults on indulgences.)

If we envisage the condition of human consciousness 500 years ago, if we envisage the intimate and essential part which religious institutions then played in daily life, we shall have no difficulty in understanding the economic necessity of the Reformation. It was doubly essential to the new-born middle class of Europe to break the power of Rome. It was essential for the most concrete and worldly reason: for the Roman Church held so much of the best land that the establishment of private profit-making agriculture, producing goods, such as wool, in bulk for exchange on distant markets, was impossible until the abbeys and the convents had been dispossessed. And it was equally essential from an ideal or spiritual point of view in order that the men of the new middle class should have the religious assurance that was necessary to them.

These tasks were accomplished in two different ways in different parts of Europe. In England during the first half of the sixteenth century the Roman Church was destroyed outright, a new State Church set up, and the Church lands made over, by that much underestimated middle-class revolutionary, Thomas Cromwell, to the new private landlords. In the Rhineland, on the other hand, the Catholic Church bent before the new forces and was not broken. The power of Rome, but not of Catholicism, was destroyed. The Church was decentralized; the local bishops set up as independent sovereigns, who themselves proved hostile to the regular orders and, more or less gradually, transferred the land to private ownership. (And here, at the outset, we come across the indissoluble connection between private property and free exchange. For there could be little buying and selling until the custom-restricted, semi-communal property of the Middle Ages had been transformed into private, individual, unrestricted property.)

The curious may trace the slow retreat of the Catholic Church before the growing power of the men of the market in the successive changes in the teaching of the Church on the question of usury. For if buying and selling connote private owning, owning in turn connotes lending. The growth of trade is impossible unless the capital necessary to its conduct can be hired by the traders. But the hiring out of capital for gain was usury: and usury was sin. So said the Church in the heydey of its power. But as in fact the technical possibility, and then the actual practice, of trade grew greater and greater, and as all efforts to suppress it failed, it became necessary for the Church to find reasons why usury might sometimes be allowed. First it was suggested that, since it was clear that one man might freely lend another capital with which to conduct a trading enterprise, if at the end of the period of the loan he received back nothing more than the original amount, then also the lender might accept, without offence, a recompense for any risk of loss that might be entailed. This was the doctrine of *Damnum emergens*. But this did not suffice: other loopholes for the charging of interest were needed. So the schoolmen invented the doctrine of *Lucrum cessens*. This meant that the lender might charge interest to cover the loss of not employing his capital himself in trade. It might be thought that this doctrine would serve to absolve most creditors. But the Church was in the end forced to go still further. Accordingly the doctrine of *Contractus trinus* was evolved. *Contractus trinus* was a threefold contract between lender and borrower: under its provisions the borrower first entered into simple partnership (which had always been allowed) with the lender: the borrower then insured the lender against loss of principal, and finally he insured him against loss of profit on the enterprise. It must have been an exacting capitalist indeed who did not find his requirements met by the provisions of one or other of these doctrines.

How necessary was this preliminary religious revolution to the growth of vigorous buying and selling may be gauged from the fact that in the one country in Europe, in Spain, where the Catholic Church was neither bent nor broken, until 1931, capitalism has never flourished. For what after all is Protestantism but the free market in God? What are Liberty of Conscience, and the principle of Justification by the unaided Faith of the individual, but claims that every man may go and fetch down God's mercy from on high, if he can, for himself? Protestantism is theological private enterprise. Thus the original monopoly, the great double monopoly of the Roman Church over the best available land and over men's spirits, was broken.

One hundred and fifty years later in the epoch of the next pitched battle for the market, in the England of 1640-1688, the terrain of the engagement had shifted (though by no means completely) from the religious to the political field of consciousness. The Crown, instead of the Mitre, had become the highest expression and the chief support of monopoly, of power without the consent of the now formidable middle class. The contest of King against Parliament was a contest between men who stood by the older ways of life against the ever-growing power of the new middle class. For the parliamentary leaders, Pym, Eliot, Hampden and Oliver Cromwell, were, of course, an agricultural middle class. These great squires, some titled, some commoners, were not feudal overlords but busy, bustling, agricultural entrepreneurs. After all their title-deeds ran back no further than Bosworth field. They did not dislike being considered to be noblemen: but they were far from refusing to be in fact merchants and tradesmen. They were the forerunners of the "Whigs," that remarkable class of Englishmen who, uniquely, have known how to combine most of the privileges, dignities and splendours of feudalism with the enterprise, vigour and acquisitiveness of commerce.

The economic motivation of the Rebellion of 1640 and the Revolution of 1688 is not far to seek. The wealth of the new commercial squires and landowners, of the merchants, of that whole new class the very existence of which now depended on the maintenance and expansion of the free market, had grown quite out of proportion to their political power. They felt threatened, and were threatened, by the arbitrary and uncontrolled power of the King; they were restricted by his monopolies and annoyed by his taxation. Their discontent was not due so much, however, to anything that the King had done to them (1600-1640 were for them exceptionally prosperous years), as to the fact that for just so long as he was out of their control he was dangerous and therefore intolerable. The King was a piper whom they paid and they would not even listen to his tune until they had called it. Moreover, although the King had in fact done little or nothing to them, it was apparent that he or rather that his man Strafford, intended much. For in each of the great European states in the seventeenth century someone, either king, or nobles, or middle class, had to act. A critical point in the development of the market had arisen. The interchange of goods, specialized production, an increasing scale of production, and the enormously increased concentration and accumulation of wealth which these things connoted, had at length made the existing form of State totally inadequate. It was imperative that someone should organize the modern State. An administrative staff, an effective and professional judiciary for the enforcement of contracts, a permanent and professional armed force for the promotion of the nation's commercial interests without its frontiers, and the suppression of dissatisfied classes at home, had become urgently necessary. Thus the burning question in every one of the rising European states was the question of *who* should create, and consequently control, this new and formidable apparatus of coercion. Different states found different answers. In France, Cardinal Richelieu's success decided that it should be the royal power which should do the job. In Britain, Strafford's failure denoted that it should be the upper middle class which should, after fifty years of struggle, forge and then wield the weapon of the modern State machine.

Thus the struggle in Britain from 1640 to 1688 was a struggle to decide which of two opposing interests should take the power necessary to create a State apparatus adequate for the new possibilities of production and of exchange. It was not in the least a question of the revolt of an oppressed class against a tyrant. It was a question of two well-matched opponents struggling for the glittering prize of being able to create and to possess a State machine which should henceforward make them almost omnipotent for the furtherance of their own economic interests. It is this fact which has enabled the orthodox school of British historians, who, naturally, express the views of the middle class, since it was in the end victorious, to pretend that the struggle was not waged for material ends at all. Mr. G. M. Trevelyan, to-day the leading British historian of this school, tells us that "in England the revolutionary passions were stirred by no class in its own material interest. Our patriots were prosperous men, enamoured of liberty, or of religion, or of loyalty, each for her own sake, not as the handmaid of class greed. Hence the moral splendour of our Great Rebellion...." (*England Under the Stuarts.*) Two pages later, however, Mr. Trevelyan forgets about the "moral splendour" and tells us what the Great Rebellion was about. "Finch," he says, "was the judge who at Hampden's ship money trial had first roused Englishmen to their senses by proving that their property was not their own but the King's." There is nothing like a threat to property for rousing moral splendour in prosperous patriots. Hampden, one of the richest men in England, would not pay his taxes because he and his class had determined that Britain should not be organized into a modern State until and unless they were able to do the organizing. For the British middle class felt itself equal to the task. It was just because they were growing richer and stronger, and yet were given no increased share of power, that the English middle classes rebelled. For although it is demonstrably true that men do not invariably act according to their individual and immediate economic interests; that classes do not rebel only because they are starving (and that no one ever suggested that they did), yet it is such growing disproportions as these between the real strength of a class and the amount of political power which is allotted to it, which cause those redistributions of power between sections of the community which are called, if they are rapid, revolutions, if gradual, reforms. And it is a change in economic conditions, a change in the methods of production, that is, which first shifts the balance of strength in the community, and so starts the whole movement.

It was precisely the growing wealth and power of the English squires, the agricultural entrepreneurs of the period, and of the merchants, that enabled them to break the power of the monarchy. It is perhaps an example of that political capacity which English Historians are ever ready to attribute to the English people, that the Whigs—as this great coalition of the champions of the market came to be called—grew to realize that it was not monarchy itself which had to be destroyed. A king was a perfectly harmless kind of a person, so long as he was *their* king. What was obnoxious, what was intolerable, was the principle of absolute monarchy, the claim that the king ruled by divine right, in other words by his own right; and what was equally obnoxious was the principle of popular monarchy, the claim that the king was the guardian and the father of *all* his subjects, and not merely of his property-owning subjects. Such claims would certainly never do. But there was no reason on that account to fly to Cromwellian extremes of republicanism. Moreover, long before the end of the seventeenth century it had become apparent that the English middle class was itself subdivided. The Whig nobles, the great merchants, Mr. Trevelyan's "prosperous patriots," had little sympathy with the small shopkeepers and yeomen, who had finally won the civil war. The new Model army was the *party*—in the most modern sense of the term—of the lower middle class, and the Commonwealth was its brief period of power. So little, however, had the Whig grandees in common with it that they preferred even a Stuart restoration. Accordingly, when in 1688 the Stuart became odious to them, they had no intention, and no need, to make another new model and another Commonwealth. The glorious revolution was anything but glorious for the lower middle class. Its interests and ideas were totally ignored in the resulting "settlement," and they remained all through the eighteenth century a dissenting and sometimes rebellious faction. The "prosperous patriots" actually preferred a monarchy, so long as they controlled it, to a republic. They disliked the principle of absolutism, not the institution of monarchy. These subtleties had been arrived at by the English Whigs of the second half of the seventeenth century, not so much by ratiocination as by nearly half a century of trial and error. They applied them in practice in 1688 and the result was that England got a start of just a century over the rest of Europe as a commercial nation. She had taken the lead in the race for the establishment of political institutions calculated to foster and promote the growth of the free market. For what after all is the substitution of a king by Act of Parliament for a king by divine right, but the application of the principle of the free market to monarchy.[1]

The French revolution and its consequential wars (the period from 1789 to 1815) saw the last and greatest of the pitched battles in the war for the free market on the European continent. There have been, of course, two pitched battles in the struggle for the free market upon the American continent, the War of Independence and the Civil War. The American Declaration of Independence was one of the great manifestoes of the free market, and Jefferson was at once one of its best theorists and sturdiest crusaders. The American Civil War, on the other hand, was the last great armed struggle fought on behalf of the free Labour market. For the American middle class could not enter fully into its enormous heritage until the dark feudalism of the Southern States had been destroyed, any more than the European middle class had been able to flourish until European feudalism had been destroyed. Once again, as in England a hundred and fifty years before, it was the increasing wealth and strength of the members of the French middle class

[1] The Dutch middle class got into power even before the English. But from sheer lack of territory and population, Holland could not become a modern great power. After an obstinate struggle designed to prevent the growth of the commerce of England, the Dutch burghers had perforce to make common cause with their rivals against the menace of a still absolutist France. And in such an alliance they inevitably took second place. Thus the exception of Holland does not in fact affect the truth of the statement that the English middle class, by the settlement of 1688—in which they actually borrowed a Dutch king—got a clear lead of the middle classes of all other nations capable of becoming great powers.

which enabled them, which in fact forced them, in defence of their wealth, to take power. By this time the issues had become clearer. The terrain of the struggle it is true was still predominantly political. But a consciousness of the economic foundation was growing. Did not Danton as his first act of power propose "that all ownership, whether territorial, individual, or industrial shall be maintained for ever"? How can the market be free, how can men buy and sell, unless free purchase and sale, and not Governmental or noble distraint, is the only method by which goods pass from hand to hand? Danton, that great bourgeois, put his finger on the very crux of the matter—on the relationship of property and the market.

Up till the end of the eighteenth century, the sanctity of private property had seemed the best guarantee of the liberty of the market. It was above all necessary, Locke, the great Whig theorist, had explained, that men should enjoy the fruits of their own labour: that they should reap where they had sown. Their property was to be the result of their labour; neither more nor less. Labour and property were to be identified.[1] Assuredly, however, men cannot live like so many Robinson Crusoes solely on the fruits of their own toil. Specialization, the division of labour, can multiply a hundredfold the general wealth. How therefore is the division of labour to be reconciled with the great necessity of the sanctity of property, with the assurance that every man shall enjoy the full fruits of his own labour? Fortunately, the new theorists believed, that greatest of all blessings, the free market solved the problem. By fair exchange, by sale and purchase, a man might enjoy if not the actual physical fruits of his own labour, yet the full *value* of that labour; if not the actual corn he had sown, yet clothing, shelter and all the other necessaries of life to the full *value* of his corn, which he had freely sold upon the market.[2]

---

[1] See, for example, Locke's *Treatise on Civil Government*, chapter v., where property is justified by explaining that it arises from men converting natural objects to their own use through their labour.

[2] Thus Adam Smith, in *The Wealth of Nations*, Book I., chapter iv., tells us that a man "supplies the far greater part of his wants by exchanging that surplus part of the produce of his own labour, which is over and above his own consumption, for such parts of the produce of other men's labour as he has occasion for." And again, *The Wealth of Nations*, Book I., chapter v., "The value of any commodity to the person who possesses it, and who means not to use or consume it himself, but to exchange it for other commodities, is equal to the quantity of labour which it enables him to purchase or command."

These theorists hardly paused to enquire, however, whether property might be of two different kinds. They did not ask whether the private possession of the objects without which those things which satisfy the wants of man cannot be produced, whether in a word, private property in the means of production, would have the same happy results as did private property in the fruits of labour. They did not differentiate clearly, for example, between private property in land and private property in corn. Nor was their failure to do so accidental. For the new theorists were the theorists of the men whose private property the land had in fact become. For them it was enough that the freedom of the market seemed to guarantee the sanctity of private property, by reconciling it with the necessary division of labour. So Locke and Smith thought, and Danton acted. And the thoughts and the deeds of the great middle class for which they stood conquered the whole earth.

The men of 1789 killed feudalism in France. The Frenchmen of the first decade of the nineteenth century broke the back of feudalism in Europe. Napoleon led the great crusade of the free market. He incarnated the fully evolved European bourgeois. We only fail to appreciate this fact if we let the garish splendour of the Emperor obscure the workaday genius of the First Consul. It was the Napoleon of the Code, however, who accomplished the mission which history had allotted to him; this was the Napoleon who began his first proclamation with the words: "The Revolution has returned to the principles with which it began: it is at an end." Danton must have applauded from the tomb, for the original principles of the Revolution had been nothing else but the realization of the battle-cry of the middle class—that the rights of private property are eternal and inviolable. It was because wherever he went he carried this slogan with him, and for this reason alone, that Napoleon was able to play football with the crowns of Europe. Into every country his armies brought the free market.[1]

It is at first glance, perhaps, surprising that in the eighteen hundreds, Napoleon, the crusader of the free market, should have found his supreme antagonist in the British, who a hundred years before were the market's best champions. In fact, however, the

[1] Stendhal's *Rouge et Noir* makes us realize what that meant to the young men of the new middle classes of Europe, still half stifled by feudal absolutisms.

interactions of the English and French middle classes between 1640 and 1840 give an instructive picture of the way in which the historical process works. First, as we have seen, England took the lead: the whole system of social relations, the political institutions and consequently the prevailing ideas, in the England of the seventeenth and eighteenth centuries were far freer, were far better suited, that is to say, to buying and selling, to the growing predominance of commerce as the national way of life, than were the institutions of France. How could it be otherwise, when the English aristocracy had gone into trade and the English merchants had been ennobled? Yet that unique coalition of forces, a commercially minded aristocracy and an aristocratic mercantile class, that great "Whig interest," which dominated England for over two hundred years, which gave her an enormous lead in the acquisition of wealth; which, in a word, founded the British Empire, had its limitations. The Whigs were too bound up with an older world to kill outright either the monarchy, or the remnants of feudalism. For, as we have seen, it was the upper middle class which had made the British revolution. Naturally, therefore, the Whigs were ever menaced on the left by the lower middle class which had largely fought their battle for them in the civil war, and had been bilked in 1688. The existence of the dissenters and the Wilkesites was a reminder that liberty should never be allowed to get out of hand. Thus the English Whigs were convinced that things must not be pushed to extremes. Justice demanded, they agreed, and the institution of private property ensured, that every man should enjoy the fruits of his own labour. There was, however, the question of inherited landed property. There were, for example, the innumerable acres of the Duke of Bedford, himself the father of all Whigs. It might be difficult to show that the Duke's gargantuan rent-roll was indeed the exclusive product of the labours of the House of Russell. Decidedly things must not be pushed to extremes. In other words, the liberty which had been established in eighteenth-century England was a liberty for the big merchants, the great landowners and the trading aristocrats. They and they alone possessed the freedom of the market.

The Frenchmen of 1789 had other ideas. The surviving absolutism of the French monarchy had prevented the emergence of a class of really big bourgeois and had at the same time kept the aristocracy out of trade. And so the French champions of the free market, when they finally took power, seemed entirely strange, and not a little terrifying, to most of their well-established English counterparts. For these Frenchmen, being in the towns for the most part petit bourgeois, and in the country small proprietors, had no use for monarchy or feudalism at all. And off went the heads of both king and nobles, a proceeding most shocking to Mr. Burke, who had succeeded Mr. Locke as the chief British theorist of Liberty. The result was, however, that in fifteen years the French bourgeoisie had more than caught up with the English middle class; had established a degree of freedom of exchange unknown before; had elaborated in the Code Napoleon a system of social relations scientifically adjusted to a modern middle-class state; had, in a word, finally done away with feudalism. The aristocratic, commercial, constitutionally monarched England of 1688-1789 had been a menace to its contemporary absolutist, semi-feudal France. They had struggled all through the eighteenth century for the vast heritage of Spain. For Spain had proved incapable of emerging even to the French degree from the fetters of feudalism. Britain had been on the whole successful just because she was less feudal than her rival. But now, in the period 1789-1815, the roles were suddenly reversed. France, equalitarian, petit bourgeois, republican, or commercially imperial France, revealed by contrast a relatively feudal Britain: menaced her power and wealth and was soon locked with her in desperate struggle.

The British coalition of ennobled agricultural entrepreneurs and merchant princes, the great Whig interest, was, however, a formidable opponent. It could even afford in its struggle with the revolution to allow its small Left wing (the famous "hackney-carriage full") to split off under Fox and show sympathy with the revolutionaries. Meanwhile the main body, with Burke, coalesced with the Tories, who by then had lost most of their old-world anti-commercial notions.[1]

After a struggle that strained but did not in itself break the old governing class, the revolution was apparently beaten and Napoleon destroyed. Britain produced in Arthur Wellesley, Duke of Wellington, the very incarnation of her "system." He summed up the British eighteenth century, just because he was not by any means an exclusively feudal personage. On the contrary, there was nothing

[1] William Pitt had been an apt pupil of the Edinburgh economists.

anti-commercial about him. He and his brother, Lord Wellesley, had been servants of the East India Company before they were servants of the State. For Britain's ultimate victory was due to her wealth. And this wealth was the result of a century of relatively free market conditions.

It is possible to observe how in fact British economic predomi-nance exerted its decisive influence. The Napoleonic system first began to weaken because the French armies which had burst out over Europe had gradually, during the Empire, ceased to be the deliverers of the middle classes of Germany, Italy and Austria; or, at any rate, they had become extremely expensive deliverers. Na-poleon had to make the delivered nations pay every penny of the cost of their liberation. For the resources of France could not pos-sibly have stood the strain. Hence the rise of nationalism which after 1810 began to give the Emperor such trouble. Moreover, the French armies had now penetrated to the two countries of Europe, to Spain and to Russia, where there existed only the feeblest begin-nings of a middle class. Hence, Napoleon found neither in Moscow nor Madrid that solid base of support which he had used success-fully in every other capital of Europe. Britain saw her opportunity and sent an army to re-deliver Spain from her former liberator. Wellington's army, however, would have been no more popular in the Peninsula than were the French, if it had not been for the cardinal fact that while the French lived on the country, Welling-ton's men paid for everything. And Britain's economy was suf-ficiently strong, owing to its imperial profits, not only to keep an army for five years in Spain, but to pay enormous subsidies to her European allies. She thus enabled the semi-feudal monarchies of Europe, whose own resources were exhausted, to do most of her fighting for her. (Britain's wealth has always enabled her to do a good deal of her fighting by proxy. Subsidies and mercenaries founded the British Empire.) Thus one may say that it was Arthur Wellesley of the East India Company—a "nabob" amongst generals —whose Indian victories were bringing home enormous profits, who beat the French, rather than that august personage His Grace the Duke of Wellington. At Salamanca, Vittoria and Waterloo, the Duke capitalized the gains of Seringapatam and Assay.

Waterloo, however, from the point of view of Wellington and his peers, was an empty victory. All through the eighteenth century

Whig freedom was doing something more for Britain than foster the large-scale agriculture and the half-plundering commerce of the aristocratic merchants. The relatively free market conditions of distribution permitted a growing concentration of the various handicrafts by which the needs of the population for industrial products were met. And, with that concentration, the change in the actual methods of production which had been slowly going on since the middle ages, suddenly gathered an altogether new speed and momentum. Productive technique—human command over nature—was able to make certain critical strides forward and modern mechanized production came to birth in Coalbrookdale in Shropshire, beside the Clyde, at Hockley Brook in Birmingham and in the valleys of Lancashire. So decisive a change in the economic foundations of a society cannot take place without necessitating a political reorganization. Moreover, the persons who benefited by the former political system will always be sure to dislike the change. There will, therefore, be a conflict of interest between them and those persons whose interests are bound up with the establishment of the new methods of production. In this instance the rise of mechanized British industry produced a working class: more immediately important in its political consequences, it produced a new middle class, unrelated to the old coalition of ruling classes.

This new industrial, as opposed to commercial, middle class found itself excluded from the rights and privileges of the State. Together with the new industrial working class, which on the whole followed their leadership, the new excluded lords of cotton and of iron set about the task of acquiring a political position adequate to their new economic status. They found important allies in that Left wing of the old Whig interest which, at the time of the French Revolution, had broken away from the main body of the governing class. And, in 1832, Grey and Russell passed the Reform Bill and admitted them to power. With perfect appropriateness it was over Wellington, himself, as the last Prime Minister of the forces of the older order, that they triumphed. From a social standpoint, the Reform Bill avenged Waterloo. Just as the failure of the Restoration, and the success of the Revolution of 1830, showed that a semifeudal absolutism could not be restored in France, so the Reform Bill proved that the epoch of the great British alliance between the aristocratic agricultural entrepreneurs and the merchant adventurers was over, and that a new epoch of the dominance of the industrial middle class had begun. The battle for the free market had been won.

It has been well said that all distinctions in nature and society are unstable and to a certain extent arbitrary. Just as in the heyday of feudalism there was a good deal of buying and selling, so at the height of the era of the free market, there were many fixed human relationships: moreover (and this will form a major theme of these pages), long before the last feudal stronghold was destroyed the first of the new enemies of the market—the new monopolists—had arisen. For no type of social order has as yet completely monopolized human relationships.

This undoubted fact has led some historians to deny the existence of all these historical categories—feudalism, capitalism, the free market, the middle class, the aristocracy, the workers—of which we have been speaking. There are really no such things, we are now told. There is just "history," a vast undifferentiated, homogeneous mass of facts which cannot possibly be analysed or classified in any way. Thus it is impossible to come to any conclusion on any subject at all. Our reply must be that, in spite of the undeniable fact that historical categories are never absolute, it should be possible for even an historian to detect a difference between the England of 1840 and the Rome of 1300, between the outlook upon the world of Saint Thomas Aquinas and that of Mr. Jeremy Bentham. It is quite true that the world of 1840 still contained conditions which would have been familiar to Saint Thomas, and that the world of 1300 nurtured shoots that Mr. Bentham would have regarded as hopeful. Is it necessary, however, to deduce on that account that there was no such thing as feudalism and that there is no such thing as capitalism?

A more serious question remains. Can we accept the general view of the course of history which is adopted in these pages; can we accept the hypothesis of this chapter as to how and why feudalism turned into capitalism, into something, that is, very much like its own opposite? The first answer to that question is that the discovery of historical truth is a more complicated matter than had been supposed. "This then is my truth," remarked Zarathustra. "Now, tell me yours." Historical truth for, say, the working class of Great Britain, may be something rather different from historical truth for the professional historians. We have been taught by the physicists that the position of the observer is an integral factor in the characteristics of the thing observed. The perspective of history is long. But the angle of vision is very important. This, however, can be said confidently. The view of history here adopted is a hypothesis which gives sense and coherence to the human past. If we reject it, then we must retire with the agnostic historians to bury our heads in enormous heaps of meticulously collected and quite unrelated facts; or, as they themselves are beginning to recommend, give up as vain the whole quest for the truth and return with the æsthetic biographers to the art of story-telling.

CHAPTER II

CAPITALISM AND THE MARKET

By the middle of the nineteenth century the battle for the market had been won. Sale on the market had become the predominant and characteristic object for which goods and services were produced. The middle class of Europe in the four preceding centuries of sanguinary struggle had done its work. In order to make room for the market, in order to render everything in life susceptible to sale and purchase, nearly every convention, every social relationship, every element of conscious co-operation, or of permanent, legal dependence, had been shattered. All men, they were now assured, were at last "free and equal": they were to approximate as nearly as possible to perfect social atoms, without ties or impedimenta, whether human or divine, bent only on one activity, namely, to produce in order to buy and to sell. Everything else, it was assumed with unparalleled confidence, would very shortly be added unto them.

Such was, of course, the theory rather than the practice of the victorious middle class. Actually, the freedom of the market was by no means universal. Feudal survivals existed everywhere (except perhaps in the United States after the victory of the industrial middle class in the civil war). In Eastern Europe, the market was never freed from feudal lumber; in France, however, the job was done with logical thoroughness; and in Britain, in spite of the survival of many feudal forms, a legal and social system was established by the new industrialists which was designed to afford the very maximum freedom of exchange. The great British extremists of the theory of the free market, Bentham, McCullough, Senior and their followers appeared. And in Cobden the market found its Saint Paul, for he preached also unto the Gentiles. At length, the last logical step was taken and the principle of the free market was extended beyond the bounds of the community. Its claim was transformed from being a claim of perfect freedom of contract and exchange between individuals within the state, into a claim for freedom of contract and exchange between states, and between individuals in different states. The theory of the free market became the theory of the free world market; became the theory of free trade.

It was perhaps natural for the European middle class to dance a dance of triumph. The war whoops and the hosannas of their spokesmen, however, do not make very pleasant reading to-day. (It is difficult for us to comprehend, and it is painful for us to remember, that Lord Macaulay, for example, was reduced to a state of lyrical optimism by the contemplation of the growth of the town of Torquay.) It is their horribly shallow optimism which now renders somewhat disgusting the writings of the great middle class economists and historians of a hundred years ago. They were too ready, indeed they were determined, to mistake the unparalleled good fortune of themselves and of their class for a proximate millennium for all mankind. (One could hear just the same opinions in our own time, and more naively expressed, in the America of 1921 to 1929.)

In Great Britain about the year 1860, the principle of free exchange must have seemed to a man of property to have something infallible about it. A detached observer, it is true, might have had some difficulty in recognizing in the existing state of affairs the ideal community of freemen to which the seventeenth and eighteenth century prophets of Liberty had looked forward. Every man, it must be remembered, was to have been perfectly free of, and legally equal to, every other. Naturally, however, they might make willing contracts between themselves by which they should exchange their goods and services. Thus, they were to enjoy the advantages both of an almost complete social independence and of close economic co-operation. The Lancashire of the eighteen-sixties did not perhaps correspond in all respects to this ideal. Perfect equality before the law did not always seem very efficacious in preventing death from starvation and overwork in the case of British freemen who chanced to be cotton operatives, while it might have been observed that the British freemen who chanced to be mill owners were entirely immune from these accidents. And the operatives, benighted creatures, prized their undoubted freedom of contract so lightly that they were always badgering Parliament to restrict their liberties—to take away, for example, their undoubted constitutional right to work for fourteen hours a day. This was peculiar. But it was incidental. And British property-owners, keeping their eyes firmly fixed upon themselves, were entirely convinced that very little now remained to be done except to convert the whole of the rest of mankind to their point of view.

Human life, however, turned out to be a more complicated matter than the English burghers of the nineteenth century supposed. Hitherto, we have emphasized the destructive struggle of the middle class against feudalism. That struggle, we have said, was fought in order to establish the principle of free exchange: to dissolve every tie, except that of free contract, between human beings. Is it possible, however, for men to live in a kind of social vacuum, without any social system at all, regulating their affairs wholly by means of private contracts between themselves? Such was the implication of the theorists of the middle class. Admittedly, some authority was needed for the enforcement of these private contracts. And is not this authority the nucleus of a new social system which the middle class must set up for itself after it has destroyed feudalism? As we all know, the middle class has created an elaborate social system which is universally known as capitalism. In this chapter, it will be our task to examine the birth process of this new social system; to show how the establishment of the free market led on to the development of modern capitalism.

The first question which we must ask is, how was it that a social system founded upon the principle of free exchange, which was established by the breaking down of almost all social ties, was yet able to provide for that high degree of human co-operation which modern methods of production obviously require? For observe how large an amount of human co-operation is needed in an industrial society. We may best appreciate this point by comparing an industrial to a peasant society. Now an industrial society differs from a peasant society in two ways. In the first place, in a peasant society nearly everybody works at the production of the same things. Each peasant produces his own food, and, in the older peasant societies, most of his clothes and household necessities. Society consists of numerous and almost identical units all engaged on the same tasks.[1] Contact between such units need be comparatively slight. Let us

---

[1] These units may sometimes be households, sometimes villages within which there exists a conventional and hereditary division of labour.

now contrast this state of things with the picture presented by an industrial society. In an industrial society the very first thing we notice is that each unit is producing different things. One factory is making boots, another paper, another motor-cars, another steel, another tin cans, another railway engines, another ships, and so on in great variety. Economists call this system the division of labour. It is obvious that such a society cannot exist for a day without continual contact between all these producers. Men cannot live by tin cans alone. As everybody knows, an industrial society in fact lives by perpetual contact and co-operation between these different producers. Now, and this is the point, the extant social system must somehow provide for this high degree of social co-operation. The producers of corn, boots, houses, paper, ink, steel, ships, printing machines and so on and so on must somehow be got together. For if these producers do not somehow or other co-operate, there is no way of ensuring that the right proportions of each of these things are produced, or indeed of ensuring that some of them are produced at all. Society might suddenly, for example, find itself with far too much paper and no ink at all.

But there is another and equally important way in which an industrial society differs from a peasant society. Not only does each peasant produce the same things as the other peasants, but also he produces them by himself. On the other hand, not only does each producer in an industrial society produce different things, but also he produces his particular product, not alone, but by association in work with hundreds or thousands of other men. In an industrial society, then, each producer is no longer a single human being, or a single human family, as in a peasant society. The productive unit is a factory: the producer, that is, is an association of hundreds or thousands, or to-day, of tens of thousands, of different human beings. The Ford worker, for example, performs one tiny operation, such as checking the clearance of a valve tappet, as the half-finished product flows past him on the conveyor belt. Yet tens of thousands of Ford workers in the Detroit plant between them make one thing only, an automobile. And collectively they make one every few seconds. Compare this to the work of an individual peasant, who successively and without any outside co-operation, ploughs, sows, and reaps his harvest.

Here then is another job, and a heavy one, for the social system of an industrial society. Not only must such a social system some-how provide for social co-operation between different producers, it must also provide for the actual day to day, and minute to min-ute co-operation necessitated by the working together of thousands of human beings *within* each producing unit. Obviously, the social system of an industrial society is going to have to be a far more complicated and effective thing than the social system which may have been all that was wanted for a peasant society.

Now, as we all know, that social system which we call feudalism was the prevailing system of the peasant societies of the middle ages. Under the feudal system, the degree of social co-operation necessary for the peasant society of the middle ages was provided for in a quite obvious and rough and ready manner. The peasants were grouped into manors (in England) and were made to pro-vide by extra work for a lord, to protect them, and for a priest to minister to them. A little less obviously, but still quite simply and understandably, they had to provide by a tax, often levied in kind, for a king and his court, and for a few judges; for, in fact, the very simple kind of social apparatus appropriate for the small de-gree of social co-operation necessary to peasants.

Capitalism, on the other hand, is the social system set up by the middle class and it is indissolubly associated with industrialism. It has had to face the two jobs which we have just defined. It has had to secure a hitherto unparalleled degree of social co-operation between the different productive units, and at the same time has had, somehow, to make it possible to mobilize thousands of sepa-rate human individuals for common work in factories, to associate them together in order to create our huge modern units of pro-duction.

How has capitalism accomplished these two tasks? Once we have grasped the nature of the question, the answer, whether we agree with it or not, is quite easy to understand. The confusion arises only if we do not know what question is being asked and answered. The importance of asking the question of how it is that capitalism achieves this double feat of social co-operation is emphasized when we recall again that capitalism was established by the same process which dissolved all previous forms of social co-operation. All these fixed legal bonds which bound peasant to landlord, landlord to over-lord, overlord to king, king to pope and so on were smashed by the triumph of the principle of free exchange. All the more, therefore, capitalism had to find new and effective methods, not only to replace, but immensely to improve upon, the old methods of social co-operation which it destroyed. We are confronted by the paradox that while the principle of free exchange destroyed almost all the extant social mechanism, it is associated with a technique of production which obviously requires a far more complex social mechanism; which imposes upon society the two new tasks of organization which we have just defined. How then does capitalism accomplish these two tasks? Let us first consider the question of how it provides for the co-operation of the different independent producers, each producing different things. For this, we shall see, is the easier task.

Under a capitalist system, this form of co-operation is provided for, as everybody knows, by the mechanism of price. It is certain, it is claimed for capitalism, that just the right proportions of the different things society needs will be produced; that there will be just enough paper to go round and just enough ink to cover it. For if too much paper is produced, the price will go down, and the paper-makers will be discouraged, and vice versa. In a word, the law of supply and demand will operate and all will be well. The method is too well known to need further words.

It must be observed, however, that the capitalist system achieves this automatic and unconscious form of social co-operation between the producers of different things only by turning everything that is produced into what is called "a commodity": that is to say into something produced not for its own sake, not to use, not for its "use-value," *but for exchange on the market.* For capitalist producers are entirely, indeed ostentatiously, independent of each other. They never come into contact at all: they disdain, they abhor, all thought of conscious co-operation. What do come into contact, however, are their products, the commodities which come pouring on to the market. Cotton goods are exchanged for coal, coal for corn, corn for timber, timber for railway engines and so on in an endless series. Thus there is no contact at all between the producers—the human beings engaged in economic activity: the only contact is between the products, the things, the commodities, which have resulted from that activity. *Thus the cardinal fact that the work of society as a whole in satisfying its wants under any sys-*

tem of the division of labour must necessarily be a work of social co-operation is masked and hidden. The fact that the producers are in intimate relation to each other is invisible: all that can be seen is the relationship of their respective products on the market. What is actually a relationship between people appears only as a relationship between things. Thus men in a capitalist society are enabled, by this peculiar masking and mystifying characteristic of the market, to think and feel as individualistically as if they were so many self-supporting peasant proprietors. Yet their economic activities have been woven together by a net of the closest mesh: they are actually, and without knowing it, engaged in a gigantic enterprise of co-operative social production. Thus the market produces at once an ever-growing, objective interdependence of the producers, while leaving completely unmodified, and indeed intensifying, their subjective, or imagined, independence. In such conditions, there is all the difference in the world between men's idea of the social system under which they live and what that system is really like.

It is in this way that capitalism achieves the necessary co-operation between the producers of different commodities. It is in this way that it accomplishes the first task.

We now come to the second task which, we saw, must be accomplished by any social system which is compatible with industrial production. And this task will prove more difficult to accomplish. It is necessary, we saw, for a social system suitable to an industrial community to achieve the daily and hourly co-operation of thousands of individual workers for the production, under modern conditions, of each separate commodity. How is this to be done? Capitalism, be it remembered, was established under the banner of the freedom of the individual. The degree of co-operative production which was achieved by the legal dependence of the serf on his lord, and the degree of more or less voluntary productive co-operation achieved by the mediæval guilds, were alike swept out of existence. How then in spite of this, did capitalism achieve a far higher and more extensive degree of productive co-operation than had been ever before accomplished? It did so by the establishment of what is known as the "labour market." Now the labour market is merely a subdivision, a very important "special case," of the market as a whole. Let us define as exactly as possible what is meant by the "labour market."

When we say that a labour market has been established, we mean that the power and ability of individuals to labour is being bought and sold. We saw that once the principle of free exchange has been established, every useful article is turned into a commodity, into, that is to say, something which is produced with the object of exchanging it for something else. When once a labour market has been established, the ability of men to work is also turned into a commodity. For it is the distinguishing characteristic of a labour market that in it people's power to work is bought and sold (that is exchanged) by the hour, day or week. When once this condition of things has come into being, a solution for the problem of mobilizing thousands of individuals for a common task in a factory or mine has been found. For so many hours of the labour of these individuals can simply be bought, and applied to the common task. We may say, therefore, that capitalism solves the problem of getting large numbers of legally free citizens to work together in factories by turning their ability to work into a commodity.

The next question is, obviously, how does capitalism manage to get people to sell their power to work in this way? How can this indispensable institution, a labour market, be brought into being? In order that a labour market may arise, it is necessary that there should appear in the community a category of persons who will, and who habitually do, hire themselves out to work in return for wages. It is significant of the degree to which the characteristics of capitalism are taken for granted that to-day most of us simply assume the existence of such persons. The very idea that it might be impossible to establish industry or commerce, not because of any technical reasons, but because no workers would respond to the offer of wages does not occur to people. Yet such was once the prevailing condition of affairs, and is still to a large extent the condition of affairs in many "primitive" and undeveloped parts of the world. In such places, to use the terminology we have adopted, no solution has been found for the second of the two tasks which, we saw, face a social system suitable to an industrial society. No method has been evolved for getting individuals together to work at a common task.[1]

---

[1] This problem arises acutely to-day in the colonies. All sorts of devices are resorted to in order to induce the native peasants, who own their own simple means of production, to come and work for wages on the white man's planta-

Now two essential conditions have to be secured before any such class of people, both able and ready to sell their power to labour, can exist. In the first place, all forms of slavery, serfdom, peonage and villainage must be abolished. For if the mass of the population belongs to certain overlords and landlords as their exclusive private property, it is no use for the enterprising entrepreneur to offer them wages in order to induce them to come and work for him. In this case the potential worker will be unable to sell his labour. Such conditions of legal dependence must therefore be broken down. This part of the job, as we have seen, the middle class effectively accomplished in its war for the market. But there may be another reason why an entrepreneur cannot get labourers to work for him. The potential worker may be perfectly free, but he may be working already. He may be working for himself. He may, for example, be a peasant proprietor tilling his freehold plot of land: or he may be a skilled artisan—a cobbler or handloom weaver— with his own tools and with ready access to the raw materials he needs. In other words, he may himself possess the means of production. And if so, why should he come and work for another? He will obviously work for nobody but himself, and will enjoy—either by consuming them directly himself, or by exchanging them for something else which he prefers—everything that he produces. For, after all, if he works for a master that master cannot possibly offer to give back to him in wages the equivalent of everything which he produces. He cannot be given back either all the actual things he makes, or all of what they are worth in alternative goods, or in money. For, if his employer did so, the worker would in reality still be working for himself. His connection with the employer would be merely nominal. The only reality would be that the employer had freely and permanently "lent" the means of production to the worker. And, as every lawyer knows, an unconditional loan for an indefinite period is tantamount to a gift. In this case, therefore, the worker will be able, but unwilling, to sell his labour.

tions. The most common is the well-known imposition of a "hut tax." A tax of a given amount is placed on a native's hut in order to make it necessary for him to earn money. He is then enabled to earn the sum of money which he must subsequently hand over to the tax-collector by working on the plantation of a white landowner. It is one of the triumphs of the League of Nations that its jurists have been able to detect a difference between this procedure and the imposition of forced labour.

How does the capitalist system solve this difficulty? What is the inducement which makes millions of men work for others in return for wages: for payments, that is, which cannot be equal to the full value of the things which they produce? It is a sufficient inducement. It is, in the first place, that for the most part they neither possess nor have access to the means of production. They are not peasant proprietors owning plots of land: they are not skilled artisans owning their own tools and with ready access to a supply of raw materials. They are workers "owning" nothing but their own capacity to work: and, moreover, unable to work until they are given access to the tools and raw materials which can alone make work possible. And it is not until such a state of things has come into being that large-scale production can begin. The establishment of the labour market, which, as we have said, is the institution by which capitalism performs its second task, requires, not only that the workers should be free—that they should not be possessed by any overlord or master—*but also that they should neither possess nor have free access to the means of production*. In other words, when the middle class freed the workers from the landlords they had to, and did, take very good care to free them from the land as well.

We must now examine the methods by which capitalism fulfils this vital condition for the establishment of a labour market. Historically, there have been two ways in which the workers can be disembarrassed of the means of production. In the first place, their tools, materials and natural resources can be quite frankly and straightforwardly taken from them. This is the older method. It is the method of the English "enclosures," for example. What happened, and went on happening quite steadily for about four hundred years, was that the land of England, which towards the end of feudalism was tending to become the property, partly the individual property, partly the common property, of the English peasants, was taken away from them by a new set of landlords. After other expedients had been exhausted, this was done in due form, quite legally, by special laws—Enclosure Acts—passed by Parliament expressly for the purpose. The new landlords were not the old feudal overlords who had in the middle ages held the peasants in various degrees of open servitude, but a new class of agricultural entrepreneurs, who had supplanted the old feudal nobiilty. True,

they were very soon ennobled, and have become the British aristocracy. But, as we have seen, their origins were highly commercial
(and this is why they never afterwards disdained trade). They
originally made their money about the fifteen-hundreds by taking
Church and peasant land and turning it into sheep-runs. They
made their money out of wool. (Thus, economically speaking, it
is not only the Lord Chancellor but the whole House of Lords that
should sit upon the woolsack.)

Stated thus baldly it seems difficult to understand how such
forcible seizures of land, which in one form or another took place
all over Europe, by a small new class, can have been possible.
Why did not the peasants rebel? The first answer is that they did
rebel. They rebelled in the long series of peasant risings which
marked the first hundred and fifty years of the process, and which
were only suppressed with difficulty.

The more interesting answer to this question, however, will lead
us on towards a consideration of the other, and to-day far more
important, method by which the means of production can be
alienated from the workers. (For cleared and drained land, on
which human labour has been expended, is of course only the
oldest and most important of the means of production.) The
English enclosures, however ruthless, were not an economically
reactionary policy. On the contrary, they were universally associated with improvements in agricultural technique. Sheep-farming,
for example, was no doubt in itself the most "economic" use that
a good deal of English land in the sixteenth century could be put
to. Again, not all the land enclosed, especially in the seventeenth
and eighteenth centuries, was laid down to sheep pasture. A great
deal of it continued to be cultivated, but to be cultivated on a far
bigger scale, far more scientifically and so more economically than
ever before. The enclosures were a great process of agricultural
rationalization. This technical progress offered at once an overwhelming incentive for the enclosures, and by increasing the real
productivity of labour made possible an advance in the national
wealth. It did so by this very act of "freeing" agricultural workers
from their work on the land; and at the same time it created the
surplus wealth (from the more profitable agricultural exploitation)
which should re-employ these new "free" hands at something else.
But before that "something else"—which could only be industry

and commerce—could develop a considerable proportion of the surplus peasants had perished. This is the first simple and frank method. It consists in just taking the means of production away from the workers.

The second method by which the worker can be dislodged from his tools is far less frank and obvious. Once the capitalist system has got going in any particular sphere of production, in agriculture, or in cotton spinning, or in building, or in what you will, large-scale technically advanced forms of production are soon established. For the growth of trade, that is, of exchanges, at once requires and renders possible an ever-growing specialization of production. Nothing, however, is more obvious than that this growing specialization and division of labour in turn promote technical development and progress. For example, the cobbler will make better shoes and will find that it pays him to use better tools in making them, for he will keep his tools in constant use, than will the peasant farmer who tries to make his own shoes in his spare time. And technical development, it is universally agreed, at once requires and promotes large-scale production. Indeed there is a well-graduated and well-known scale in the size of the unit of production all the way from the Ford works at Detroit to the hand-loom of Mr. Gandhi's model peasant. It is, on the average, a quite direct ratio: the more complicated, the more mechanized, are the methods of production at a given time and place, the larger are the constituent factories, mines, workshops, the more capital they embody per unit of production.

After some considerable amount of capital, some considerable collections of the means of production, that is, have once been got together, the products of these new technically advanced wage-worker-employing enterprises begin to compete on the market with the products of the individual handworkers, who still own the far simpler means of production which had formerly been all that had been necessary in the trade in question. There can of course be only one end to such competition. The handworkers are first reduced to starvation and then driven out of the market. They have to sell their now hopelessly obsolete means of production for scrap: they become the raw material of wage-workers, namely workers with no power to produce for themselves, and with only their power to labour to sell. The classical example of this process is the ruin of the handloom weavers by the rise of the large-scale mechanized Lancashire textile industry. Observe, however, the fundamental difference in this method of divorcing the worker from his means of production and the former direct method of primary accumulation. In the case of the former method, it was the new landowner, a definite human person, who did the job—by, for example, putting up a most tangible fence round the land he was enclosing. In the second case, however, no particular person appears on the scene at all. The handloom weavers were not dispossessed, in any direct visible way, by the Lancashire millowners. What seemed to them to be ruining them were not the millowners, but the millowners' products: not the cotton kings themselves, but their cotton cloth. (And the early revolts of the industrial workers were directed against the machines which produced the stream of commodities which seemed to be dispossessing them, instead of against the machine-owners.) Once again a relationship between people disguised itself as a relationship between things. And this second method is the way in which in recent times by far the greater proportion of the workers have been divorced from the means of production. The method is obviously in every way preferable to the dispossessors. It has all the impressive impersonality of a law of nature. Indeed, it is always spoken of by the theorists of capitalism as "an inevitable process." It has, too, an air of voluntariness about it. There is nothing, the lawyers will assure him, to prevent the handworker from continuing to work for himself with his own tools, and thus continuing to enjoy the full product of his labour. It is merely that there is now a wealthy gentleman in the field, who will offer him a rate of wages which, though admittedly it means a profit to the wealthy gentleman, may exceed what the worker can now make for himself. But it is entirely a matter of free choice for the worker.

The worker has, of course, only this choice—to go and work for wages or to starve. For the competition of machine-made products has reduced the value of what he can produce himself, with his own tools, to below what he can possibly live on. Since, however, this is a form of economic instead of legal compulsion it does not officially exist. The worker does not know what has hit him: he only knows that from being an independent unit of production working on his own for the market, he has suddenly become a propertyless man; that he has now no way of earning his living but to induce an owner of the modern and efficient means of production to employ him for wages.

By these two methods then, and principally by the second one, the capitalist system "frees" the worker from his means of production. The second condition for the establishment of a labour market is thus achieved. It is at this precise point, when a large mass of "free" workers—free, indeed, of everything except their skins—has at length been created that the market becomes sufficiently free to allow of the functioning of a fully developed capitalist system. Capitalism may be said to exist when the principle of the free market has been extended to the labour market: when, by the freeing of the workers, alike from serfdom and from their ability to work for themselves, a large mass of workers willing to hire out their power to work has come into existence: when man's ability to work has, therefore, become a commodity to be bought and sold on the market. For then and not till then, does large-scale capitalist production become possible. It is appropriate to begin to use the word capitalism to designate this particular stage in the development of the market, since, as it marks the achievement of large-scale production, it also coincides with the mobilization of large pooled aggregates of capital, either in the hands of an individual entrepreneur, or a group of entrepreneurs, or latterly, by means of the sale of shares, in the hands of wide sections of the possessing class. Henceforward, it will be necessary to own large aggregates of capital—large, complex and expensive means of production, that is—before independent production for the market is possible.

It was then by these summary methods that capitalism solved the second great problem of social co-operation. That problem was how, after the dissolution of all feudal ties, the thousands of now free and independent workers were to be induced to engage in the collective labour of the modern factory. The solution is clear. The worker is brought into the factory by being prevented from working, and so sustaining life, outside it. And this is accomplished by a small number of persons appropriating, originally by the use of force (usually the force of the State machine of which they have got control), the increasingly centralized means of production. Once the process has begun, however, it extends itself automatically, since the new comparatively large-scale, centralized means of production in the hands of the few send their relatively "mass produced" products into the market to compete with, and so drive off the market, the products of the small decentralized means of production which still remain in the hands of the many. Thus the number of workers continually being "freed" for involuntarily co-operative production in the centralized factories of the few, is constantly being increased. A labour market, in which these workers must perforce sell their power to work, establishes itself. And once a condition of things has grown up in which a large class of persons habitually do sell their power to work, the problem of securing collective work at a common task has been solved. For once a man has sold his power to work, he has relinquished any pretensions to controlling what tasks he shall work at. He, and any desired number of his fellows, are set to work by the purchaser of their labour power at any given common task.

If we consider this whole process from another point of view, we shall see that it is the process of the accumulation of capital. Capital accumulation is also of two kinds. There is first the process which is usually described as primary accumulation. This is the other aspect of that direct, forcible, dispossession of the workers from the means of production which we have described. It may take several forms: the necessary capital may be acquired by the plunder of peoples subjected by conquest. This was the method of Cortes, Pizarro and the other Conquistadors in the Americas, or of Cromwell in Ireland. Or, the means of production may be acquired by the usurpations of nobles who enclose the land of peasants. (Virgin land is not a means of production, any more than is coal lying unworked in the earth: but cultivated, drained land with agricultural equipment upon it, does constitute an essential instrument of production.) What then constitutes the category of primary accumulation? It is that the accumulation is accomplished not by the extinction or absorption of small masses of capital by the competition of big, but by the initial, forcible, collection of the relatively big masses of capital necessary to start the competitive process.

When once this primary stage is over, the accumulation of capital goes on, as we have shown, automatically. For the further accumulation of capital is identical with the second method of freeing the workers from the means of production. We showed that the bigger masses of capital will inevitably accumulate faster than the smaller, because the bigger will be able to produce goods cheaper than will the smaller, and so will make more profit. But this is only another way of saying that the owners of these bigger masses of capital will retain for themselves a higher proportion of the values created than can the owners of the smaller masses of capital. Thus, the accumulation of capital, and the creation of a free market in the power of men to work, are one and the same process looked at from two different points of view.

We have now described the methods by which capitalism accomplished the two tasks, which, we saw, faced a social system compatible with large-scale methods of production. It was by these means that the middle class solved the problem of organizing production. The job has only been done by means of the appropriation of the means of production by a single class. Thus, alone, have they been centralized: thus, alone, have enough of them been accumulated to make modern large-scale production possible.

The process has involved the splitting up of society into two opposed classes. Capitalism has only secured collective labour at the common tasks of factory and mine, by creating, on the one hand, a category of persons who live by virtue of their ownership of the means of production, and, on the other hand, a category of persons who live by selling their power to labour. A society, totally different from any which might have been expected to result from the overthrow of feudalism, has been created.

The early theorists of the middle class—especially the most influential of them, Rousseau—had envisaged that after the fall of feudalism there would arise a society of small independent producers for the market. We have seen, however, that no sooner had the middle class succeeded in dissolving the social ties of feudalism, than the growth of large-scale industry, itself inevitably springing from the competition of free producers for the market, involved the concentration of the instruments of production which had been scattered and individualized at the fall of feudalism. And so, before ever the relics of feudalism had been cleared away, there began to appear, not a homogeneous society of free and equal producers for the market, but its very opposite. There began to appear a society sharply split up into two classes: on the one hand, the owners of capital, and, on the other hand, the wage-workers. Such was, and is, the fundamental character of the society called capitalist, which has succeeded feudalism. It bears no resemblance to the promised land of Rousseau and his disciples. Instead of the destruction of all monopoly, a new category of monopolists, the monopolists of the means of production, has arisen. Instead of personal freedom for all men, there has been created for the great majority of men a new and far more extensive form of dependence, all the more extreme for being concealed. Instead of civil liberty, there is a daily and hourly compulsion upon the great mass of the population which is much more pervasive and effective because it is economic instead of legal. Instead of the principle of private property guaranteeing to the worker the fruits of his labours, that very principle has become an impassable obstacle for ever preventing him from obtaining them.

Thus, when the accumulation of capital brought the middle class face to face with the necessity of organizing large-scale production, it was only able to achieve its purpose at the cost of repudiating, in economic practice, all those principles of social justice to which it had appealed so successfully in its struggle with feudalism.

In this chapter, an analysis has been submitted of how the overthrow of feudalism, and the establishment of the free market, has resulted in that system of society under which we live to-day. For our society is certainly very different from anything which might have been expected to result from such a process. We have suggested that the fundamental fact about capitalism is that, although it was established in the name of free exchange, although its armies fought under banners inscribed with the words Liberty, Equality and Fraternity, yet it has inevitably developed into a society sharply divided into antagonistic classes. For the members of the middle class, having destroyed the feudal monopolists, became themselves the exclusive owners of the means of production: they became, in fact, the capitalist class as we know it to-day, and henceforward we shall use this term to describe them. For after the fall of the feudal aristocracy, the term middle class becomes misleading.

PART II

CAPITALISM TO-DAY

CHAPTER III

MONOPOLY

"He [J. D. Rockefeller] is the supreme individualist working out
individualism to its logical end in monopolization."

MR. H. G. WELLS in *The Work, Wealth and Happiness of Mankind.*

IN this part of our argument we are not concerned with any
theoretical analysis of the inherent characteristics of capitalism.
This chapter, and the three which follow it, are, on the contrary,
devoted to a discussion of what has happened to capitalism during
the period in which it has constituted the world's predominant
economic system. We shall describe, in the first place, the condition of capitalism to-day and, secondly, the views and theories of
capitalist economists as to how the present difficulties of their
system can be surmounted. Then we shall be in a position to see
whether these difficulties bear any relation to the foregoing account
of the birth of capitalism.

Now it will not be disputed that capitalism is to-day showing
certain marked characteristics. First, there exists a strong tendency
to the growth of monopolies of various sorts. Second, nationalism
has become a dominating factor in the world situation. Third,
what appears to many observers to be a technical defect in the
working of capitalism has become more and more apparent: money
has become to an increasing extent what is called "unstable." And
fourthly, capitalism has become more and more subject to the
recurrence of crises, during which production is seriously interrupted. We shall discuss these phenomena in turn. And we shall
enquire whether they bear any relation to each other.

The subject of this chapter is the growth of monopoly. We are
not here concerned with monopoly in the sense in which we used
the term in the preceding chapter. It is not a question of the
owners of the means of production having collectively, and as a
class, monopolized those means of production. What we are here
concerned with is the possibility of one particular owner, or one

particular association of owners, monopolizing the production of a particular commodity. And by monopolizng that commodity, we shall mean securing a sufficiently exclusive share of the existing means of production of that commodity to suspend, more or less completely, the ordinary laws of competition. Thus the price of the monopolized commodity will no longer depend on the law of supply and demand. On the contrary, within wide limits it will depend on the variously motived decisions of the monopolists. Whenever a monopoly is created, the price-determining mechanism of the market is destroyed in that particular field of economic activity. Monopoly then is the deadly enemy of the market. Indeed, in the form of feudalism, monopoly was, as we have seen, the original enemy of the market. Feudalism had to be vanquished before the market could be established. But monopoly is like Cerberus: strike off one of its heads and a new and yet more terrifying one grows instantly in its place. Even before feudalism had finally vanished, vast monopolies, in a new form, had begun to arise.

It does not, surely, to-day require demonstration that a whole new category of capitalist monopolies has in fact arisen. It would be alike tedious and unnecessary to write many pages enumerating the names of existing monopolist and semi-monopolist organizations. For no one will be found to deny the existence of trusts, cartels, state monopolies, municipal monopolies, banking monopolies, holding companies, interlocking directorates, price-fixing agreements, and all the other almost innumerable *forms of combination* which are to-day one of the most striking facts about the economic organization of the world.

Let us first, very briefly, describe the factors which have led to the rise of these monopolistic organizations. We can then consider the question of the *extent* to which monopoly has, in fact, superseded free market conditions.

The older economists of capitalism used themselves to point out that, "wherever there is competition there can be combination." There can be, and there is. No sooner has capital been accumulated to a considerable extent than the free and independent producers for the market, who are not now, as we have seen, the individual citizens of the community, but are the individual capitalists, each with his retinue of dependent wage-workers, begin to "get together." They do so for several excellent reasons. In the first place, the combination of independent entrepreneurs is, in fact, simply a continuation of that tendency towards the accumulation of capital for large-scale production which is a consequence of the establishment of the market itself. For large-scale production needs large and expensive means of production, that is to say, it needs a large amount of capital. This capital may be obtained in the course of the productive activities of one particular successful business.[1] In this case it is obtained from that part of the values created which the owner of the means of production does not pay back to the workers. A part of this annual surplus is put back into the enterprise each year as new capital.

Another method, however, is to pool the resources of two hitherto competing enterprises. A successful firm which is in any case rapidly expanding its capital equipment, as a result of its own operations, will like to absorb a smaller competitor. For, by doing so, it can hasten the speed of its own development. The smaller, less successful, firm has often no choice in the matter. It is being left behind in the race for more and more elaborate equipment. Thus its competitive power is decreasing. Sooner or later it will be bankrupted by its more successful rival, if it does not sell out while it still has something to sell. It must be eaten now or die out in the cold later on. Thus both firms have good reasons for combination. And such combinations are, in fact, continually taking place. Capital, then, is continually being *concentrated:* more and more of it, that is, is used in any given enterprise. And at the same time capital is being *centralized;* that is to say, it is passing into the hands of fewer and fewer effective owners. And the two processes hasten each other.[2]

---

[1] Here and throughout, I follow the usage of most writers on economics of whatever school and make the term "productive activity" cover such work as the transport and distribution of goods.

[2] It is quite true that claims to a participation in the profits of the great modern centralized and concentrated enterprises are now, by means of the sale of shares, quite widely distributed amongst members of the property-owning class. But it is very naive to suppose that this constitutes any diffusion of effective ownership or control. A small shareholder, or indeed the whole body of small shareholders collectively, in a great modern company, have about as much control over it as they have over the Grand Lama of Tibet. They take what dividends the directors, who own the controlling blocks of shares, like to pay them, and read, devoutly, the financial columns of their newspapers, where city editors tell them what the big capitalists want them to think.

Thus far, however, the process of combination can go on without the realization of monopoly in the supply of a given product. When, however, the twin tendencies of concentration and centralization of capital have gone a certain distance, the units of production in the given industry will have become large and few. Yet competition among these large remaining units will still be going on. Now, however, it is a case of competition among a few formidable competitors. The stakes of the contest will have been raised. For each of the remaining firms will have made heavy capital investments. If they are defeated in their trade war, they stand to lose many thousands of pounds. Thus the hazards of unrestricted competition will decreasingly appeal to them.

Free competition, the classical economists teach us, is "the antiseptic of trade." This wonderful device, we are told, prevents the selfish instincts of individual business men from exploiting the community. The free play of competition ensures that all economic activity shall be automatically directed to the maximum possible benefit of the community. To business men, however, engaged in a hazardous and desperate trade war, in which all they possess is at stake, competition is more likely to appear as a very hard master. In fact, the uncontrolled play of the market affords a very rough and ready method of adjusting the unco-ordinated activities of the producers to the needs of society. It does so only by periodically bankrupting a certain number of them. Thus business men, in a genuinely competitive industry, are kept in the fear of imminent ruin—in a state, that is, of the greatest possible instability.

Now that production has become very large in scale, however, instability is a much more serious difficulty than ever before. The huge expensive plants which have become necessary bring ruin, not wealth, to their owners if they cannot be operated steadily and regularly. Such regularity, and the security which it alone can bring, can only be achieved, it seems to business men, by the abolition of competition within their branch of production. Is this, however, so difficult? Surely not, say up-to-date capitalists, intent upon the making of "mergers." The producers in the particular industry in question have been reduced to a small number of large concerns. Let them but "get together," either by outright amalgamation or merely by a cartel or price-fixing arrangement, and all the terrifying dangers and chances of competition can be eliminated.

In practice, moreover, no rigid written agreement may be necessary. When the number of competing firms has dropped to, say, half a dozen, competition may simply die out of the industry of itself. A conventional price for the product may be established. Different territorial divisions of the market will become more and more the exclusive property of particular firms. And all the organizations concerned dreading the rigours and risks of renewed strife, may be glad, for a time at any rate, to become economic pacifists, content with a share of the market rather than willing to risk all to gain all.

Hence *the desire for stability,* grown stronger with the growth of large-scale production, is one of the most important motives for the elimination of competition and the formation of monopolies.

Secondly, there exist many spheres of economic activity within which the principle of competition cannot operate, at any rate fully. There is, for example, a special tendency to monopoly in the case of the supply of gas, water, and electricity to a given city or part of a city, and, to a large extent, in the case of railway transport between great cities. For in these fields competition is especially wasteful and the technical advantages of providing the service by means of a single unified organization are especially great. In many cases, these activities were carried on by monopolies from the beginnings of capitalism. Thus they served as examples of monopolies, and their advantages to their owners. Moreover, and this is an exceedingly important point, they drew the State towards an intervention in economic affairs. For clearly the persons who happened to own these technical monopolies could not be left to exploit everybody else at their own sweet will. For example, it has been from the outset necessary to regulate railway charges by law. The existence of this special tendency to monopoly in certain economic activities qualified from the beginning the application of the principle of free exchange. The State was, in fact, unable to maintain that perfect aloofness from economic affairs which was prescribed for it by the theorists of the market. And these initial examples of State interference led to wider interferences later on.

Last but not least, of course, business men form monopolies in order to get monopoly profits. They feel the whip of competition most cruelly upon their backs. They dream of a stable, easy, quiet, and limitlessly profitable world, from which the demons of price-cutting and competition in all their forms, have been finally exorcised. They innocently suppose that they have only to combine instead of to compete in order to achieve such a capitalist paradise, that the process of amalgamation has only to be pushed to its logical conclusion in order that all capitalists should enjoy the pleasures and profit of monopoly. They have no suspicion that such a conception is self-contradictory: that existing monopolies only find themselves in a favourable position just because the rest of production is still being subjected to the pressure of competition. A monopolistic industry sucks its extra profits from other free competition industries around it. (For example, a mining monopoly could fix the price of coal at a figure which would appropriate all the profits of the steel industry.) But if all industries were monopolies, there would be no areas of free competition to exploit. We shall examine this whole question, however, at a much later stage in the argument.

It is only necessary for our immediate purpose, to prove the inevitable character of the growth of monopoly. For the fact of its growth is not in dispute. For example, an eminent ex-official of the League of Nations, Sir Arthur Salter, has recently published a book on the present crisis, under the optimistic title *Recovery*. We shall refer to his arguments on several future occasions; his evidence is of special interest, since he is a devoted supporter of the principle of free exchange by means of the mechanism of the market. On the question of monopoly, he writes:

"In every form of human activity indeed there is an instinctive dislike of standing completely naked before the full blast of competition. The etiquette of professions like the Bar, medicine or the Stock Exchange, the growth of combines, controls, monopolies and understandings as to prices, are examples within the sphere of private organization. And this has been supplemented by an ever-increasing use of the power and mechanism of the State, which has given the protection of tariffs and the aid of bounties. The full flood of competition has been canalized, locked, dammed and diverted from its natural course."

We now come to a consideration of the extent to which combinations of all sorts have, in fact, abolished the free market.

Let us first consider the growth of combination in the land of the purest and least qualified form of capitalism, in America. Now one of the most reliable indications of the growth of combination is to be found in the efforts of the rest of the community, fearful of exploitation, to restrain that growth. In particular, the old independent producers for the market, above all the agriculturalists, are sure to put up a fight against the rise of industrial monopolists. Hence, just as America is the home of the trust, so also is it the home of the "trust busting." Towards the end of the last century, American trusts had become sufficiently threatening for the independent producers, who were still politically dominant, to attempt to stop their growth once and for all. They succeeded in passing the Inter-State Commerce Law of 1887 and the Sherman Anti-Trust Law of 1890. Had these measures been observed, they would have prevented anything like a nation-wide, or Federal Trust. Partly no doubt by means of the successful "lobbies" of the trusts, these laws were for a time allowed to fall into disuse. Then, just after the turn of the century, they were suddenly revived and their enforcement attempted by President Roosevelt. This was no doubt a piece of presidential demagogy, yet Roosevelt, who was a most accomplished demagogue, would never have chosen such a policy if there had not been strong forces remaining in America which feared and hated the trusts. And he actually succeeded, be it observed, in breaking up, at any rate nominally, some of the greatest of these organizations, including the vast Standard Oil Company. This success marked the high-water mark of the efforts of the anti-trust forces. There had been before, however, and there were to be again, similar movements on the part of the independent producers west of the Mississippi. These movements, it is interesting to observe, reached their peak point of activity at the bottom of every cyclical trade depression and were dispersed almost completely by the warm waves of prosperity at the top of every boom. Thus, we have the Granger movement of the seventies, struggling against railway monopoly; the Populist or non-partisan movement of the nineties and the Farmer-Labour movement of the early nineteen-twenties. All these movements marked the efforts of the small independent producers to protect themselves against the monopolists. Their forces comprised the farmers, the smaller industrial producers, the lower middle class generally; and, to a large extent, they carried working-class support with them. Between them, they managed to achieve the intermittent enforcement of the Sherman Law. Open amalgamations creating anything like a nation-wide monopoly were, and still are, fairly effectively forbidden. Nor is this the only anti-monopolist provision of American law. Almost equally important is the prohibition of branch banking, so that nothing like the "big five" British Joint Stock Banks, with their virtual monopoly of all internal banking operations, can be created.

The Sherman Law, and the further anti-trust provisions are, however, to-day the subjects of hot debate in American business circles. The trusts are pressing for their abolition. It is true that ways and means of circumventing them have been developed. Still they represent a real hindrance to the further development of monopoly. And, for the first time, monopoly is the open and avowed object of one school at least of the leaders of American capitalism. Not that they use the term. On the contrary, the arguments of this school do not lack plausibility. Some of the most up-to-date American business men can often be heard to express themselves somewhat as follows. "Competition and the free market in modern conditions of ultra-large-scale production, involved intolerable instability. They precipitate appalling economic crises, such as the crisis of 1930. Is not the only way to avoid such crises to set to work consciously and systematically to plan our economic system? Planning is the keyword of future economic development. By the consciously planned development of America's unrivalled natural resources, the future of the Republic can alone be secured. In order, however, to achieve such planning—to fit production to demand, to share out raw materials, to dovetail industry and agriculture, to ensure the right proportion between the production of capital goods and consumers' goods—you must give us leave to combine and to merge to a far greater extent than ever before. For example, you must abrogate the Sherman Acts, the prohibition of branch banking, and the Inter-State Commerce Commission must allow wholesale railroad mergers." (The best exponent of this policy is Mr. Owen D. Young of the General Electric Corporation.) Such ugly words as monopoly are never mentioned, be it observed. Yet the realization of monopoly is, of course, the underlying object of the whole programme. And necessarily so.

For Mr. Young and his colleagues are quite right in saying that economic planning is quite impossible while capitalist competition exists. (But has Mr. Young ever asked himself whether anything would be left of capitalism, if competition was eliminated?)

Considerable obstacles still exist, however, to the realization of any such programme. America is still an agricultural country as to some 25% of its population and her farmers are most justly suspicious of entrusting their supply of essential industrial goods to a series of gigantic, interlocked, and tariff-protected capitalist monopolies. The old creed of American Populism is still strong in Congress. The whole American hinterland west of the Mississippi is still deeply suspicious of the new scientific "planners." (And it may be that in the autumn of 1932, Governor Roosevelt, a soberer Bryan, will ride to success on the waves of petit bourgeois discontent, to become that somewhat rare and usually most unfortunate creature, an American Democratic President.[1]) Thus it is very doubtful if this new school of "business executives" will succeed in obtaining a sort of legal enfranchisement of the trusts. It does not vitally matter to them, however, whether they succeed or not. (And so their efforts in this direction will probably not be unduly persistent.) The Sherman Law, it is true, does fairly effectively prohibit the simple, direct merging of one company in the same line of business with another—steel company with steel company, oil company with oil company, etc., etc., at any rate on a nation-wide scale. These plain, straightforward, "horizontal" amalgamations are often to-day legally impossible. But "the resources of civilization are not exhausted," as Mr. Gladstone once remarked on a less important topic. Let us give an imaginary example: Company A cannot marry Company B. A stern (fairly stern) judiciary forbids the banns. Company A, however, banks with the great New York finance house of X. In the course of time and overdrafts the finance house X comes to own and control Company A. Is there now anything in statute law or in equity which forbids the finance house X from acquiring 51% of the shares of Company B and thus controlling it also? There is not. And if X equals Morgan's, it does so. By what it may be pardonable to describe as a morganatic marriage, Companies A and B are united, and presumably live happily ever afterwards. Innumer-

---

[1] Written before the presidential election of 1932.—Ed.

able such marriages have taken place and ever new ones are being arranged. In general, therefore, it may be said that though American companies and corporations appear on the surface to stand in splendid isolation, their roots interlace and intertwine in an incredible labyrinth. It is impossible to follow every hidden root, but visibly a high proportion of them draw their nourishment from one or two great central reservoirs of capital, the Eastern Banking and Finance Houses. Moreover, the great banks themselves are not necessarily independent institutions. Such and such a bank is "a Morgan firm," another "a Rockefeller institution," a third "a Mellon house." I make no pretensions of offering a thread to the labyrinth. Some of the greatest corporations are, however, well known to be anything but independent. U. S. Steel, for example, which is perhaps the largest single industrial enterprise in the world, is a "Morgan" firm. The Rockefeller Bank—the National City—is certainly not unconnected with those various Standard Oil Companies into which Mr. Rockefeller, obedient to President Roosevelt, ostensibly split himself up. Naturally this remarkable process of weaving together the entire economic life of a continent is far from complete. There are still outstanding examples of independence. Mr. Ford, we know, is genuinely independent. The very prominence of that example, however, betrays its loneliness. Nor is any simple formula, such as "The banks own the industries," or "The industries own the banks," or "Morgan owns the whole country," an adequate description of the situation. Sometimes the banks own the industries, sometimes the industries own the banks, sometimes there is an alliance. Sometimes the point of junction between the banks and the industries is a single human being (Mellon); sometimes it is a family (the Rockefellers), which owns both banks and industries. What, however, is indisputable is that the whole of American economic life is steadily coalescing and congealing into a vast conglomerate mass from which competition tends to be expelled. And this vast organization is ever striving to become coterminous with the State itself. Hence, it does not seem that the trusts will fight to the death against the Sherman Act, and the other anti-monopoly statutes. They can pursue their policy, less conveniently and directly, but far more discreetly, by more devious courses: by fusion with the banks and finance houses; by the close interlocking of directorates; by a dozen devices suggested by the ingenuity of corporation lawyers.

We have taken America as an example of the growth of monopoly within a capitalist state, partly because of the particularly dramatic way in which events have developed there, and partly because of an interesting point which American experience goes far to prove. It is often said that the growth of monopolistic forms and the curtailment of competition and the free market generally is due to Government interference with business—to tariffs, subsidies, municipal development, chartered enterprises and the like. Yet, with the important exception of tariffs, America has been the classic land of *laissez faire*. The Government has kept most strictly out of business. (It would not, however, be true to say that business has kept out of the Government.) Yet America has been the continent of the trust. True, there has been the tariff, and undoubtedly the tariff has sheltered and fostered the trusts. Historically, however, it was the trusts (under the leadership of Mark Hanna) which created the tariff, not the tariff which created the trusts. In any case, the U.S.A., as the free traders used, before 1929, to remind us so often, is "the largest free trade area in the world." Consequently, it seems clear that the growth of the trusts, and the whole tendency to monopoly is, as we have argued, something inherent in the development of capitalism, and not something imposed on it by the State.

Let us now consider the growth of monopoly in Great Britain. No one denies that the State often does play a very large part in the promotion of combination. In post-war Britain, for example, it has played a very large part indeed. There is, it is true, plenty of private amalgamation going on. And in some instances, at any rate, such direct private amalgamation has secured an effective monopoly in the production of a range of commodities, viz. the national monopoly of the chemical industry achieved by Imperial Chemical Industries and the virtual monopoly in the supply of a basic commodity, soap, achieved by Messrs. Unilevers. Innumerable "interlacings" have taken place throughout industry, while Joint Stock Banking has passed into the hands of five large undertakings which limit competition among themselves to minor points. More striking, however, than the rise of these purely private monopolies is the fact that the State has actually set up monopolies to take over whole new branches of production. Four great State-created, and State-protected, monopolies have been established since the war. Imperial Airways practically monopolizes British civil aviation; Imperial Cables monopolizes intercontinental telegraphy; the British Broadcasting Corporation monopolizes the transmitting side of the wireless industry; the Central Electricity Board monopolizes the long-distance distribution of electric current. Meanwhile, the railways have been regrouped, put under a greater measure of State control, and subsidized (1929 Development Act); and a measure of State control, especially designed to limit competition and output, has been established over the vast British coal-mining industry (1930 Coal Mines Act). Last but not least a tariff, fairly low as yet but showing remarkable powers of growth, has been built round these new monopolies for their protection.

The recent economic history of Germany, however, provides the most extreme example of State-formed monopolies. A whole new flora of economic forms has blossomed there in the last decade. State monopolies, "mixed enterprises," in which the State holds some of the shares and private capitalists the rest, municipal enterprises, mixed private and municipal enterprises, State-controlled trusts, State-controlled banks which in turn control private trusts, uncontrolled private trusts, cartels, price-fixing agreements—a whole bewildering variety of forms has arisen, forms which have only this in common, that they are all designed to limit free competition. Moreover, the remaining ostensibly independent firms are interlocked by the German industrial banks which stand behind them all, and to a varying degree control them all. In fact, German economy in 1932 does seem to have come near, though it has not reached, the theoretical goal of the monopolists, viz. a unified whole, with the municipalities and indeed the State itself as integral parts. (It is worthy of note, however, that even when this extreme degree of what can only be called economic coagulation has been reached, the dependence of the whole system upon the market has not, apparently, been even decreased. For German capitalism has suffered fully as much from the crisis of 1930 to 193? as have the least highly organized capitalisms.)

Thus it is clear that in those most advanced industrial states of the world, the United States, Great Britain and Germany, the

growth of a variety of forms of combination and monopoly is undeniable. And the same thing is true, though in a less degree, of
other capitalist states such as France, Japan, Belgium, and Czecho-
Slovakia. Moreover, it is clear that, at any rate in Europe, the State
is becoming more and more enmeshed in these new economic
organizations. Optimistically inclined gentlemen of socialistic views
often see much to rejoice at in all this. It marks, they suppose, a
great advance towards socialism when the State becomes an integral
part of this vast new capitalist network. Thus if Herr Schmidt, or
Sir Algernon Smith, in his capacity as Director of Bank X or Trust
Y, lowers the wages of half a million workers, it is, they feel, a
monstrous tyranny. If, however, this able gentleman joins the
Government, and as Minister of Commerce takes the same decision, all is well. If a country's economic life is carried on by private
and independent trusts, that is capitalist tyranny. If, however, the
State acquires an interest in the trusts, then that is socialism. These
optimistically inclined "socialists" may not have noticed, however,
that this never happens until some time after the trusts have taken
the precaution to complete their control of the State.[1]

As a matter of fact, the question of whether the trusts tend to
take over the State apparatus or the State apparatus to take over
the trusts is quite an unreal one.[2] What actually happens is that a
closer and closer identity between the trusts and the State grows
up. Naturally they never formally fuse. It is merely that the two
administrative machines—that of the State on the one hand, and of
the trusts on the other—are increasingly manned and directed by
the same persons. The same men pass backwards and forwards
between the Ministers' rooms in the great departments of State and

[1] This fact is illustrated by a probably apocryphal story which used to be told
of Britain's richest man, Lord Rothermere. Lord Rothermere, to satisfy a private
whim, on one occasion "took up" Hungary, and published a series of articles on
Hungary's wrongs from his own pen. The Hungarian Government, grateful but
ill-informed, committed the extraordinary blunder of offering his lordship some
pecuniary compensation. They were informed by one of Lord Rothermere's junior
secretaries that while in Balkan and barbarous parts of the world it might be the
custom for Governments to buy newspapers, in all really first-class states it had
long been the practice of the newspapers to buy the Governments.

[2] The State is to-day merely the crowning form of the organization of the
capitalist class. The committee meeting held, usually bi-weekly, at No. 10 Downing
Street, is the board meeting of the directors of Great Britain Ltd.

the chairmen's rooms in the great corporations which carry on the nation's economic life. It is the most pathetic example of the worship of forms to suppose that anything is altered when the State, as it exists to-day, takes over the running of an industry. All that has happened is that the capitalist class has found it more convenient to conduct this particular industry through its governmental apparatus instead of through the apparatus of some trust. Since the capitalist class owns and controls the governmental apparatus in every whit as real a sense as it owns the apparatus of the trust, the change makes no important difference to anybody.

Nor, of course, is competitive private enterprise entirely extinguished. It flourishes—indeed, it is cultivated—in all the minor branches of production and distribution. A whole class of small entrepreneurs continues to exist—a class which cherishes many illusions as to its own importance and the most servile loyalty to the leaders of industry on whose large-scale enterprises its own little ventures largely depend. These fringes of competition are merely supplementary to the trusts, and serve both to carry on the less profitable or more risky spheres of economic life and to screen the real state of affairs from too curious scrutiny.[1]

It is not, of course, suggested that the logical result of all these monopolistic tendencies has yet been attained anywhere, or that indeed it ever will be attained. Nor have certain qualifications been ignored. Of these, by far the most important is the undoubted tendency of the great trusts to link up internationally across the State boundaries with their counterparts and competitors in other countries, as an alternative to fusing with their own State apparatus. This important question is considered in the next chapter. We may observe, however, that while this tendency no doubt exists, it is being increasingly overshadowed by the tendency to fusion between the State and its own trusts. As a matter of fact, international trustification was on the whole a phenomenon of capitalism immediately before the war, rather than of post-war development. Inter-imperial antagonisms appear to have been sufficiently strong,

[1] For example, they enable Mr. Walter Runciman (a British capitalist of the Liberal tradition) to tell us that so many thousand independent firms, with so many thousands of small capitalists attached to them, still exist. This gives Mr. Runciman great pleasure since he believes that he thus refutes the view that capital is becoming more concentrated.

in the post-war period, to canalize increasingly the development of combination along national lines.

What has been here submitted is that there exists an inherent tendency of individual producers to amalgamate, to form monopolistic enterprises, and subsequently for these monopolies to meet and pool their resources with those of the national States.

CHAPTER IV

NATIONALISM

THE second marked characteristic of present-day capitalism is, we suggested, nationalism. Now it will probably be widely agreed that the nationalism of all states, great and small, presents to-day a major obstacle to the successful working of the capitalist system. For the universal growth of nationalism is having catastrophic consequences upon the exchange of commodities in the world market. And the creation of the world market was, we saw, the crowning application of the general principle of freedom of exchange.

By 1914 the world market, which made possible a real international division of labour, had become a dominating fact in the economic life of all the more important States. The enormous scale of the international exchange of commodities; the transference of large masses of capital from the old industrial States for investment in new or backward countries, and the emigration of workers to countries of higher wage standards, had gone far to make the whole world into a single market—to fuse the national markets. The working of this world market was, it is true, hampered and menaced from the outset by the nationalist policy of nearly every State. Interferences with the free play of the market, by tariffs and by many other less obvious examples of the exercise of the power of the State, were perpetual. And such interferences were growing.

Yet on the whole up till 1914, such was the volume and vitality of international exchanges that they flowed over and under these interferences. And their volume grew steadily. Then came the war. Its coming shattered the world market, and the economic history of the post-war years has largely consisted in the attempt to rebuild it. About the year 1929, it seemed to many observers that this attempt had succeeded. The volume of international trade was again steadily expanding. In spite of every difficulty, it appeared as if the old system of the international exchange of commodities, with a superstructure of capital import and export, of emigration and immigration, was re-establishing itself. In 1932, everyone knows better. International trade has not only failed to expand, but has sunk disastrously both in volume and value. At the moment of writing, it is drying up in large and important parts of the world. Even if recovery comes before capitalism is overthrown in any state, it is clear that almost all the work of reconstruction has been undone, and that the capitalist world is back where it was in 1921.

Nearly all orthodox economists are agreed in substance on what has caused the catastrophe. The present (1932) world economic crisis is, they tell us, the cumulative effect of all those varied, numerous, and extremely vigorous measures of economic national-ism which have been adopted by almost every nation in the world during the last ten years. How much more widely extended throughout the world, how immeasurably more intense these measures have been than any which have ever been attempted be-fore is still hardly realized. A certain British economist is said to keep a "tariff map" of the world. Along the now innumerable frontiers he despondently lays little raised paper walls of varying heights, indicating the scale of the tariffs of each State. Europe, on his map, now resembles nothing so much as the cross section of a prison, with each nation cowering immured in its own little eco-nomic cell.

Tariffs, moreover, are only the very beginning of the economic expedients of nationalism. A whole science, designed for maxi-mizing the exports and minimizing the imports of each and all of the nations of the world simultaneously, has now been elaborated.[1] Import "Quotas," import licenses, export bounties, subsidized rail-way rates to the frontier, penal railway rates from the frontier. subsidies to export industries of every kind, subsidized advertising of "home" produced products, the systematic placing of all Govern-ment and municipal contracts "at home," regardless of comparative costs, a whole labyrinth of measures for the restriction of interna-

---

[1] Mr. Neville Chamberlain told us in so many words that this was the principal objective of the new British tariffs, which he introduced into the House of Com-mons at the beginning of February 1932. No statesman, however, has as yet proposed the obvious method of making possible a universal, simultaneous, and yet successful, adoption of this policy, viz. the creation of an international dump for commodities somewhere in the middle of the Atlantic. This project might be placed on the agenda of the League of Nations under the heading of "How to make Dumping Safe for Democracy."

tional exchanges has been elaborated by the patient and devoted civil servants of every nation. Yet even this "administrative protection," as it is called, still deals only with the interchange of commodities.

The next category of the measures of economic nationalism consists in the obstacles which have been placed in the way of the import and export of capital. Capitalist economists consider them to be particularly disastrous since international capitalism, as the world knew it before 1914, is, they say, unworkable unless the highly developed countries of the world will allow their annual surplus of wealth to leave their shores in search of the higher rate of profits obtainable in backward countries.

Great Britain before the war habitually exported her surplus capital. She did not confine this export to her own empire. Nor did she immediately or invariably attempt to establish political hegemony over the countries in whose industries she had invested. Naturally this moderation was merely relative. British imperialism, based in the last analysis on this power to export capital, was sufficiently predatory. Egypt was absorbed, the South African republics crushed, China dominated, India held in a tightening grip. Still vast quantities of capital were invested in Europe, in the United States, and in South and Central America, without too blatant an attempt to dominate the Governments of the recipient nations. The decencies were to some extent preserved.

Now, however, the predominant power to export capital is passing into the hands of the United States and France. And in both cases the investing classes of these countries, and their respective Governments, are either refusing to use that power at all or are only using it as a direct and open instrument of their political policy. France, of course, is an old exporter of capital. She has not, however, been a very successful one. A high proportion of her pre-war export was lost (in Russia, in particular). Her peasants have been bitten, and are now exceedingly shy. They prefer the modest stocking. Hence, her export of capital is certainly far below what it could be in quantity. And what there is of it, is directed quite openly for her own political ends. Some of it goes to her empire and most of the rest goes to her little circle of "clients" in Europe—Jugo-Slavia, Poland, Roumania, Czecho-Slovakia. These States are now entirely

dependent upon her and hardly even pretend to an independent
foreign policy.

The United States, on the other hand, is a comparatively new
comer to the field of the export of capital. Up till 1915, she was
still a capital importing (a debtor) nation. To-day, however, those
great masses of new capital which should be, we are told, revivifying
world capitalism can come from her alone. Yet as a matter of fact,
hardly a dollar emerges! For about four years (1923-1928), it is
true, America appeared to be taking to capital export on a fairly
large scale. And to an extent which is usually ignored the temporary
world capitalist revival of those years took place on the basis of
this export. Some of the dollars went to South America, and they
carried with them the usual implications of political domination.
They arrived, as it were, in the eagle's beak. (American commercial imperialism was, however, no more predatory than its British
equivalent in this sphere.) For the rest, American capital went into
Germany on a really considerable scale.

And then, suddenly, the whole outward-flowing stream dried up.
At first, before the crash, this was because a mania of speculation in
the shares of home industries that seemed, through the beaming
spectacles of the advertising men, to be illimitably profitable, had so
seized the whole nation, that, say, an American aeroplane share
yielding ½% per annum seemed more attractive than a German
Government 7% loan at par. Moreover, the undoubted fact that the
world had never regained the degree of political stability achieved
before the war, did justly diminish the attractiveness of foreign
investment to the American and French investing public. The two
factors began to react on each other. The world remained poor and
unstable, for lack of new capital, and new capital was not forthcoming because the poverty and instability of the world frightened
off the potential investors. Finally, as the new loans, which continued to be made until 1928, failed to restore the economic stability
of the borrowers, it became clear that their total indebtedness had
made their position hopeless. The interest charges had mounted
to a figure which could not be paid—or which could only be paid
by a fresh loan. Thus, in any case, slump or no slump, the Americans were sooner or later bound to get tired of making new loans
to enable their debtors to pay them the interest on old ones. And
now, after the great crash, the very idea of sending his money thou-

sands of miles across the sea sends shivers down the back of the petrified American investor. Above all, it would be unpatriotic, it would be, oh! awful word of opprobrium, "Un-American," to invest abroad at such a time as this. Far better leave the money lying in an American bank (until, of course, that bank fails—when the problem of how to dispose of the money solves itself).

Thus, in the field of the export and import of capital also, it has been, according to the orthodox economists, the spirit of nationalism which has shattered the world market. The United States Congress, for example, is at the time of writing (Spring of 1932) solemnly engaged in pillorying the New York bankers who conducted the export of American capital up till three years ago. How vile of these Wall Street harpies, it is now said, to have lent those good American dollars to corrupt and vicious Europe and rebellious South America! How vain for the bankers to try to explain that the cessation of that lending (however corruptly it was carried out) was an important cause of the slump. Happy Congressmen from broad Middle-Western acres, you may turn from "grilling" your "international financiers" for lending to Europe; and from preventing in advance any signs of generosity in the matter of the repayment of war debts on the part of your President, to putting in an honest day's work at raising the tariff on the more important products of your State. Nor is there the least fear that the possibility of there being anything contradictory in these activities will ever enter your heads.[1]

An ultra-nationalistic capitalism without a considerable flow of capital across national frontiers has been, however, suggested. (And it is clear that the prohibition of international movements of capital is the logical corollary of the present attempts to obstruct the international movements of commodities.) A certain American writer, Mr. Lawrence Dennis, has actually advocated something of the sort in a book which has just been published in New York.[2] Mr. Dennis devotes a great deal of time to proving successfully that the principal of foreign loans can never be repaid. He also shows that interest charges can only be paid while fresh borrowings are

[1] Sir Arthur Salter suggests that the only way foreign lending can be re-started is for the American and French Governments to guarantee the foreign loan. One would like to see Sir Arthur Salter explaining his proposal to the Senate in Washington and to the Chamber in Paris!

[2] *Is Capitalism Doomed?* (Harper's).

being made, or if the lending country is willing to allow a permanently "unfavourable" balance of trade.

Mr. Dennis is able to prove the final logical contradictions inherent in foreign lending: but he ignores the fact that capitalism knows no other method of developing the backward areas of the world. He can show that foreign lending must always lead to a crash. But he is not entitled to deduce from this that capitalism could get on better without it. On the contrary, international capitalism can only exist by means of foreign lending, and the increase in such lending is one of its essential methods for staving off crisis.

We realize this when we compare the views of a capitalist writer who is, like Mr. Dennis, a strong nationalist and is quite unconcerned with the fate of capitalism elsewhere, if only his own country may be benefited, with the views of a capitalist theorist concerned for the welfare of world capitalism as a whole. Sir Arthur Salter proves quite irrefutably that world capitalism must break down unless a perpetual flow of foreign lending is maintained. There existed, he tells us, on the authority of the British Committee on Finance and Industry (the so-called Macmillan Committee) a "gap," some two thousand million dollars wide, between what the debtor countries of the world could (in 1927) pay to the creditor countries and what they owed them. This "gap" could only be bridged by that amount of annual foreign lending. And when, in 1928, foreign lending stopped, world capitalism fell headlong into the "gap." For the actual detonation of the acute stage of the crisis was due, Sir Arthur Salter considers, to the cessation of foreign lending ("the financial crisis was due to its [foreign lendings] sudden cessation"). Sir Arthur Salter exactly describes the nature of the capitalist dilemma when, on page 110 of his book, he tells us that the basic cause of the crisis was excessive foreign lending, and that the cure is a resumption of foreign lending.

We have now, perhaps, established the fact that the systematic and successful obstruction of the movement of both commodities and capital across national frontiers is one of the most striking characteristics of present-day capitalism.

Many capitalist economists themselves point out this disastrous tendency and, as we have said, they attribute it to the growth of nationalism. In Great Britain, in particular, where Liberalism, so long as it is impotent, is still a respectable opinion, this identification of nationalism as the villain of the piece is quite familiar. Liberal statesmen and economists, for the most part out of place and power, are often to be heard wailing dolefully in this strain at public meetings in idle industrial centres. It is natural that it should be in Britain that these bemoaners of the Golden Age of free international competition are most vocal. For Britain, though no longer as she used once to be the inevitable victor in such free competition, is yet the world's merchant and the world's carrier. Hence the plague of economic nationalism which rages with ever-increasing violence through the world is least infectious for her. (For she suffers worst of all from the consequences of the disease in others.) Now at length, however, she is showing the well-known symptoms. She is engaged in reproducing the protective systems of her neighbours; and her Liberal economists have yet another reason for despair.

These Liberal economists say that it is the spirit of nationalism, and its economic consequences, which have prevented a re-establishment of the world market since the war, and have thus kept the world poor, divided, distracted, fear-ridden and on the edge of another war. For them, however, the plague of nationalism seems to have descended upon the world out of a blue sky. They see no reason, apparently, why the nations of the world should not be trading together at least as amicably as they did seventy years ago. Economic nationalism seems to them to be just one of the inexplicable manias of mankind. It cannot be analysed or accounted for in any way. And yet if the Liberal economist would examine the phenomenon a little more closely they would find a quite simple explanation of its sudden and alarming increase. Thus they would be spared the expenditure of a great deal of energy in resisting a tendency which, if the cause cannot be removed, is quite irresistible.

What after all is the object of measures of economic nationalism? Demonstrably their object is to favour arbitrarily the interests of the property-owning citizens of one particular nation at the expense of the interests of the property-owners of some other nation. What is this, however, but to confer on the favoured property-owners some of the privileges of monopoly? And this in fact is what is done by tariffs, administrative protection, politically selective capital exports, and the like. In other words, economic nationalism attempts to set up a special form of monopoly. Hence nationalism and monopoly are by no means unrelated characteristics of capitalism.

This conclusion naturally leads us to enquire whether economic nationalism is not the logical and inevitable consequence of the growth of monopoly within each state. After all, is it not natural that a progressive change in the character of each state, a change which gradually transforms their very natures, should change the relationship between different states? Nor is it difficult to see exactly how and why the growing element of monopoly within the various national capitalisms has changed, and changed radically for the worse, the relationship between them.

The growth of monopoly, not so much of any one particular monopoly; the growth not of this or that trust, but the general weaving together of once competitive units of production, is changing the very nature of the modern state. The nineteenth-century conception of the capitalist state was that of an arena for the free competition of its citizens, or associations of citizens. Its functions were largely confined to the modest office of keeping the ring. It is clear that the external relationships of such a loose association of producers as the national states then were, could be comparatively peaceful and non-competitive. When the growth of international exchange brought, say, British producers, who were already in genuine and active competition with each other, into contact with French or American producers in the same line of business, all that any of them noticed was that the area both of their market and of competition had been widened. It made very little difference that some of their new competitors were located within the areas of sovereignty of other states. The activities of Governments were so limited that the nationality of a firm was hardly noticed. How very different is the position to-day. From being an arena for the competitive activities of its citizens, the state is becoming a federation, a sort of syndicate, representing the combined interests of its property-owning citizens. In particular, it is becoming the culminating organization of its federated entrepreneurs and financiers. The character of the external relations of these radically modified states is necessarily new also. For example, far from the nationality of a firm encountered on the international market being an irrelevance, it has now become one of the most important facts about that firm. For it will imply that behind that particular firm, with its limited means of competition, will stand some State apparatus, with its vast resources. And the competitive power of the firm will depend to a considerable extent on the power of the state of which it is a constituent part. Instead of playing a negligible part in the economic life of the world, the capitalist states are now becoming more and more active. The common interests of their constituent economic organizations tend more and more to overshadow the competition of these organizations. The associated entrepreneurs of to-day have long ceased to think of the State as a policeman set up by them to see that they all observe the rules of the game. They have come to regard the State apparatus as an essential expression of their joint wills, as one of the most important instruments by which their mutual prosperity may be enhanced. The State's economic activities, far from being dreaded by the capitalist class as they once were, are becoming a necessary and very welcome part of the general system. Tariffs, for example, and all the devices of "administrative protection," appear as the natural support of the monopolies or virtual monopolies which have been nationally created; since without tariffs the home market would be exposed to the products of rival foreign firms in the same line of business, and the possibility of monopoly profits diminished.

The attachment of political considerations to the export of capital is also inevitably associated with internal monopoly. If the heavy industries, generally, and in particular those branches of industry catering for large capital constructions of every type (iron and steel, heavy engineering, armaments, etc.), are highly organized and integrated, then the attachment of conditions to foreign loans will be strongly pressed. The condition that a high proportion of the loan must be spent in the lending country may be explicitly exacted. More generally, however, it will be a vital interest to the federated firms of the heavy industries that "their" state should manage to get for them the right to undertake major schemes of capital development in newly opened up or backward countries. And this, of course, envisages that large and suitable portions of the undeveloped globe should belong to their state. Thus, inevitably the struggle for the acquisition of colonies arises. The most obvious feature of imperialism begins to appear. For imperialism is nationalism on the offensive. It is the final and most ferocious form taken by the rivalry of the modern monopolistically organized states.

It is now less difficult to understand the condition of acute international tension into which the world has fallen. The monopolistic tendencies of modern capitalism were bound to produce just those symptoms of relentless international rivalry which are to-day threatening the very existence of capitalist civilization. For, in a sense, it is true that the uncompromising nationalism of every great state is one of the factors which is making a revival of capitalism impossible. It is, in a sense, true that it is nationalism which makes insoluble every one of the capitalist world's economic problems: that it is nationalism which keeps the world permanently shivering on the brink of another and far greater war. All this, as we have seen, is recognized in even the Liberal diagnosis of the situation. But what makes these last Liberal voices so futile, and indeed so irritating, is that they ignore the indissoluble connection between the whole inevitable drift to monopoly *within* states and the intensification of enmity *between* states. They all refuse to realize that if they wish to abate international rivalries, and so rescue the world free market, they must first restore freedom of competition within all the home markets. Until and unless they can do this, all the Liberal denunciations of nationalism and imperialism are either humbug or nonsense.

A valuable analysis of the inevitability in modern conditions of these three stages in the self-destruction of capitalism, which we may call respectively economic nationalism, imperialism and war, has lately appeared from the pen of Mr. R. G. Hawtrey, the economic expert of the British Treasury, whose words we have already had occasion to quote.[1]

We have seen that the growth of nationalism is based upon internal unification and monopoly. We have seen that modern capitalist states now consist of more or less unified groups of entrepreneurs and financiers. We must now consider the objects for which these groups compete with each other, the methods of their struggle, and its consequences. Let us follow Mr. Hawtrey's admirable study.[2]

Now it will be agreed that the group or category of citizens who predominantly influence their country's Government (that is to say

---

[1] It is true that Lenin and Bucharin had achieved a comprehensive analysis of these tendencies as early as 1916. We have, however, adopted the policy, in this section of the argument, of following up to their logical conclusions the hypotheses of the economists of capitalism. Hence we shall here attempt no more than a purely preliminary treatment of the whole vital question of imperialism. Lenin's conception of imperialism is discussed in Chapter XII.

[2] *Economic Aspects of Sovereignty* (1929).

the rich) always entertains the goal of further self-enrichment. Indeed, the rich have been taught that by seeking this goal untiringly, they will most benefit the community. But why should this in itself lead them on to a nationalistic and so warlike policy? War, it has been argued, by many Liberals, most notably by Sir Norman Angell, always impoverishes all the parties to it. Hence, it is the "great illusion," as Sir Norman Angell called it, of the capitalist class of each country to think that their interests are served by nationalism and militarism. In particular, Sir Norman Angell's argument continues, the economic gains supposed to be derived from the annexation of new territory, are illusory. They are based upon a confusion between property and sovereignty. It is thought by the imperialists that by acquiring sovereignty over a portion of the globe, property rights—a real enrichment—are also gained. This is not so, and if only it were possible to induce the property-owning classes of the great powers to take a clear view of their own interests, they would cease to be military and imperialist.

To this very popular argument, Mr. Hawtrey applies his quiet and careful criticism. In the first place, he shows that sovereignty and property are more closely related than the Liberal pacifists admit. "Sovereignty is not property, but it carries with it important economic rights which are closely related to the rights of property." These rights of property which appertain to sovereignty also, are, he explains, of the nature of a landlord's interest in an estate which is about to be developed by entrepreneurs who acquire portions of it from him on lease. In the case of the annexation of new territory by a capitalist power, private entrepreneurs will apply for the right to acquire land, etc., from the imperialist Government which has annexed the territory. Now the mere right to invest capital in the provision of the essential services of a new country—in making the railways, sinking the mines, draining or irrigating the land, supplying electric power—is in itself an extremely valuable thing. For the average rate of profit obtainable by investment in new or undeveloped countries will be certainly higher than the rate obtainable in a fully developed capitalist country such as that from which the entrepreneurs with their surplus funds will be sure to come. (No abstruse economics are needed in order to realize why this must be so. For, in a well-developed country, there will be, by definition, a good supply of capital equipment, and at the same time a large amount of new capital seeking investment. While in an undeveloped country there is, also by definition, a shortage of capital equipment and very little available new capital. Therefore the price of capital, which is simply its average rate of profit, will be high in the new country where the supply of it is short and the demand for it urgent, and low in the old country where the demand is less urgent and the supply more abundant.)

Hence, people with money to invest are always looking for nice new countries, bare of railways, mines and power stations, etc., to invest it in. As we have seen, however, they must first get the consent of the Government which possesses sovereignty over the new country in question. Now this Government will have to choose which enterprising entrepreneur it will select as the "concessionaire" who is to build and afterwards own some railway or power station in its colony. On what principle do Governments in fact proceed in the granting of these valuable concessions? Mr. Hawtrey, who after sitting for many years in Treasury Chambers, Whitehall, London, has seen a good many of them given, tells us quite clearly.

"The principles," he writes on page 23, "on which applicants are favoured may never be publicly formulated at all. It may be a matter of tacit understandings. But the tendency almost invariably is to follow a nationalist policy. The Government favours applicants from among its own people, and lays its plans to suit their interests.

"This nationalist policy has far-reaching effects, in that it makes sovereignty over new or undeveloped countries an object of cupidity. The profit seekers are usually in a position to exercise influence over their own Governments, and Governments regard the support of their profit seekers' activities in every part of the world as a highly important aim of public policy."

Hence, it is by no means an illusion that the annexation of territory by a great power enriches the individual capitalists who control the Government of that power.

"What I have said," Mr. Hawtrey continues, "as to the need of the profit-making exploiter to obtain rights and concessions from the sovereign authority would not in itself weaken Norman Angell's argument. In most people's eyes it would strengthen it.

If the sovereign power is to be used, not to promote the interests of the community in general, but to line the pockets of a limited number of people, who will have been very rich to start with, that in itself seems to be an abuse. If the State is to be involved in disputes arising out of the rival ambitions of different sets of exploiters, and such disputes are to lead on to war, surely nothing more than a public exposure is required for all those concerned in such events to be treated as criminals and enemies of the human race.

"But is not the fault in the system? If I may criticize Norman Angell, it will be for arguing that the system does not involve these consequences."

That is the whole point. What Mr. Hawtrey calls "the system" —that is, the present-day imperialist or monopolistic phase of the capitalist system—*does and must* involve predatory adventures upon the part of the Governments of the great powers, in order to acquire territories in which their capitalists may invest. The rest of Mr. Hawtrey's argument is devoted to showing, with faultless lucidity, that these inevitable imperialistic adventures must in theory, and do in practice, involve the great powers in war. If, he says, "welfare," the economic well-being of its citizens, that is, were the main object of the public policy of the great states, war between them would not be inevitable. Power, however, and not welfare is the real object of their policy.

"We are accustomed to think of economic ends in terms of welfare, but in matters of public policy that is never the whole story. To each country power appears as the indispensable means to every end. It comes to be exalted into an end itself.

"So long as welfare is the end, different communities may co-operate happily together. Jealousy there may be, and disputes as to how the material means of welfare should be shared. But there is no inherent divergence of aim in the pursuit of welfare. Power, on the other hand, is relative. The gain of one country is necessarily loss to others; its loss is gain to them. Conflict is of the essence of the pursuit of power.

"If it has constantly been an aim of public policy to use the authority of the State to favour the activities of those who undertake economic development, even to the extent of acquiring undeveloped territory as a field for their activities, and possibly risking war in the process, that is because this policy has been believed to further the power of the State."

And the pursuit of power must, we are further shown with impeccable logic, sooner or later involve the Governments of the great states in war. For, as Mr. Hawtrey points out, there is no other conceivable method by which in the last resort this competition for power can be decided.

"If war is an interruption between two periods of peace, it is equally true that peace is an interval between two wars. That is not a mere verbal epigram. It is significant in a very real sense. War means the imposition of the will of the stronger on the weaker by force. But if their relative strength is already known, a trial of strength is unnecessary, the weaker will yield to the stronger without going through the torments of conflict to arrive at a conclusion foreknown from the beginning. The reputation for strength is what we call *prestige*. A country gains prestige from the possession of economic and military power. These are matters partly of fact and partly of opinion. Were they exactly ascertainable and measurable, conflicts of prestige could always take the place of conflicts of force. But it is not possible to measure exactly either the wealth of a country or the degree of its mobility, and even if the military force that could be maintained were precisely known, there are imponderables to take account of, the military qualities of the men, the proficiency of the leaders, the efficiency of the administration, and, last, but not least, pure luck. Prestige is not entirely a matter of calculation, but partly of indirect inference. In a diplomatic conflict the country which yields is likely to suffer in prestige, because the fact of yielding is taken by the rest of the world to be evidence of conscious weakness. The visible components of power do not tell the whole story, and no one can judge better of the invisible components than the authorities governing the country itself. If they show want of confidence, people infer that there is some hidden source of weakness.

"If the country's prestige is thus diminished, it is weakened in any future diplomatic conflict. And if a diplomatic conflict is about anything substantial, the failure is likely to mean a diminution of material strength.

"A decline of prestige is therefore an injury to be dreaded. But in the last resort prestige means reputation for strength in war, and doubts on the subject can only be set at rest by war itself. A country will fight when it believes that its prestige in diplomacy is not equivalent to its real strength. Trial by battle is an exceptional incident, but the conflict of national force is continuous. That is inherent in the international anarchy."

Nor can preparations for this inevitable conflict be avoided.

"An end which can at one time be thus paramount cannot be disregarded altogether at other times. War is an industry, and, like other industries involving the use of plant and capital equipment, it requires an interval of time between the beginning of the productive process and its culmination in the delivery of the completed product. The completed product is organized force. Time in war is precious and may be decisive. Delay in making force effective may mean irreparable disaster at the outset. Any deficiency in the prior preparations may mean some shortcoming in the field of battle which cannot be made good in time.

"Even if war were a visitation comparable to an outbreak of fire, and disconnected with the events preceding it, this question of preparation could not be neglected. The cost of armaments in peace-time is often compared to a premium of insurance against fire. The comparison would be more convincing if it did not imply that the fire insurance companies are the principal incendiaries."

We perceive that there is a perfect chain of logic between the existence of what Mr. Hawtrey calls "the system"—that is, capitalism in its present imperialist phase—and the present condition of the capitalist world, heavy with armaments, and racked by the foreboding of its own doom in a new war.

Capitalism, we see, is coming more and more to mean monopoly at home and ferocious competition abroad. The acquisition of territory in order to acquire monopoly rights of exploitation is a major object of the competing national groups of entrepreneurs. The object of the individual entrepreneurs may be the apparently harmless one of enriching themselves. They know, however, and their knowledge is no illusion, that the acquisition of power through the use, or the menace, of the armed forces of their state is to-day an essential prerequisite to the acquisition of wealth. Hence, the organized force alone possessed by the Governments of the great powers is of necessity pressed into their service. Were any such national group of capitalist entrepreneurs to deprive themselves, on Sir Norman Angell's advice, of this armed force they would quickly be excluded from all opportunities for really profitable investment by other groups of entrepreneurs who had not been so quixotic. Once this had happened, their helplessness would be apparent and what meagre revenues they, and the wide sections of the population of their nation who had become dependent on them, retained would be on sufferance from the entrepreneurs of some still warlike power. Hence, they and their states are inevitably involved in a perpetual struggle for power. In peace-time, this struggle is conducted by menace—as by the display of force in great armaments. Every now and then, however, the need must arise to make good the menace, by the actual use, of force. And too great an apparent reluctance to use force will always be taken as a lack of confidence that the force is really there to use. Liberal pacifists should read, and then re-read, Mr. Hawtrey's book.

There exists, however, another school of thought which takes an optimistic view of the prospects of world peace under capitalism. This school starts with a very great advantage over the Liberal pacifists, in that its adherents have at any rate realized the intimate connection between the monopolistic tendencies within, and the political relations between, capitalist states. They take the view that, while admittedly the prospects of war are greatly increased by the formation of national monopolies, and that these prospects have been in fact increased in so far as this tendency has existed, yet the consequential imperialist and nationalist phase of capitalism is a passing one. And, pointing to the existence of international monopolies, they look forward to Combination instead of Competition amongst the great powers themselves. Imperialist adventure and war, they agree, are nothing but capitalist competition on an international scale. In the same sense, a world federation of the great powers, of which the League of Nations is the beginning, will be the political expression of capitalist combination on a world scale. This theory which, like most theories, has been most fully elaborated in Germany, looks forward to a time beyond the present imperialist phase, when "ultra-imperialism," as it is called, shall have brought the peace of mighty united international trusts to the whole earth. This point of view is certainly ahead of Liberal pacifism in that it does suggest some material basis for its optimistic forecasts of a pacific capitalism. Its adherents do not, like the Liberal pacifists, simply suppose that the attainment of peace is a matter of a sufficient number of speeches at public meetings.

No one indeed denies that there are signs of international as well as national combination in the world to-day. There is perhaps only one well-developed world trust—Kreuger and Toll's, the Swedish match monopoly.[1] There exist, however, numerous cartels and working agreements as to price between big producers of the same commodity in different nations (e.g. the European Steel Cartel). The question at issue boils down to a purely factual and quantitative one. If the tendency to international monopoly is running more strongly than the tendency for monopolies to cluster and cling round the national State organizations, then certainly it is possible to look forward to a growth of pacifist sentiment, and even practice, in the governing classes of the world. This question, however, has only to be raised for the answer to become obvious. No one can possibly doubt that to-day the predominant tendency runs strongly the other way. The international organizations are comparatively few, and are most unstable. They are apt to break up, under patriotic pressure, for instance, especially during slumps. (A good example

[1] The first draft of this chapter was written before the suicide of M. Ivar Kreuger, the collapse of his organization, and the discovery that the whole trust had been a gigantic fraud from its inception. No more striking confirmation, however, of the view that international trusts are inherently unstable could have occurred. In December 1931 Mr. T. G. Barman, writing in the *Fortnightly Review* could found a whole political philosophy upon the beneficial activities of Messrs. Kreuger and Toll. These activities were to inaugurate here and now, and without the slightest inconvenience to anyone, the era of pacific ultra-imperialism. Again, Sir Arthur Salter had the misfortune to publish his book on world recovery just before Mr. Kreuger's demise. In it he deplores the fact that "good constructive loans, like those arranged by a man of such creative vision as Mr. Ivar Kreuger, are threatened with the bad." No one will deny that "creative" was the *mot juste*. For it now transpires that Mr. Kreuger had been, ever since 1925, creating Italian Government bonds by the simple and direct method of printing them.

of the national resistance to international participation in share capital is afforded by the rules which the British General Electric Company has adopted in order to prevent control passing into American hands. Again, the employment of even those liquid funds awaiting investment, which are to-day gathered in the three financial centres of New York, Paris and London, is becoming more and more determined by nationalistic considerations. Thus French balances in London are regularly used by the French Government to influence British policy.)

The best answer to the theorists of ultra-imperialism is not to be found, however, in any detailed enquiry into the actual number and importance of national as opposed to international trusts. For the connection between the rate of growth of the two forms of economic monopoly and the possibilities of peace or war under capitalism is not in dispute. The ultra-imperialists admit that peaceful developments are only to be expected in so far as monopoly becomes international and that warlike symptoms must follow the growth of national monopolies. Hence, an agreed test of which economic tendency has in fact predominated can be found by estimating whether signs of international co-operation or of international rivalry are growing in the world to-day. And who in their senses can doubt the answer to that question? (We might in order to weigh the two tendencies put the Japanese Manchurian adventure of 1932 into one scale and the Disarmament Conference of the same year into the other.) Hostility between the great powers is growing almost month by month. If the present (1932) world slump is surmounted, it will only be after the wholesale adoption of measures of economic nationalism. Tariffs, administrative protection, quotas, export bounties —every conceivable form of interference with economic internationalism, is growing at an unparalleled rate. Great Britain has become a protectionist country. Desperate efforts are being made to isolate the British Empire from the current of world trade. And these efforts are themselves being thwarted by acute national rivalries within the Empire. A frenzy of nationalism has seized the United States Congress. The states of Eastern and Central Europe are starving in the midst of the bitterest internecine hostility. France and Germany are still in irreconcilable dispute. International lending is almost at an end. Does this look like the laying of the economic foundations of an ultra-imperialist, peaceful, phase of capitalism? It does not.

The truth about this possibility of a peaceful world trustification of capitalism, a "golden international" which shall both end war and preserve capitalism for ever, is that it is a theoretical possibility, and nothing more. There is nothing in pure theory which makes it inconceivable. It is not out of the question in the same way that the Liberal dream of a peaceful world, combined with the present nationally monopolistic organization of capitalism, is out of the question. On the other hand, the evidence of what is actually happening in the world proves that things are going in precisely the opposite direction. We may be told that this is merely "a phase"— that sooner or later the world will be quite peacefully and nicely "trust up." Yet, even if this extremely far-fetched proposition be admitted, we may be sure of one thing at least. Even if we admit that capitalism is on the way to world monopoly and so to peace, yet the whole condition of the world assures us that the road it has taken does not lead through gentle mergings of trusts and scientific federations of nations. On the contrary, if it leads to the peace of world monopoly at all, it does so by a series of the most gigantic and devastating wars between the great monopolist groups, and the nations which they own. It leads only to a desert peace, established by some victor empire after the last supreme war of the world. Thus, and thus alone, could capitalist peace be established upon the earth.

CHAPTER V

UNSTABLE MONEY

THE third of the four marked characteristics of present-day capitalism which we are examining in turn, is unstable money. Now the most important conclusion of the last two chapters was that the two capitalist characteristics discussed, viz. monopoly and nationalism, were closely interrelated. Our conclusion as to the instability of money, however, will be that, on the admission of the leading capitalist economists themselves, unstable money is purely a symptom, and not a cause of the present difficulties of the capitalist system.

It is necessary, however, to examine the question of monetary instability and to demonstrate that its symptomatic character is now admitted by all serious students of the subject. For there exists a whole school of thought which clings to the comforting illusion that one particular difficulty of capitalism at least, namely, the recurrence of crises, can be eliminated by what is called "monetary reform." The members of this school of thought call attention to the fact that the chief symptom of these recurrent crises is a simultaneous fall in prices. They attribute this symptom to a defective working of money. And they propose various measures by which money can be reformed so that it can become "stable": so that all prices, that is, shall never simultaneously rise or fall. Were this view well founded, the possibility of the continuance of the capitalist system—the question to which the whole first half of this book is devoted—would be profoundly affected. Hence it is necessary to dispose of it conclusively.

Now, for a writer of the year 1932 to describe the characteristics of a commercial crisis, and its appalling consequences upon the prevailing economic system, would be, for his contemporaries, a superfluous task. For the whole capitalist world is, as he writes, still plunged into one of the more violent and disastrous of such crises. The general price-level of staple wholesale commodities has fallen 42 points, from 100 in 1927 to 58 in July, 1932. This catastrophic *fall* in the prices of things and equally catastrophic *rise* in the price of money, is a symptom of human frustration, suffering, privation, actual starvation and death, on a scale unparalleled in any previous crisis.

The one overwhelming characteristic of such a crisis in capitalism is waste. To-day waste, on a scale unparalleled in the history of the world, is the dominating fact of life. The most striking and visible form of this waste is perhaps the waste of human beings— what we call unemployment. This wastage, the enforced physical deterioration, that is, of millions of human beings, goes on before our eyes. According to the League of Nations, there are about thirty million unemployed men and women in the world to-day, whose mental and physical powers are slowly being wasted by the denial of the opportunity for their exercise, and by their consequent inability to provide themselves and their dependants with the necessaries of life. But the immeasurable waste of a great crisis is not confined to human beings. On the contrary, at the same time as these millions lack most of the necessaries of life, all over the world to-day vast stocks of commodities, redundant harvests, rotting goods, rusting machines are gradually deteriorating *into* uselessness.

Moreover, waste is now being consciously and systematically organized. For example, during 1931, the American Board of Agriculture advised American cotton growers to "plough in" every third row of their cotton crops. This advice did not, however, succeed in sufficiently reducing the crop. Accordingly, it is now suggested that the great cotton pest, the boll-weevil, should be protected—preserved like partridges in England—so that some part of the unsaleable crops at any rate should be destroyed. Similarly, it has been suggested that suitable pests should be introduced into the rubber plantations. Again, the Brazilian Government, which has been systematically burning coffee for some time, is now said to be about to adopt a plan by which the coffee grains can be used as fuel for its locomotives. Examples of such carefully and ingeniously organized waste could easily be multiplied.

And yet all but a comparatively small proportion of the world's population still exists miserably without a sufficiency of even bare necessaries. For example, the London *Times* of April 4th, 1932, tell us that:

"Telegrams received in London in the last few days from Sir John Hope-Simpson, in China, report that cholera has broken out in a camp of 104,000 refugees near Hankow, and that over 80% of the cases have proved fatal. Funds are not available to provide a hospital or medical relief. In North Anhwei food supplies are exhausted, and nothing is left to sell except children, who are sold at the rate of six Chinese dollars (9s) for a boy and ten Chinese dollars for a girl. All dogs have been eaten."

On June 8th, 1932, the Tokyo correspondent of the same newspaper writes as follows:

"Painful details of rural destitution are extracted by the vernacular newspapers from preliminary reports of officials sent by the Ministry of Agriculture to investigate four rural prefectures.

"They state that many villages are almost moneyless, that petty trades are done by barter, and that people are eating the roughest grains and bracken roots, even beancake being cooked. The police cannot control thefts of food, and incendiarism for insurance is said to be rife. Worst of all, girls are being virtually sold."

Nor is such overwhelming poverty a mere legacy from the epochs of real scarcity. Nor is it confined to India, China, and the regions of the world in which modern productive methods have not yet been systematically applied. On the contrary, at this moment when in Western Europe and America men are striving desperately to destroy the products of their marvellous machines, and to nullify the embarrassing fertility of nature, mankind in general is becoming progressively poorer month by month.[1] Even in the regions of a comparatively high standard of life such as Europe, the symptoms of mass starvation are beginning to appear. Thus the Committee of Inquiry, set up by the clergy of Newcastle in Great Britain, reported that "what was really most needed was food. Mothers were suffering from undernourishment." In March 1932, the London *Times* reported that the inhabitants of the considerable Austrian town of Steyr had now killed all their dogs for food, while in Buda-Pest one

[1] "Never was nature so generous in her gifts: never was man so equipped in skill and scientific resources to utilize them. Ours is a problem of the impoverishment which comes with plenty."—Sir Arthur Salter in *Recovery*.

whole area of the city consisted of shelters half dug out of the ground. In the Czecho-Slovakian province of Ruthenia, a skilled observer, Mr. Gerald Hamilton, reports that:

"I have seen famine in India and China, and was in Germany during the starvation blockade of 1918. Never have I seen hunger and want so appalling. Rescue service has completely broken down. The children are so undersized through lack of nourishment that six-year-olds present the appearance of babies."—*Daily Express*, March 11th, 1932.

At the same time, obsolete pre-industrial economic methods begin to reappear since the new technique is being deliberately destroyed. Hungary, the London *Times* also informs us, has already almost abandoned motor transport and returned to the horse. Great areas of Central and Eastern Europe are returning to darkness and primitive destitution.

Thus the capitalist world presents us with an astonishing spectacle. The perfection of its technique of production is only matched by its inability to produce. The abundance and superabundance of everything which men need, is only matched by the destitution of half mankind.

Few will, perhaps, deny that the cause of a phenomenon which can, and not for the first time, produce such effects is worth looking for. It is, therefore, essential that we should arrive at an understanding of the nature of capitalist crises and so form our conclusions on the question of whether there is any possibility of their elimination from the system. Let us deal with the arguments of those who suppose that monetary reform provides a solution. Let us first examine the nature of money.

The true nature of the money which is used by the great powers to-day is a matter of dispute amongst capitalist economists. The historical origins of money, on the other hand, and the nature of nearly all money until recent times, is not open to question. Money originated out of barter. Every text-book on economics describes to us the obvious inconveniences of barter. Thus, in a barter economy, if you had more boots than you needed and not enough bread, you had to find a barefooted baker, or go hungry. But once money has come into existence, you can *sell* your boots to anyone, and with the money he gives you, *buy* your bread from any baker—no matter whether the baker wants boots or a ticket to a circus. Money, in a word, enables you to split an exchange into two halves, buying and selling, and to effect the two halves of the exchange with different people at different times.

Thus the *need* for money is obvious. But when and how in fact did mankind become possessed of this remarkable contrivance? The answer is that we do not know when money appeared: it appeared before recorded history begins, at any rate. But we do know, from the evidence of all recorded and surviving primitive communities, *how* money originated. Man first made money by putting aside one particular commodity and agreeing that this commodity should be the "general equivalent" of all other commodities. That is to say, it was agreed that this particular commodity—usually at first the most important commodity used in the daily life of the community —should always be accepted by everybody in exchange for anything else. Let us straightaway call this specially selected commodity gold. (Not that gold is ever in fact the commodity first selected to serve as money. Cattle, shells, goats, tobacco, cotton, rice, iron, copper, silver and all sorts of things have been and still are used by men for this purpose.)

The predominant money commodity is now, however, gold. So let us say, for simplicity, that gold is chosen right away. At once a new question arises. We have said that everybody has agreed to give and to take gold in exchange for anything else. But how much gold? How much gold will your customer give you for your boots? How much gold must you give the baker for his bread?

We see that with the emergence of gold as the general equivalent in exchange, the price of everything must be reckoned in ounces of gold. Gold becomes the standard of the price of fish, of bread, of tickets to circuses, and, for that matter, as we had occasion to observe in Chapter I, of tickets to heaven too.[1]

[1] *Gold! Yellow, glittering, precious gold! ...*
Thus much of this will make black, white; foul, fair;
Wrong, right; base, noble; old, young; coward, valiant;
... What this, you gods? Why, this
Will lug your priests and servants from your sides,
Pluck stout men's pillows from below their heads.
This yellow slave

Thus bread is exchanged for fish, fish for clothes, clothes for fuel, fuel for shelter and so on and so on, but all by means of gold. That is to say, by each commodity actually being exchanged in the first instance for gold, and in the second instance, by their comparative prices all being reckoned in quantities of gold.

Thus gold has become money and certain quantities of it—viz. so many ounces, or fractions of an ounce, of gold—have become the units of money. For coinage and coins have really nothing to do with the matter. Pounds sterling, shillings and pence, are simply names that have been given to so many ounces, or fractions of an ounce, of gold.

This is how money originated. And this original kind of money is most conveniently called "commodity money." For that name makes it clear that money is simply a commodity like any other— but a commodity which has been, as it were, seconded for special duties. The chief of these duties are, first, to serve as a means of exchanging all other commodities; and, second, to serve as a substance which can be infinitely subdivided into quantities, so that

> *Will knit and break religions; bless the accurs'd;*
> *Make the hoar leprosy ador'd; place thieves,*
> *And give them title, knee, and approbation,*
> *With senators on the bench; this is it,*
> *That makes the wappen'd widow wed again....*

It is difficult not to believe that this is one of the passages which Shakespeare wrote into the MS. of *Timon of Athens*. Marx quotes it in *Capital*. Incidentally it is not usually observed that Marx was a keen Shakespearean. The first 150 pages of *Capital* have four Shakespearean quotations alone. Shakespeare, himself, who stood just at the watershed between feudal and modern life, had the keenest possible sense of the fatal and overmastering power of economic necessity, both for the individual and for the community. A whole sequence of the sonnets is after all nothing more than an echo of Hamlet's answer to the question of why he was melancholy: "Why, sir, I lack advancement...." Mr. Keynes, however, points out that Shakespeare was in the end able to achieve "advancement" and died rich. As Mr. Keynes says, he could hardly help doing so, since he lived at a time when immense profits were being reaped by the Elizabethan governing class at the expense of the workers and peasants by means of rapidly rising prices. Mr. Keynes goes on to swallow whole in one footnote the materialist conception of history, stated in rather an extreme form. He makes the suggestion that "by far the larger proportion of the world's greatest writers and artists have flourished in the atmosphere of buoyancy, exhilaration and the freedom from economic cares felt by the governing class, which is engendered by profit inflations." (*A Treatise on Money*, Vol. II, p. 154.) It would almost seem that Mr. Keynes believes that "profits do make poets of us all." Marx never went as far as that.

the price of everything can be reckoned by comparing it to a particular quantity of the money commodity.

Whether or not this primal type of money, commodity money, is still the only actual type in use is another matter of dispute between capitalist economists. (As a matter of fact, as we shall show, there is not the slightest doubt that money is and always must be, so long as capitalism endures, a commodity.)

Let us, for example, consider for a moment the view of the nature of money taken by the most optimistic of all capitalist theorists, Mr. J. M. Keynes. The text which immediately follows is a summary, and so necessarily a rough and ready, account of his view of the functions of money and the possibilities of monetary reforms as exposed in the early chapters of his two volumes entitled *A Treatise on Money*. If we come, by following this guide, to any conclusions unfavourable to the possibilities of monetary reform, we shall know that if we had instanced the work of other capitalist economists, such as Dr. Hayek or Mr. D. H. Robertson, we should inevitably have come to conclusions still more unfavourable.

Mr. Keynes' view is selected for discussion, not because it is necessarily the soundest, but just because it does hold out the maximum possible hope of capitalist revival by way of monetary reform. Meanwhile, some attempt will be made in the footnotes to keep an eye on the views, at least of Dr. Hayek who represents a school of monetary thought which is particularly interesting for our purposes. These footnotes, since reasons of space forbid an exposition of another monetary theory, will inevitably assume a much greater familiarity with the subject than does the main text. Perhaps those readers, who do not happen to have made a special study of a subject which Mr. D. H. Robertson calls "a field of appalling intellectual difficulty" will not take offence if it is suggested that the footnotes in this and the following chapter can, if the reader prefers it, be neglected altogether without breaking the continuity of the argument.

Mr. Keynes considers that there exist to-day no less than four kinds of money. He calls them Commodity money; Fiat money; Managed money; and Bank money.

Let us take these kinds of money, one by one. Commodity

money we have already considered. Fiat money is what people usually call "inconvertible paper money."

Managed money is also paper money, but it is a paper money which the authorities undertake to manage in such a way as to maintain its value at a constant level in terms of some commodity. For instance, Great Britain had Managed money between 1925 and 1931. Her citizens used paper notes, but the value of each pound note was kept equal to a given weight of gold. This was ensured by giving everyone the right to convert one of these notes into this weight of gold. In order to be able to do this, the State has to refrain from issuing too much of this money.

Now it will be observed —that these last two kinds of money, Fiat money and Managed money, are both issued by the State. Therefore they may both be classified as kinds of State money.

Lastly, Mr. Keynes distinguishes Bank money. Bank money is in one sense another kind of money altogether. It is a kind of money, moreover, which performs only one of the two essential functions of money which we defined above. It acts perfectly as a medium of exchange. But it cannot possibly be a standard of price. Bank money is a kind of private, irregular money, which has grown up behind the back of the State. For it is the State, as we have seen, which creates Fiat and Managed money, and even, when it coins it, recognizes Commodity money with the official stamp of its blessing at the mint. Private Bank money, however, is a very old institution: it dates from the time when men discovered that the acknowledgment of a good and reliable debt was just as good a thing to own as the amount of the debt itself. Bank money is, in fact, simply a gigantic system of I.O.U.s which are passed about from hand to hand by means of cheques and "bills." For example: A wants to buy a dog from B for £10. Instead of giving B ten one-pound notes, A writes a bill, or letter, to his banker, who keeps A's money for him, telling him to pay B ten one-pound notes at any time that B likes to call. But B, as it happens, is buying a table from C, also for £10. So instead of taking the trouble to go to A's bank and get the notes, he writes a sort of postscript to A's letter to his banker (endorses A's "bill," as we say), telling the banker to pay the notes to C instead of to himself. C, however, wants to buy something from D, and again passes A's acknowledgment of a debt of £10—for that is what a "bill" is—on to D: and so on and so on without anyone ever troubling to go to A's bank and get the notes. Thus we see that these *acknowledgments of debts* can circulate on and on exactly as if they were money. And in fact it is calculated that about nine-tenths of the money which we use to-day is this kind of "Bank money."

Observe, however, two important limitations which attach to Bank money. In the first place, the whole system depends on everybody's confidence in everybody else. Unless B believes that A really has got the ten one-pound notes in a bank, the acknowledgment of the debt, however precise, is valueless. For in that case it would be A who had sold B a pup. Hence, Bank money depends on the exchangers having confidence in each other's stability and integrity. In the second place, Bank money, the acknowledgment of debts, cannot itself be the standard of price. The amount of the debt must be reckoned in terms of something other than itself. It is, of course, reckoned in money, that is, in units of one or other of the particular kinds of money which are in use in the community. You cannot, in other words, pay a man in "bills" or "cheques." You pay him in a cheque of, say, £10. There must always be some monetary units to write on the face of the cheque.

These then are Mr. Keynes' four existing types of money. Is it not already clear, however, that the last three types Fiat, Managed, and Bank money are, in fact, a mere superstructure built on the essential and original type, Commodity money? And is it not clear that they cannot exist without Commodity money as their foundation?

For we have seen that Bank money, in spite of the undoubted fact that it is the predominant form of money current to-day, cannot, on Mr. Keynes' own showing, be the only or exclusive money of the community. Some other form of money must underlie it. Now Managed money is clearly derivative from Commodity money. It is not identical with it, but it cannot exist unless Commodity money exists too, unless, that is, there still exists some commodity (or, as will appear, commodities) which has been picked out as the general equivalent. For, as we saw, it is of the essence of Managed money that it is managed with reference to the value of some commodity. And this is shown by another name which can be given to Managed money. For Managed money is a particular type of "Representative money." It is, that is to say, money which consists of something (say, paper) which is made to represent another thing (say, gold). Hence, it is clear that Representative money cannot exist without something to represent. As to Fiat money, Mr. Keynes himself admits that it cannot exist for long without breaking down. That is to say, the mere decree, the arbitrary "say so" of the State, cannot for ever, or universally, make pieces of paper which have no fixed quantitative relation to any commodity, carry out the functions of money. Sooner or later such Fiat money, for the value of which there will be no criterion, which may rapidly become more or less valuable to any extent, will cease to perform the functions of money. For people will no longer accept it in exchange for anything else. They will not reckon the value of everything else in terms of its units. It will cease to be money.

Therefore, it is surely impossible to deny that Mr. Keynes' own train of argument leads to the conclusion that the original form of money—Commodity money—is the only form. All the rest are superstructures upon the top of it. For it is agreed that Fiat money will only function so long as there lasts, what we may call, the momentum of goodwill of the Commodity money which it has succeeded. As for Managed money and Bank money, they are merely ingenious and important extensions of Commodity money: extensions, however, which cannot possibly exist without their base. Hence, in one form or another, Commodity money is the essential basis of all money. And yet Mr. Keynes says that the era of Commodity money is finally over. Surely he is guilty of a quibble. For he tells us that our modern money is "Representative money." Agreed, but representative of what? Obviously of some commodity. No one, of course, is suggesting that we use directly Commodity money to-day, in the sense that given weights of the chosen commodity circulate amongst us. But is it not obvious that Representative money betrays by its very name that it is only Commodity money at one remove?

Now, if money is a commodity, the particular commodity which has been selected to be money has a price—like any other commodity. And that price will be immediately determined by the supply of it and the demand for it. Therefore its price can, and will, fluctuate. Gold, as we have seen, is to-day the commodity chosen by the most important countries of the world to be their money commodity. And the price of gold can and does fluctuate widely. But what does this mean? What effect does it have on the mechanism of the market when gold—the commodity chosen to be the general equivalent of all other commodities—when money itself, fluctuates in price? Before answering that question, let us at once define this paradoxical conception "the price of money." I use it throughout this chapter to mean the exact converse of the phrase "the general price-level." The way in which to think of the "price of money" is to read a price-list from right to left instead of from left to right. Then we realize that it is just as true to say that you can buy a certain amount of money with a certain amount of goods, as vice versa. All that is necessary is to think of goods buying money instead of money buying goods. For a change in the price of money is the same thing as a simultaneous, and opposite, change in the price of everything else. For money, as we have seen, is amongst other things the measuring-rod of the economic world. And if the measuring-rod grows longer in the night, everything else is reckoned to be shorter next morning.

Now the inconveniences and distresses of changes in the price of money are all too well known to the modern world. We need not labour them here. Suffice it to say that in principle it is clear that if money itself is, for example, going up in price, then obviously the process of exchange will be slowed down. For when a man has only completed half of an exchange, when he has sold but not bought, he has money in his hands. But if that money is going up in price, he will hold on to it and not buy until he can get more commodities for his money than he would have previously.[1] Conversely, if the price of money is going down, he will hurry to buy and the process of exchange will be speeded up— unless indeed its price is falling so catastrophically that the other man, with whom he is exchanging, is holding on to his goods, since they are now rapidly increasing in price.[2] Thus, in either

[1] This is above all true when the purchase which he contemplates is a purchase of an investment. But to develop this point would be to anticipate the argument of the next chapter.

[2] Why, however, is it universally observed that men are more anxious to hold on to their money when prices are falling than to hold on to their goods when prices are rising? The answer is, no doubt, that money is the universal "good," the fetish of wealth, which gives its possessor the choice of any particular "good." Once he has spent it, he has only the particular good he has bought and no others. His boundless choice has gone.

case, unstable money ceases adequately to perform its function as a medium of exchange.

Again, of course, a rise or fall in the price of money prevents it from properly fulfilling another major function which arises out of its function as a standard of price. This third function of money, which for simplicity's sake we have not yet considered, is to serve as a reckoning of the amount of the debts people owe each other, and as a means of paying these debts when the agreed time of settlement arrives. Now the chief way in which debts are contracted is for a seller to deliver commodities to a buyer, and for the buyer to postpone, by agreement, his payment for them. This function of money, which is to bridge the gap of time which often in practice must occur between the two halves of an exchange, is sometimes alluded to as the function of money as a means of deferred payment: sometimes, as "a store of value." It is obviously this function,—above all important in the modern world—that changes in the "price" (the buying power) of money impair most of all. For how can money measure truly the amount of a debt over a space of time, if over the same space of time a given amount of money is itself changing in price? Again, unstable money upsets the necessary calculations of all entrepreneurs, since their function of producing goods takes time. If they buy raw materials, when prices are high, and if, when they come to sell the finished product, there has been a sharp fall in the level of price while they were busy producing, they may be ruined. These are naturally only the most obvious cases of the damage caused to the mechanism of the market by unstable money.

But we have already been driven to the conclusion that money is, and must always remain, just one particular commodity—or, and this is the same thing, must be kept convertible into one particular commodity at a fixed rate. Hence the price of money must vary with every variation in the price of the chosen commodity. For example, if the chosen commodity is gold its price will (and did, in fact) go down if a new and more easily worked gold field, or a cheaper way of working the present ones, are discovered. On the other hand, if the demand for gold is increased by more communities adopting it as the basis of their money, or if important new industrial uses for it are discovered, and the supply of it does not proportionately increase, its price will go up.

Thus the price of any Commodity money can only remain stable in the unlikely event of the supply of the selected commodity happening to increase or decrease exactly in the same proportion as the demand for it, both as money and as an ordinary useful commodity. This has never happened, and money has never in fact been stable in price. It has not, however, been as unstable as might be supposed from this analysis. If the increased demand for money which arose during the last hundred years as a result of the enormous increase of the number of exchanges which took place—that is, the vast increase in the world's trade—had been allowed to have its direct effect on the price of gold, gold would have risen (and everything else would have fallen) in price to such an extent and with such rapidity that trade would have become impossible.[1] As a matter of fact, however, vast "economies," as the economists call them, were effected in the use of gold. In the first place, it was found that it was not necessary for actual gold to circulate in order to effect exchanges. Pieces of paper would do as well, and it was found possible to keep those paper notes stable in price in terms of gold—"to maintain convertibility"—even though more notes (in moderation) were issued than there was gold to back them with. This, as we have seen, is the economy of Managed money.

Far more important, however, was the economy effected by the growth of Bank money. Even in countries, like nineteenth-century Britain, in which actual gold circulated as coin, this did not mean that a direct Commodity money was being used as the predominant current money. For much the larger proportion of the actual money necessary to circulate commodities did not consist in nineteenth-century Britain of these bits of gold. On the contrary, it consisted of Bank money, i.e. of acknowledgments of debts passed from hand to hand in the form of cheques and "bills." This Bank

[1] Dr. Hayek (see *Prices and Production*) denies this, and considers that a fall in prices due to increased trading with the same amount of money is always healthy. It would be interesting, and not perhaps impossible, for an historical statistician to calculate the fall in the price-level which would have been necessary to carry on the increase in trade between say, 1800 and 1900, had there been no increase in the circulation of money. Perhaps even Dr. Hayek would admit the catastrophic social consequences of such a fall in prices, even though he might still be able to show that by having allowed it to take place "the structure of production" would never have been distorted and so crisis avoided.

money, however, had to be kept stable in value with gold. This was done by making it convertible into gold. Hence the authorities had to see that they did not create too much of it, lest it lose its value. For in that event everybody would try to convert their Bank money into gold and Bank money would go out of use. It was only by means of the unparalleled growth in the use of this Bank money as a circulating medium that a gold famine was averted. Naturally, however, there was nothing to ensure that these economies in the use of gold, plus any increase in its supply, would always equal the increase in the demand for money, caused by the enormous increase in exchange transactions. Yet this coincidence alone could have allowed general prices to remain stable. (And even this coincidence, as we shall see, would not have *ensured* a stable price-level. Far from it. All the more disastrous fluctuations in prices, the so-called Credit Cycle, could, and would, have taken place just the same. But without this coincidence in the net supply and demand of gold, general prices *must* have moved. Their equality was a prerequisite, not an assurance of general price stability.) In any case, the coincidence did not occur.

From the middle of the last century, for twenty-five years to 1875, prices rose. This was, no doubt, due partly to the growth of the use of Bank money and partly to the discovery of fresh gold fields, which enabled capitalism to finance many more exchanges. Later on in the century (for another twenty-five years, 1875-1900) prices fell. But whether this fall in prices, which was the main symptom of the great depression of the early eighteen-nineties, was, in fact, due to the demand for gold exceeding the supply, or to other non-monetary factors, which we have not yet considered, is another matter. The latest opinion amongst capital economists themselves is inclined to the view that the demand for, and the supply of, gold had much less to do with it than had been formerly supposed. Mr. Keynes and his contemporaries, however, have only half transferred their attention from the monetary mechanism to events in the outside world. They have only got to the half-way house which we shall describe in the next chapter.

There is little doubt as to what was the fundamental cause of the business depression of the end of the nineteenth century. What happened was that the products of two formidable new industrial nations, Germany and the United States, began at that time to appear upon the world market and to compete with the products of Great Britain. Undoubtedly, such competition had its repercussions in monetary affairs. The new industrial nations naturally insisted upon setting up their own gold reserves independently of the Bank of England. And this helped to cause that shortage of gold, and consequently of money, which on a superficial view appears to be the reason for the depression. Even such a realist as Bismarck, the leader of one of the new industrial competitors, seems to have been content to regard the competition for gold as the important thing. Hence, his well-known remark that the powers, each trying to accumulate gold, were like a number of men, lying in the same bed, and all trying to cover themselves with one blanket. The comparison is just, if the blanket symbolizes not merely the world's available gold supply but the world's available markets. It was the general competition of the powers, not merely their competition for gold, which was the cause of the depression.

But if this was the cause of the depression of the eighteen-nineties, what was the cause of the comparative revival which occurred in the early nineteen-hundreds? Why did not the depression, and with it the competitive rivalries of the great powers steadily worsen, until the logical end in war was reached at about the turn of the century? How are we to account for the breathing-space of almost a decade and a half, from 1900 to 1914, which was given to world capitalism? Here, again, there are non-monetary factors to account for the phenomenon. There is above all the fact that in the eighteen-nineties there were still large areas into which the rival imperialist powers could expand without immediately colliding with each other. Africa could be, and was, partitioned, South America and China opened up, India more intensively exploited, Burma annexed. There is no doubt that it was this phase of all-round imperialist expansion which played the greatest part in the revival of the nineteen-hundreds.

It must be admitted, however, that the check to the fall in general prices about 1900 coincided with the opening of the South African gold mines, and the sudden improvement in gold mining technique which occurred at the same time. (The master patent of the cyanide process is dated 1890.) Thus, although we must not for a moment neglect the non-monetary factors, there is little doubt that the actual increase in the production, and above all *decrease in the cost of production,* of gold around 1900, did play a part in the recovery after 1900.

In general, then, although changes in the price of the commodity used as money have undoubtedly changed the general level of prices, they have not, thanks to the immense growth of Bank money and Managed money, changed it with such violence as to dislocate the mechanism of the market.

We have arrived then at the first of the consequences of the conclusion that, under capitalism, money must always be a commodity. General prices can never be made stable. For if, for example, the commodity selected be gold, then the price of money will vary with the price of gold. Need the commodity selected, however, be gold? Gold was not by any means the original, nor need it necessarily be the ultimate, money commodity. The proposal is now seriously made by the most advanced theorists of capitalism, that gold should be dismissed from its monetary throne and a new commodity raised up in its stead. More exactly what is proposed is not to select any one new commodity but to construct from the basis of *all* the most important existing commodities a new synthetic or artificial commodity to serve as money. What is proposed is that a table of the prices of say sixty of the chief commodities in use in the world to-day should be kept; and from this table an average price should be read off each day—or each week.[1] When once this new "tabular" commodity, as it is called, is established, a system of Managed money (inevitably consisting predominately of Bank money) is to be imposed on top of it. That is to say, the money of the community, which under a "gold standard" was managed so as to keep £1 always equal to a given number of ounces of gold, is now to be managed so as to keep £1 always equal to so many units of this new composite commodity. In other words, money is to be so regulated as to keep the index number of the prices of the sixty commodities selected always the same.

[1] The actual compiling of an index number of prices is by no means a simple matter. It is above all necessary to "weight" the commodities selected in accordance with the amount which they are actually used. Jevons, Edgeworth and the older economists used to hold that this was unnecessary. But Mr. Keynes has shown, I think conclusively, that they were misapplying a law of physics to the problems of economics.

The first observation to make about this proposal is that its adoption is not in essence inconceivable. The establishment of a "Tabular Standard" for money is conceivable, since, under it, money still remains in the last resort a commodity.

The second observation to make is that a tabular money could not eliminate changes in the price-level due to changes in the price of the money commodity. For, even if we assume that it proved quite possible so to manage the new money that it retained a constant purchasing power in terms of the sixty commodities selected, the price of these commodities themselves could, and certainly would, vary in relation to the prices of all the other almost innumerable commodities and services which exist all over the world. Just because the Tabular Standard is a Commodity money, it does not escape the objection to all forms of Commodity money, namely, that the selected commodity—or in this case commodities—will vary in price. The most that can be claimed is that this disadvantage of Commodity money may be diminished by a Tabular Standard. Since the changes in the prices of the individual commodities composing the table would, it is hoped, tend to "average out" and so produce stability.

An apparently obvious way out of this difficulty will at once occur to the reader. Why restrict the composition of the new composite money commodity to sixty important commodities? Why not include in it all commodities? Why not take an average of all prices and so manage your money that it keeps these prices stable? And this is what is meant, in fact, by those persons who advocate the adoption of a money managed, not by the price of any one commodity, or even list of commodities, but by the price of commodities in general. The objection to this solution is that it is in fact impossible to find a common measure for all objects of expenditure all over the world, on the basis of which to construct an average of price. The conception becomes so general as to lose all meaning. Mr. Keynes devotes Book II of his *Treatise on Money* to this subject and concludes characteristically that "we are not in a position to weigh satisfactions for similar persons of Pharaoh's slaves against Fifth Avenue's motor-cars, of dear food and cheap ice to Laplanders against cheap fuel and dear ice to Hottentots." In other words, the conditions under which human beings live vary so greatly at different points in space, and have varied so greatly at different points in time, that the degree of urgency of their wants is incommensurable. Hence, Mr. Keynes suggests that money should in future be managed so as to keep its price (its buying power, that is) stable in terms of a relatively simple list of say sixty important commodities, even though this would by no means ensure that changes in the prices of the monetary commodities would never affect general prices.

In any case it is now admitted by Mr. Keynes and most other serious economists of capitalism that this question of the stability of the price of the commodity, or commodities, upon which money is based is a much less important one than had been supposed. We have seen that when, as in the last century, the price of money (the price-level) was made dependent on the demand and supply of even one particular commodity (gold) alone, the fluctuations in prices which could possibly be attributed to changes in the price of gold were not the important ones.

Just in the same way the changes in the average price of sixty commodities chosen to serve as the basis of a new tabular money, and any future changes in the demand for money, would not be the predominant influence acting upon the price-level. Therefore, it is scarcely worth the while of the economists to attempt to discover a monetary commodity which will remain stable in price. For changes in the price-level are, in fact, predominantly due to non-monetary causes. We shall devote the next chapter to showing that this is now an agreed point. It has now been discovered by the capitalist economists themselves that the fluctuations in the price-level which really matter, and which mark the recurrent crises of capitalism, are not due to changes in the price of money at all. On the contrary: the movement of the general price-level up and down the credit cycle, is the effect and not the cause of commercial crises. The instability of money is due to the crisis, not the crisis to the instability of money.

To sum up. It is a characteristic of all money that it varies in price. (This is merely another way of saying that under capitalism the general price-level can never be stable.) This is due to the fact that money is a commodity, and all commodities are liable to changes in price owing to changes in the cost of their production or in the amount of the demand for them. Modern money has, however, departed a considerable distance from its commodity basis. It is now only indirectly a commodity. This has made it possible to minimize the effect of changes in the price of the money commodity. This has been possible even when money has been based on a single commodity, gold. It is now proposed to base money on the price of a composite commodity averaged from the prices of the principal individual commodities.

Such a reform would do nothing, however, to prevent the recurrence of capitalist crises. The next chapter will be devoted to a demonstration of the fact that this is now admitted by even the most optimistic of the economists of capitalism themselves. We shall show that it is now agreed that a perfect tabular money would not even help to eliminate crises.[1] For it has been discovered that prices go up and down in the disastrous economic switchback of the credit crisis for reasons which are not monetary at all. In other words, commercial crises (such as the present one) are not due to prices going up and then down: but, on the contrary, the movement of prices is the result of the crisis.

[1] Dr. Hayek would go further than this and would say that the very attempt to eliminate changes in prices "on the side of money," as he calls it, would, in times of technical progress, actually *cause* commercial crises.

CHAPTER VI

CAPITALIST CRISIS

WE are now in a position to examine the true causes of the recurrent crises of capitalism. If even the most optimistic of capitalist
economists are agreed that crises are not caused by the instability
of money, what are they caused by?

Now we have indicated in the last chapter that the truth of the
matter is that the recurrence of crisis is inherent in the whole
character of a system of private enterprise and competition. The
phenomena of crises can be shown to be the inevitable consequences
of the essential features of capitalism, of the fact, that is, that capitalist production is carried on without plan, that its only regulating
mechanism is the mechanism of the market, and that the wealth of
the community is concentrated in the hands of the small class of
persons who own the means of production. What we shall be concerned with in these chapters, however, is to show that the economists of capitalism have, themselves, been driven to this conclusion.
Let us, therefore, continue to follow up Mr. Keynes' thesis.

Mr. Keynes considers that, broadly speaking, the price-level depends upon one particular thing—upon, that is, *the proportion of
savings to investments*. In order to understand what he means by
this, it is necessary to know the two broad categories into which
economists divide all commodities. These categories are investment,
or capital, goods and consumption goods, respectively. Investment,
or capital, goods are, as the name implies, such things as looms,
land drains, and power stations; and consumption goods are the
cotton cloth, agricultural produce and electric current which these
capital goods help to produce.[1]

In any capitalist society, the modern capitalist economists continue,
there are two streams which flow through the body politic. There
is a stream of money ceaselessly passing from hand to hand and

[1] I am deliberately neglecting, as unnecessary to my argument, the further
distinction between investment and capital goods, on Mr. Keynes' definition.

there is a stream of goods and services, also circulating until they drop out of the process by being consumed: and both these streams are subdivided. The stream of money is subdivided into the money which people save and the money which people spend; the stream of goods is subdivided into capital goods and consumption goods. Now it is clear that there must be a connection between the spending part of the money stream and the consumption goods part of the goods stream, on the one hand, and between the savings part of the money stream and the capital goods part of the goods stream on the other. For investing is just spending your money on capital goods instead of on consumption goods. If, for example, you have spent £5 on a suit of clothes, you have bought £5 worth of consumption goods. But if you saved the £5 and invested it in one of the loans of the British Central Electricity Board, you would really have bought £5 worth of the "pylons" which are to-day bestriding the British countryside. For when the Central Electricity Board got your £5, they would use it to buy £5 worth of that particular kind of capital goods. And so one would suppose that the amount people saved, the amount they invested, and the demand for capital goods would always be equal. In the same way, one would think, the amount people spent and the demand for consumption goods would be equal too. What then do economists mean when they talk about the proportion of savings to investments? What, above all, do they mean when they go on to say that the price-level depends on the proportion of investments to savings? They tell us that they mean that the price-level depends upon whether the proportion of the community's savings to its spendings exceeds or falls short of the proportion of consumption goods and investment goods which it produces. (It may help the reader to realize that what is being compared is *a proportion to a proportion*. That is to say, it is $\frac{\text{spendings}}{\text{savings}}$ which ought to be equal to the production of $\frac{\text{consumption goods}}{\text{investment goods}}$. The real equation is not quite so simple as this.)[1]

Now a moment's thought will show us why prices must move if these proportions are not equal. For clearly if we all devote, say, a

[1] In Mr. Keynes' words, "The question whether the price-level of the goods which are consumed is in fact equal or unequal to their cost of production" (when it is equal, the price-level will be stable) "depends on whether the division of income between savings and expenditure on consumption is or is not the same as the division of the cost of production of output between the cost of the goods which are added to capital and the cost of the goods which are consumed."

quarter of our productive resources to producing investment goods and three-quarters to producing consumption goods, then, in fact, and whether we subsequently like it or not, we have "saved" one quarter of our income. For only three-quarters of the possible amount of consumption goods will have been produced; and we shall only have this three-quarters to consume. But is there any guarantee that at the same time we shall all have only spent three-quarters of our money income and have saved the other quarter? And if there is no such guarantee, what happens? As a matter of fact, there is not the slightest reason to suppose that we shall always save and spend in an equal proportion to our production of capital and consumption goods. For, and this is the real point, under capitalism, the decision as to how much of our productive energies we shall put into making investment goods and consumption goods respectively, and the complementary decision as to how much of our income we shall save and how much we shall spend are made quite independently and by different sets of people. Naturally, therefore, the two decisions do not keep step. The decision as to how much new capital is to be created is, of course, made by the capitalists or entrepreneurs. It is they who decide whether new factories shall be built, new mines sunk, new land drained and cleared. And, naturally, they make the decision depend on whether they anticipate that these new capital goods will, if they create them, bring them in a profit. And this decision of theirs, be it observed, is the decision upon which the proportion of the community's energies which shall be devoted to the production of investment goods as against consumption goods, depends. For if the entrepreneurs employ, say, one-quarter of the available labour and other means of production, of the "factors of production," as the economists call them, on making investment goods, then there will be only three-quarters of the factors of production left for making consumable goods.

But is it the entrepreneurs who make the other decision as to how much of the community's money income shall be spent on consumable commodities, and how much of it shall be saved? They do not. On the contrary, everybody—all recipients of money incomes, that is—decides that for themselves. So what happens if, when the entrepreneurs have decided, and have proceeded in fact, to use a quarter of the factors of production for investment goods, leaving only three-quarters to produce consumption goods, the public decides only to save one-eighth of its money incomes and to spend all of the remaining seven-eighths on consumption? *Naturally the only result can be a rise in the prices of all consumption goods.* For the entrepreneurs have only produced three-quarters, while the consumers are demanding seven-eighths of the possible output of them. Hence, demand exceeds supply, and prices rise. Conversely, if the entrepreneurs had decided to employ only one-eighth of the factors of production on producing investment goods, and seven-eighths on producing consumable goods, and the public had saved one-quarter of its money, and had, therefore, only three-quarters of it left to spend, the prices of consumable goods must fall. For there will be more of them and less money to buy them with, viz. supply will exceed demand. This proposition is the foundation of a whole school of thought which, in one form or another, is being expounded by several capitalist economists.[1] It is, on the other hand, very far from being the whole story. (The prices of investment goods them-

[1] The version of the theory propounded by Dr. Hayek and his school sounds very different from Mr. Keynes' version. It approaches the problem from another angle, and Dr. Hayek takes a much less optimistic view of the possibilities of remedial action. But on the broad facts of what happens in the credit cycle they are, as I understand them, in agreement. For Dr. Hayek's version of the theory relies equally with Mr. Keynes' on the proportionate demand for capital and consumption goods, respectively, as the key to the situation. Certainly Dr. Hayek's conception of "the structure of production" which exists at any given moment is a useful one. His point is that there are not two broad categories of goods, capital goods and consumption goods. There is an infinitely graded hierarchy of goods, from machine tools at one end to a toothbrush at the other. Moreover, he points out that many goods can be used at one time as capital goods and at another time as consumption goods. Thus he considers that the effect of, say, an increase of saving with its consequent decrease in demand for consumption goods, and increase in demand for capital goods, alters "the structure of production" by making it longer and narrower—by pulling it out like a concertina, or, as Dr. Hayek puts it, most elegantly, as befits a Viennese, by opening it like a fan! (Dr. Hayek seems to slur over a point which we shall consider in a moment, of whether new savings do always increase demand for capital goods by increasing investment.) Now "the structure of production" is simply the way in which things are produced at a given moment. That is to say, if it is long it means that production is a long, elaborate, highly mechanized business, employing a great deal of capital. If short, that it is a simple, direct, relatively unmechanized business, with little capital. Thus an increase in demand for investment goods—an increased use of capital in production—is what he calls lengthening the structure of production.

(All this seems to be merely an approach towards the Marxian conception of "the higher organic composition of capital." And Dr. Hayek is quite right, if hardly original, in saying that this tendency is at the root of some of the worst troubles of capitalism.)

selves, for example, are said to depend upon a different, though related, combination of factors. Again, we have not yet taken any account of another factor, which, according to Mr. Keynes, is equally important—namely, the behaviour of the banking system. It is clear, for example, that *the price* which entrepreneurs have to pay for the credit which can alone enable them to take command of, say, one-quarter of the factors of production and turn them on to producing investment goods, will have a vital bearing on the matter. But more as to that later.)

All the same, once this basic proposition has been grasped, it is not difficult to understand the new explanation of the recurrence of sharp fluctuations in the general price-level and so of crises. For, it is clear from the above that broadly speaking whenever the entrepreneurs are producing capital goods to a greater amount than the public is saving, prices must rise, and whenever the opposite is happening prices must fall. Now it is suggested by Mr. Keynes that a capitalist community saves a surprisingly constant amount of its income from year to year. The factor which changes suddenly is that of investment. For entrepreneurs may easily wish to invest far more one year than they do the next. A vital new technical discovery may suddenly offer them the expectation of high profits. (The invention of steam railways acted in this way in Great Britain in the last century. The invention of the motor-car had the same effect in America this century.) Or a new country may, as we have seen, be suddenly "opened up" and made safe for every kind of investment; or a war, requiring immense quantities of munitions and supplies, may break out. On the other hand, conditions may suddenly become unfavourable for investment. For example, political and social instability may quickly increase the risk of long-term investment to a prohibitive point. Or again, and this factor is consistently neglected by capitalist economists, the competition of some new group of producers may begin to drive down the prices of several important commodities to a point where investment in their means of production is unattractive. This factor is becoming, as capitalist methods of production become universal, the dominating fact of the whole situation. Thus, the factor of investment is a highly variable one, while the factor of saving is relatively stable. Hence, we should expect, and we do actually find, that investment sometimes greatly exceeds and at other times as greatly falls short of saving: and that, accordingly, the price-level moves sharply up and down.

It would be out of place to describe the considerable intricacies of this theory of price determination in any but a specifically economic work. All the more so since, as I have already complained, there is no agreement in detail among the numerous economists who are now offering us various versions of it. Substantially, however, it should, I have personally no doubt, be conceded that orthodox economic science has at length approached the diagnosis of the real cause of capitalist crisis. Whether, however, this diagnosis is as new as the capitalist economists, who are scrupulously ignorant of any but "respectable" economic views, suppose, is another matter. For what in the end does the new theory amount to? It amounts to the discovery that the ruinous crises, the catastrophically sharp changes in the price-level, to which capitalism is subject, are not due to the misbehaviour of money, to the instability of the weather, or even to the malice-aforethought of bankers, but to the inherent character of the capitalist system.[1] For it is now agreed, as we have seen, that the price-level moves whenever investment ceases to equal savings, and that investment does constantly differ from savings because quite different and unrelated people do the investing and the saving, and do them without reference to each other's actions. In other words, it is now admitted that capitalist crises are due to the anarchy of production which must always characterize any system dependent upon the mechanism of the market. It has now been in effect admitted by the leading capitalist economists themselves that the true cause of the periodic breakdown of their system is the planlessness with which production is undertaken. Nor can this state of things be altered so long as capitalism endures. For if the amount of saving is not left to the free will of individuals and groups of individuals, and investment—that is, the initiation of new enterprises—to private entrepreneurs, what is left of capitalism?

[1] Whole schools of amateur economics and sociology have been founded on the view that "it is all the fault of the bankers." All the various varieties of "social credit" movements, all the types of "currency cranks" for several generations have taken the view that the bankers are exclusively to blame for the instability of capitalism. If only the bankers could be persuaded, or forced, to be more generous with credit, all would be well. The enormous potential productivity of modern technique (which the currency cranks do at any rate recognize) could be released, social antagonisms could be painlessly removed and poverty abolished. *Et ego in Arcadia vixi*—I too have lived in this economic Arcady.

Indeed, propagandists of both sides often pick out this particular feature of capitalism as its essential characteristic, and refer to "the system of private enterprise."

Some capitalist economists, however—notably Mr. Keynes—do go on to suggest a method by which, they claim, the recurrence of crises can be avoided and yet "private enterprise" retained. They suggest, however, that this can be done only if certain very notable measures are taken by the Governments of the world. Let us follow up Mr. Keynes' suggestions, for they raise very sharply the whole question of the possibility of the continuance of capitalism. Moreover, they reveal the interconnection of the recurrence of crises, the fourth characteristic of present-day capitalism, with our other three characteristics, unstable money, monopoly and nationalism.

Mr. Keynes, as we have seen, considers that crises occur when investment ceases to equal savings. Now this can happen either by a change in the amount of savings or in the amount of investments: but in practice, savings, we noticed, were the more stable factor and the typical fluctuation begins with a sudden change in the amount of investment.[1] This is very often due to a change in the conditions of production—to a new invention or a sudden increase or decrease in political stability. For these changes increase or diminish the investing entrepreneurs' expectations of profit. But their expectation of profit does not depend uniquely on the returns which they anticipate. It depends also on the cost of investment.

[1] Dr. Hayek dissenting. Dr. Hayek usually starts off the process with a change in the volume of savings—in practice, I should have thought, an unusual occurrence. He does not mention, at any rate in *Prices and Production,* the possibility of the original impetus coming from a change in the urge to investment on the part of the entrepreneurs. This is, I take it, because this urge can never take effect unless the bankers "accommodate" the now eager entrepreneurs. And if the bankers do accommodate the entrepreneurs this is tantamount to the process of change starting by the "injection," to use his words, of new money in the form of producers' credits—a case which he does consider.

Yet it seems far fetched to describe, say, the railway boom of the last century as being *due* to an "injection" of new money in the form of producers' credits! Surely it would have required bankers of that super-conservatism, of which Dr. Hayek fondly dreams, but frankly admits that he may never live to see, to have refused to allow railways to be built because there had not been sufficient prior voluntary saving to pay for them? In a sense, however, Dr. Hayek may be right in saying that that would have been the only way to mitigate recurrent crises under capitalism. For this almost amounts to saying that the way to have prevented crises in capitalism was to have prevented capitalism from ever arising. And there is a lot in that.

That is to say, it depends on the rate of interest which the entrepreneurs have to pay when they come to borrow the money necessary for the production of investment goods. For in modern conditions, the entrepreneurs do not, in the typical case, own the very large sums of capital necessary for considerable new enterprises. Even if, exceptionally, a group of entrepreneurs do themselves own sufficient resources to finance their proposed enterprises, it makes no real difference, for their money will already be employed elsewhere and it will cost them the prevailing rate of interest to withdraw it from its present employment and devote it to the new enterprise. Thus we may say that entrepreneurs borrow from the whole property-owning community, either, in the case of a short loan, through the banks acting as middle men, or, in the case of a long loan, by an issue of bonds (or sometimes shares), with an "issuing house" acting as middle man. Naturally, therefore, the question of whether some new enterprise, or piece of investment, shall be undertaken or not depends in fact on whether the rate of profit which it is expected to yield exceeds, sufficiently to cover the risks involved, the rate of interest which the entrepreneurs will have to pay on the money borrowed to undertake it. Thus the volume of investment does not depend simply on the expectation of profit, but on the proportion of the expected rate of profit to the current rate of interest. Hence, the volume of investment can change, not only because of a change in the expectation of profit, but because of a change in prevailing rates of interest on borrowed money.

Can anyone, however, control the prevailing rates of interest? The answer to this question is vital to Mr. Keynes' argument, for clearly, if there exists anyone who can effectively control the rates of interest, he may be able to control the volume of investment. Since even though he would not be able to control the expectation of profit—and so the inducement to investment—he would be able to control the second determinant, the cost of investment. Hence if, for example, he wished to keep the volume of investment constant, for every change in the entrepreneurs' expectations of profit, he might be able to make an equal and opposite change in their costs of investment. In other words, there will always be, in pure theory, a change in the rate of interest on borrowed money which will just balance any change in the entrepreneurs' expectations of profits. Hence, if savings are constant, this change in the rate of interest will keep the volume of investment equal to the rate of savings. This rate of investment, Mr. Keynes calls "the natural rate of interest." If "the market rate," that is the actual rate prevailing, is the same as the natural rate, then, investment will equal savings. And if investment equals savings, the price-level, Mr. Keynes believes, will be stable.

Hence, it is alleged that he who can control the rate of interest, and so the volume of investment, controls the price-level. Mr. Keynes' answer to the question of whether anyone can actually control the rate of interest is unequivocal. He believes that the bankers, ultimately the central bankers, can and sometimes do control the rates of interest. He considers that the central banks—that is, in Great Britain, the Bank of England; in America, the Federal Reserve Board; in France, the Bank of France; in Germany, the Reichsbank, and so on—by altering their rate of short-term lending —their "bank rate" or "re-discount rate," as it is called—can, in fact, control all rates of interest.

This is a somewhat surprising claim, but some evidence can be brought in support of it. Indeed, I think that the chain of reasoning by which Mr. Keynes connects the bank rate with what he calls the "bond rate," that is the prevailing rate of long-term borrowing, is in itself sound. The chain, however, is very tenuous in the sense that it is very abstract. Even if it be admitted that in a social vacuum, any change in bank rate will sooner or later be reflected in a change in bond rate, that does not in the least mean that in the real world we need always expect that the one will follow the other. On the contrary, there are always so many hard and intractable "other factors," so many wars and rumours of wars, successful and unsuccessful imperialist adventures, successful and unsuccessful strikes by the working class, so many changes and chances, that the establishment of the fact that a change in bank rate, if nothing else interferes with the process, will result in a change in the bond rate, has only a very qualified importance. Let us, however, for the purposes of following Mr. Keynes' argument to its logical conclusion, assume that the claim is justified. If we make this assumption we shall find that Mr. Keynes' argument has led us to the conclusion that central banks can, by always keeping the market rate of interest equal to the natural rate, maintain a stable price-level. Hence, Mr. Keynes' view is that although the cause of these short, sharp, and altogether disastrous fluctuations in the price-level which we call crises, are not monetary; that, on the contrary, they arise from the fact that under a system of private enterprise the function of investment is inevitably separated from the function of saving, yet a monetary cure is possible. For the central banks can by appropriate variations in the rates of interest always *offset* the inherent instability of the system and so maintain equilibrium.

Is there the slightest justification for this claim? [1]

Now, it may be that enough has already been said to show that Mr. Keynes' claim is quite unjustified; that it neglects the most important factors of the situation. At the same time, instead of attempting its detailed refutation, let us assume for a moment that Mr. Keynes' theory is sound. For the surprising thing is that it will still be possible, even on the basis of this assumption, to prove that in fact no improvement in the mechanism of capitalism is possible along these lines.

Let us assume then that a central bank, acting on Mr. Keynes' instructions, could indefinitely maintain a stable price-level within the community over the currency of which the central bank in question presided. Let us, in other words, give capitalism the full benefit of assuming that a very great improvement in its present organization is possible. Let us then follow out, always on the basis of this assumption, the possible effects in the world of to-day of a

---

[1] Dr. Hayek does not think the claim to be justified. He thinks that the best bankers could do for capitalism even in theory, and he despairs of them doing so much in practice, is to keep the rate of investment down to the rate of savings and so prevent any booms developing. And this indeed is "a hard saying" for it would mean keeping the business world in what business men would certainly consider a permanent state of depression, with, in times of technical advance, a steadily falling price-level. (Incidentally Dr. Hayek has not a word to say about the automatic and perpetual increase in wealth which such a policy would bring to all creditors and *rentiers,* or about its social consequences at all.) As Dr. Hayek puts it, with a certain ferocity of manner, "bankers need not be afraid to harm production by over-caution, even in times of general depression." But once any expansion has begun nothing can be done and a crash is bound to come. As to how the crash actually does come both Mr. Keynes and Dr. Hayek point to a sudden deficiency of working capital. (See *Prices and Production,* pages 81-87.)

Moreover, when the crash has come, Dr. Hayek sternly forbids any attempt at recovery by monetary expansion. We must wait for the slow adaptation of the structure of production to the new situation. Nothing we can do can hasten the time when it will again be possible to employ all the factors of production. Or, rather, if we do try a little monetary expansion we shall get a temporary boom but only at the cost of a worse crash later on.

central bank regulating its rates of interest so as to keep invest-ment equal to savings. Now it can only do this by varying the market rate of interest every time the natural rate changes, that is to say, every time that the expectation of profits for entrepreneurs from new investment either grows or diminishes. (Or, of course, every time that the rate of savings grows or diminishes. But in practice this is a much more stable factor.)

Now as a matter of fact, central banks do no such thing.[1] They change their rate of lending in such a way as to protect their reserves of liquid cash. Therefore, if they are members of an international gold standard system, if, that is, their bank money is convertible into gold, and there is no prohibition of the export of gold, they lower their rates of interest when they are attracting plenty of gold, and raise them in order to stop an outflow of gold. Thus, just as soon as we consider the possibilities of applying the new theory we come up against the international question. We must, therefore, consider the international use of money for a moment before going on with our attempt to follow up the consequences of applying Mr. Keynes' theories in practice.

Now what is the essential difference between the use of money within a country and its use for the purpose of exchanges between countries? We have seen that the predominant current money within all the big capitalist states to-day is Bank money. In other words, we exchange our commodities amongst ourselves by handing around acknowledgments of debts. And we have gradually learned to rely on these memoranda of debts always cancelling each other out if they are given long enough to do it in. Thus actual payment

---

[1] Dr. Hayek in several passages seems to assume, on the contrary, that they always do so (see *Prices and Production,* page 75 *et infra*). This is no doubt be-cause he writes as if the rates of interest, or to use his phrase, "the loan market" was a perfect market, which responded perfectly to the supply of savings and the demand for capital. In that case, of course, the bankers would be mere automata and the market rate of interest would in fact always be the natural rate. Yet, even apart from the complication of international factors, which we are just going to consider, is not this a most artificial assumption? For in that case, as was suggested in the case of the invention of railways, bankers could never allow of the development of any major technical discovery unless there happened to have been a *previous* increase in the rate of savings. (For presumably the existing rate of savings was absorbed by existing capital development and renewal—leaving nothing over for sudden new technical progress.) Thus what Dr. Hayek really proves is that there can be no rapid technical progress under capitalism without forced savings, booms and consequently crises.

in cash is *never* demanded (Bank notes and coins have become, in fact, merely the small change of Bank money). And the system works. The payments do balance each other, because the percentage of default is negligible and (this is the real point) there are no serious interruptions in the never-ending flow of exchanges. The velocity of the flow may vary but that is all.

All this, however, only applies to a limited degree to international trade. It is true that Bank money is now extensively used for international trade (above all, until this year at any rate, the sterling bill on London was the predominant instrument). But it is not used exclusively as it is in internal trade. That is to say, payments are not allowed to run on for ever in the perfect confidence that they will balance themselves at infinity, if not before. When at any given moment the balance of payments stands high against one country, and high in favour of another, the latter country, under the gold standard system, in effect declares that the payments have ceased to balance and that consequently the balance must be paid! And paid it is in hard cash by the shipment of gold coin or bullion from one country to another.

It is not difficult to see why these periodic international "settlement days"—for that is what it comes to—are considered necessary to international trade. It is natural that people should have less confidence—and be willing therefore to allow less credit—in international transactions than in national ones. For the exclusive use of Bank money, without periodic payments of balances in cash, obviously depends on all parties having confidence that the flow of exchanges will never be interrupted: that they are in commercial relations with each other for ever. Clearly, however, this is much less true if the transactions involve moving commodities over national frontiers; if, in fact, the trade is international. The numerous areas of absolutely independent sovereignty into which the world is cut up enormously increase the risk of sudden interruptions of exchanges. It is not necessary to speak of the absolute interruption of international exchange which is effected by the outbreak of war. Even in peace-time, and to an ever-increasing extent, as we saw in Chapter IV, interferences with, and interruptions of, international exchange are becoming part of the deliberate policy of all states. Tariffs, "administrative protection," restrictions in dealings in foreign exchange, import licenses, export bounties and a host of

130 THE COMING STRUGGLE FOR POWER

other devices are, we saw, part of a highly developed policy of economic nationalism adopted by almost all states.

No wonder that traders have no confidence that payments between nations will always in the end balance each other. No wonder they have no confidence that the flow of exchanges will continue indefinitely, and that there will always be time and opportunity to offset any temporary debit balance. They know that the flow of international exchanges is constantly subject to partial interruption, and may at any moment be stopped altogether by war. No wonder, therefore, they are increasingly determined to get their cash while they can, decreasingly willing to let bills "run" for long periods.[1] Hence, the international gold standard is a device by which international balances are automatically settled in hard,

[1] Marx, of course, twice expressed this point most forcibly. Thus in the *Critique of Political Economy,* page 197, he writes: "Therefore, whenever such a thing as a chain of payments and an artificial system of settling them, is developed, money suddenly changes its visionary nebulous shape as a measure of value, turning into hard cash or means of payment, as soon as some shock causes a violent interruption of the flow of payments and disturbs the mechanism of their settlement. Thus, under conditions of fully developed capitalist production, where the commodity owner has long become a capitalist, knows his Adam Smith, and condescendingly laughs at the superstition that gold and silver alone constitute money or that money differs at all from other commodities as the absolute commodity, money suddenly reappears not as a medium of circulation, but as the only adequate form of wealth, exactly as it is looked upon by the hoarder.... This sudden reversion from a system of credit to a system of hard cash heaps theoretical fright on top of the practical panic; and the dealers by whose agency circulation is affected shudder before the impenetrable mystery in which their own economical relations are involved."

Again in *Capital,* on page 120 of Eden and Cedar Paul's translation of Volume I, where he restates the argument of the earlier book, he writes even more aptly of what is actually happening to-day: "Whenever there is a general disturbance of this mechanism, and no matter what its cause may be, money suddenly quits the ideal form of money of account and materializes as hard cash. Profane commodities can no longer replace it. The use-value of commodities becomes valueless, and their value is routed by their own form of value. A moment earlier, the bourgeois, drunk with the arrogance of prosperity, was ready to declare that money was a pure illusion, and to say that commodities were the only money. Now, when the crisis comes, the universal cry is that money alone is a commodity. As pants the hart for cooling streams, so does his spirit pant for money, the only wealth."

In these passages Marx does not confine the need for an ultimate concrete means of payment to international trade. He shows that need arises whenever there is an interruption from whatever cause to a chain of payments; and this may happen within a country if a crisis becomes sufficiently severe. But as he points out a few pages later, in *Capital,* the risk of such interruptions is greatest in international trade.

golden cash whenever the balance of payments tilts more than a little against one nation and in favour of another.

The gold standard works very simply. Say that the balance of payments tilts against Great Britain. This means that the value of all kinds of imports exceeds the value of all kinds of exports, including all the services which we do for foreigners. Foreigners selling goods in Britain are paid in pounds and then sell the pounds to buy units of their own currencies. British exporters, on the other hand, are paid in foreign currencies and buy pounds in order to bring the money home. Hence, if the value of imports exceeds the value of exports, more pounds will be sold than bought. Therefore, the price of pounds in terms of other currencies will fall. But both pounds and the other currencies are, under the gold standard, convertible into gold at a fixed rate. Hence, if pounds get cheaper and other currencies dearer, it will pay the foreign importer to convert his pounds not straight into, say, dollars, but first into gold and then to take the gold across the Atlantic and convert it into dollars. And in fact as soon as pounds have got cheaper and dollars dearer to a sufficient degree to make the difference cover the cost of shipping the gold, an export of gold occurs.[1]

Now the central bank uses its power to vary the rates of interest in order to protect its reserve of liquid cash—consisting chiefly of gold. Hence, when an export drain of gold occurs, the rates of interest inside the country which is losing gold are put up. But how do these higher interest rates stop the export of gold? In the last analysis (and neglecting many complicating but inessential factors) they do so by decreasing the volume of investment and so depressing the price-level. For a lower price-level will, of course, necessitate lower money costs of production. In plain English, a

[1] I am deliberately neglecting the complication introduced by the question of foreign lending. As we noticed in Chapter IV, the export of capital from state to state is an essential part of modern capitalism. Hence, what really constitutes international equilibrium is that the value of a country's exports (of all kinds) and interest on previous foreign loans should equal the value of its imports, of all kinds, plus the annual rate of its foreign lending of capital. The point is an important one in practice since the export of capital will sometimes go on after there is no real balance of payments to justify it. Thus, a central bank's real task is to make its state's foreign lending equal its foreign balance of payments. The immediate effect of an increase in bank rate is not to attract gold by altering the balance of trade, but to do so by checking foreign lending and/or increasing foreign borrowing. This complication does not, however, alter the general principles involved.

lower price-level necessitates lower wages, and it secures them by inflicting losses on entrepreneurs until they get wages down. (But this, as Mr. Montagu Norman, Governor of the Bank of England, discovered in 1926, is neither an easy nor a safe process.) And lower wages, other things being equal, increase a country's competitive power in the world market, and thus lower imports and increase exports. Equilibrium in the balance of payments is re-established and the "gold drain" stopped. Presumably that drain started, by costs of production having gone down in some foreign country, or having gone up at home, thus upsetting the relative price-levels. Hence, the international gold standard may be regarded as primarily a device for ensuring that central banks, in fact, vary their rates of interest in such a way as to keep costs of production of their respective states on a level.

We can now return to our attempt to follow up the consequences of applying Mr. Keynes' theory in practice. How is the above compulsion upon central banks consistent with Mr. Keynes' instructions that they should in future vary their rates of interest so as to keep investment equal to saving in their own country? The answer is that it is not consistent at all. For variation in the urge to investment, owing to changes in the expectation of profit, are essentially *national* phenomena. They occur quite unevenly over the world's surface. For example, conditions may be such that American entrepreneurs are all "bulls," that is to say, they all believe that the production of any amount, and any kind, of new capital goods will bring them in immensely high rates of profit. In this case, it will be necessary for the Federal Reserve Board to make them pay very high interest rates if it is to prevent them from investing far in excess of savings. At the same moment, however, conditions of great political instability may have arisen in, say, Germany, so that German entrepreneurs are all "bears," and nothing but the establishment of very low rates of interest by the Reichsbank will induce them to keep the rate of investment up to the rate of saving. Yet if the Reichsbank does in such a situation bring down interest rates to this low level, the effect under a gold standard will not be primarily to increase investment in Germany at all but merely to lose gold to America. And the receipt of that gold by America will tend to make the Federal Reserve Bank, not raise its interest rates, as the American internal situation demands,

but lower them and so add fuel to the flames of the American
"bull" movement. And this will cause American investment to run
still further ahead of savings. To use Mr. Keynes' terminology,
"the natural rate of interest" (i.e. that rate which will keep investment equal to savings) varies *nationally*. Hence, the price-level
tends to vary nationally also. Yet the gold standard enforces an
international price-level. Hence it forces a central bank to vary its
interest rates not in order to keep its own country's price-level
stable, but actually and deliberately to *alter* that price-level in conformity with changes which are spontaneously occurring in other
countries.

It is easy to see, moreover, that this difficulty is deeply rooted
in the national capitalist system of to-day. It is an expression of
the fact that while most economic factors are determined nationally,
the monetary system is (or was) international. Mr. Keynes, himself, acknowledges this when he raises "a doubt whether it is wise
to have a currency system with a much wider ambit than our
banking system, our tariff system and our wages system." [1] It is,
in fact, the *nationalism* of the banking, tariff, wages and general
economic policy of the modern capitalist states which causes many
of these sharp oscillations in entrepreneurs' expectations of profit.
Hence, the inducement to invest, and consequently the natural
rate of interest, varies sharply between different nations at the same
moment. And so central banks would be confronted with an impossible task if they were asked to combine internal and external
price stability. Yet, as we have noticed in preceding chapters, the
national rivalries of all states are bound to increase and not
diminish.

In fact, of course, the rivalries have reached, at this time of
writing, to such a point of frenzy that within thirteen months
of Mr. Keynes raising his doubt (September 1930) as to the possibility of an international currency standard in a nationalist world,
the then existing golden international standard has been shattered.
International exchanges had been so hampered and harried, the
normal balance of payments between nations so disturbed, that
huge balances began to pile up against some countries—notably,
against Great Britain. (Britain was hardest hit partly because she
had not in any case fully adjusted her price, wage, and costs sys-

[1] *A Treatise on Money*, Vol. II., page 334.

tem to that of the rest of the world when she returned to gold at the old parity in 1925.) Such balances are, as we saw, automatically paid in gold, while the standard is preserved, and accordingly an unparalleled export of gold from the Bank of England began. This drain drove Great Britain, and following her example, half the rest of the world, off the gold standard in the autumn of 1931.

It is worth while to notice why, in fact, Britain abandoned the gold standard. She abandoned the standard in order to preserve the gold. She ruptured the convertibility of sterling into gold in order to *preserve* the remaining stock of gold in the Bank of England. In one sense, Britain, therefore, did not so much abandon gold as resolve to cling desperately and at all costs to what gold remained to her. This consideration may not be without significance in determining what other standards, or whether no international standard at all, are practicable alternatives to gold.

We have now come to the conclusion that the attempt to avoid crises by the adoption of the maintenance (by savings and investment parity) of a stable *internal* price-level, as the objective of central banks, is, in the nationalistic world of to-day, quite inconsistent with the maintenance by them of the international gold standard.[1] Mr. Keynes is aware of this; and he is unable to do much more than suggest certain devices for minimizing the difficulty; and for the rest, he hopes for the best. He hopes, that is, for a time when the great states will be more "reasonable." We have seen, however, that the great states are inevitably getting more and not less nationalistic—more "unreasonable."

Thus the capitalist world to-day is facing a dilemma. How is the most vital device of the system of free exchange—how is money—to be controlled? Three possible alternatives exist.

---

[1] Dr. Hayek would say, and American experience in 1929 seems to bear him out, that a crisis can occur even when the central bank has managed by luck or skill to keep the price-level stable. For in this case what has happened is that the market rate of interest has exceeded the natural rate, investment has gone ahead of savings, and so the structure of production has been distorted. But this laxity and over-lending on the part of the banks has not resulted in the obvious symptom of a rising price-level. For the tendency of prices to rise has been balanced by technical progress, and so a reduction in real costs, which, had the banks not overlent, would have resulted in a falling price-level.

But even if Dr. Hayek is right, this does not alter the fact that it will be impossible for the banks to combine external and internal stability, even if we understand by internal stability a slowly dropping price-level.

First alternative. The first alternative is that the international gold standard should be re-established where it has broken down and maintained where it still exists. All the more conservative theorists, and certainly many of the very ablest theorists, of capitalism, together with nine-tenths of the practical bankers and financiers, advocate this course. Its great recommendation is that it does at all costs maintain the world market. It provides, in gold, some objective commodity in which in the last resort international balances can be settled. Thus it provides an international means of payment. And a means of payment is the essential device for allowing some credit in exchanges. Without it no debt can be allowed to arise, and exchanges (since payment must always coincide in time with delivery) become little more than barter, with the prices of the commodities exchanged reckoned in a money of account. The fact that it was known that international balances would be automatically settled in gold at no very distant date has been the ultimate and indispensable basis of confidence without which these balances would hardly have been allowed to arise at all.

On the other hand, the preservation of the international gold standard means the abandonment of any opportunity even to attempt to apply Mr. Keynes' policy for the maintenance of a stable internal price-level. Hence, it means abandoning any attempt to free the capitalist system of the recurrence of crises.[1] But can capitalism stand the continual repetition of such crises? Many even of

---

[1] Mr. Keynes, himself, supports this view. He tells us that nothing short of the regulation of the value of new investment by the rate of savings, *throughout the world*, could preserve the world from recurrent crises. The regulations of the supply of new gold would, he thinks, keep the long-term trend of prices stable. But, then, he admits that the long-term trend of prices is comparatively unimportant.

"Thus an appropriate regulation of the new supplies of gold would leave us still exposed to the full blasts of every credit cycle which blew, unless some further mitigating action were taken by the central banks acting in unison and with well-directed purpose."—*A Treatise on Money*, Vol. II., page 281.

And Dr. Hayek is, as usual, even more pessimistic: "It is probably an illusion to suppose that we shall ever be able entirely to eliminate industrial fluctuations by means of monetary policy. The most we may hope for is that the growing information of the public may make it easier for central banks both to follow a cautious policy during the upward swing of the cycle, and so to mitigate the following depression, and to resist the well-meaning but dangerous proposals to fight depression by 'a little inflation.' ... Under existing conditions, to go beyond this is out of the question. In any case, it could be attempted only by a central monetary authority for the whole world: action on the part of a single country would be doomed to disaster."—*Prices and Production*, page 109.

its warmest supporters now admit that it cannot. Let us then examine the consequences of embarking upon the policy of attempting to mitigate commercial crises according to the new technique.

The second alternative. The second alternative is to break up the international gold standard and to attempt to establish no international substitute for it. In the case of Great Britain and of more than half the rest of the world, such a course would to-day be to acquiesce in an existing state of affairs. Thus it is now an easy—indeed the easiest—course and is therefore of much more practical interest and importance than seemed possible before 1931. The advantages of this course are clear. It would admit the unhampered application by central banks of a policy designed to keep their national rate of investment equal to their national rate of savings, and so, on Mr. Keynes' theory, to maintain a stable internal price-level. In that case we could have a practical test of Mr. Keynes' view.[1] (The attractiveness of this prospect is, it is true, a little marred in practice by the reflection that probably no central bankers [with the possible exception of one or two directors of the Bank of England] believe in this policy, and that very few indeed of them have ever even heard of it.)

At the moment, however, we are conducting our discussion on the assumption that the theory is sound. We are assuming that its adoption would, at least, mitigate the severity of crises. But even if this assumption were justified, the cost to world capitalism of its application would be prohibitively high. This cost has been alluded to indirectly when we considered the advantages which international trade derived from the use of gold as an international means of payment. What would be the consequences of having *no* international means of payment? For that is what the permanent and universal abandonment of the international gold standard

---

[1] Dr. Hayek is against any attempt on the part of central banks consciously to follow such a policy. He would rather they stuck more or less blindly to restriction even as he says "in times of general depression." This appears to be the result of his, no doubt well-founded, phobia of inflation due to painful experience of its effects in Central Europe during the last ten years.

Indeed, the conclusion which emerges most strongly of all from a comparison of the views of Mr. Keynes and Dr. Hayek is that Mr. Keynes has lived in a country which has experienced the ills of capitalist deflation, while Dr. Hayek has lived in a country which has suffered the ills of capitalist inflation. It is not inexplicable that they make very different practical suggestions from the basis of what appears to be fundamentally the same analysis.

implies. This would be a very different matter than for one or more countries temporarily to abandon the convertibility of their currencies into gold. For if there exists no international standard, money becomes a purely national affair; international money has, in fact, ceased to exist. It would be too much to say that the destruction of international money would prevent international exchanges altogether. Certainly, however, it would go very far indeed to break up the world market. It might be expected increasingly to reduce international trade to an elaborate kind of barter in which delivery of the goods and payment for them must always coincide in time, if not in place. In 1932, however, this matter is only partly one for speculative theory. The gold standard has actually broken down over a large section of the globe. What are the effects? Writing in 1932, it is too early to appraise more than the early symptoms. So far, however, they appear to be exactly of the character which we should anticipate. International trade is, in fact, rapidly diminishing. And already the question of international barter has been raised. Whether any system of barter will actually arise is, of course, much more doubtful. After all, although the gold standard is badly tattered it does still exist. Half the money of the world is still convertible into gold. So long as this is the case, even those currencies which have lost convertibility can still be to some extent used as international means of payment. For their value can still be, and is, reckoned in terms of the gold currencies. The difficulty is, of course, that their value, expressed in gold, changes from day to day. This, however, is a serious inconvenience and no more. But what if all countries "went off gold"? Then, indeed, there would be no longer any gold currencies in terms of which the others could be reckoned.

Paradoxically enough, I believe that if this happened, gold would immediately re-appear as the sole international money. For none of the national moneys would have any calculable relationship to each other. Thus, the only money which international traders could use would be gold. We should have reverted to the conditions of the Middle Ages, when international commerce was carried on by means of gold or silver measured by weight as the medium of exchange.[1] It is by no means impossible that something of this sort

[1] Cf. the pound "banco," the instrument by which the bankers of Hamburg and Amsterdam effected international payments before the emergence of stable

may happen. Another possibility is that the world will break up into a number of economic areas, each with a money of its own. Thus, the British Empire is now widely suggested by British imperialists as such an area. Other British theorists wish to include Scandinavia and the Argentine—indeed any country which will adopt sterling as the basis of its money. France would then, no doubt, make another such closed economic area, America another and so on. The money of each area could be based on some quite separate standard. One group of powers might be using gold, another silver, a third might experiment with a tabular standard. And each area would have great difficulty in trading with any other except by some form of barter.

The consequences of such a breakdown of international money would be disastrous for world capitalism as a whole. All those tendencies towards economic nationalism which, as we observed, are already so strong, would be enormously reinforced. The great states, empires, or groups of states, would move far more rapidly than ever towards becoming self-contained monopolistic units. These monopolistic empires would strive towards economic self-sufficiency. On the other hand, just because their foreign trade would be so restricted they would be aggressive and imperialistic to an unparalleled degree. For it would be of paramount importance to them to annex to their areas of sovereignty territories providing supplies of important raw materials and valuable natural resources. In such a world, peace would be a rare exception. And there are few, surely, who believe that capitalism can indefinitely survive a recourse to major wars.

The third alternative. The third alternative is to attempt to combine the advantages of both the former. The problem is to provide an opportunity for experimenting with Mr. Keynes' technique for avoiding crises and yet at the same time to preserve an international means of payment. Nor is it difficult to state the conditions upon which alone this problem can be solved. There must be established a supernational central bank which shall enjoy in respect of existing national central banks

currencies. The trader took his silver coins, of no matter what denomination, to the bank: they were then weighed and he was credited with so many pounds weight of silver. These were pounds "banco" and thus an international means of payment was created.

the same authority as these in their turn now enjoy in respect of their own national member banks. Thus, there would be established internationally the same currency system which exists nationally to-day. The supernational central bank could vary its rate of interest in such a way as to preserve the equality of world investment to world savings. At the same time, it would not have to fear any outside interference—for the simple reason that there would be nothing outside of its control. Thus, it is quite easy to say *how* this great reform can be achieved. But, so soon as one has done so, it becomes perfectly apparent that it is absolutely impossible to achieve it at all. For the demand for a supernational currency authority is, in fact, nothing more nor less than the demand for the world state. It is quite true, of course, that the inevitable centralization of authority could be disguised. It is quite true that there are all sorts of intermediate forms and halting-places, represented by National Federations, Leagues of Nations and the like; but the fact remains that in so far as an effective supernational financial authority was established, the reality of national sovereignties would be abolished. For only by the abolition of national sovereignties can the need for an objective international means of payment, such as gold, be avoided. It is only by abolishing national sovereignties, by removing the possibility of national Governments suddenly impeding and preventing the flow of international exchanges, that periodic settlements of international balances in hard cash can be rendered unnecessary.[1] If the world had come under one effective sovereignty, then a world Bank money, based on no matter what commodity or commodities, would serve. For men would feel no more need to settle international balances than they now feel to settle internal balances. There would be no danger of the interruption of world trade.

When we have said this, however, we have shown the extreme unreality of Mr. Keynes' whole proposal, even on the assumption that his theoretical argument is sound. For the world is, in fact, rushing in exactly the opposite direction. We have already considered, in Chapter IV, the whole question of the possibility of the emergence of a capitalist world state. We saw that it was part of the whole question of ultra-imperialism. Thus the solution

[1] "An international money system, or bank, can never function in a nationalist world."—Sir Arthur Salter.

of the question of money ultimately depends, even on Mr. Keynes' own showing, upon the possibility of capitalist unity. We concluded that, although that possibility could not, as a question of pure theory, be denied, yet it was quite clear in practice that capitalism was becoming almost daily more hopelessly disunited. Moreover, we saw that the road toward capitalist world unity was not, even in pure theory, the road of peaceful federation. The way in which capitalism could just conceivably secure world unity would be by a series of unparalleled wars from which an ultimate victor empire might emerge. The road would lead via Shanghai, not Geneva. In practice, however, what would emerge from such a series of imperialist wars, if capitalism were to be left unchallenged to wage them, would not be a victor empire, with central bankers well versed in Mr. Keynes' hopes and Dr. Hayek's doubts, but a new dark age of barbarism, hunger and ignorance. The alchemist rather than the scientific central banker would be the final inheritor of capitalism's attempt to establish a stable money.

CHAPTER VII

BACK TO THE MARKET?

THE last four chapters have been devoted to a description of the four major characteristics of present-day capitalism. A chain of cause and effect was discovered. We saw that the growth of monopolistic tendencies within each state leads inevitably to the growth of a ferocious nationalism in the relations between states: and that, in turn, this plague of nationalism prevents capitalism from finding solutions to its problems. We concluded that, in particular, it was this unappeasable rivalry between the great states and empires which forbade any attempt even at the solution of one of capitalism's most pressing problems, namely, the elimination of crises.

Now these facts are not invisible to the more clear-sighted and realistic theorists of capitalism. More especially during moments of extreme capitalist crisis, such as the present (1932), the capitalist economists see that "things cannot go on like this." And all sorts of remedies and reforms are suggested. Nine-tenths of these suggestions are not worth even a moment's consideration, since solutions are arrived at by the simple method of assuming away, one or other, or all, of the tendencies in capitalism which have produced the problem.

There have arisen to-day, however, at least two comparatively realistic schools of thought amongst orthodox theorists. For both these schools see clearly and face frankly the present crisis in capitalism. Both admit that the present situation is impossible. But each proposes a remedy which appears to be antithetical to the other's. One school proposes to attempt to restore the free market in all its pristine purity: the other proposes to hasten forward the process by which the freedom of the market is being curtailed. We may, perhaps, call the adherents of the school which wishes to re-establish full free market conditions, the "market restorers" or the "free traders," using the words free trade to mean not merely the absence of international tariff barriers but to imply every kind of freedom of exchange. The school which wishes further to curtail the market, we may call "the national planners."

Let us consider first the solutions proposed by the "free traders."[1] Now it is clear that the "free traders" are facing very great practical difficulties. They avowedly wish to revert to a previous condition of affairs. Hence, existing tendencies are dead against them. Their theoretical position, however, is strong (stronger, I shall submit, than that of any other capitalist school). Let us look for a moment at their aims and at the arguments which, they claim, show that their policy offers a solution for capitalism.

They diagnose the malady from which capitalism is suffering as being due to interferences with free exchange. Hence, they believe that the cure is to be found in the abolition of these interferences, and the restoration of the nearest possible approximation to what the economists call "a perfect market" (that is, a market in which the laws of supply and demand work upon price without check) all over the world. They would not claim that such perfect market conditions had, in fact, ever existed. They admit that the new tendencies to interference with freedom of exchange had arisen long before the old restrictions had been dissolved. But this is no reason, they feel, why something much nearer a perfect world market than has ever before existed should not now be established. For economic science has made great strides. In the outside world the market is becoming, it is true, less and less perfect; but in the brains of the economists it is becoming more and more perfect. And so the "free traders" consider that the time has at length arrived when the perfect market can be established. All that is necessary is that the statesmen of the world shall listen to the advice of the economists. If only they will do so, mankind may be led back from the edge of the abyss into a promised land of economic progress and stability. Modern economic science, the free traders assure us, is now able to offer the complete "blue prints" of a world market, not only far superior to anything which survives to-day, but much more subtly perfect than was ever dreamt of

[1] Professor Lionel Robbins, the vigorous young economist of the London School of Economics, holds and preaches the kind of views which I have in mind as typical of the "free traders."

in the philosophy of Mr. Cobden. It is now up to the statesmen to begin to construct it, and so to save civilization.

Modern "equilibrium economics" is indeed an intellectually delightful system (intellectually delightful and well rounded, just because it is tautologous), and if only the capitalist system, which it seeks to explain, does not finally break down in the meantime, it will soon reach perfection. "Equilibrium economics," in effect, offers us a picture of a perfectly self-adjusting social automaton. If only the compensating motions of this automaton are not interfered with in any way, a stable and yet economically progressive society will result. The wants of individual consumers will automatically exercise just sufficient influence, and no more, upon "the structure of production" to ensure that they are satisfied in the order of their urgency. Fallible human reason will be wholly excluded from the task of determining to what purposes the limited productive resources of the community should be devoted. An infallible mechanism will ensure that they shall be invariably devoted to satisfying those wants which the members of the community most want to satisfy. Exactly the correct amount will be saved and spent. Just that proportion of their energies which, it turns out, the citizens of the community desire, will be devoted to satisfying their present and their future needs respectively. Every part of the mechanism will react perfectly on every other. There can never be a serious disturbance of equilibrium since a dozen variable "rates," each finding its own natural level in a perfect market, will at once offset any tendency to disharmony. The long-term rate of lending, the short-term rate of interest, the average rate of profit attainable in different industries in the same country and in different countries at the same time, the price levels of different categories of commodities, wage rates, "the money rates of the efficiency earnings of the factors of production," and a host of other variables, will all move gently and harmoniously against each other in order to maintain an ideal and perpetual balance. And all that the human beings, who form what one might call the connective tissue of the whole machine, need do, is each and all to follow exactly their own personal and pecuniary interests. Indeed, it is precisely if they attempt, impiously, to do more than this that they will disorganize the subtle mechanism. Let them strive to respond perfectly and automatically to the pull of profit and loss; let them be but reeds swaying in the winds of the market; and they will have the felicity of knowing, both that they themselves as individuals are becoming richer at the maximum possible rate, and that society as a whole is becoming "bigger and better" more rapidly than it could do under any other conceivable arrangement.

Such is "the vision of the market" held up for our admiration by devout economists. Some of them even go so far as to suggest that such a condition of affairs has in a past "golden age" actually existed. Sir Arthur Salter, in *Recovery,* for example, thus lyrically describes the pre-war world.

> "Over the whole range of human effort and human need, demand and supply found their adjustments without anyone estimating the one or planning the other.... So supply and demand would circle round a central, though moving, point of equilibrium—tethered to it by an elastic though limited attachment.... And what changing prices would do for commodities, changing rates of interest would do for capital.... The economic and financial structure under which we have grown up was indeed, at the moment of its greatest perfection, more like one of the marvellously intricate structures built by the instincts of beavers or ants than the deliberately designed and rational works of man."

(The admission of the unconscious nature of economic life, as a whole, under capitalism is worth noting.) Why is it, it may be asked, that British economists like Sir Arthur Salter, describe with such peculiar enthusiasm the beauties of free exchange? The reason is not difficult to find. When British economists hymn the virtues of free trade, they are in truth commemorating the days of Britain's industrial and commercial hegemony. Sir Arthur Salter writes as if the last century had been a sort of commercial Arcadia, in which willing buyer met willing seller, each possessing equal bargaining power, neither in a position to impose an inequitable contract on the other. Nothing, of course, could be further from the truth. The last century was the epoch during which Great Britain enjoyed what approached a monopoly in the provision of many important goods and services. She could impose almost what conditions she chose upon her customers. Moreover, the wealth created by the extremely favourable terms of trade, which she did impose, enabled her to develop, though not without constant wars, an empire which gave her traders a privileged, if not a monopoly, position in a large part of the globe. So, in fact, the system which British economists find so beautiful was to a large extent one of free exchange for everybody else, and of monopoly for Great Britain. No wonder they bitterly regret its passing.

This consideration should be borne in mind throughout the contrast which we are drawing between the "free trader" school and the main body of British middle-class imperialist thought. The kind of free trade which the free trader economists dream of returning to is a free trade in which the scales which measure exchanges have been weighted in Great Britain's favour. And this should warn us not to push the contrast too far. The most ardent British free traders are loyal imperialists. The most extreme British imperialists now call themselves Empire Free Traders. It is clear that the difference between the two schools is one of methods, not ends. Still, the difference exists and is well worth analysis, for it reveals the present position of the British governing class.

Sir Arthur Salter's description of the perfect market is typical of the views of British free trader economists, and, compared to the real world of capitalist catastrophe which we inhabit, his description certainly sounds most attractive. It is comprehensible that the economists, having proved to their own satisfaction the theoretical possibility of such a system, sincerely believe that the best interests of humanity will be served by efforts to bring this ideal and perfect market into existence, or, at any rate, to return to a state of things in which its most elementary and essential conditions are not, as they are to-day, universally flouted. For the best of them see and are horrified by the chaos and devastation, the stupendous waste of desperately needed wealth, which is going on around them to-day. And it is natural that they should suppose that all these disasters are a punishment to the nations which have abandoned the one true god—the perfect market—and have worshipped false economic deities. And so they arise like the prophets of old to warn a stiff-necked and hard-hearted generation to return to its forsaken faiths.[1]

We will now briefly consider whether a restoration of the market is in the abstract desirable. We shall then go on to the more practical question of whether it is possible. In a sense it is true that the recent disasters of capitalism are the result of gross infringements of the market principle. But, these ever-growing infringements of the principles of free exchange are not due to the folly of statesmen, but are the consequence of the inevitable emergence of characteristics which were all along inherent in the capitalist system. This, however, the economists do not believe, for they have for the most part very little interest in historical considerations.

Moreover, they cannot conceive of the world without markets. They are appalled at the thought of the problems which would arise if the market were to be abandoned. They see, quite correctly, that the rival school of reformers, the "national planners" are weaving schemes which would have consequences far beyond anything of which they dream: which would raise problems for which the national planners have not the vestige of a solution. For it is quite true that the question of the abolition of the market raises the most fundamental and far-reaching problems that can possibly arise for human society. (We shall postpone the discussion of the schemes of the national planners until we have finished our consideration of the whole subject of the present condition of capitalism. We shall return to them in Chapter XII.)

The free trader economists believe, in effect, that men cannot do without the market: that they are not yet old enough and wise enough to organize their productive activities without the guidance of "consumer preference"—without, that is, allowing the free choice of the ultimate consumer to determine, by the mechanism of the market, what commodities shall be produced. Men will make, they suppose, appalling mistakes if they attempt to decide in advance what commodities, and what proportions between commodities, shall be produced, without the guidance

[1] Marx long ago observed the theological character of much of the thought of capitalist economists: "Economists are like theologians for whom there are only two kinds of religion. Every religion other than their own is the invention of man, whereas their own particular brand of religion is an emanation from God." —*The Misery of Philosophy*.

given by the inducement of profit and the corrective of loss, which the market alone can provide. Yet this is precisely what must be done in any society which is not individualistically organized and guided by the "motives of the market." In that case, some kind of "Planning Commission" or "Supreme Economic Council" or whatever you like to call it, composed of fallible human beings, will have to settle what commodities shall and shall not be produced in the next year—or five years—or whatever period is chosen. And this is a task which, the free trader economists inform us, mankind is simply "not up to." They cite the alleged inefficiency of the economic activities which an army carries on: the difficulty of making decisions: the arbitrary nature of what decisions are arrived at. In general, the tasks involved by the conscious organization and direction of the gigantic economic process, necessary to the life in a modern community, appals them. And even if they do not deny, as fifteen years after 1917 they can hardly do, that such a task is within the range of human possibility, they believe that the quality of organization achieved by conscious planning will produce economic results far inferior to those possible under a capitalist system. What will turn out in the light of future demand to have been the wrong things will, they say, be produced: and they will be produced in the wrong relative quantities. Then, again, there will be no variety and idiosyncrasy about the commodities produced under a planned economy. Fashion, charm, gaiety, fantasy, they allege, will be banished from life. "We shall all have to wear standardized suits." In fact, the free traders allege, any attempt to do without the market is foredoomed to failure: and, if it did succeed, the results would be unpleasant. Let us rather return, they urge, to the guidance of the market. All our misfortunes have come upon us because of our infidelities to the great principle of free exchange. At all costs, we must get back to it. Whatever obstacles stand in the way must be swept aside. Let us fight under a banner inscribed with the device "Back to the Market."

Such views may be quite comprehensible on the part of well circumstanced economists. Yet, in fact, they represent nothing but a sort of prostration before the market. Mankind must and can do without the guidance of the market. It is true that the establishment of a planned economy does presuppose a complete transformation of the structure of society. Without such a social revolution, the economic revolution involved in the abandonment of the market is unthinkable. And after it has taken place, men will not at first consciously organize their economic activities to the best possible advantage. Mistakes and costly mistakes will be made. It may even be that in its early years a planned economic system will not utilize the "factors of production" so advantageously as they would be utilized under an ideal system of the perfect market, as envisaged by the free trader economists. But is this the relevant standard of comparison? On the contrary, since the vision of the perfect market remains, and always will remain, merely an idea in the heads of the economists, the actual comparison which a planned economy must bear is with capitalism as it exists to-day. And, on that standard of comparison, who in their senses can doubt the immense superiority of a planned system? Indeed, when we look at the world in 1932, we are tempted to say that no planning authority, however foolish, myopic, or even corrupt, could achieve quite so grandiose a misdirection and waste of the world's productive capacity as is achieved by the present phase of capitalism. It is difficult to believe, for example, that any planning authority could be engaged in deliberately destroying the crops of one half of the world, while the population of the other half is dying of starvation.

It is no doubt true that the great advantage of the planned system of a classless society is its ability to satisfy, regularly and securely, the basic demands for necessaries on the part of the whole population. It might well prove at first inferior to even the existing capitalist system in providing an immense variety of pleasant but unnecessary articles. And the comfortably circumstanced economists, living for the most part in what are still after all the relatively "millionaire" spots on the earth's surface, such as Great Britain, America or France, are really much more interested in this latter capacity. What they are really doing when they show their remarkable predilection for the market is, *in the abstract,* grossly to over-estimate the importance of the economic factor in life: while, *in actual concrete here-and-now fact,* they as greatly underestimate it. Thus, they tell us that a planned economy must be rejected because of its alleged inability to provide the infinite variety of commodities which, they say, are necessary to the maintenance of civilization. In what sense, we may ask them, is civilization dependent upon the mountain of what we can only call knickknacks, some of them pleasant, some æsthetically attractive, some useful and convenient, many more of them, however, useless and hideous, which form the stock-in-trade of all the great commercial areas of the great cities of the capitalist world? What would the world lose in civilization if Fifth Avenue and Disraeli's famous quadrilateral, bounded by Oxford Street, Piccadilly, Regent Street and Park Lane, plus the Rue de la Paix, were all taken up and shaken as a woman shakes a cloth, until every commodity they contained had fallen out of them? And how much would civilization decline if to this holocaust of frankly luxury goods were added the contents of the great middle-class stores, the stocks in trade of Harrod's, of Saks, or Macy's, of the Galeries Lafayette? The middle classes of the West would certainly lose a good deal of comfort. But that is about all. (And who knows but that a little loss of comfort might not revive to some extent those intellectual activities of which that class was at one time undoubtedly capable?)

In any case, what would be the balance of advantage to civilization if the planned economy of a classless society, while failing to keep up the variety of such luxuries and conveniences, secured, as it undoubtedly could secure, to every single citizen of the community an adequate supply of the necessities of life? Of course, the mere psychological gain in the removal of the neurosis of anxiety which to-day prevents about two-thirds of the population of even the richest communities from ever being able to attend whole-heartedly to anything but their daily bread, would make possible a quite unparalleled advance in civilization. (It is not necessary even to speak of the actual physical improvement which adequate food, clothes, and house-room would achieve.) When once people *know* that by working a reasonable number of hours they can assure adequate and satisfactory food, housing and clothing for themselves and their dependents, the provision of further commodities should become a quite secondary social objective. And yet while the free trader economists condemn planned economy because it might not, at first, be able to provide all the frills of life to which they are accustomed, they tolerate and defend a capitalist system which is failing utterly to provide the necessaries of life to perhaps half the population of the world. In practice, we suddenly discover, they seem to attach as little importance to the provision of the necessaries of life (to others) as any stoic. In theory, they put the maximum possible production of wealth before every other consideration. We must, at any cost, restore perfect freedom to the market because we can thus, they claim, produce wealth faster than in any other way. Yet they defend a system which, in practice, produces a state of poverty for 80% of mankind, which would have done credit to Diogenes himself. But then the existing market system merely enforces destitution upon the mass of the population of the globe. A planned economy might neglect to produce the comforts of those, at present, well circumstanced. Thus, it is not difficult to account for this absurd deification of the market on the part of the free trader economists.

There is nothing absurd, however, about these economists' conviction that the only way in which capitalism as they have known it can be preserved is to restore, at any rate, some approximation to free market conditions. In this contention, they are entirely justified. Capitalism is doomed unless it can curb and restrain the enormous and now almost universal interferences with freedom of exchange, the manifold distortions and dislocations of the market, which to-day characterize the policy of every important state. For not only would the restoration of free market conditions be essential to any hope of preventing the periodic crises of capitalism from becoming more and more catastrophic: it would also be the only possible way in which a whole series of new wars, in which capitalism is certain to perish, could be postponed. It is essential, therefore, to consider, not as we have done up till now the relatively academic question of the desirability or the reverse of the restoration of the market, but the immediate and practical question of whether the market can be, and if so, how it can be, restored.

There are four major reforms, which it will perhaps be agreed, must be accomplished if the world free market is to be restored.

They are: first, the restoration of the normal flow of commodities between countries by the levelling of tariff barriers and the reversal of the whole tendency indicated by the term "administrative protection"; in fact, the establishment of world free trade. Second: the break up of the great trusts; the reversal, that is, of the whole tendency towards monopoly and towards the fusing of the commercial apparatus with the state apparatus of every major nation. In fact, freedom of exchange must be restored within, as well as, between states. Third: the reversal of the whole tendency towards the establishment of social services, giving a new and secure source of income to the working class, and to state and trade union protection of wage rates. For social services and static wage rates are progressively "freezing" one of the most important variables of the market into a disastrous immobility. In fact, the restoration of the free market in labour must be accomplished. Fourth: the establishment of some sort of monetary control on a world-wide scale which can attempt, at any rate, the task of mitigating commercial crises. In fact, the restoration of the stability and continuity of international exchange must be accomplished.

It will scarcely be denied that these are tasks which confront any body of men who wish to accomplish the restoration of a greater measure of freedom to the market. It is not of course necessary that all these tasks need be accomplished in their entirety in order that a workable free market may be restored. Yet, certainly, substantial progress must be made with each of them, if disaster to capitalism is to be averted. Let us, therefore, turn our attention to the question of how the market restorers propose to effect these reforms.

In the first place, how are the tariff barriers of the world to be levelled, or at any rate diminished? And who is to do the job? For let us remember that disastrous as tariffs may be to world capitalism as a whole they are of enormous benefit to particular capitalists. It may be true that "everybody" (that uninspiring abstraction) would be much richer in a free trade world. But that does not alter the fact that those very wealthy, and influential capitalist gentlemen Herr Schmidt of Düsseldorf, Sir Algernon Smith of Birmingham, Henry T. Smith of Pittsburgh, and M. Durand of St. Etienne, would all be immensely poorer. In other words, the general enrichment which free trade would bring could only be achieved at the cost of a gigantic redistribution of existing wealth, both between individuals within communities and between communities as a whole. For not only would individual capitalists be ruined, but whole industrial areas, which have grown up behind the protection of ever-rising tariff walls, would be laid desolate. If the free trader economists, or anybody else, are to be given the power to scale down tariff barriers, they will be given the power, here, to bestow immeasurable wealth, there, to deal destruction and ruin. They will be opposed by most powerful and well-organized forces, by the organized entrepreneurs of every state, fighting a life-and-death struggle for very existence. Certainly this task is not a light one.

Again, let us consider the problems presented by the urgent necessity of breaking up the trusts and the other monopolistic organizations within the state. Somebody will have to go and beard the great monopolists in their dens. Somebody, for instance, must inform the Morgan partners that they must now reveal exactly what companies, banks, private firms and finance houses they control both in the United States and in the rest of the world, and that they must forthwith dissolve the bonds which hold together their unique organization. Somebody must have a few words with Mr. Mellon and with the Rockefellers on the same subject. In Great Britain, the directors of Unilevers, of Imperial Chemical Industries, and of some at any rate of the other private trusts must be compelled to dissolve their organizations. Of far greater importance, however, both in Britain and on the continent of Europe, will be the task of reversing the whole tendency to transform the State itself into an association of federated and interlocked entrepreneurs and financiers. Those fields of production which the State has itself monopolized in Great Britain, as we saw, civil aviation, the distributive side of wireless, the long-distance distribution of electric current, cable communications (and in Germany far wider fields of production), must be restored to the competition of the market. In general, the State must recede into its former position of a referee presiding over the competitive struggles of its citizens. It must abandon its newly assumed function of attempting to bring these competitive citizens into combination: indeed, it must reassume as one of its most important duties, the function of forbidding future combinations, and dissolving combinations which already exist. For by pursuing this policy alone can it reverse the progressive curtailment of the area of the internal free market.

Thus, in order to attempt the first two reforms, it will be necessary to challenge all the most formidable capitalist interests; it will be necessary to reverse all the most marked tendencies and forces which exist in all capitalist communities to-day. A powerful movement of reform, it will be admitted, must be mobilized for these two purposes alone. Great leaders backed by whole sections of the community acting with the utmost determination will be needed. And we have only as yet considered half of the measures which we saw to be essential. After having challenged every interest in capitalism, the free trade restorers of the market must next proceed to take away everything which the workers have gained by a century of effort. For it is of little use to restore the freedom of the exchange of commodities both internationally, and within each nation, if trade in one vital commodity, human labour, is to remain hedged about by every kind of restriction and restraint. The free market cannot function properly, the glittering mechanism of the economists' perfect market can never work, unless *all* its interconnected parts are movable. If one of them sticks, then naturally the whole machine will jam and ruin itself. Thus it is essential that the price of that universally necessary commodity, human labour power, should vary with perfect freedom according to the supply of it and the demand for it. Every calculation of equilibrium economics is based upon the assumption that it does so. The price of human labour power, like any other commodity, must be made to vary freely with the ratio of supply and demand and it must vary to any extent. The only limiting factor, and this is no limit for short periods, is the necessity that its price should cover the cost of production. And the cost of production of human labour is clearly the cost of maintaining the labourer at such a standard of life as will enable him successfully to reproduce his kind. Thus, in particular the price of labour must be free to fall to this point whenever the supply of it exceeds the demand for it.[1]

And yet as everyone knows a hundred provisions have been devised to prevent this very thing from occurring. Powerful trade unions have to some extent succeeded in creating monopolies in certain types and categories of labour and so in obtaining monopoly

[1] Sir Arthur Salter gives an excellent illustration of this point. He is writing of Britain's return to the gold standard at the old parity in 1925. "In a flexible system, an increase in the exchange value of sterling would have transmitted an equivalent reduction in terms of sterling throughout the price, wage, and costs structure. Only in this way could the change have been effected without loss of competitive strength in the world market. But at every stage fixed wages, based on wage agreements, and prices held up by semi-monopolistic organizations and understandings, resisted the influence of monetary action."

prices for it. Moreover, the State has itself stepped in and, in certain trades, actually fixed artificial minima below which wage rates cannot fall, no matter what the conditions of the market may be.

Even more disastrous to the mobility of the price of labour, however, has been the tendency of the State to establish the so-called "Social Services." These social services consist in the provision by the State of income for the labourer additional to the income which he derives from the sale of his capacity to work. This additional income takes the form of old age pensions, payments during sickness, payments to widows, and, most serious of all, payments during periods of unemployment. Part of all of these forms of income is subsidies paid out of general taxation. The effect of these payments in retarding the tendency of the price of labour (in ordinary language, of wages) to fall to its "natural" level is obvious. The "natural" level of wages, whenever the supply of labour exceeds the demand for labour, is as we have said, the cost of maintaining and reproducing the labourer. Naturally, both during all commercial crises, and in periods of rapid technical progress, when a given output of commodities can be maintained with ever less and less labour, the supply of labour always will exceed the demand for it. At these times, therefore, the price of labour (i.e. the rate of wages) ought always to be falling towards the cost of its production. And it is essential to the mechanism of the market, to its power of recuperation from crises, to its ability to minimize crises, that it should do so. But if the worker is receiving additional income, if in particular he is receiving income when he is unemployed, which is itself a sign that this critical condition, when the supply of labour has exceeded the demand, has arisen, he will be enabled to resist wage reductions. He will stand out for the former rates. And his standing out will dislocate the whole delicate mechanism of readjustment.

Hence, it is imperative that all such gross interferences with the freedom of the labour market, as Trade Boards, Old Age Pensions, Health Insurance, and Unemployment Insurance, and the activities of such disastrous "associations in restraint of trade" as the Trade Unions, should be abolished, or, at any rate, greatly curtailed. Thus, the market restorers must fight a head-on engagement with labour as well as with the capitalists. Truly, their god is a jealous god, who brooks no rivals in the field.

It might be supposed, of course, that the market restorers would, at any rate, have the assistance of all the capitalist forces in this crusade for the freedom of the labour market. And to some extent, no doubt, this is the case. Not all, even of the forces of capitalism, however, would support them. Some of the more moderate and sagacious minds in capitalism have been, until recently, inclined to maintain and even extend the social services, if this was in any way possible. They did not share the free traders' enthusiasm for the perfect market in labour. They supposed that the growth of the social services, the grant, that is, of small doles from the surplus wealth which society creates, is in fact the only thing which has hitherto kept the workers of the capitalist communities of Europe relatively passive in times of crises. And, even now, they feel no stomach for a policy which promises them a perfect market at the cost of making the workers feel, directly and without cover or protection, the effects of every breakdown in capitalist stability.

Finally, since even the most ardent of the market restorers cannot suppose that the rest of their programme is practicable without a notable increase in the stability of capitalism as a whole, we come to the last necessity—the establishment of some sort of world monetary system designed to secure approximate stability of trade.[1]

We have already discussed the practicability of this proposal and found that in fact it involved nothing less than the demand for a world State. The establishment of a world monetary authority, that is, invested with powers adequate to attempt the task of business stabilization is flatly incompatible with national sovereignty. Thus, any attempt to establish it will at once run up against the intransigent and ever-increasing jealousies, hostilities and fears of the rival empires of the present world. For example, the most

[1] I think that Dr. Hayek and probably Mr. D. H. Robertson would say that trade stability would automatically follow from the successful accomplishment of the first three restorations, and that accordingly there would be no need for world monetary control. They would mean by trade stability, however, that capitalist economy would, in such conditions, be so elastic that, while violent slumps would occur, a tendency towards recovery would be almost immediate and would work very rapidly. Surely, however, they would concede that such a system of naked *laissez faire* would create revolutionary conditions at once, and that some attempt at world monetary control designed to prevent and not to cure crises, would be absolutely necessary to capitalist survival?

elementary necessity for such a world central bank must be that all states shall entrust their gold reserves to its keeping, and submit to it determining their bank rates. Thus, in addition to their tasks of world tariff levelling, world trust busting and world trade union smashing, the market restorers must induce French bankers and American senators to part with their gold reserves and deposit them in Geneva, or wherever else is thought convenient.

We envisage these not inconsiderable tasks, and then we look round for the men who are to attempt them. At first sight no one seems to be available—except perhaps the professors of the London School of Economics.[1] Yet the execution of such a programme cannot even be attempted unless some powerful class, or coalition of classes, is solidly behind the attempt. How can the market restorers hope to find such a basis of support? Only by finding a class whose interests would be promoted, whose wealth and power would be aggrandized, by the restoration of the market. Does such a class exist? Surely it must, for if there were no such class at all the very idea of the restoration of the market would hardly have arisen. That class is the remnant of the old middle class of small-scale producers for the market. Naturally, this now disregarded and diminishing class yearns after the days when it was the dominant class in the community. Naturally, its members dream of a sort of small bourgeois restoration in which all their enemies, the big monopolistic capitalists who are crushing them out, the trade unions, which are hampering them, the tariff barriers which hem them in, the recurrent crises which ruin them in the night, shall all be abolished. Nor do their dreams lack verisimilitude. For it is from this particular class that many of the ablest theorists and economists derive. And they can show that compared with the hell which the large-scale imperialistic capitalists are making of the world, the reign of *their* class was, in some ways, comparatively tolerable.

Observe, however, how pitifully small is the element of genuine class support upon which the market restorers can rely. It is by no means co-extensive with the whole of the petty bourgeoisie.

[1] No economist who has had the practical experience of world affairs can quite bring himself to be a market restorer. Thus Sir Arthur Salter writes: "We cannot return to the unregulated competition of the last century; an unwillingness to accept some of the social consequences and the development of modern industrial technique together make that impossible."

Large elements of quite "small" people, in Great Britain especially, are wholly opposed to such a programme. Far from being free trade liberals, they are the most violently jingoistic of imperialists. They are, in fact, not so much petty bourgeois as petty *rentiers*. They live, that is, not by small-scale independent production, but by enjoying a small *participation* in the profits of great monopolistic imperialist enterprises. This category of persons is of enormous importance in the oldest and largest of empires, the British Empire. From the retired colonel, living on an Indian pension, and the salaried technician or accountant in a trust, to the widow with a few shares in the Hong Kong and Shanghai Bank, they will all be natural imperialists, tariff reformers and, if they are intellectually active, "national planners." The free trade market restorers will get no help at all from them. Nor can they depend even on all the remaining free producers. Those of them whose business is, in fact, wholly parasitic upon a trust, will naturally acquire the outlook of their overlords, usually in a somewhat crude and exaggerated form.

There is, however, one other and unexpected source of support for British market restorers. From over the Channel, hands are held out to them. For if we shift our attention from Great Britain, Germany and America, from the lands of large-scale capitalism, to such countries as Austria and France, we shall find that the point of view of the market restorers has a much wider basis of support. For example, Dr. Hayek shows in the concluding sentences of his books, *Prices and Production,* from which we have already quoted so freely, that he is a market restorer.

"And there is still another and perhaps no less important reason why it seems dangerous to me to overstress at the present moment the urgency of a change in our monetary system; it is the danger of diverting public attention from other and more pressing causes of our difficulties" (page 111).

And these causes are then, somewhat darkly, indicated.

"It would be easy to demonstrate by the same type of analysis which I have used in the last two lectures that certain kinds of State action, by causing a shift in demand from producers' goods to consumers' goods, may cause a continued shrinking of the capitalist structure of production, and therefore prolonged stagnation. This may be true of increased public expenditure in general or of particular forms of taxation or particular forms of public expenditure. In such cases, of course, no tampering with the monetary system can help. Only a radical revision of public policy can provide the remedy" (page 111).

In plain English, what this means is, of course, that the real way to get out of the crises is not to tinker with money but to stop the excessive demand for consumers' goods caused by social services.

Again, most French economists, notably M. André Siegfried, at any rate when dealing with the problem of other countries, are keen market restorers. And this is natural because in fact the comparatively backward development of large-scale production in France has still left extant a freedom of exchange unknown in Britain, Germany or America. Thus M. Siegfried's remedies for the plight of British capitalism, as expounded in his well-known work *England's Crisis,* are simply those of a market restorer. Curiously enough, however, the best individual expression of market restoring views has been made by an American. Mr. Lawrence Dennis, whose book *Is Capitalism Doomed?* has already been cited, wishes, he implies, to return to the America of Washington and Jefferson; that is, to an America of small-scale independent producers for the market. He feels that in order to do so, he must stop the farmers from borrowing in order to expand and mechanize their farms: must apply crushing taxation to big fortunes, in order to prevent the large-scale accumulation of capital which makes monopoly possible: and he must build a Chinese wall around the Union so that neither mass-produced foreign goods shall come in, nor American capital go out.

Now Mr. Dennis is admirably realistic when he is showing the fatal contradictions inherent in large-scale capitalism. He is especially powerful in his exposure of the rapidity of the present drive towards war.

"The American people have now admitted that they are going to do nothing about unemployment. War, therefore, is the inevitable solution. It will impose itself by the force of economic and political events brought to bear on statesmen who do not know what it is all about. The more our statesmen talk peace, and the greater their sincerity of belief in what they say, the more inevitable becomes the war issue."

The only alternative which he offers, however, is his programme of a return to modest, small-scale, early capitalist methods. And he is most unrealistic in dreaming that the American people will ever return to such conditions. Indeed, he half admits this himself:

"The criticism of this book is not destructive. Capitalism is destroying itself or disintegrating with age. The book advances suggestions of moderation and restraint which might, if followed—and they probably will not be—prolong and render more pleasant the old age of capitalism."

All the same, Mr. Dennis has written a far more penetrating analysis of the crises than has been achieved by any professional capitalist economist.

We may estimate then that the real amount of support behind the market restorers is just about enough to conceive of the idea of such a restoration of the market, but is not enough to move a single step towards its accomplishment. This in no way disproves, however, the arguments by which they demonstrate that the only way in which the present capitalist system can be preserved is by the restoration of the market. Their arguments cannot, in fact, be disproved. They remain impeccable.

We arrive at these conclusions. The free traders are able to prove that their solution is the only one; yet they have not the slightest prospect of being able even to attempt to apply it; hence, capitalism cannot in fact be much longer maintained in existence.

It is sad, though it is explicable, and indeed inevitable, that so much talent should be lavished by these able economists on a cause lost these thirty years. Let us erase from our minds for a moment all that has been said of the practical impossibility of restoring the market. And let us envisage the psychological task which would be involved. Let us consider the dying faiths which would have to be revived, the worn-out political watchwords recoined, the strange outdated weapons of social struggle refurbished, if the free trader economists could by some stroke of magic have their way. In order that the free market might flourish again, that whole system of ideas which reached perhaps its highest point in nineteenth-century Britain, and its very apogee in nineteenth-century Lancashire, would have to be raised from the dead. Out of the Lancashire of to-day, out of the now silent mills, out of the empty weaving sheds, the very machinery of which has been sold off to Allahabad or to Shanghai, would have to emerge, as from the grave, a new generation, with the unquestioning faith of their grandfathers in the principles of democracy, the British Parliamentary system, the Protestant faith, and a total absorption in self-enrichment as a religious duty. Even the ghosts of these ideas do not walk. They are laid for ever. For the epoch of human history and the material conditions which alone gave them life have passed away down the irreversible stream of time. Only the least historically minded men on earth, only English economists, could dream of their resurrection.

PART III

THE DECAY OF CAPITALIST CULTURE

CHAPTER VIII

RELIGION

THE capitalist system is dying and cannot be revived. That is the conclusion to which any honest investigator of the actual facts and possibilities of the present situation must be driven.

The end of that phase of the history of the peoples of the West which began five hundred years ago, carries such enormous implications with it that nearly everyone stands too dumbfounded to admit what is happening. And even those who do admit the fact of finality, are reluctant to realize a tenth of its consequences. The gradual and fatal decay of all those societies which are based upon the capitalist system of production, and the rise of another and alternative way of carrying on life, are the two sides of a process, too gigantic to be easily apprehended. But we may be assured of one thing: the death of capitalism and the substitution of another economic system in its place, will leave no single side of life unaltered. Religion, literature, art, science, the whole of the human heritage of knowledge will be transformed. For no aspect of human life can remain unaffected by a change in the way in which human life itself is maintained. And the new forms, whether higher or lower, which these principal concepts of man's imagination will assume, will depend on what new economic system will succeed the capitalist system. On the character of this new basis will depend whether human knowledge and skill flourish and expand so that a new and less miserable, or (if you prefer it) more glorious, epoch in human history is made possible, or whether they relapse and decay, as they have done so many times before, until nearly all the little gains which men have so painfully won are lost again, and the slow long task of revival from a very simple level of life has to be begun again.

We shall discuss below the question of what form of economic organization will succeed present-day capitalism. The question of whether it is to be an improvement, or the reverse, has still to be decided. It is the destiny of the men of the twentieth century to decide this very question. But it is, in any case, certain that the whole structure of that civilization, which has been built up upon capitalist production, is crumbling. For that structure—that "culture," as the Germans would call it—was adapted to an age of individualism and "freedom" alone. And the age of individualistic freedom is very nearly over.

We are told to say nothing but good concerning the dead, and it would be foolish to say nothing but ill of the dying. It is true that the age of individualistic freedom has been for the vast majority of mankind merely a mockery of its own name. But so long as we clearly recognize that this epoch is over and that efforts to revive it are utterly futile, we should be foolish to deny the achievements of the culture of the capitalist period. Certainly this was a stage through which mankind had to pass. Lenin says that capitalism is hell compared to socialism, but heaven compared to feudalism. And his testimony is weighty; for he was one of the very few men who have ever lived under all three systems. The Russia of his youth was at least semi-feudal, the Western Europe of his years of exile saw the long rich afternoon of capitalism, and the last seven years of his life were spent in the labour of clearing the ground for the foundations of the first considerable attempt at the establishment of socialism. And no doubt Lenin was right. Feudalism sounds comparatively pleasant to Western Europeans across the gap of five hundred years. But, compared to it, even capitalism did mean the emancipation of, at any rate, one class of mankind. The European middle class was enabled to rise and to build up what has been, on the whole, the most brilliant, if by no means the most stable, civilization that the world has as yet known. It is undoubtedly true that the cause of individualistic freedom is to-day the cause of everything that is reactionary, stupid, barbaric and repressive in the world, and that it can only triumph by destroying civilization and pulling us back into an age of darkness. But that does not mean that it was not in the past the best cause for which men at that stage in human development could fight. The achievements of the age of individual freedom were real enough. Moreover, it would be especially foolish for a British writer to deny the function of the capitalist system in laying down that material basis which can alone make higher achievements possible. For undoubtedly Great Britain played a leading part in "the fight for freedom." That fight was, of course, only the fight for the free market, the struggle for the right to buy and sell; the struggle, in the final analysis, for the right to exploit. All the same it was a fight that had to be won. Victory in it marked a stage in the history of man. The wiser part for a British writer is not to deny the achievements of the capitalist epoch but, in recognizing unhesitatingly that that epoch is over, to hope that his countrymen will play an equally important part in the struggle to achieve a new and higher form of society in the new epoch which is visibly and inevitably upon us. Unfortunately, an appallingly large number of even the best intelligences are not to-day engaged in the task of burying the vast and slowly expiring body of capitalist culture. They are taking no part in the essential work of clearing the ground for the new order. Unfortunately, the great majority of Western intellectuals are engaged in useless and indeed pernicious task of trying to carry on a little longer the culture of capitalism. And yet one might have supposed that there was ample warning to be had from the desperate condition of every extant system of ideas; warning enough from the present state of religion, philosophy, art, literature and science, that it was impossible under the existing social system to prevent a progressive decay from invading every one of these fields of intellectual activity.

The systems of ideas with which men strive to comprehend the world are, it will scarcely be denied, dependent upon the society which gives them birth. And the health and vitality of these concepts and ideas are essential to the health of that society. For although the economic activities by which men keep alive must be the foundation of any society, they are only the foundation. And men do not live on foundations alone. There is no need to deny the importance of the social edifice simply because we have at length discovered what its foundations are made of. And if a dry rot, starting quite explicably in those foundations, spreads, as it must, to the whole great structure of civilization, if it lends the odour of decay even to the highest pinnacles of thought, to the philosophical, religious, æsthetic and scientific concepts which crown the whole building, then certainly the decay of these higher parts will be scarcely less fatal to the building than was the original decay of the foundations. The decadence of the ideas of a given system of society can, and do, themselves react on the economic basis. Once the process of change has begun, action is reciprocal. When the movement is upwards, when the society is expanding, the growing wealth and vigour of the basic economy makes possible ever new achievements in the field of ideas: and these theoretical and psychological achievements themselves, by freeing the human mind from prejudices and fears, make possible a new expansion in the economic base. On the downward slope, the process is the same. Not only does decay transmit itself from the shrinking economy to the structure of ideas above it, but the weakening grip of these now enfeebled ideas over the hearts and minds of men make them decreasingly capable of maintaining and preserving even that contracted economic basis which still remains to them. Action, both of growth and of decay, is reciprocal between the economic foundation and the ideal structure.

In these pages, there has been submitted a demonstration that the capitalist system has now far passed its meridian and is dropping steeply and irretrievably into the shadows. If this diagnosis is justified, we should expect to find not only those symptoms of economic disorder and contraction which we have already discussed, but a parallel decline in the vitality and creativeness of the systems of ideas to which capitalist society gave birth.

Now a characteristic system of ideas, religious, philosophic, æsthetic and scientific, has been the contribution to human civilization of the capitalist classes of the Western world. It is, however, a commonplace of even the capitalist theorists themselves that in every one of these fields the existing system of ideas is being held together with great and ever-increasing difficulty: even though overt collapse is averted, the hold of these ideal systems over men's minds becomes continually weaker.

Hence, for the purposes of our estimate of the position and prospects of the extant social order, it is necessary to attempt some examination of present conditions and tendencies in the field of ideas.

Hitherto the supreme expression of the spirit of every epoch of human history has been the religion which the men of that epoch have succeeded in evolving.[1] In the major historical epochs great religious systems have been established. By a marvellously elaborate and, at the height of the given epoch, a marvellously satisfying arrangement of symbolic acts, closely associated with an equally elabo-

---

[1] Hence, as Marx says, "The criticism of religion is the beginning of all criticism."

rate and satisfying mythology, it has been possible to express the contemporary interpretation of man's place in the universe. And men have been able to express themselves by means of this religious method with a thousand times greater force and richness of content than they would have achieved, if they had attempted to express themselves intellectually. In every age and place, men have rightly concluded that their religion was the central feature of their civilization. They knew that it represented the richest expression which they all collectively, and generation by generation, had been capable of giving to the fundamental assumptions of their civilization.

Such assumptions, such prerequisites, of civilization have hitherto contained two main strands of feeling. On the one hand, men have imperatively required some assurance that they are not altogether helpless and alone in the face of the gigantic and perilous indifference of the natural forces which surround them. Such assurance religion supplied by personifying these forces so that, at least, they might be invoked, cajoled and propitiated. On the other hand, it was imperative to the stability of the human communities of the past that the strongest possible prohibitions should be placed upon some of men's strongest instincts. This need religion also supplied, by providing that these very natural forces of which men were principally afraid should, in their personified form, as the gods, or as God, forbid the "anti-social" acts. Thus, a sanction far more awful than any that could be provided by a human tribunal was secured for the tabus necessary to the main forms of civilization which have hitherto existed. For it was necessary to convince the great majority of men, by means of a partly conscious act of deception on the part of their rulers that they would in their own persons be certainly, dreadfully, and eternally punished, if they committed acts which tended to make the then existing type of community life impossible.

Of these religious expressions of the characteristics of the human communities of the past, the Christian religion has been one of the greatest. Above all, it has been one of the most flexible. The same elements of mythology, even the same symbolic acts, have been capable of wide adaptations. Different versions of Christianity have served the religious needs of the various forms of society which have existed in Europe, and latterly, in America, during the last 2,000 years. Moreover, widely different forms of the religion have been used by different classes existing simultaneously in time and place within the same society.

Roman Catholicism has been the predominant version of the religion during most of the 2,000 years of its currency. Catholicism, however, has not been the expression of Christianity especially suitable to the capitalist form of society evolved by the Western world. On the contrary, it is an historical commonplace, which we repeated in Chapter I, that the middle class in its first great battle for the freedom of the market found its major opponent in the Catholic Church. It is characteristic, however, of the flexibility of Christianity that, although its established form was the arch enemy of the new form of society, which a changing technique of production was making necessary, yet the very authors of this new society fought under the banner of a new variety of the old religion. The middle class of Europe in their long struggle showed no signs of inventing a new religion for themselves.[1] The men of the market found that a new form of Christianity, namely Protestantism, served their purpose very well. Indeed, as Marx points out, this form of Christianity "with its cult of the abstract human being"[2] is an ideal religion for a society based upon private property. With capitalism, Protestant Christianity flourished. For it was the Protestant virtues which were at once the product and the support of the capitalist system. Thrift, self-denial, self-reliance, sobriety, industriousness—these virtues built alike the Protestant churches and the railway system of the world. Accordingly, it is significant that it is precisely this final form of Christianity, that it is Protestantism in all its sub-varieties, which is to-day in the most rapid and obvious decline.

Nor did the rise of capitalism affect the fortunes of Christianity by creating the Protestant schism alone. With the very first appearance of merchant capital in the thirteenth century, the character of Catholicism itself began to change, and has been changing ever since. With the rise of the merchant guilds, of the individual merchants, and later, of the merchant bankers (to use a modern term), Catholicism itself became, under the influence of the Franciscan

[1] Robespierre's Goddess of Reason and, at a later stage, the Positivism of Comte are a very illustrative kind of exception. They showed, by being conceived of at all, the theoretical possibility of a new special religion for the triumphant middle class, and by their complete failure, the practical redundancy of any such new religion.

[2] *Capital,* Vol. I., page 53.

movement, a personal and not, as it had been before, an essentially communal religion. When the individual, as trader and producer, instead of as formerly, the feudal association, became the basic unit of society, religion had to become the religion of that individual's salvation. This "Protestantization" of the Catholic Church, if we may be permitted the paradox, culminated in the seventeenth and eighteenth centuries with the Jansenist movement, and the heyday of merchant, as distinct from industrial, capital.

Since then, and this is of especial interest, the Catholic Church has been getting more Catholic again. After the low-water mark of Catholic power at the end of the eighteenth century, Catholicism has recovered ground, if only relatively to the other Churches, both in intellectual prestige and in temporal power. And this, of course, is just what we should expect. For life, with the growth of large-scale production, is becoming less and less individual and more and more communal again. Thus, for anyone who can achieve religious belief at all, the Catholic form of Christianity is becoming increasingly appropriate. To-day, the point has been reached where a highly intellectual neo-Catholic, and significantly, neo-Thomist, movement is evidently reaching back for the pre-Franciscan, predominantly communal form of the faith.

The present crisis in religious belief goes far deeper, however, than the decay or revival of any of the sub-divisions of Christianity. A religion, it has been suggested, is the supreme collective expression of a community's view of man's place in the universe. And yet, by a crucial paradox, it is essential to the existence of any religion that its adherents should not consciously realize that this is the function of their faith. If they did so, they would inevitably attempt an intellectual instead of a symbolic and mythological statement of their philosophy of life. For the very fact that they had become capable of standing critically outside of their religion and of realizing what in fact its function was, would mean that they were ready for explicit and rational statement: it would mean that they had ceased to *believe*. And straightforward belief in the literal and overt truth of what a religion teaches about the nature of the universe, and not any esoteric recognition of the services which it is performing to the community, is what keeps a religion alive.

This straightforward belief in the essential claim of all varieties of religion to be supernatural, has become extremely difficult for men to-day. In that melancholy book, *The Future of an Illusion,* Dr. Freud, himself one of the last great theorists of the European capitalist class, has stated with simple clarity the impossibility of religious belief for the educated man of to-day. The traditional claims of religious dogma are, he tells us, three in number.

"They [the dogmas of religion] deserve to be believed: firstly, because our primal ancestors already believed them; secondly, because we possess proofs, which have been handed down to us from this very period of antiquity; and thirdly, because it is forbidden to raise the question of their authenticity at all."

Dr. Freud then examines these claims.

"This third point cannot but rouse our strongest suspicions. Such a prohibition can surely have only one motive: that society knows very well the uncertain basis of the claim it makes for its religious doctrines. If it were otherwise, the relevant material would certainly be placed most readily at the disposal of anyone who wished to gain conviction for himself. And so we proceed to test the other two arguments with a feeling of mistrust not easily allayed. We ought to believe because our forefathers believed. But these ancestors of ours were far more ignorant than we; they believed in things we could not possibly accept to-day; so the possibility occurs that religious doctrines may also be in this category. The proofs they have bequeathed to us are deposited in writings that themselves bear every trace of being untrustworthy. They are full of contradictions, revisions, and interpolations; where they speak of actual authentic proofs they are themselves of doubtful authenticity. It does not help much if divine revelation is asserted to be the origin of their text or only of their content, for this assertion is itself already a part of those doctrines whose authenticity is to be examined, and no statement can bear its own proof.

"Thus we arrive at the similar conclusion that just what might be of the greatest significance for us in our cultural system, the information which should solve for us the riddles of the universe and reconcile us to the troubles of life, that just this has the weakest possible claim to authenticity. We should not be able to bring ourselves to accept anything of as little concern to us as the fact that whales bear young instead of laying eggs, if it were not capable of better proof than this."

It is on account of these simple considerations that what we have called straightforward religious belief becomes ever more impossible to-day. But, it may be objected, is not this a very naive form of religious belief? Have not intelligent men always believed in religion on quite other grounds? Have they not always privately known that their belief was pragmatic, not evidential: that it was the essential service which religion could perform to society which made it worthy of their adherence, and not its literal truth? Dr. Freud examines this question also.

"The second attempt is that of the philosophy of 'As If.' It explains that in our mental activity we assume all manner of things, the groundlessness, indeed the absurdity, of which we fully realize. They are called 'fictions,' but from a variety of practical motives we are led to behave 'as if' we believed in these fictions. This, it is argued, is the case with religious doctrines on account of their unequalled importance for the maintenance of human society. This argument is not far removed from the *Credo quia absurdum*. But I think that the claim of the philosophy of 'As If' is such as only a philosopher would make. The man whose thinking is not influenced by the wiles of philosophy will never be able to accept it; with the confession of absurdity, of illogicality, there is no more to be said as far as he is concerned. He cannot be expected to forgo the guarantee he demands for all his usual activities just in the matter of his most important interests. I am reminded of one of my children who was distinguished at an early age by a peculiarly marked sense of reality. When the children were told a fairy tale, to which they listened with rapt attention, he would come forward and ask: Is that a true story? Having been told that it was not, he would turn away with an air of disdain. It is to be expected that men will soon behave in like manner towards the religious fairy tales, despite the advocacy of the philosophy of 'As If.' "

Thus beyond doubt, and beyond recall, the possibility of religious belief is leaving Western man. But what does this mean? It means

that man is at length alone with the universe. He is at last free to
face those natural forces which are so unbearably careless of his
fate. He can no longer pretend, as he used in his childhood, that
these natural forces can be made, if suitably invoked, to co-operate
with him. Nor can he now, as he did in his youth, invoke the aid
of a celestial and omnipotent ally to fight on his side against the
stars. At last, he is old enough to bear the thought that upon himself
alone depends the issue of the struggle between life and death. For
he has at length thought this fatal thought and so he must bear it.

The ebb of religious belief brings man face to face with his environment; but it also brings him face to face with the necessity of
remodelling that environment. For unmodified by man, the world
is intolerable. It must be recreated, if not in fancy by the comforts
of religion, then in fact by the hand of man himself. Fortunately,
by the inevitable intertwinings of historical cause and effect, that
very growth of knowledge which has robbed man of his protective
cloak of religious illusion, gives him in compensation the power to
refashion the earth. It is precisely because man is at last in sight of
being able to control nature himself that he now can neither maintain, nor should he need, the illusion that nature is controlled by
God.

If this were all, all would be well. The illusions of childhood
would be slipping from man, not a moment before he was able to
dispense with them. But now we come on an astonishing paradox.
It might seem that once he had achieved technical mastery over
nature, as he has so largely done, man would have nothing more to
fear. There would be nothing left unknown, incomprehensible and
so uncontrollable, to impose the arbitrary and terrifying hand of
necessity upon him. As he became every day more sure of his
technical powers, he would become in exact measure more free,
more fearless and less in need of ghostly comforts. Man would have
grown up. His life would be within his own control, free from his
long serfdom to his environment. And this, indeed, is the vision of a
millennium which has floated before the eyes of some of the noblest
thinkers of mankind. It is a vision which has been seen for the
last 200 years; ever since, that is, it became clear that man was
winning his struggle with nature. It was this vision which inspired
the great eighteenth-century French rationalists; which sustained
the somehow less estimable English liberals of the nineteenth cen-

tury (less estimable because they were already beginning to be able to know better); and which flickers on, even to-day, in the minds of such belated prophets of the capitalist class as Mr. H. G. Wells.

To-day, however, one would have supposed that the naivety of the vision would have been apparent to everybody. Man's conquest of nature is already far advanced. But where is the millennium? It is almost out of sight. In practice the technical progress of man, his machines, his science, his general command over nature, far from having created a universe sufficiently habitable for him to dispense with the consolations of religious illusion, have left him almost, if not quite, as miserable and terrified as ever. The knowledge which he has acquired has indeed made religious belief almost impossible. But the application of that knowledge has not as yet made a world in which the need for that consolation is much if any the less urgent. The promises of the scientists and the rationalists seem to have been all false. Man has, at their bidding, eaten of the tree of knowledge and so conquered his environment. And yet, in some mysterious and incomprehensible way, nature remains as cruel, arbitrary and terrifying as ever. Man now knows how to grow his food with one-tenth of the labour that he used before. And yet, inexplicably, he remains as hungry as ever. He can clothe, warm and shelter himself with one hundred times the ease he could. Yet he remains almost as naked, cold and ill-housed as before. No wonder that a profound sense of disappointment and discouragement pervades the Western world. No wonder that in spite of the intellectual suicide involved, an increasing number of men turn away from science and reason, and seek again in desperation to believe in the consoling myths of the childhood of the race.

How can this tragic paradox have arisen? How can man have gained the knowledge which makes illusion impossible, and which should make it unnecessary, and yet find himself still in as great a need of it as ever? Surely, the answer to the riddle is not obscure? We have said that man has progressed a good way in the conquest of his environment. But were we right? Truly, he has learnt how to control the forces of nature quite sufficiently to enable him, if he would, to make his life incomparably more secure, less arduous, longer, healthier, more civilized in every respect, than it has ever been hitherto. But does this conquest of nature in fact constitute a victory over his environment as a whole? Does nature in fact constitute the whole of man's environment? Is man himself something apart from nature, something contraposed to it by antithesis? Certainly, he is not. Man is himself a part of nature, a part of his own environment. For each man, all other men, all of humanity, are part of his external environment. And man's conquest of the whole of his environment necessarily involves man's self-conquest. In other words, the comprehension and so control of his fellow-men must be a part of any control over his environment as a whole. Man, before he can achieve anything substantial, must learn to control not only nature but also the social organizations, the relationships between man and man, which are necessary to his control over nature.

It is no longer difficult to understand how the present pitiful condition of man in the capitalist world has come about. Man has subdued nature. But he lives in the most abject servility to the social organization, the various associations with his fellows, which he has been led to make in order to accomplish his conquest of nature. He has learnt how to control the production of almost anything he desires. But he is obviously and shamefully controlled by the means of production. He is acquiring a clear and rational understanding of his relationship to nature. Therefore he has that relationship under his control. But he does not and cannot comprehend his relationship to other men, to society as a whole. Hence he cannot control that relationship; on the contrary, it unmercifully controls him, forcing him to starve miserably in the midst of the plenty he has created. While his relationship with nature is bathed in the clear light of science, his social relationships, his relationships to his fellow-men, are still shrouded in obscurity and mystification. Man, in a word, has not really conquered his environment at all. He has only conquered the non-human part of his environment. He is still, in the main, as ignorant as any terrified savage of the nature of his relationship with his fellow-men. And not until he makes this second conquest: not until he has understood the nature of his relationship to his fellow-men and has acted on that understanding, will he be able so to refashion life that he will be able to do without the comforting illusions of relgious belief.[1]

---

[1] Lenin perfectly expresses this point in an article in the newspaper *Proletarii*, written in 1909: "In modern capitalist countries the basis of religion is primarily *social*. The roots of modern religion are deeply embedded in the social oppression

In fact, what has been accomplished by science is largely to remove the need for what we have called the first strand of feeling expressed by a religious system; but it has failed to remove the need for the second strand. Men need no longer fear nature as they did before. But they need to fear their fellow-men as much as ever. Thus the second function of religion, which was to give a supernatural sanction to the prohibition of anti-social acts, seems to be as much needed as ever.

What, however, are anti-social acts? If men have not yet discovered, or at any rate recognized, any science which will give them an understanding of the nature of society, how can they know what acts are indeed incompatible with society itself, with any form of civilization, and what are merely incompatible with the form of society under which they happen to live? May it not turn out, on closer investigation, that the awful sanctions of religion are really being used to restrain the great majority of men from committing acts of rebellion against the particular form of society under which they live? May not many of what Dr. Freud calls the "instinctual privations" of men be, not the inevitable price of civilization, but the price of a civilization which solves the problems of organization for production by creating two opposed classes in society?

Dr. Freud, in some passages, seems to recognize this.

He writes:

"If we turn to those restrictions that only apply to certain classes of society, we encounter a state of things which is glaringly obvious and has always been recognized. It is to be expected that the neglected classes will grudge the favoured ones their privileges and that they will do everything in their power to rid themselves of their own surplus of privation. Where this is not

of the working masses, and in their apparently complete helplessness before the blind forces of capitalism, which every day and every hour cause a thousand times more horrible suffering and torture for ordinary working folk than are caused by exceptional events such as war, earthquakes, etc. 'Fear created the gods.' Fear of the blind force of capital—blind because its action cannot be foreseen by the masses—a force which at every step in life threatens the worker and the small business man with 'sudden,' 'unexpected,' 'accidental' destruction and ruin, bringing in their train beggary, pauperism, prostitution, and deaths from starvation—this is the *tap-root* of modern religion which, first of all, and above all, the materialist must keep in mind, if he does not wish to remain stuck for ever in the infant school of materialism."

possible a lasting measure of discontent will obtain within this culture, and this may lead to dangerous outbreaks. But if a culture has not got beyond the stage in which the satisfaction of one group of its members necessarily involves the suppression of another, perhaps the majority—and this is the case in all modern cultures—it is intelligible that these suppressed classes should develop an intense hostility to the culture; a culture, whose existence they make possible by their labour, but in whose resources they have too small a share. In such conditions one must not expect to find an internalization of the cultural prohibitions among the suppressed classes; indeed they are not even prepared to acknowledge these prohibitions, intent, as they are, on the destruction of the culture itself and perhaps even of the assumptions on which it rests. These classes are so manifestly hostile to culture that on that account the more latent hostility of the better provided social strata has been overlooked. It need not be said that a culture which leaves unsatisfied and drives to rebelliousness so large a number of its members neither has a prospect of continued existence, nor deserves it." (*The Future of an Illusion*)

If we may turn his own weapons of analysis against him, may we not observe that the form in which Dr. Freud pays his tribute of recognition to the inherent instability of class society is highly significant? "It need not be said," he writes. But surely this particular sentence in which he actually says that a class society neither can nor should survive is just what *does* need to be said. It needs to be said all the more because Dr. Freud seems, once he has put these words on to paper, to forget all about them for the rest of his argument. He shows no further recognition of the fact that certainly the great majority and, for all we know to the contrary, all of the "instinctual privations" of man would be inevitable in a classless society. And this is all the more strange in that Dr. Freud comes to the conclusion that the experiment of educating a generation of men free from belief in the illusions of religion both must be tried, and may produce startlingly good results. For he attaches the utmost importance to the damage which is done to, what he calls, "the radiant intelligence of a healthy child" by instilling into the child's mind the intellectually untenable dogmas of religion. Indeed, he goes so far as to suggest that it is largely this which accounts for the relative degeneration to "the feeble mentality of the average adult."

But is this not exactly what Marx said, somewhat more forcibly, when he called religion "the opium of the people"? Dr. Freud considers that if this intellectual damage is not done to children, they may well remain sufficiently intelligent to fight the battle of life without needing the illusions of religion. It is not difficult to agree with him. But would not these intelligent adults use their mental powers to acquire an understanding of the social relationships which to-day so painfully constrict the lives of the great majority of them? And is it not precisely the fear that this would happen which makes the present rulers of the world so insistent on the need for the maintenance of religious belief? It is because he does not even ask these questions that Dr. Freud remains, for all his great intellectual powers, the last major thinker of the European capitalist class, unable to step outside of his class limitations.

The nature of these social relationships has been the subject of these pages. The key to their understanding is, of course, that they are all, by derivation, productive relationships.[1] That is to say, men find themselves associating with each other in social arrangements to facilitate the production of the things they need. And consequently the forms which these associations take will vary and alter as the methods which they use for production vary and alter.

But until men understand this, and until they begin to act on this understanding, their social life will remain wrapped in impene-

---

[1] It is possible that some of the earliest social relationships were not productive (i.e. economic) but sexual in origin. Certain anthropological, and indeed zoological, researches (for these relationships were in fact mostly pre-human) seem to indicate this. But these researches also indicate that these pre-human and semi-human relationships were tenuous—precisely because they were not productive. Again, Professor Malinowski's vivid description of social relationships amongst comparatively developed communities such as the Trobrianders show how important is the sexual strand in the human connections of these islanders. But they also show that these sexual relationships are themselves closely bound up with economic factors, viz. customary gifts of great value at marriage, etc. There seems to be no conflict at all between the results of these researches and the contention that the predominant social relationships in all modern communities in the last 3,000 years in Europe, let us say, have been in fact relationships for the purposes of production, and that, consequently, these social relationships must and do vary with the methods of production. At bottom, of course, the economic and the sexual impulse are not separable. The impulse to maintain life is the same as the impulse to produce life. Production implies reproduction.

trable mystery. Being mysterious, it will be uncontrollable, and being uncontrollable, it will continue to play havoc with their lives. Men's forms of association, which are to-day companies, trusts, banks, trade unions, states and empires, will continue as they do now, not so much to further the productive purposes for which they have evolved as to thwart and render useless the marvellous new methods of production which men have come to possess. And so long as this remains, so men will need, perhaps more desperately than ever, the religious consolations which their new knowledge has made almost unattainable. Marx had a sentence which, published nearly seventy years ago, gives us a key to the whole condition of discouragement which pervades the capitalist world to-day. "Such religious reflections of the real world will not disappear until the relations between human beings in their practical everyday life have assumed the aspect of perfectly intelligible and reasonable relations as between man and man, and as between man and nature." [1] The relations between man and nature are now becoming every day more "perfectly intelligible and reasonable": the social and political relations between man and man in society remain, in the capitalist world, almost as mysterious as they were when Marx wrote in 1867. And so long as these vital relationships remain in obscurity men will attempt, even if vainly, or even at the cost of all intellectual integrity, to regain the comforts of religion.

Marx says elsewhere that "the demand that one reject illusions about one's situation, is a demand that one reject a situation which has need of illusions." Man's situation, which under capitalism is now growing worse and not better, has, therefore, more and not less need of that greatest, dearest and most comfortable of all illusions: the illusion of religion. Only by a realization of the need to do away finally with the capitalist form of society, which to-day forbids the creation of the new civilization which has become attainable; only by the destruction of that worn-out set of social relationships which are year by year thrusting us all back into chaos and barbarism, can the need for illusion be removed. The passage quoted from *Capital* continues: "The life process of society, this meaning the material process of production, will not lose its veil of mystery until it becomes a process carried on by a free association of producers, under their conscious and purposive control." When that

[1] *Capital*, page 54 of Eden and Cedar Paul's translation.

has been accomplished, man will not, to be sure, have immediately solved all his problems. His situation in the universe will still be daunting enough. Human life will remain for a long time a hasty and precarious affair. The conquest by comprehension of man's relationship to man, when it has been added to the conquest of man over nature, will not automatically usher in any impossible millennium of universal happiness. It would be childlike to believe any such thing. But it will make possible a whole new era of civilization, an era based upon the full use of man's ever-growing power and knowledge; a civilization far richer, because a civilization which will embrace whole communities and not merely certain classes within communities, than any we have yet known.[1]

[1] This is the answer to make to such nihilistic pessimism as Dr. Freud has expressed in his other semi-sociological work *Civilization and its Discontents*. He finds that the burden of sustaining, by the repression of anti-social instincts, the weight of the existing form of civilization is becoming ever more intolerable to men. And is this to be wondered at, since the overwhelming majority of men draw little and ever-decreasing benefits and carry an ever heavier weight? It is not encouraging for the worker rigorously to repress his private pugnacity in order, as a reward, to fight and die in an imperialist war: to curb the egotism of his unconscious in order to make possible a community life from which he draws only a grotesquely unequal share of the benefits. To-day the vast majority of men have almost all of the burden and very little of the civilization. Is it then so remarkable that Dr. Freud finds that the weight is becoming intolerable?

CHAPTER IX

SCIENCE

An explanation has been offered both of the decay of religious belief and of the painful consequences, so long as capitalism endures, of that decay. This is no place (nor have I the equipment) to consider that somewhat equivocal sphere of human thought, philosophy. Philosophy seems to have been, on the whole a kind of grandiose attempt on the part of men for whom what we have called straightforward religious belief had become impossible, to spin out of their own heads a satisfying substitute for faith. Such an attempt marked, however, a stride forward in the liberation of the human intelligence. It marked the point at which it had become necessary for the leading minds of the race to attempt an explanation of the universe by intellectual methods. For although it is only now that the amount and the diffusion of scientific knowledge has made religious belief almost impossible to wide sections of men, there have long been individuals who have found it impossible to accept the credentials of any of the divine revelations.

Philosophy sets out to be the critique of human knowledge as a whole: the science of the sciences. That school of historically minded philosophers which culminated in Hegel, approached, I take it, the realization of this high claim, and then drew back in terror.

No other philosophers, however, have ventured so far. And to-day a large part of official academic philosophy is in full retreat from the attempt to use the intellect in order to comprehend the universe, and is engaged in no other task than the reintroduction of theological methods. The present tendency is to "reconcile science and religion": to attempt, that is, not to comprehend science, but to prove that science can "really" tell us nothing about life. But science can tell us this at any rate, it can tell us how to change life. And it does not seem unreasonable to suppose that understanding a thing and changing it are interdependent acts. If, as we have suggested above, it is impossible to change life until we have begun to under-

stand it, it is also impossible to understand life unless part of our
effort to understand it is also and at the same time an effort to
change it. (This after all is simply the method of everyday common
sense. If, to use a homely illustration, any of us really want to understand, say, the carburettor of a motor-car we take it to pieces, put it
together again, *at the same time* looking at the handbook to see if
there is anything wrong with it, and if so, putting it right.) It is
also, of course, the experimental method of science. The manipulation of an object must be a part of a successful attempt to understand it.[1]

Until philosophy adopts this, the characteristic outlook of healthy
science, it will remain, however brilliant and subtle its practitioners
may be, half buried in a mediæval scholasticism. Some idealistic
philosophers, it is true, claim to be able to change the world by
means of their moral exhortation. Indeed, as they believe that "the
idea" is the basis of "the thing," and not the thing of the idea, moral
exhortation leading to a "change of heart" on the part of all men,
is the only dynamic method open to them. All that we need say as
to this claim is that experience has shown, after a trial of some 3,000
years, that it is unjustified. Naturally, however, as long as philosophy
continues to exist in the world of capitalist decline, it cannot possibly adopt the outlook of healthy science. On the contrary, it will
continue to become, as it is doing to-day, less and less scientific,
extrovert, objective and vigorous, and more and more theological,
introvert, subjective and impotent.

What, however, is the effect of the decline of capitalism on science
itself? Does science alone manage to remain immune? Now science
was once the favourite son of capitalism, its supreme intellectual
achievement. The growth of scientific knowledge alone enabled
capitalism to make its dramatic achievements in the conquest of
nature. Each time that capitalism encountered some obstacle to its
development, science was called in to solve the problem. Had the
opening up of new markets far outstripped the possibilities of production, science could be relied upon to, and did, double production
by new methods. Were the means of transport inadequate to dis-

[1] "The philosophers have merely interpreted the world in various ways: the
thing is to change it."—*Eleventh Thesis on Feuerbach*, Marx.

"The problem of the cognition of the external world is an integral part of the
problem of its transformation. The problem of theory is a practical problem."—
Theory and Practice from the Standpoint of Dialectical Materialism, Bukharin.

tribute the products of an improved industrial technique? Science found new methods of transport and distribution. Were the possibilities of profitable investment at a given level of industrialization in a given place reaching exhaustion? Science produced inventions which made it profitable to scrap whole categories of productive equipment and to replace them by new machines. Did the demand for labour tend to exceed the supply and thus enable the worker to command better wages? Science produced automatic machinery, by which an increased level of production could be maintained by perhaps two-thirds of the former amount of labour. Nor were the capitalists ungrateful. We can catch a glimpse of their former attitude to science in the works of Dr. Ure, that delightfully naive rhapsodist of the rising industrial system. In his *magnum opus, The Philosophy of Manufactures,* published almost a hundred years ago (1835), Dr. Ure tells us again and again of the gratitude which is due to the scientists, both for reducing the demand for labour, and for "disciplining" what labour might still be necessary. Thus, he tells us, that "the constant aim and the tendency of every improvement in machinery is, in fact, to do away entirely with the labour of man, or to lessen its price by substituting the labour of women and children for that of grown men, or of unskilled for that of skilled workmen." Again, there is nothing like a good dose of science for overcoming recalcitrance on the part of workers in accepting the terms of employment offered. Thus, the benefits conferred on humanity by the invention of the self-acting mule are described by Dr. Ure as follows: the mule, he says, is "a creation destined to restore order among the industrial classes. This invention confirmed the great doctrine already propounded, that when capital enlists science into her service, the refractory hand of labour will always be taught docility." [1] Is it strange that in the hot youth of an expanding capitalism, science was a best belovèd son?

Now, as we have seen, capitalism has exhausted the possibilities of its development. It has reached an economic impasse and cannot use the enormous capacities for production which science has already given it. Still less does it know what to do with the ever new and

---

[1] For the changes that have taken place in capitalist views on science, Professor Hessen's brilliant paper, "The Social and Economic Roots of Newton's 'Principia'" (published in *Science at the Cross Roads*), should be consulted. See, also, for Dr. Ure and his school of thought, the first volume of *Capital*.

more fabulous powers which science is pressing into its hand. May we not expect some change in the attitude of the capitalist class to science? We may expect it in theory, and we can discern it in fact. Science has now definitely ceased to be the admirable genie which, produced from its lamp at the correct moment, can solve every problem. The capitalists find themselves rather in the embarrassing position of the sorcerer's apprentice. To-day, when they call on science to solve their problems of production, they get more than they ask for. What, for example, is a harried capitalist who cannot sell, say, 10,000 tons of steel a year, to say to the scientists who can tell him how to produce 100,000 tons? What thanks will the agricultural expert, who can double the yield of wheat, get from the farmer who has just gone bankrupt because he has grown too much of it? It is only natural that the modern capitalist is coming to have a new view of his scientific assistants. A decided coldness is developing. The capitalist's father may have been all on the side of Huxley in his famous controversy with the bishops. But the son, when he looks around him at the dangerous chaos of the world to-day, is apt to think that the conservatism of the ecclesiastics had a good deal to be said for it.

An excellent example of this coldness towards science is afforded by a speech which that able, and always up-to-date, spokesman of French capitalism, M. Caillaux, delivered in London on the World Crisis on February 29th, 1932. M. Caillaux said:

"At the present time an urgent task is to stop this war of technical appliances, but it, too, is a difficult problem. First of all I must destroy any illusions you may have. It is purely chimerical to imagine that time will cure all and that producers themselves will moderate the application of scientific discoveries to industry; even if they wished to, they could not do this. We must realize that the authorities must be called upon to intervene. Employers, financiers, and merchants will have to be compelled to co-operate in the home markets of their own countries and later beyond their frontiers, to get together to adapt production to consumption, to co-ordinate their forces, to unite, to rationalize, if this barbarism is preferred, their technical appliances. But this must be carried out in such a manner that individual enterprise, which will always be the great motive force in human progress, does not become less, in such a manner that the public authorities do not exceed the scope of the only part which is theirs to play, that of encouraging and controlling."

How fiercely M. Caillaux demands that scientific advance should be "moderated"! He is even prepared, for this destructive purpose alone, to see an intervention of the State in economic affairs. But he realizes that he is here on dangerous ground. Was he not after all delivering the fourth annual "Richard Cobden Lecture"? Once the State has compelled producers to arrest technical progress, it must step back and allow "individual enterprise" to act once more as the "motive force of human progress." To such intellectual depths are even the more talented spokesmen of capitalism reduced, by their efforts to solve the insoluble problems which their system presents to them.

And this new coldness on the part of capital towards science is a very serious matter for the latter. The scientists are, for the most part, rather simple-minded fellows outside of their laboratories. Ever since the days of Dr. Ure and his friends, they have gone ahead with their researches in the confident assurance that they were conferring inestimable benefits upon mankind. But now it appears that, on the contrary, all they are doing is to make chaos worse confounded. In a world already half smothered in commodities which it cannot distribute or consume, they are discovering how to double the production of new commodities. In a world where thirty or forty million men and women are condemned to the agony of unemployment, they are discovering how to dispense with half of those who are still employed.

No wonder that they get no more panegyrics. On the contrary, doubt and hesitation has, if we may judge from the columns of the most responsible British scientific organ, from the columns of *Nature* itself, spread even to the scientists themselves. For example, under the somewhat ambiguous title of "Unemployment and Hope," *Nature* writes: "There is, indeed, in the present situation much to excuse a passing reflection that perhaps, after all, the people of Erewhon were wiser than ourselves in destroying their machines, lest, as Marx predicted, the machines reversed the original relation and the workmen became the tool and appanage of a lifeless mechanism." [1] This is indeed a new note! Where now are the dithyrambs of a Ure, the thundering hosannas of a Huxley? *Nature,* moreover, follows up the argument with some practical proposals. Not content with a "passing reflection" that the application of every principle for which it has stood since its foundation has proved disastrous, *Nature* begins to make some concrete suggestions for undoing its own work. The writer continues as follows:

> "The aims of industry are, or should be, chiefly two: (1) to furnish a field for ... growth of character; and (2) to produce commodities to satisfy man's varied wants, mostly of a material kind, though of course there are large exceptions outside the material category, and the term 'material' is here used in no derogatory sense. Attention has hitherto been directed mainly to (2), and the primary aim of industry has been ignored. Such a one-sided view of industry coupled with a too narrow use of the much-abused word 'evolution' ... has led to over-concentration on quantity and mass production and a ridiculous neglect of the human element, and there can be no doubt that had a little thought been given to the first aim then the second would have been much more completely and satisfactorily attained; also unployment would not have been heard of...." [2]

All this means (although one must admit to an element of guesswork in interpreting the passage), that all our efforts to produce commodities with the minimum expenditure of human energy have been a mistake. What is really wanted is a type of production which will produce a correct frame of mind in the worker (will "furnish," that is, "a field for growth of character").

We are next informed that in future the aim of science must not be, as heretofore, to achieve large-scale efficient production. The new aim is to be "elasticity." And elasticity is then defined as follows:

---

[1] Marx, of course, said just the opposite. He said that, under capitalism, the workmen had become the tools and appendages of machines, but he predicted that, under communism, the position would be reversed and the machines become the tools and appendages of the workmen.

[2] The apology, in a scientific journal, for such an indelicate suggestion as that man has material wants which, after all, may sometimes need a little attention, is particularly charming.

"Elasticity further means the possibility of reviving, under new and improved forms to meet modern conditions, two at least of the older types of industry which are supposed to have been superseded or rendered obsolete by modern large-scale production, namely: (1) small cottage industries or handicrafts; ... (2) a combination of manufacturing with agricultural or garden industry.... Industry still has its roots firmly and deeply rooted in the past, and foolishly to tear up a great part of those roots as old and useless is the surest way to weaken the industrial tree. Perchance the source of the unemployment curse is to be found here.

"The restitution of these two principles of an older industrial order, so essentially and characteristically English, under improved forms made possible by modern scientific achievement, including notably electrical power distribution, would furnish, in the first place, a new and almost infinite field for human employment of all kinds, absorbing all or most of the present unemployed."

This passage, at any rate, is clear. What is wanted is to go back to pre-industrial methods of production. Scrap your huge large-scale factories: prohibit mass production by law: and return to "small-scale cottage industries, or handicrafts," with a little gardening thrown in. (It is true that the use of electrical power is suggested for the cottage industries. But this is obviously a mistake. For clearly much more employment will be given if all forms of mechanization are prohibited.) Samuel Butler certainly never foresaw that, within thirty years of his death, those proposals for universal machine-wrecking, which he put forward as a literary fantasia, would be seriously advocated as a practical solution for the problems of the day by the leading organ of British science. How much that last phrase about these revived handicrafts furnishing "a new and almost infinite field for human employment" would have delighted Butler's restless irony. He might have written to *Nature* to enquire why its leader writer stopped short in his beneficial proposal. Why should handicrafts be permitted? Why should specialized tools, such as hammers, saws, spades, forks, planes, awls, and the like, all displacing an immense amount of labour, be allowed? Why not return at any rate to the level of the technique of, say, the older stone age? Then the leader writer could drop that weak word "almost" and boldly write that he had discovered a method for furnishing an "infinite field for human employment."

The state of mind of the author of "Unemployment and Hope" is, no doubt, an extreme example of the intellectual catastrophe which has overtaken some of the spokesmen of modern science. But it is none the less deeply symptomatic of the growing loss of self-esteem and self-confidence which they are feeling and which they must continue progressively to feel in the capitalist world. What has happened is undeniable, for its consequences cannot be escaped. The existing system of society has ceased to be suitable for the extant methods of production; for the general level of technique which science has achieved. There are only two things to do about it. Either the system of society must be changed, and a form of society adopted which is compatible with modern science; or, conversely, modern science must be destroyed, or, at any rate, artificially put back to, and kept at, a point where it will again be compatible with capitalist society. When faced with this choice the author of "Unemployment and Hope" has no hesitations. The hope which he brings to the unemployed is the hope of the destruction of science. If he has to choose between capitalism and science, he chooses capitalism every time. For he is a spokesman of the capitalist class, long before he is a scientist.

It is naturally in the field of the applied sciences that we should expect to find the first symptoms of discouragement. For the applications of scientific advance increasingly dislocate the social system. Thus I understand that in a recent meeting of the chief Association of American Civil Engineers—certainly the most powerful, and hitherto the most self-confident body of scientific technicians in the world—a proposal was lengthily discussed in a private session, that the only real contribution which engineers could make to the economic problem was to close the United States Patent Office for a hundred years. Again, examples of the suppression of new devices and inventions by vested interests which would be adversely affected by their application could, of course, be given in very great numbers. Indeed, many inventors have now become, in effect, licensed blackmailers of the trusts. They do not dream, having perfected a device, of putting it on the market. On the contrary, they take it to the existing trust, certain that they will be "bought off" for a good round sum. This, however, is a hackneyed theme. Mr. Bernard Shaw summarized the matter neatly in his play *The Apple Cart*, in which he described the great firm of Breakages Ltd., which undertakes all the repair work of the nation—and suppresses all the devices for making commodities unbreakable.

At the same time, it is not merely in the applied sciences that symptoms of faint-heartedness begin to appear. Many eminent physicists now make a regular practice of, and in some cases a regular income by, excursions into idealistic philosophy. Again, it is natural that official scientific bodies should show particularly marked signs of intellectual reaction. For example, the British Association, with a perfect appreciation of the trend of the times, chose as its annual President in its centenary year (1931) General Smuts. It is not until we come to enumerate the qualifications of this well-known soldier that a full realization of the adequacy of this choice is realized. In the first place, General Smuts is a General. Thus the martial application of so many of the recent triumphs of chemistry and mechanics is emphasized. In the second place, General Smuts has become a great imperialist with impeccable views on the fundamental inferiority of "native" races. Thus a tribute is paid to the impartiality of modern anthropology. Thirdly, General Smuts is a philosopher, and moreover an idealistic philosopher, whose doctrine of "Holism" lays down that everything is one indivisible whole, incapable of analysis, and therefore not susceptible of scientific investigation. Thus, the graceful admission of the science of modern capitalism that it cannot "really" tell us anything about anything is recognized. And fourthly, of course, General Smuts is a statesman, whose historic achievement it was to insert into the Treaty of Versailles those stipulations which set the amount payable in reparations by Germany at an order of magnitude hitherto more familiar to astronomers than economists. Thus, the assistance which scientific conceptions can now render to the art of politics is recognized.

All the symptoms of doubt and hesitation, which are growing up in the minds of scientists, should not, however, in themselves induce us to expect any immediate slowing up of the advance of scientific knowledge. Science is, increasingly, not merely a subjective process which goes on inside the heads of scientists, and is dependent upon their state of mind; it is an objective large-scale semi-industrial activity which, once it has been started, acquires a very great momentum of its own. The recent advances in the fields of chemistry and physics, in particular, depend to a great extent upon the actual laboratories and equipment provided, the endowments received and the number of research workers trained in the universities. Thus, we must expect a very considerable lag between a change in the attitude of the governing class towards science, or in the self-confidence of scientists themselves, and any falling off in the rate of scientific progress. In fact, the decade immediately after the Great War, 1918-1928, was a period of quite unprecedented scientific advance. It is true that this decade was on the whole one of capitalist recovery. And it is not without interest to observe the extremely close correspondence which now exists, not only between science and industry as a whole, but between particular sciences and particular industries. The unparalleled progress of physics during the last fifteen years has been quite demonstrably dependent upon the rise of the electrical industry. For the great electrical firms, such as the American General Electric Company, the Phillips Lamp Company (lately employing some forty professors directly), the British Metropolitan Vickers and the German electrical trusts, have provided practically all of the large sums of money which are needed for modern physical research. They have both maintained large laboratories themselves and have also made substantial grants to universities for physical work.

Nor is it difficult to discover the basis of the other great scientific success of recent times: the advance of biology. The money for this work has come, partly from imperialist Governments, and partly from the great coporations such as the British trust, Unilevers, which are vitally concerned in opening up tropical areas. There has been nothing in the least accidental about recent scientific progress. It has been closely correlated with the fortunes of capitalist industry. Where capitalism has prospered, science has progressed. If even these sections of capitalist enterprise cease to make progress, we may expect a corresponding stagnation in science.

For the post-war recovery of capitalism was a very relative recovery; it was extremely patchy; while some industries, such as the electrical industry, went ahead, others were stagnant or regressive. It is not surprising that symptoms of psychological decay in the attitude of mind of scientists were apparent before the end of this decade. Even now, however, the rate of scientific advance has hardly, if at all, abated. We should expect the effect of the changed attitude of the governing class to make itself felt in the end, indeed, by the gradual drying up of the funds provided for scientific work: and we should expect the subjective degeneration of scientists gradually to begin to affect the quality of their work. (And this latter consequence, in contrast to the former one, would presumably show itself first in the failure to advance any further the most abstract and theoretical concepts of science. Many observers do claim that this is already occurring in the form of a "crisis" in the basis of mathematical thought.)

Both these factors will take effect over the decades rather than over the years, however. In the meantime, too, there are counterbalancing factors. Even though modern capitalism finds science an embarrassment rather than a help in the field of production, modern imperialism has still—has indeed increasingly—a need for science. The progressive banishment of competition from the field of commercial rivalry between firms and companies, and its reappearance in the form of international or rather inter-imperial rivalry, while destroying one field for the application of science, creates another—the field of war. Thus, at any rate to those branches of science which may increase the power of the state in war (and which may not?) the governing classes of the great empires will still be liberal. Altogether, therefore, we may say that while science is most vitally affected by the fact that capitalism has reached an impasse, yet there is no reason to suppose on that account that there will be an immediate slowing up in its rate of advance.

Yet for the moment at any rate, we may expect such a retardation: and that for a very concrete and objective reason. The present capitalist crisis has gone so far that the actual funds available for many forms of scientific work are drying up. Modern scientific research in many of its aspects is a costly affair and it can only be carried on in the capitalist world by the trusts and corporations and by the State itself. Both the trusts and their States are to-day feeling the pinch very badly and the actual basis of scientific work is narrowing. Thousands of scientific workers are themselves becoming unemployed.

Disquiet is growing in the minds of many young scientists: they are beginning to show a new interest in political and economic questions. Their necessarily specialized training seems, however, to have an only limited application to these questions. Their approach is, for the most part, unhistorical. Hence, there seems to be a danger that the energy and enthusiasm of the younger scientists, who are genuinely in revolt against the uses to which their work is at present being put, will be dissipated in impracticable schemes. Some of them, for example, talk of inducing all scientists to refuse to do work which can be used for war purposes. Apart from the technical difficulty of finding much scientific work which could not be so used, it should surely be apparent that there is not the slightest hope of inducing scientists as a whole to take up such an attitude. Most scientists have exactly the same political outlook as that of other professional men and they are, as the last war showed, quite as susceptible to patriotic appeals. They are caught within the net of existing social relationships just as much as lawyers, doctors or civil servants. There is not the slightest possibility of their taking up an independent revolutionary role. What is possible is for individual scientists to realize the incompatibility of capitalism and science, and to throw in their lot with the forces of the working class—as some of the most distinguished of the older Russian scientists have done. To do so involves, however, a recognition of the overriding strength of historical forces which it seems particularly difficult for scientists to make. Most of them prefer to take up the much easier attitude that politics are all nonsense; that science is the only reality. (Mr. J. B. S. Haldane, for example, has often expressed this view.) They appear to suppose that science exists in a sort of vacuum unaffected by the social struggles of the present epoch. Truly, we may confidently rely on coming events rather than on argument to shatter this delusion. But, unfortunately, it will then be too late for such genuinely well-intentioned scientists to make their contribution to the working-class cause. Only a serious study of history and economics could convince them that the working class is the only objective force which can possibly avert the destruction of civilization and science in the wars of imperialism. And very few scientists see the need for such a study.

Again, the very forms under which modern scientific work is organized are well designed to shut off scientists from contact with the outside world. The grouping of scientists around universities, without any contact at all with productive industry, is clearly a relic of the literary tradition of learning. In another sense, however, scientists are brought into close touch with reality: they are forced to consider the fact that the principal way in which they can earn an income to-day is to obtain one of the university appointments which are open to them. As their confidence in science as a bene-factress of the human race is undermined by the frustrations of capitalism, they are more and more tempted to subside into not uncomfortable academic chairs.

Thus it is inevitable that many scientists, when they realize the incompatibility of the present social system and even the present achievements of science, will, like the author of "Unemployment and Hope," humbly conclude that the social system is perfectly in the right, and that the applications of science must at once be re-stricted in order to conform to the exigencies of capitalism. Some, however, may come to the conclusion that another remedy is to adapt the social system to the advance of science. For some scientists may, when they have to choose, prefer science to capitalism.

CHAPTER X

LITERATURE. I

IT is not, however, in the enfeeblement of belief, alike in religion and in science (for the victor in that once famous contest has not long survived the vanquished), that we shall find the most sensitive reflection in the world of ideas of the impasse which confronts capitalism to-day. We shall look for it rather in that wide and ambiguous tract of human thought which is called literature. "Literature" is perhaps the most remarkable of all the ideal constructions which the human mind has begotten. It is a great sea into which for centuries have been poured all those thoughts, dreams, fantasies, concepts, ascertained facts, and emotions, which did not fit into any other of the categories of human thought. Into literature have gone philosophical ideas too tenuous for the philosophers, dreams too literal for plastic expression, ascertained facts too uncorrelated for science, and emotions too intertwined with the particular instance to find expression in the glorious and precise abstractions of music.

While the other arts, music, painting, sculpture, are the algebra of emotional expression, literature is the arithmetic. Music and the plastic arts seek to express the generalized essence of man's predicament in the universe. Literature, for the most part, attempts to illuminate some particular predicament of a particular man or a particular woman at a given time and place. Literature is something of everything: its borders march on one side with science, on another with music, on a third with the plastic arts; and they touch the kingdom of religion itself. For the purposes of these pages, we shall take the widest possible definition of literature and include in our discussion the works of a novelist turned historian, Mr. H. G. Wells, of an economist turned social critic, Mr. Keynes, and of a poet philosopher, Nietzsche. To take this very wide view of literature is, after all, only to accept literature's traditional claims. Traditionally, the boundaries of literature were coterminous with those of human knowledge itself. Up till the sixteenth century, the poets felt that there was nothing on earth or in heaven which their art could not comprehend or express. When Bacon said that he had "taken all knowledge as his province," he did not, we may be sure, feel that he had overstepped the boundaries of literature.

What we are concerned with is to mark the reactions of some of the major writers of present-day capitalism to the social and economic conditions which surround them. For these writers are certainly amongst the most gifted and sensitive men of their time, and what they feel and express cannot fail to tell us a good deal about the state of the society in which they live. Let us examine first of all the work of three contemporary social theorists. If we deal first with the social theorists, that is not because more can be learnt about the conditon of a society from those of its writers who consciously criticize its characteristics, than from those writers who, fondly, believe that they are writing "pure literature." It is arguable that we may learn more from the unconsciously assumed attitudes of the "pure" writers. All the same, let us begin by considering such a writer as Mr. Wells, in order that we may not be obliged to push out at the very beginning of our investigation on to the uncharted, and unchartable, sea of "pure" literature. We shall undertake that voyage in the next chapter.

Mr. Wells has shown himself, more especially in the work which he has done in the last five years, to be the heir of a long and important tradition. By the publication of his three *Outlines*—of history, of science, and of economics, respectively—he has shown himself to be a modern encyclopædist. He is the last of that long line of the theorists of the capitalist class which stretches back in Great Britain, through Herbert Spencer, through the younger Mill, through Godwin, to Locke and Hobbes; and which in France springs from the encyclopædists and physiocrats, from Condorcet, Montesquieu, Quesnay, Condillac, d'Alembert, Helvetius, Holbach, Diderot and Voltaire himself. And if it seems somehow odd to compare Mr. Wells to these venerable figures, that is the consequence of his environment rather than of any lack of talent in the man himself.

Mr. Wells' own recent development in self-consciousness has been significant. It is curious to remember, for example, that until the last decade Mr. Wells used to consider that he was a socialist.

As, however, the real nature of the issue between capitalism and socialism has become inescapably clear, Mr. Wells has at length realized where he stands. He has grasped the fact that he heartily dislikes communism, socialism or any form of working-class collectivism. His major works, in fact, mark the close of the exactly antithetical tradition: they are the *vale* of English liberalism. It was the touchstone of communism in practice—of the Russian Revolution—which enabled Mr. Wells thus to find himself. About 1921, he went to Russia, interviewed Lenin and Trotsky, came home to compose his diatribe against Marxism in *The World of William Clissold,* and discovered that salvation lay in the beneficent trustifications of big business. He became, though he does not seem to have been quite conscious of this, or ever to have read his Kautsky or Hilferding, an ardent disciple of the school of ultra-imperialism: of the world state to be achieved by the coagulation of the capitalist classes of all nations.

And it is not really Mr. Wells' fault if he has in consequence become involved in the most extreme contradictions. For the contradictions were inherent in the situation of capitalism, and could not be avoided by anyone who sought a capitalist solution. The basic contradiction in Mr. Wells' attitude, from which all the others flow, is that while he represents the final expression of the tradition of liberal individualism, he is compelled to become an advocate of big business monopoly. And this is a form of economic organization which, as we shall show in the following chapters, must stamp out ruthlessly the last traces of liberalism.

Mr. Wells, in 1926, revealed himself in a novel called *Meanwhile,* dealing with the British General Strike, as the arch anti-Fascist: yet at the same time he supports that growth of big business monopoly which inevitably creates Fascism as its political instrument. At last, in 1932, as if wishing, himself, to sum up his own contradictions, he appealed to the Liberal Summer School at Oxford, for "Liberal Fascists. He wanted them to be the Western response to Russia." (*Observer,* July 31st, 1932) Mr. Wells has been the untiring champion of the rights of oppressed nations: yet he must now champion a cause which involves the forcible subjugation of every other nation in the world by some one victor state. He has been the strenuous opponent of imperialism, yet he must now champion the ultimate right of whichever empire proves itself the strongest to possess the whole earth.

With such contradictions underlying his position, it is to be expected that Mr. Wells will instinctively abstain from driving his investigations too deep. And, indeed, they have become painfully superficial.

The Outline of History is Mr. Wells' most considerable work. For, in spite of everything, the fact remains that it is, for the ordinary reader, the only outline of world history which as yet exists. (A world history written from the standpoint of dialectical materialism—which alone could make the dynamics of history comprehensible—has yet to be written.) By writing it, Mr. Wells made good the claim to be ranked in the list of the chief living theorists of the capitalist class. For a Universal History is the appropriate definite expression of the "world view" of a class: it is a sort of summing up of the culture which that class has been able to achieve. And Mr. Wells' *Outline of History*, both in its qualities and its defects, is an almost perfect expression of the final stage of the Anglo-Saxon part, at any rate, of capitalist culture.[1]

We can attempt here no detailed discussion of *The Outline of History* as a whole. Our best method will be to give one or two examples of the rigid limitations which the circumstances of capitalist decline have put upon Mr. Wells' thinking; limitations which they put on the thinking of any man who is determined to see a hopeful outcome for capitalist civilization. Let us take Mr. Wells' treatment of what is after all the key question of our day,

---

[1] Many people will no doubt object that a far more worthy summary of capitalist culture has been made by Oswald Spengler in his *Decline of the West*. Herr Spengler's book is, in effect, another universal history, and it is a much more erudite, cultured and literary one than Mr. Wells'. (Although it has a whole category of defects from which Mr. Wells' history is free.) It would, of course, serve as a more obvious example of the case which I am making in these chapters, as Herr Spengler, being a far more philosophically minded man than Mr. Wells, comes himself to the conclusion that the era of capitalism is over. He is consciously writing its epitaph. It is for this very reason that I prefer to instance Mr. Wells' history. Just as in Chapters V. and VI. I took Mr. Keynes' thesis on the possibilities of monetary reform because it was the most optimistic, so now I take Mr. Wells' history because it too represents the most favourable case that can be made for capitalism. The two alternative German theses—the monetary thesis of Dr. Hayek and the historical thesis of Herr Spengler—thus remain as *a fortiori* reinforcements of the argument of these pages.

the question of imperialism, and then let us follow his argument on this one point, at any rate, in some detail.

Now, curiously enough, it was precisely in respect of imperialism that Marx's views did need amplification. For imperialism, as a dominating factor in the world situation, had not arisen in his lifetime. And both Lenin and Bukharin, realizing this, set themselves, with the outbreak of the Great War, to achieve a richer and more complete understanding of the nature of imperialism. Hence, as Mr. Wells was setting up as a critic of Marx, an analysis of imperialism gave him an opportunity. What has he to offer us? In an interesting preface which Mr. Wells has added to a newly revised edition of *The Outline of History,* published in 1930, he tells us that in 1918 everyone was "thinking internationally" and asking such questions as "What was an empire? How had empires begun?" Now, if the submissions made in Chapter IV. of this book have any validity, "everyone" was entirely justified in raising this particular question at that time, for upon the answer to it the future of capitalist civilization depended.

Naturally therefore one might expect that an answer to this question would form an important part of Mr. Wells' concluding chapters. And in fact, we find Chapter XXXVIII. of *The Outline of History* entitled "The Catastrophe of Modern Imperialism." What, therefore, must be our astonishment when we search the chapter in vain for a rational explanation of the rise of imperialism. We are given instead a vivacious account of the psychological effects upon the European capitalist classes of the formation of the German, British and French empires. And then, by a complete inversion of reality, it is implied that these psychological effects are themselves the explanation of imperialism. Here, for instance, are the two paragraphs which Mr. Wells devotes to explaining the growth of imperialism in Britain.

"The old tradition of the English, the tradition of plain statement, legality, fair play, and a certain measure of republican freedom, had faded considerably during the stresses of the Napoleonic wars; romanticism, of which Sir Walter Scott, the great novelist, was the chief promoter, had infected the national imagination with a craving for the florid and picturesque. 'Mr. Briggs,' the comic Englishman of *Punch* in the 'fifties and 'sixties, getting himself into Highland costume and stalking deer, was fairly representative of the spirit of the new movement.

"It presently dawned upon Mr. Briggs, as a richly coloured and creditable fact he had hitherto not observed, that the sun never set on his dominions. The country which had once put Clive and Warren Hastings on trial for their unrighteous treatment of Indians was now persuaded to regard them as entirely chivalrous and devoted figures. They were 'empire builders.' Under the spell of Disraeli's Oriental imagination, which had made Queen Victoria 'empress,' the Englishman turned readily enough towards the vague exaltations of modern imperialism."

The inadequacy of the last sentence fairly takes one's breath away. If we were to take Mr. Wells at his word, we should have to say that he considered that modern imperialism was "a vague exaltation" and that its rise in Great Britain was due to the fact that that country once had a Prime Minister whose Oriental imagination enabled him to weave spells.

In Mr. Wells' whole account of the transformation of the hitherto comparatively liberal phase of capitalism into the present phase of rampant bellicosity, which he fully recognizes to have taken place, and which he so much deplores, there is not one sentence (or, to be precise, there is one half of a sentence) to show *why* this happened. For Mr. Wells apparently it just happened. Disraeli suddenly wove an Oriental spell, and modern imperialism was born. Somebody else apparently happened just then to weave corresponding spells in France and Germany, and a little later in America and Japan, and the modern world situation was complete. This is, indeed, the "spell-binding conception of history." There is, however, just one half sentence in which a hint is given of *why* these imperial spell-binders got to work at this particular moment. We are told that "the new British imperialism found its poet in Mr. Kipling"—and then in a sort of aside—"and its practical support in a number of financial and business interests whose way to monopolies and exploitations was lightened by its glow."

Now this is really very curious: for this phrase, if we look carefully enough into it, does actually mention some of the real elements of modern imperialism. As Mr. Hawtrey has explained to us so lucidly it is just this business of the granting of necessarily monopolistic rights of exploitation, in developing territories, which forces the great powers to undertake imperialist adventures. It is as if semi-consciously Mr. Wells did really know what an empire was. But his "censor mechanism," to borrow one of Dr. Freud's earlier concepts, knows quite well whither a statement of this concrete material explanation of the rise of imperialism would lead. And so Mr. Wells' semi-conscious knowledge of the real facts only escapes in queer little asides like the one we have just quoted. We can only conclude that while Mr. Wells and his friends had, in 1918, just got to the point of asking the question— "What is an empire?" they have not yet found an answer. As a matter of fact, Lenin and Bukharin had found the answer a year or two before Mr. Wells had found the question. In their two classical studies on the subject, both produced during the war years,[1] they showed the real connection between the change in the character of capitalist production and the growth of imperialism. According to them—and indeed according to a capitalist economist like Mr. Hawtrey—modern imperialism is not a "vague exaltation," but is the inescapable concomitant of a vast increase in the scale of capitalist production, amounting tendenciously to the creation of national monopolies. Thus imperialism, as Lenin summed it up, is the monopolist phase of capitalism. The vast expenditures and the great hazards of imperialist adventure have not been undertaken by all the great states because of Disraeli's or anybody else's imagination and eloquence: they have been undertaken, and are still being undertaken, because they were, and they are, the only remaining method by which the capitalist system could, and can, be kept going. This explanation does not appeal to Mr. Wells. For if the growth of imperialism cannot be attributed to the eloquence of Disraeli how can we expect that even the eloquence of Mr. Wells can restrain it? If imperialism and its horrible consequences, which Mr. Wells admits, are not the result of some malign accident, or of some appalling misdirection by the leaders of humanity, but are inherent in the development of large-scale capitalism itself, of the creation of those huge monopolistic businesses which Mr. Wells so particularly admires, what hope is there of persuading capitalism into peace? Is it not

[1] *Imperialism* by Lenin. *Imperialism and World Economy* by Bukharin.

possible that this is the reason why Mr. Wells finds all Marxian theories so repulsively scholastic, so unrealistic, so absurd?

On page 1063 of *The Outline of History* we are told that "Italy, too, caught the imperial fever." On page 1065, we find that at the same time "by an odd accident America had produced in President Roosevelt a man of an energy as restless as the German Kaiser's, as eager for large achievements, as florid and eloquent; an adventurous man with a turn for world politics and an instinct for armaments." For Mr. Wells, then, the simultaneous appearance of imperialism all over the world is just "an odd accident." We can only say that it is an accident that is likely to prove fatal to the continued existence of capitalism. We must in fairness, however, continue the passage on America which we have just quoted, for Mr. Wells is arguing that Roosevelt did not in fact produce an American imperialism. Although Roosevelt was, he says, "the very man, we might imagine, to have involved his country in the scramble for overseas possessions," he did not do so.

"There does not appear to be any other explanation of this general restraint and abstinence on the part of the United States, except in their fundamentally different institutions and traditions. In the first place, the United States Government has no foreign office and no diplomatic corps of the European type, no body of 'experts' to maintain the tradition of an aggressive policy. The President has great powers, but they are checked by the powers of the Senate which is directly elected by the people. Every treaty with a foreign power must first receive the assent of the Senate. The foreign relations of the country are thus under open and public control. Secret treaties are impossible under such a system, and foreign powers complain of the difficulty and uncertainty of 'understandings' with the United States —a very excellent state of affairs. The United States is constitutionally incapacitated, therefore, from the kind of foreign policy that has kept Europe for so long constantly on the verge of war."

Mr. Wells' contention that America did not become imperialistic under Roosevelt is of course simply an error of fact. One has only to think of the story which they tell in Washington of the occasion on which Roosevelt was fomenting a revolution in the Republic of Colombia in order to annex the canal zone. The President wished to go through some rather absurd formalities about taking the territory. He was rebuked by his Attorney General, Philander C. Knox, with the question, "Oh, Mr. President, why bring the taint of legality into it?"[1] Active American imperialism dates, of course, from the Spanish American War. It is quite true that it developed somewhat later than the European imperialisms. For the American homeland is far bigger, and there was therefore far more room for the internal expansion of American capitalism. But that phase of internal expansion seems to have ended with a jolt, in 1929. American imperialism is comparatively young yet, but Mr. Wells should give the boy time. America will yet "show the world" in this field also. Then Mr. Wells will see what his pathetic reliance on the republican institutions of America is worth.[2]

To what extraordinary lengths of formalism his line of argument leads Mr. Wells, is shown by his chief suggestions for checking imperialism. He now gives no hint of there being any connection whatever between the economic and social structure of states and their "method in world politics." On the contrary, imperialism, he implies, is all the fault of certain institutions which, by ill luck, one supposes, most states have established. It is, in particular, the creation of certain diabolical places known as

[1] Mr. Wells' account of this Panama incident is prudent. He writes: "Here we will not enter into the political complications attendant upon the making of the Panama Canal, for they introduce no fresh light upon the interesting question of the American method in world politics." And, of course, America has a Foreign Office. It happens to be called "The State Department," which simple disguise has, it seems, confused Mr. Wells.

[2] The sudden love for America, which has become a discernible trait of some English liberals such as Mr. Wells, Mr. Harold Laski or Dr. Jacks, is, of course, quite comprehensible. For it is quite true that the decay of the whole structure, both material and ideal, of capitalist civilization has not in many respects gone so far in America as in the Old World. Thus a visit to America offers Mr. Wells, for example, something of the services of his own "time machine." He is enabled to escape back into a less painfully decayed, less ferociously imperialistic, social system. But his affection is likely to be short lived. Things move very quickly in America.

The obverse of this attitude is shown by English social democrats, who have become professionally anti-American. What they are really doing is, of course, to follow the lead of the British governing class in its life-and-death struggle with American capitalists. But they find an admirable excuse for this in pointing out all the characteristically unpleasant symptoms of capitalism in America—while retaining a very tolerant heart for the very same symptoms, usually exhibited in a still more unpleasant form, at home.

"embassies and foreign offices." Here, for example, is a sentence (page 1063) in which Mr. Wells both defines imperialism and suggests his remedy.

> "Modern imperialism is the natural development of the Great Power system which arose, with the foreign office method of policy, out of the Machiavellian monarchies after the break-up of Christendom. It will only come to an end when the intercourse of nations and peoples through embassies and foreign offices is replaced by a federal assembly."

Thus, in Mr. Wells' view, imperialism is the product of embassies and foreign offices. The whole of a great phase in the history of man, the whole of that continuous conflict of national force, which to-day shakes the earth, is the product of one of the minor instruments by which each empire, in times of peace, carries on that conflict. In the same way, one supposes, *The Outline of History* is the product of Mr. Wells' pen.

The third of Mr. Wells' *Outlines,* entitled *The Work, Wealth and Happiness of Mankind,* has just (1932) been published. It marks quite a new stage in his intellectual surrender to the pretences behind which capitalism has now to conceal its real nature. It is not possible to say what Mr. Wells' new book is about. He devotes a chapter, twenty-six pages in length, to the attempt to inform us; but it cannot be said that he succeeds. What he tells us is that the three *Outlines provide* "a complete modern ideology," and that history, biology, and economics are the three main factors in such an ideology. Since, therefore, *The Outline of History* and *The Science of Life* account for the two former factors, we might reasonably expect that this new work would be devoted to economics. But of its eight hundred odd pages, only a few contain anything about economics at all. Indeed, the only specifically economic chapter in the book is Chapter IX. This consists of an exposition of Mr. Wells' views on monetary problems. Mr. Wells has just reached the point of an unquestioning belief in an application of the Quantity Theory of Money, as a cure for all the ills of capitalism. No doubt Mr. Keynes has, perhaps wisely, refrained from trying to tell him about the proportion of savings to investments. "All this so far is fairly simple," Mr. Wells writes at the end of his exposition of monetary theory, "and, now universally admitted to be entirely false," we must add.

If, however, Mr. Wells' book is not about economics, what is it about? Some hint of an answer may perhaps be found in another phrase which he uses in telling us of the object of his work. It is, he writes, "some explanation of the toil and motives that bind mankind together in an uneasy unity." We began to realize the extreme confusion of purpose which lies behind the book from the queer conjunction of these words "toil and motives." If Mr. Wells had written *an analysis of the motives of mankind,* he would have written a work of psychology and economics. If he had written *a panoramic description of the toil* of mankind, he would have written a work of popular technology. As it is, he has never made up his mind as to what kind of a book he was trying to write. This is not to object, however, to Mr. Wells' attempt to broaden capitalist economics, to break down the barriers which its more academic professors seek to erect between it and politics. Mr. Wells rightly implies that one of the reasons why capitalist economics, however subtle and accurate their chains of reasoning may be, are entirely sterile, is because of the ludicrous falsity of their underlying psychological assumptions. For capitalist economists heap the whole of humanity, worker, peasant, merchant, entrepreneur, *rentier,* landlord, and aristocrat into one mass. They treat them all as an undifferentiated pile of human atoms reacting similarly to similar stimuli. Mr. Wells admits that this is false; that we get nowhere until we have divided mankind up into groups and categories. And he further acknowledges, though most grudgingly, that it is the Marxists alone who have done this.

"The Marxist indeed makes some pretensions to psychology with his phrases about a 'class conscious proletariat' and a 'bourgeois mentality,' and the like. He shows, at least, an awareness of difference of persona. But under the stresses of political and social combat such phrases have long since degenerated into mere weapons, aspirations and terms of abuse. So discredited and warped are they that they will be of no use to us here."

Elsewhere, he tells us that his book is "to supersede the vague generalizations on which Marxism rests and concentrate and synthesize all those confused socialist and individualist theorizings of the nineteenth century which still remain as the unstable basis of our economic experiments." All this means, we gather, that Mr. Wells rejects the Marxian categories of social classes and will substitute new ones of his own. What has he to offer us? A little talk about "persona." (A term taken from Dr. Jung but applied quite newly by Mr. Wells.) These "persona" are men's ideas of themselves; and there exist the following personas: the peasant persona, the nomad persona and the educated persona. A more lively bit of nonsense could hardly be imagined than Chapter VIII, in which Mr. Wells plays with these three social categories of his own invention. And these are the new concepts which shall replace the visible, palpable realities of the Marxian social classes!

As soon as Mr. Wells comes to any descriptions of existing society, his new categories cease to fit and he forgets all about them. Thus Chapter X is headed "The Rich, the Poor, and their Traditional Antagonism." This sounds a little more like reality; and so it is. With the exception of some particularly silly, and in some instances self-contradictory, anti-Russian propaganda,[1] this is the best chapter in the book. Reality, it seems, has literally forced itself upon Mr. Wells' attention. He actually says this himself:

"We began this work as a survey of productive activities. It was only as our study became closer and more searching that this contrast of the rich who have got the money and the poor who have not, came, almost in spite of our design, athwart the spectacle. Gradually we have been forced to recognize that in the course of twenty-five centuries or so, the ancient rules, servitudes and tyrannies of mankind have given place, step by step, by the substitution of money for other methods of compulsion, to the rule of wealth."

Here is the truth, excellently expressed. In spite of all Mr. Wells' wonderful fertility of invention; indeed precisely because, in the last resort, he is unable wholly to disregard the main facts of the subject which he has under discussion, the contrast between

[1] Thus, on page 797, we are told that in Russia "to point out defects in the Five Year Plan is a crime." On page 509, however, we had been told that "the frank admission of difficulty and disappointment is not the only virtue of the Bolshevik."

the rich who have got the money and the poor who have not, "forces itself athwart" his description of the work, wealth and happiness of mankind. But in so far as it has done so, the reader cannot but see beneath Mr. Wells' pleasant picture, the real unemployment, poverty and misery of mankind.

Such passages of strangely frank admission as the above, and the sentence hinting at the real basis of imperialism, reveal the constant struggle between Mr. Wells' sharp intellect, which finds it difficult always to disregard all the facts, and his overpowering capitalist instincts, which simply cannot endure the implications of these facts.

It has been worth while to follow up the efforts of one of the most gifted of the remaining theorists of capitalism to analyse and to comprehend the phenomena of to-day. If those efforts led only to the strangest contradictions, that is certainly not the fault of Mr. Wells. Mr. Wells has abilities not inferior in many respects to those of the men who laid the theoretical basis of the capitalist system. He is involved in his contradictions because it has become impossible to comprehend or order the phenomena of our times without the use of the hypothesis of dialectical materialism.[1]

A more curious example of the effect on its writers of the phase which British capitalism has passed through during the last fifty years is afforded by the case of Mr. Bernard Shaw. Mr. Shaw is probably regarded by educated public opinion, at least in Great Britain, Germany and America, as the foremost writer of our day. And he too, like Mr. Wells, has applied himself both indirectly and directly to the study of society as a whole. Endowed with mind of keener edge than his contemporary, he was one of the few Englishmen to read and understand the first volume of *Capital* in the first decade after its publication. But his reaction to that experience was a very strange one. It induced him to join the Fabian Society! And yet to do so was in a sense logical; it showed at any rate Mr. Shaw's shrewd grip upon immediate reality: his almost—if not quite—commercial sense of what was immediately

---

[1] How categorically Mr. Wells rejects the materialist conception of history can be gathered from his quotation of Lord Acton's (the Catholic historian) remark: "It is our (the historian's, that is) function to keep in view and to command the movement of ideas, which are not the effect but the cause of public events." "That is precisely where we stand" is Mr. Wells' comment (*The Work, Wealth and Happiness of Mankind*).

possible. It is an interesting speculation to consider what would have happened if, in the 'seventies of the last century, Mr. Shaw had become a revolutionary instead of a Fabian. It is very possible that he would to-day be in secure possession of immortal fame as one of the two or three great Europeans of the recent centuries. But it is also probable that he would already have been dead for some considerable time. His life would have been far less successful, easy and economically secure. He would probably have been denied even persecution; and if he had died, say about 1913, he would have died as Marx himself died in the 'eighties, in what would have seemed to the capitalist world to be failure and neglect. There is little doubt that Mr. Shaw foresaw all this more or less clearly. He grasped the inherent contradictions of capitalism, the impossibility of any solution short of communism. But he also grasped the fact that British capitalism at any rate would last his time.

And Mr. Shaw, as he has himself told us, had the most passionate desire for success, for fame, money, power, and for the enjoyment of these good things in his own lifetime. He has triumphantly secured them, and if he has paid as a price his opportunity of immortality, he may well tell us that he is satisfied with the bargain.

Thus Lenin's epigram remains the definitive description. He called Mr. Shaw "a good man fallen amongst Fabians." And Lenin, no doubt, meant not merely that Mr. Shaw had fallen amongst the members of the Fabian Society. He meant that it was Mr. Shaw's destiny that his life's span should fall in the Fabian epoch of British capitalism: that his whole youth should be spent in that long and marvellous afternoon of British governing-class civilization, before the inevitable growth of imperialism had brought on the thunder of evening: before it had brought on that thunder of shattering high explosives which Mr. Shaw himself hears so well, and which he makes us hear in the last act of *Heartbreak House*.

The third social theorist of our epoch, whose views we may take as a sample of the effect of our present environment on its writers, is Mr. J. M. Keynes. Mr. Keynes is the ablest of the surviving economists of the British capitalist class. We saw in

Chapters V and VI whither we were led by following his main line of argument in his own special field of monetary theory. Mr. Keynes is, however, much more than a specialist on monetary problems. In fact, he is more than an economist in the narrow sense of the word. He is, as we have suggested, a major social and political theorist of the English-speaking capitalist class. (Moreover, if command of the English language is to be the test, then certainly much of Mr. Keynes' work must be called literature.) As it happens, it is at the moment particularly convenient to take a look at his more general views, since he has recently (1932) republished all his more important occasional papers, composed over the last ten years, in a volume entitled *Essays in Persuasion*.

In the preface of this work, Mr. Keynes tells us that he has been a Cassandra "who could never influence the course of events in time." And it is essential that this remark should be kept in mind as one reads Mr. Keynes' various prescriptions for the survival of capitalism. The application of the measures of "intelligent management" which he suggests will ensure, he is convinced, that in about a hundred years' time capitalism will have carried the human race into an era of universal plenty and security. For, needless to say, the thesis which runs through Mr. Keynes' collected papers is the exact antithesis of these pages. We have sought and, it is submitted, discovered, a direct causal connection of a necessary and predicable character, between the inherent characteristics of capitalism and the present disastrous condition of the world; and we have discovered in particular a connection between these characteristics and the recurrence of crises such as that which began in 1931. We submit, further, that it is possible to predict future and far worse consequences from these characteristics of capitalism. Naturally, therefore, we draw the conclusion that the only hope for the dawn of that day when man shall have finally reached (to use Mr. Keynes' definition of Utopia) a level of civilization at which the economic problem is no longer his chief concern lies in the overthrow of capitalism. For Mr. Keynes himself rightly says that such a level of civilization is now becoming a technical possibility.

Mr. Keynes, on the contrary, finds no causal connection whatever between the character of our economic system and the pres-

ent condition of affairs. On the contrary, he says, again in the
preface of his book, that his "central thesis" and his "profound
conviction" is that

> "the Economic Problem, as one may call it for short, the prob-
> lem of want and poverty and the economic struggle between
> classes and nations, is nothing but a frightful muddle, a tran-
> sitory and *unnecessary* muddle."

Mr. Keynes is a most satisfactory writer: he says clearly and
forcibly what the other theorists of his class merely mumble and
mutter. For example, it is perfectly consistent with the above
expression of opinion that he has not the slightest use for the
Marxist case. He calls *Capital* "an obsolete economic text-book
which I know to be not only scientifically erroneous but without
interest or application for the modern world." And as we read
Mr. Keynes' always reasonable, persuasive, and logically, self-
consistent pages, we are driven more and more to realize that
it is precisely his basic eclecticism, his profound antagonism for
the only unitary theory which will account for the political and
economic phenomena of the modern world, which renders so
academic, so beside the real point, nearly all of his suggestions.
Has he never, one cannot help wondering, paused to enquire
why his *Essays in Persuasion* have been so uniformly unpersua-
sive: has he never asked *why* he has always been unable "to influence the course of events in time"? If, indeed, his proposals
for the salvation of capitalism are sound, as in one sense, as in isolation, taken as logical propositions independent of time and place,
some of them *are* sound, why have they never anywhere been
applied? Surely, the leaders of capitalism all over the world are
not all so foolish or so ill-advised, as to ignore in their desperate
need, such hopeful advice; and to rush wilfully upon their own
destruction? And yet this is just the hypothesis that Mr. Keynes
and all "enlightened" capitalist opinion has to resort to in order
to account for the present situation. It is felt that capitalism is a
perfectly sound system which by some dreadful mistake the capitalists are themselves now wilfully smashing to pieces.

Nothing could be further from the truth. The leaders of capitalism are not fools: they are for the most part very able men strug-

gling against overwhelming difficulties. There is, in fact, a complete contradiction between our diagnosis of the present situation and that of Mr. Keynes. And this contradiction arises precisely from a basic difference of opinion as to whether there is a causal chain between the historical development of capitalism and the recurrence of crisis and war, or whether their coincidence is, as Mr. Keynes says, "nothing but a frightful muddle." There is this further point, however. The causal chain which we have attempted to trace has not been exclusively composed of material links (using the word material in its narrowest sense). It has involved the view that certain economic and material conditions determine certain mental and psychological points of view: and these mental and psychological points of view, in their turn, determine by reaction further material developments. In the causal chain, each economic link has been followed by a mental and psychological one: it has been a chain of action and reaction between the economic basis and the ideal structure, which has been built on that basis. To instance a few successive links, the growth of large-scale production caused certain consequences in the minds of entrepreneurs which made them strive towards the formation of monopolies. The formation of monopolies in turn caused, for reasons which we gave, certain changes in the minds of statesmen which caused them to undertake imperialist adventures. The existence of empires causes certain further tendencies in the minds of the governing class which must sooner or later involve them in war. And no one denies that wars, in their turn, cause marked economic changes.

The whole contradiction between the thesis subscribed to in these pages and the point of view of the theorists of the capitalist class arises from the fact that they do not accept this, or any connection between economic cause and psychological effect. For Mr. Keynes, there is evidently no connection whatever between the new forms which capitalism is visibly assuming and the policies which its leaders adopt. Thus, in his well-known paper *The End of Laissez-Faire,* he tells us that his own view is that "capitalism, wisely managed, can probably be made more efficient for attaining economic ends than any alternative system yet in sight." But the argument of this book is that the character of capitalism is such that it is inconceivable that it can be "wisely managed": that the development of world capitalism into a series of rival imperialisms was a development inevitable from the very nature of the system. Indeed, Mr. Keynes himself defines "modern capitalism" as "without internal union, without much public spirit, often, though not always a mere congeries of possessors and pursuers." How can he speak of possessors and pursuers "wisely managing" each other?

Let us take, as a further example of this failure to think of mental and material phenomena with some comprehensive unity, Mr. Keynes' extraordinarily unrealistic treatment of the question of imperialism. There is, for instance, his well-known view that the wealth of the modern world is due to the "magical" operation of compound interest. Thus he calculates, perhaps half playfully, that part of the booty brought back by Drake in the *Golden Hind,* which was invested by Queen Elizabeth in the Levant Company, the profits of which were in turn reinvested in the East India Company, has by the accretion of $3\frac{1}{4}\%$ compound interest added up to the present (1929) total of British foreign investment. Could there be a more perfect example of the abstraction of every element of reality from a proposition under discussion? Think for a moment of the aggressions of Chatham, of the guile of Clive and Hastings, of the slave ships out of Bristol, of reaction incarnate in William Pitt, of the cold territorial acquisitiveness of Lord Salisbury, of the bluster and corruption of Rhodes, to name a few examples at random, which have in fact alone enabled Drake's £42,000 to grow into the £4,200 millions, which is the present (1929) foreign investment of Great Britain! Must we not stand aghast when Mr. Keynes quietly tells us that the accumulation of Britain's imperial wealth is due to the magical operation of the law of compound interest? Such disingenuousness is almost majestic.

In the essay entitled "Am I a Liberal?" Mr. Keynes writes:

"As regards the empire, I do not think that there is any important problem except in India. Elsewhere, so far as problems of government are concerned, the process of friendly disintegration is now almost complete—to the great benefit of all."

Are we to suppose then that the tremendous efforts being put forward by the governing classes of all the imperialist states to extend and consolidate their empires, almost at any risk, are simply a mistake? This is the old liberal pacifist view again—a delusion surely unworthy of a man of Mr. Keynes' calibre? No, the leaders of all the great nations of the world are not fools, wilfully destroying their own system. They are men in the grip of destiny. They are obliged to perform acts which are disastrous to their own larger interests because their own minds have been conditioned by the previous economic developments of capitalism. They are able to act in a certain way, and only in that way, because they themselves are a part of, and, on the whole, are an unconscious part of, their own economic system.

Thus, the philosophical basis upon which Marxism rests: the view which attributes unity, though not identity, between the material and the ideal, between theory and practice, is not without its practical application. But for Mr. Keynes there is no such unity. Any kind of economic system may be combined with any kind of point of view amongst the men who control it. He admits, indeed, that "the economic problem, the struggle for subsistence, always has been hitherto the primary, most pressing problem of the human race." And yet he believes that the kind of solution which men have found for this problem has little or no effect upon their general point of view: that it has no perceptible influence in determining what kind of men they become. True, with another part of his mind he knows that capitalism has consequences in the realm of ideas which are "extremely objectionable." [1] He thinks, however, that by subjecting ourselves to these "extremely objectionable" consequences for another hundred years or so, we shall solve our economic problem. Can he not see that even if we could do so, "we" should not be there at all at the end of a hundred years: that these capitalist values, which he himself calls "detestable," would long before then have made us totally unfit for the promised land of economic plenty? Indeed, they would have so degraded—nay they are even now so degrading—the whole race that, far from attaining any promised land of plenty, the race would certainly lose in titanic wars that level of civilization which it has.

This extreme indifference to the real drift of events—this conviction that the crisis in capitalism is not only a "frightful" but a "transitory and unnecessary" muddle, has hitherto allowed Mr. Keynes

---

[1] For further evidence that Mr. Keynes, like Mr. Wells, really knows better: that he does sometimes see the effect of economic change on ideas, see the historical chapter of his *Treatise on Money*.

to believe in a kind of restoration of the world free market. Now, however, he is becoming a little more realistic, and is inclining towards that school of thought the existence of which we noticed in Chapter VII, and which we called "the national planners." And again in this field, his blindness to the political consequences of economic tendencies will for some time yet enable him to plan nationally without ever definitely answering his own question "Am I a liberal?" with a negative. When that moment does come, however, the next question which Mr. Keynes will have to ask himself will be "Am I a fascist?" And the answer will be in the affirmative.

CHAPTER XI

LITERATURE. II

In discussing such sociological writers as Mr. Wells, Mr. Shaw and Mr. Keynes, we have not yet even mentioned what literary people call literature. Let us therefore continue our somewhat circumspect advance towards the writers of "pure" literature. And let us, as our next stage on the ascent, consider for a moment a younger generation of writers who, though still sociologically minded, are so to a far lesser degree than are, for example, Mr. Wells and Mr. Shaw. Of these writers let us select more or less arbitrarily, of course, but also because these three seem the most considerable, Proust, D. H. Lawrence, and Mr. Aldous Huxley. In a sense, no three writers could have less in common. Yet all three reflect in a kind of agony the characteristics of the epoch in which they live. Each of them, no doubt, would say that this was the agony which every man of perception from Lucretius to Pascal had felt when he began to comprehend the nature and necessities of man's life in the universe. And in one sense this is no doubt true. At all times in the past the conditions of man's life have been the subject of tragedy. The expression of the tragic view of life: that point of view which is the one thing which all the great writers of all the ages have had in common, is an effort to ameliorate the lot of man, not by seeking to deny or conceal what have been the well-nigh unbearable necessities of man's existence, but by offering to us the example and consolation of ill fortune faced consciously and stoically by undeceived men. And each of these three modern writers has shared in the tragic view.

Can it possibly be denied, however, that there is another strand in their pessimism? In so far as they are great writers, they share in the tragic tradition of the race. But do we not all feel that each of them is only partly a great writer? They are men possessing talents not inferior to the representative writers of other times. And yet, somehow, is there not a question-mark to be put after their

names? Is there not something doubtful, something mixed, about
their achievement? And does not this doubt, on closer inspection,
derive from the very nature of the material on which they have
had to work? For every writer, no matter how much he likes to
deceive himself on this matter, can only work on the material which
the life of his time presents to him. If, as in the case of the three
writers in question, their work consists in a commentary, either in
the form of the novel, or still more directly in the form of essays,
on the actual social intercourse of their times, there can surely be
no argument about this contention.

Of the three writers, Proust has achieved the most complete work.
Yet it was just in his case that the social necessities of the time and
place of his life played the most important role. For Proust's enormous work, besides being so much else, is quite undeniably the
odyssey of snobbery. It is, moreover, in one aspect the final proof
of the absolutely necessary and praiseworthy character of snobbery in
a class society; it is the justification of raising the impulse to social
success to the level of one of the great elemental passions of humanity. To a French bourgeois who died in the third decade of
the twentieth century, snobbery was, Proust demonstrates, an elementary duty.

Proust's almost infinitely prolonged and infinitely subtle quest
for how he has spent his life, discovers that in the end he has spent
it in just this one activity: in the realization of social success. And
he concludes that on the whole it has been a well spent life. For
the little boy of *Du Côté de chez Swann* there was no other way of
living so fully and completely, of experiencing all that there was at
that time and place to experience in life, as by entering successfully
that great world which at first sight seemed to be represented by
Swann but which turned out to have, Chinese boxlike, so many
ranks within ranks, so many distinctions, real and false, so many
tantalizing false horizons and unexpected withdrawals, that a lifetime was needed to explore it. And if, in the end, the whole explora-
tion proved to have been vain, if when the ultimate arcana had been
reached its inmates proved to be not the magically refined and
delightful persons of imagination, but to be every whit as hard,
cruel, crude and *lâche* as everybody else; if the Duchesse de Guermantes could not attend to the fact that her dear friend Swann was
dying because she was late for a ball, that did not mean that any

better results could have been obtained by devoting one's life to any other purpose. If every one of these "people of the world," whom we are first shown in such excruciatingly desirable a guise, are very gradually divested, by the light yet inexorable fingers of the narrator, of every element of beauty, charm, or wit, nay even of the most elementary human decencies; if Odette de Crecy, from being an angel who can illuminate a whole park with her beauty, becomes the archetype of all stupid, grasping, demi-mondaines; if Madame de Villeparisis, from being the most delightful of grandes dames, is discovered first to be by no means smart—for she commits the sin of publishing memoirs—and is seen finally as a dreadful banal old woman with eczema all over her face; if the aristocracy turns out to be not by any means the unapproachable pinnacle it once seemed; if the arch-bourgeois Madame Verdurin suddenly becomes an arch-aristocrat and Princesse de Guermantes; if Proust's snobbery is given not a moment's peace by his implacable intellect, which exposes with a fiendish self-torturing delight the vulgarity and baseness of the social values which he has spent a lifetime, first in exploring and then in expounding, that does not mean that there was anything else to do with his life but thus to explore and to expound. By devoting it to the social passion he had at any rate penetrated to what was, presumably, the highest and most cultivated point in the society of the most profoundly civilized nation on earth.

Thus the discovery that this refinement and cultivation was all a sham did, at any rate, assure him that nowhere else was there anything better. The note of lamentation which rises throughout the concluding phases of Proust's work is a lamentation for a society which is on the road to dissolution. One recalls that passage in *Le Temps Retrouvé* in which Proust meets again the characters of his work after the interval of the war. He has the momentary illusion that the experience may have improved them. He discovers that, on the contrary, it has made them all worse not better, narrower, more selfish, less humane. Proust, in truth, sang a long agonised requiem mass over the highest expression of human life of which French bourgeois society under the Third Republic had been capable.

Mr. Edmund Wilson, the American writer, to whose penetrating work of criticism *Axel's Castle,* I, and every student of the mental life of to-day, are deeply indebted, sums up the work of Proust in this eloquent passage:

"Imaginatively and intellectually, Proust is prodigiously strong; and if we feel an element of decadence in his work, it may be primarily due to the decay of the society in which he lived and with which his novel exclusively deals—the society of the dispossessed nobility and the fashionable and cultivated bourgeoisie, with their physicians and their artists, their servants and their parasites. We are always feeling with Proust as if we were reading about the end of something—this seems, in fact, to be what he means us to feel; witness the implications of the bombardment of Paris during the war when Charlus is in the last stages of his disintegration. Not only do his hero and most of his other characters pass into mortal declines, but their world itself seems to be coming to an end. And it may be that Proust's strange poetry and brilliance are the last fires of a setting sun—the last flare of the æsthetic idealism of the educated classes of the nineteenth century. If Proust is more dramatic, more complete and more intense than Thackeray or Chekov or Edith Wharton or Anatole France, it may be because he comes at the close of an era and sums up the whole situation.... Proust is perhaps the last great historian of the loves, the society, the intelligence, the diplomacy, the literature and the art of the Heartbreak House of capitalist culture; and the little man with the sad appealing voice, the metaphysician's mind, the Saracen's beak, the ill-fitting dress-shirt and the great eyes that seem to see all about him like the many-faceted eyes of a fly, dominates the scene and plays host in the mansion where he is not long to be master."

No contrast could seem more profound, nor could prove more superficial, than the contrast between Proust and the English novelist, D. H. Lawrence. Lawrence was the one copious and vital writer which England has produced since the war: the one man who still wrote as if he knew that it was worth while to write. He suffered, however, both personally and as a writer, to the most intense degree from the nature of his environment. Lawrence was by origin a worker, the son of a Nottinghamshire miner: a man from the very heart of England, a man from that section of the English working class, the miners, who have to the greatest degree succeeded in maintaining a life of their own. Lawrence, until, at any rate, the very end of his life, was not consciously interested in politics. He felt that he had no time for them. He knew politics, it seems, only in the form of English party politics, and his piercing eye saw through their pretences at a glance. But he was extremely interested, both consciously and unconsciously in class, and in class relationships. It would be hardly too much to say that class relationships obsessed him. For the same theme recurs over and over again in his novels. A young, vigorous, unself-conscious worker is thrown into governing class society and has a love affair with an aristocratic woman, who has up till then been unawakened by the men of her own class. For example, *Aaron's Rod* and *The Ghost,* one of his best short stories, contain this theme: it appears again in his posthumous story *The Man Who Died,* where his proletarian hero is by trade a carpenter. And it is given its clearest expression in that curious tract-like novel *Lady Chatterley's Lover.* In this case, the governing-class husband is made actually, as well as symbolically, impotent and crippled by the war. The proletarian hero is always, of course, Lawrence himself.

Thus, after all, we find that Lawrence's fancy ran in the same direction as Proust's. Lawrence also, if not in his own person then in the world of his fantasy, climbed the social heights of existing society, to see if by chance something living might be at the top. And Lawrence also comes back with the report that there is nothing. The half-Jewish French bourgeois and the Notts miner both made the same pilgrimage: they both went "du côté de chez Swann" and "du côté des Guermantes." And, no doubt, they were in a sense quite right. If one rejects politics; if one rejects, like the philosophers, the proposal to change life; if one seeks only to explain it, then truly the best thing that one can do is to seek out what is highest, and so presumably best, in the old society. But both Proust and Lawrence had the misfortune to see through their social ideal. Indeed, it was unavoidable. They were born out of due time: too early to have abandoned the social ideals which still existed, too late to find those ideals in a condition of preservation which could satisfy them.

Lawrence has a passage in one of his short stories in which he describes admirably the degeneration in the quality of the old English governing class, how the cultivated, well-educated, wise and careful (though, of course, quite ruthless) men of the type of Mr. Asquith were supplanted in 1916 by a cruder type of big-business Philistines, represented by Mr. Lloyd George. He saw that the war had driven British capitalism to resort to methods which lowered the whole level of such civilization as it had created. He saw its coarsening, and cheapening, going on steadily in the years after the war. The spectacle nauseated him and finally killed him. For somehow he does not seem to have ever even conceived of any alternative. The only alternative which he saw was the Labour party, and this he rightly rejected at once as a device to castrate, as he might have put it, his own class. For in a kind of semi-conscious way he had faith in the victory of the workers. Indeed, if you like to read them so, his novels with their recurrent theme of salvation for the lovely woman of the governing class by the worker who at once captures and rescues her, are myths of the young worker revivifying society; as, truly, the workers alone can do. His novels get their incomparable vitality from this theme. But somehow it never quite came up into the conscious; and Lawrence, instead of standing outside of capitalist society and drawing strength and assurance from its decline, became himself inextricably involved in that decline. Hence his agony, his tortured excursions into a queer and, after all, rather amateurish sort of sexual mysticism; hence, the terrible sense of frustration which sometimes overshadows even his incomparable passion.

Between Mr. Aldous Huxley and Lawrence there is a great contrast, far more profound than that between Lawrence and Proust. Mr. Huxley has won his position in English letters by his erudition, wit and power of intellect rather than by any gifts of intuitive imagination. Mr. Huxley's greatest advantage is that he is free from that taint of provincialism which mars the work of so many of the most eminent English writers. He is at home in European civilization: he has at his command the whole range of that not inconsiderable culture which the European capitalist class has built up for itself during the period of its domination.

It is appropriate that it should be a Huxley, a member of one of those principal English middle-class families, which formed and still form, one of the main pillars of the British capitalist system, who would most consciously describe its closing period. And what a description it is! In a series of novels and essays, Mr. Huxley has sent the long, delicate, probing fingers of his analysis into every corner of the life of capitalist society. His findings are always the same. Go where you like, "do what you will," you will never escape from the smell of ordure and decay. Mr. Huxley would, I think, deny that this has anything whatsoever to do with the characteristics of the present economic system. He believes that it is a characteristic of human life itself. And to be sure, no one denies that a part of the horror of life (and part of the joy of life too) is irradicable, is independent of any social system.

On the other hand, it is surely demonstrable that many of the characteristics of life which in particular make Mr. Huxley resort to his now almost automatic gesture of holding his nose, are the direct products of the specific phase of capitalist civilization in which he lives. Let us take his latest work—a Utopia, entitled *Brave New World*. Not that it is of comparable importance to much of his earlier writings. Books about the future, however, generally tell us a great deal about their author's opinions of the present. Under the shelter of scientific fantasy they are able to express, partly unconsciously no doubt, what they really think about life as it exists here and now. In *Brave New World,* the typical Huxley hero naturally appears. Bernard Marx, the lonely, physically handicapped, intellectual, is not more difficult to identify than the club-footed Philip of *Point Counter Point,* or than are those innumerable small, dark proletarians who swarm amorously through the works of D. H. Lawrence. (Not that these self-portraits are identical with their authors: often they are caricatures, often idealizations.) But what are significant are Bernard's misadventures in Utopia. For they are the misadventures of the typical intellectual in the Europe of 1932. *Brave New World,* indeed, marks the point at which the Utopists, they too, turned pessimistic.[1]

It is instructive, for example, to compare *Brave New World* with one of Mr. Wells' Utopias—with, say, *Men Like Gods.* Mr. Huxley's book is naturally far more sophisticated, rusé, knowledgeable. It makes Mr. Wells seem very simple-minded. But is it as a matter of fact any more objective, any more self-consistent, any less completely a projection of the author's subjective reactions to present-

---

[1] A very well constructed, pessimistic Utopia, entitled *The Question Mark* by Miss Jaeger appeared some years before Mr. Huxley's book. It followed the same main theme, that is the splitting up of the race into sharply divided "castes."

day life? Does Mr. Huxley's belief that science is about to produce a nightmare world rest on any closer examination of the factors which determine the nature of the life of a community, than does Mr. Wells' faith that science will soon make us like gods? For example, why is there no indication in *Brave New World* of how the gigantic new scientific means of production which have been created, are owned? No doubt such a question would seem childish to Mr. Huxley. He would say that by the date of his Utopia the whole question of ownership will have long ago disappeared. The workers have, as he shows, been degraded by careful pre-natal deformations to a psychological condition exactly appropriate to the performance of menial labour. Very well then, but in that case why are we introduced to a symptom which could only arise in a society based on profit making, derived from the ownership of the means of production? We are told that one of the chief duties of the citizens of the world state is compulsory consumption. For example, we are informed of the duty of throwing away old clothes as soon as they are at all worn, and of the sinfulness of mending. These duties are hypnotically inculcated into all citizens. Again, children are encouraged to play only such games as require expensive and elaborate apparatus. For the "prosperity" of industry depends upon keeping up the rate of consumption.

If the incomes of the ruling class depend, as to-day, upon a profit derived from the ownership of the instruments of production, it would be, of course, quite logical for them to inculcate such doctrines. But there is no suggestion in *Brave New World* that this is the case. Indeed, the "Alphas," as the governing class are called, are represented as salaried workers. And Mr. Huxley is quite right in assuming that in a planned world state the concept of profit must disappear. The governing class (we are presuming, quite contrary to the facts, that a governing class could maintain such conditions) would simply appropriate what wealth they chose. But if this is so, what conceivable advantage would they derive from unnecessary consumption by the lower-grade workers, involving unnecessary production? Here, obviously, Mr. Huxley has simply taken one of the characteristics of the particular organization of mechanized production in which he lives, and applied it to mechanized production in general.

There is another contradiction in *Brave New World,* which is

similarly significant. We are asked to believe in the production of
masses of low-grade workers, carefully rendered half, third and a
quarter witted, the "Gammas," "Deltas" and "Epsilons," as they
are called, to perform necessary manual work. But at the level of
scientific knowledge which Mr. Huxley depicts, the necessity for
anything like this amount of manual labour would have long ago
disappeared. It would be far more economical to produce mechanical automata to undertake these tasks than to breed, by the elaborate and expensive process which he describes, these pre-natally
(or, pre-"decantingly") conditioned, and highly perishable, workers.
Again, of course, what Mr. Huxley is really thinking of is the
mental and physical deformation of its manual workers which capitalism perpetrates here and now. And if he had said this, and
shown that no degree of scientific advance under capitalism would
ameliorate this state of affairs, but would rather tend to make it
worse and worse, he would have written a clear and valuable book.
But for Mr. Huxley, it is not science in the hands of a profit-making
class which must deface the mind and bodies of the workers; it is
science in general. For he has never conceived of the possibility of
another form of society. He has never applied his mind to the question of in what manner, and to what extent, the particular method
adopted for organizing the social production necessary to life, conditions the character of life itself.

Since Mr. Huxley is a generation younger than Mr. Wells and
cannot possibly share the latter's obdurate, if now somewhat frayed,
optimism about the effects of the growth of scientific knowledge
under the existing social order; since he cannot help seeing the ever-
sharpening contradiction between modern science and a system of
society based upon the private ownership of the means of production; and since he does not imagine a classless society, he comes to
the conclusion that the contradiction will be solved by a pooling of
the ownership of the means of production, not amongst all the
members of the community, but amongst the members of the ruling
class. (We shall examine this conception in a later chapter and
show its inherently self-contradictory character.) Mr. Huxley, however, is not blind to the consequences of the present appropriation,
and consequent distortion, of science by a class. He sees the loath-
some sort of world which it produces. Hence, his mounting pessi-

mism. Hence, his tendency, which will no doubt increase, to join the anti-scientists, the machine wreckers. For *Brave New World* is, in effect, an anti-scientific tract. Its whole influence must be to make people feel that if this is whither science is leading them, then science must be put a stop to. (One might be tempted to hope that this new anti-scientific tendency might gain the mastery in the great capitalist states: that they should in fact take *Nature's* advice and, imitating the inhabitants of Erewhon, destroy their machines. For then, indeed, the balance of power would tip very quickly in favour of the ever-growing scientific power of the communist sixth of the world. It is to be feared, however, that capitalism will always retain an affection for one science at any rate, the science of war.)

These three writers, Lawrence, Proust and Huxley, all exhibit at least one characteristic in common. They all take the tragic view of life. They are inheritors of the great tradition of literature. They are undeceived as to the realities of man's situation in the universe. And yet, as we noticed above, the reader cannot help feeling that there is some other and far less estimable element in their pessimism; he detects something febrile, at its worst, something petty in their attitude to life. It is as if there was some element of confusion, of unconscious deceit indeed, about the picture of human life which they paint. This element, it has been submitted, arises from the fact that they all confuse the unavoidable tragedies of human existence in general, with the entirely evitable, but at present growing and deepening, tragedies of a specific system of society in a period of decay. They make no effort to show that the present horrible frustrations, deformations and agonies of men are due to the fact that they are for the most part still living under the degenerating capitalism of the twentieth century. Moreover, since by this suppression they in effect preach that ills that are quite curable by a change in the character of society are man's hard, inevitable lot against which it is futile to kick, they serve a very useful purpose to the governing class. And this is the reason for that element of inferiority which we all feel about them, in spite of their, in many ways, actually superior intelligences, as compared with the writers of the vigorous youth and of the high noontide of capitalism. For since they do not extricate themselves from present-day society, since they are unable to stand outside of it, conceiving of a new basis for human life, they are themselves, inevitably, infected by their surroundings of decay.[1]

Even now, however, we have not entered the domain of pure literature. These regions are guarded by the poets, and these guardians defy the investigator. Their territory is, and must ever remain, they tell us, a separate and secret island of escape, with no contaminating contacts with the mainland of human affairs.

And if an Englishman ventures to call in question any of the claims of poetry, he does so with trepidation. For poetry, for "pure" literature in its widest sense, has been by far the greatest æsthetic achievement of the English. Laggards and dunces at the plastic arts, heirs to a tradition of native music which somehow died before it had had the opportunity to come to maturity, the English have century after century poured their fancy into a golden stream of poetry, which is without rival in the world. For the English nature, like that, indeed, of all the major peoples of the world has contained, as well as its predominantly extrovert strain, an element of profound, subtle and dreaming contemplation. Keats was as typical an Englishman as Wellington—D. H. as T. E. Lawrence. From Chaucer to Shelley the stream flows unbroken. Then it begins to trickle. The nineteenth century produced its great poets; men as gifted as their ancestors. Yet somehow they all, Tennyson and Browning, Arnold and Swinburne, failed to establish their place in the essential tradition. And as the old century closed and as the new one began, a new and strange thing happened. It was not that poets failed to appear: it was not, principally, that their quality deteriorated. It was rather that they began to shrink in size. The poets were there all right, but they became smaller and smaller—till now most of them are hardly visible to the naked eye. Beautiful and satisfying individual poems are occasionally still written: but they appear at longer and longer intervals, and with, it seems, greater and greater difficulty: more and more tortured efforts are

[1] Lenin remarks that Tolstoy owes his immense stature in literature to the fact that although he had no conception of any other society, though he sought desperately and futilely for a basis for such a new society amongst the peasants, to the very end he refused to accept in any way, theoretically or practically, the existing life of his times, but always stood outside it. To Lawrence alone, of the three writers we have considered, and to him only in a more limited degree, could these words be applied.

necessary to write them, and one or two short books are the most that any individual poet achieves.

Mr. A. E. Housman is the very last of the English classical poets: and one of the most typical. But what a little one! Two tiny volumes are all that he has written. And the second is called, conclusively, *Last Poems.* The lovely and sombre verses which it contains are indeed ultimate in a larger sense than that they are all that we can expect from Mr. Housman. They are the last streamlet of that glorious river of verse, in which the joy of man in nature, a simple and yet satisfying philosophy, and an abounding, untamed fantasy have mingled to refresh the lives of successive generations of Englishmen.[1] And if we are apt to prize Mr. Housman above his real worth, it is because:

> *No spring, nor summer beauty hath such grace*
> *As I have seen in one autumnal face.*

True, a new school of poets has arisen in the last decades. They are, however, in spite of their deep appreciation of, and erudition in, the English classics, a new species, sharply different from any which have ever appeared in England before. They admit to the impossibility of the old tradition of poetry. This is a place totally inappropriate for a discussion of their work.[2] The most considerable product, however, of this school, Mr. T. S. Eliot's poem *The Waste Land,* is such an extraordinarily vivid example of the reactions of a sensitive man to the decay of the whole system of society into which he has been born, that it cannot be overlooked. It was published in 1922, and was, therefore, written at the most acute point of the post-war crisis of capitalism. *The Waste Land* is the most considerable poem produced in English in our day. It expresses the whole agonizing disintegration of an old and once strong social system with the greatest poignancy. The sad purpose of the poet is perfectly served by the poem's very form. It has a lack of formal

[1] Thomas Hardy, and even Bridges, have a few lines in the great tradition. So has Mr. Davies and Mr. De La Mare. These are but lingering drops.

[2] Mr. Max Eastman has written a sensible study of what the modern poets are and why they write as oddly as they do. He comes to the conclusion that when a mountain of pretentious nonsense has been stripped off them, some of their work does really represent an attempt to create the only kind of literature which will, in the immediate future, be possible. His account of the literary man's reactions both to the growth of science and to the ever-increasing crisis in capitalism is valuable. See his book, *The Literary Mind.*

eloquence; it has queer, haunting, broken, almost furtive, numbers which are for ever rising towards a passage of classic eloquence and are for ever falling back before they have achieved it; which are scattered into fragments, dismembered into snatches of song, as if they were themselves disenchanted of the possibility of all achievement and completion anywhere, any more, on the whole earth. Naturally, there is a more personal side to the poem. In many earlier, and far inferior poems, Mr. Eliot had shown himself not much more than a typical New England Puritan, lamenting delicately over lost opportunities. [1] Mr. Prufrock (prudent frock?), his favourite impersonation of himself, is little more than this. And it is, of course, quite legitimate to identify *The Waste Land* with this side of Mr. Eliot's character instead of with contemporary society. And yet, as a matter of fact, what the poem itself tells us is quite simply that the Waste Land is London. (And the poem will always remain supremely moving to Londoners on that account.) London, and the life being led to-day by different classes of people in London is quite straightforwardly and directly the subject of almost every one of the five sections of the poem. Even towards the end of the first introductory section, after a little comment on the "stony rubbish" of contemporary European life, we come to the first invocation of the city—

> *Unreal City*
> *Under the brown fog of a winter dawn.*
> *A crowd flowed over London Bridge, so many,*
> *I had not thought death had undone so many.*

The second part is the simplest and most direct of all. It consists entirely of two sections contrasting the lives of the rich and the poor, and finding them both hideous. It begins with a passage of sustained eloquence describing an exquisite setting for the life of a rich woman, and then breaks up sharply into dismembered futility.

> *"My nerves are bad to-night. Yes, bad. Stay with me.*
> *Speak to me. Why do you never speak? Speak.*
> *What are you thinking of? What thinking?*

[1] Mr. Eliot's feverish erudition is characteristically American. In *The Waste Land*, for example, he does not so much use the accumulated culture of the Old World, as ransack it. Yet perhaps it is just because he is an American that he has had the courage and energy to write the epitaph of the culture of the Old World.

What?
I never know what you are thinking. Think."

I think we are in rats' alley.
Where the dead men lost their bones.

"What is that noise?"
  The wind under the door.
"What is that noise now? What is the wind doing?"
  Nothing again nothing.
                                        "Do
You know nothing? Do you see nothing? Do you re-
     member
Nothing?"

.   .   .   .

"What shall I do now? What shall I do?"
"I shall rush out as I am, and walk the street
With my hair down, so. What shall we do to-morrow?
What shall we ever do?"
                    The hot water at ten.
And if it rains, a closed car at four.

Then comes the life of the poor—the conversation between the women as the pub is closing.

When Lil's husband got demobbed, I said—
I didn't mince my words, I said to her myself,
HURRY UP PLEASE IT'S TIME
Now Albert's coming back, make yourself a bit smart.
He'll want to know what you done with that money he gave
     you
To get yourself some teeth. He did, I was there.
You have them all out, Lil, and get a nice set,
He said, I swear, I can't bear to look at you.
And no more can't I, I said, and think of poor Albert.

There follows a long, terrible catalogue of the premature ageing of the women of the working class, enforced by poverty, igno-rance, clumsy abortions and the like. The section ends with a half-ironic, half-tragic use of Ophelia's farewell.

HURRY UP PLEASE IT'S TIME

Goonight Bill. Goonight Lou. Goonight May. Goonight.
Ta Ta. Goonight. Goonight.
Good night, ladies, good night, sweet ladies, good night, good
      night.

Part III. is all London again. The Thames in Autumn gradually clearing itself of the debris of the river parties—

> *The nymphs are departed.*
> *And their friends, the loitering heirs of city directors....*

And then the invocation again.

> *Unreal City*
> *Under the brown fog of a winter noon*
> *Mr. Eugenides, the Smyrna merchant*
> *Unshaven, with a pocket full of currants*
> *C.i.f. London: documents at sight....*

There follows the famous scene of lower middle-class life, in
which the bored, tired, typist is, meaninglessly, futilely and therefore horribly, possessed after tea in her bed-sitting-room by the
"small house-agent's clerk," "carbuncular."

At this point appears the poet's romantic longing for a less arid
and intolerable past. We get the memory of London as it had
been when Elizabeth and Leicester sailed the Thames, and, with
Part IV., of the days when tragedy was at any rate beautiful and
fertile, the exquisite short lyric of the "Death by Water" of
Phlebas the Phœnician.

Finally, in Part V., we have repeatedly expressed the falling
apart and dying of everything that the poet knows.

> *He who was living is now dead*
> *We who were living are now dying*
> *With a little patience.*

> *Falling towers*
> *Jerusalem Athens Alexandria*
> *Vienna London*
> *Unreal.*

London Bridge is falling down falling down falling down.

There are, of course, other elements in the poem. There is the theme, as we have suggested already, of Mr. Eliot's personal predicament, and there is the theme which foreshadows the mystical solution which he has since found for both his own problems and society's. But perhaps such quotations as have been given are sufficient to demonstrate beyond argument the overruling influence of current social decay on the first poet of the day.

Since writing *The Waste Land* Mr. Eliot, encouraged no doubt by the 1922-1929 period of capitalist recovery, has left the despair of the Waste Land behind him and taken up the typical position of a highly intellectual reactionary. He has become, he tells us, "a classicist in literature, a royalist in politics, and an Anglo-Catholic in religion." (Why cannot he be, at any rate, a real Catholic? Becoming an Anglo-Catholic must surely be a sad business—rather like becoming an amateur conjurer.)

The other great figure of contemporary letters is Mr. James Joyce. Mr. Joyce is undoubtedly a great poet, whose gifts would be accounted precious in this or any other age. Mr. Joyce's work remains, and will I imagine always remain, memorable. It will mark as aptly the end of that vast literature in English which was the chief achievement of the English-speaking men of the last five centuries, as Proust's novel marks the end of the corresponding French tradition. For *Ulysses* is not only a sort of summary of English literature (it contains conscious imitations of almost all the principal English prose styles): it is also the antithesis of the spirit of English letters. It marks the end of lyricism in verse, and of clear, simple, logical statement in prose. It has the same qualities of synthesis, of scholasticism as the work of the great mediævalists. Mr. Joyce's playing with the methods of all previous authors, the very plan of *Ulysses* itself with its incredibly elaborate parallelism to Homer, and above all the actual use of cryptograms in his later work, as when he weaves the names of five hundred rivers into his "Anna Livia Plurabelle," are irresistibly reminiscent of the mediævalists, and still more of the Byzantines. All this has nothing whatever to do with the tradition of the great writers of the epoch of self-confident capitalism. Mr. Joyce's work, indelibly marks the exhaustion of a whole range of possibilities. To say this is naturally to praise, not to disparage it. It is just the fact that Mr. Joyce has realized, more clearly than anyone else perhaps, the utter futility, the æsthetic impossibility, of going on writing in the old way, which makes him the profoundly significant figure which he is. For it is Mr. Joyce's superb achievement that he has succeeded in breaking through into a new kingdom in which literature and poetry may still reign supreme. There is no preferable method, indeed there is no other method at all which can tell us so much about the almost infinitely complex and, as yet, unclassifiable, interdependencies of human existence; the infinitely interwoven "point events" of, say, twenty-four hours of a few human lives, as does the poetic method which Mr. Joyce has discovered in *Ulysses*. He has succeeded for the time, at any rate, and in one particular respect, in reasserting the old high claim of literature to be the prime method of enriching our knowledge of the external world. In this sense, Mr. Joyce, in spite of the extreme Byzantinisms of his later works, is less of an end and more of a beginning than Proust. But if his work is a beginning as well as an end, it is the beginning of something which has little or nothing to do with the culture of the last five hundred years of Europe.

À la Recherche du Temps Perdu and *Ulysses* stand like massive boulders marking the end of a long tradition, blocking the old road, and pointing, not very certainly, in some new direction. If it is possible that there can be another major work in the old tradition, in the classical literature of the capitalist class, it must come from America.[1]

[1] In this connection it would be tempting to discuss the work of Mr. Faulkner, the young novelist of the American Southern States. His remarkable book, *Sanctuary*, depicts a state of violent social disintegration—a kind of rottenness developed before maturity has been even approached, that more vividly than any other book of our day makes one realize how comparatively short the noontide of American capitalism is likely to be. One lays Mr. Faulkner's book down with the conviction that this state of things is already the prolegomena to communism. Naturally Mr. Faulkner's own attitude is quite unpolitical. He is merely obsessed by the intolerable horror of what is. Politically speaking, he is the American equivalent to Dostoievsky. Yet from the point of view of literature the comparison, in spite of Mr. Faulkner's real talents, is just a little absurd. Will the American capitalist class ever have the time to find authors to express the tragic contradictions of the Republic's present period, which are no less grandiose in scale than the contradictions of nineteenth-century Russia, with the adequacy of the great Russian authors?

There is far less chance of any work on the grand scale in England. As a matter of fact, quite the best—and in many ways actually the most accurate—account of present-day English society, written by an author with something of Mr.

One more poet of the departing epoch remains for our consideration. And it is significant that Nietzsche, the last world poet of capitalism, died over thirty years ago. The most perceptive men of each phase of a civilization often express in their work, not so much the prevailing consciousness of their contemporaries, but the consciousness of that phase of their culture which will immediately follow them. Their greater insight seems to enable them to anticipate the reflections in consciousness which social tendencies, still only nascent in the actual world of things, will produce, when these tendencies have come to maturity.

Thus Nietzsche expressed not so much the ideas appropriate to the still comparatively pacific capitalism of the eighteen-eighties, but rather the ideas of the last desperate and tragic phase of the capitalist-imperialist system in which we live to-day. (Naturally his works were almost incomprehensible to all but a handful of men for twenty years or so after their publication.) The same thing is true of Marx himself. The conditions for the fulfilment of his prognosis of the overthrow of capitalism by the working class are being fulfilled, not in 1848, but in the first half of the twentieth century. The minds of the most exceptionally endowed men seem, as it were, to be able to move faster than time, and swimming up the stream as it runs ceaselessly past us, to come back to us with news of events which will soon come down the current and be upon us.

Plekhanov called Nietzsche "the arch-bourgeois," and if he meant that the poems of Nietzsche (and all his most important works are essentially poetic) are some of the greatest ever written by any capitalist author, he was right. The supreme effort of the theorists of the European capitalist class at systematic synthesis is, no doubt, represented by the works of Hegel. But Hegel's embittered opponent, Nietzsche, achieved the last and one of the greatest of their flights in the domain of the human imagination. Indeed, Nietzsche's work was the "limiting case" of poetry. For he him-

Faulkner's capacity for still being appalled by his surroundings, is contained in Mr. Evelyn Waugh's two humorous books, *Decline and Fall* and *Vile Bodies.* After writing these books, Mr. Waugh had clearly only three alternatives open to him. He could either commit suicide, become a communist, or immure himself within the Catholic Church. He chose this last (and easiest) alternative. As we come to consider these younger writers our choice of examples becomes almost wholly arbitrary, however.

self stood half outside poetry, deploring the fact that he was a poet
("and verily I am ashamed that I have still to be a poet"). He was
already unconsciously hungry for the ascertained fact.

Let us consider his central doctrine, the doctrine of the eternal
return of all things. It may be instructive to compare this pessimistic and mystical doctrine with the Marxian dialectic. The
dialectic is a sort of social X-ray apparatus, enabling us to see
the very bones of human society; and to see how they move. Once
we are in possession of this hypothesis, we see that the history
of man has been no smoothly flowing river of progress. An undeniable ebb and flow; complex forms of reciprocating movement,
in which a whole epoch is succeeded not by another epoch which
produces the former's tendencies to their conclusion in infinity,
but which starts a movement in the opposite direction; within
these main epochs innumerable minor movements, backwards and
forwards; the subject; the negation of the subject; and then the
negation of the negation of the subject—these are the undeniable
characteristics of the human past. Two men of the last century,
Hegel and Marx, together discovered this, the deeply buried and
gigantic pattern of history.

Hegel first described the phenomenon. He presented it more
or less mystically. For him, there was no very clear reason why
history was made up of this particular pattern of events. For
him "the idea," by which he meant in the last resort, people's
opinions, coming presumably either from nowhere, or from God,
was the motive force of the whole process. But since Hegel's
dialectic was at any rate dynamic—even though mystically dynamic;
since there was a prime mover, even though a distant and divine
one, the whole process was not merely circular. The negation of
the negation did not bring you back just where you started
from—as it would in formal logic. Human society has evolved,
Hegel agrees. Each phase, though antithetical to the last, has not
been a mere repetition of the one before that. Elements, achievements, of the previous phase become embodied in its successor.
Each successive phase is a correction of the former one, rather than
its blank negation. There is a progressive growth in the complexity, in the richness, of the forms achieved. The movement is
that of a spiral rather than that of a circle. It is true that for Hegel
the whole process comes to a dead stop with the Prussian nine-

teenth-century state. The historical process, he taught his disciples, having created perfection had finished its work. Up till that point, however, the process had been genuinely dynamic.

Marx supplied a real instead of an ideal prime mover for the whole construction. He showed that human societies have developed dialectically because of the interactions between the continually changing methods by which men have performed the most essential business of their lives—have kept alive—have, in a word, *produced,* and the tendentiously static forms of the societies which they have organized. Thus, the new methods of production have continually had to break down old societies. It has been to clear the ground for the construction of new social forms compatible with the new methods of production. Thus Marx stood the dialectic upon good, sound, material feet and, as he says, made it "a scandal and an abomination to the bourgeoisie and its doctrinaire spokesmen, because, while supplying a positive understanding of the existing state of things, it, at the same time, furnishes an understanding of the negation of that state of things, and it enables us to recognize that that state of things will inevitably break up; it is an abomination to them, because it regards every historically developed social form as in fluid movement, as transient; because it lets nothing overawe it, but is in its very nature critical and revolutionary." [1]

In the case of Nietzsche's doctrine of the eternal return of all things, however, there is neither the divine prime mover of Hegel nor the real one of Marx. Nietzsche did not believe in Hegel's disguised deity; and yet he had not the slightest interest in changes in methods of production. It would not be true to say that he did not realize that methods of production determined the character of every civilization. On the contrary, his classical studies showed him quite clearly that slavery was the necessary basis of all the ancient civilizations. And he at once concluded and preached that some form of slavery for the mass of mankind was the necessary basis of all culture. (And if you grant him the implied hypothesis, namely, that methods of production have not changed since the days of Pericles, he is in a sense right.) For Nietzsche seems never to have noticed the existence of a machine in his whole life. A

[1] Preface to the second German edition of the first volume of *Capital*.

South German, from what was then one of the most technically backward parts of Europe, he seems to have recognized no improvement in the human command over natural forces, since the introduction of agriculture at any rate.

Nietzsche, then, rejected both of the motive principles of history. Men were neither pulled forward by a God—more or less philosophically disguised—nor were they impelled to elaborate their social relations by the growth of what we have called their own comprehensive command over their environment. And yet Nietzsche saw through, and exposed, with unmatched vigour of bitter raillery, the shoddy, unhistorical, impoverished philosophy of nineteenth-century liberalism. He knew perfectly that, whatever else was the pattern of history, it was not a straight line of automatic and uninterrupted progress. What other view of human history could he take, therefore, than the terrible one which he announced; the view that it was the destiny of men ceaselessly and eternally to tread a circle, in which the past was always but the mirror of the oncoming future: in which past and future were but the deceptive sectors of a circle round the circumference of which the human race must for ever, wearily run its race?

In fact, the doctrine of the eternal return of all things is a static, and therefore pessimistic, despairing version of the great truth that the problems which history presents to men recur and recur. For it fails to recognize that they recur to men who may be better equipped to deal with them. Nietzsche, however, since he was a man of a culture which the next turn of the wheel must supersede, could not comprehend this. His discovery of the ineluctable conditions of destiny caused him the utmost agony, for he mistook the doom of his particular category of civilization for the doom of civilization itself.

And yet this was only one side of Nietzsche. Side by side with the doctrine of the eternal return of all things and, in spite of all denials, contradicting it flatly, there is the doctrine of the superman. Super to what? we enquire. And the only answer must be that the superman is above just precisely this recurrence of destiny: that he is superman just in so far as he is freed by knowledge and conscious power from the necessities of fate. For, as Engels wrote, freedom *is* the knowledge of necessity. Thus, Nietzsche, the last philosopher-poet of European capitalism, sometimes reached out unconsciously beyond the limitations of his time and place. To use his own terminology, "he reached beyond himself."

Nietzsche has been for many European intellectuals, especially for English intellectuals, with their cloying tradition of liberalism, a bridge which had to be crossed before they freed themselves of illusion. He has been a guide to the tragic view of life. For it is impossible to achieve the ultimate, though always caustic, revolutionary optimism unless the mind has first been purged of the facile optimism of nineteenth-century liberalism. The necessity of an objective force incarnated by a specific social class in order to achieve a new type of society, the futility of supposing that sweet reasonableness can solve the iron contradiction of our extant social order, these things cannot be understood unless some cauterizing flame has passed over the mind.

Friedrich Nietzsche was the last major poet of the culture of the capitalist class. He reflected the violence and despair of the final imperialistic phase of capitalism. But at the same time he shattered for ever the shallow hypocritical optimism of capitalism's earlier period. And, thus, with his destructive vigour, he unconsciously performed a service to the nascent forces of the workers, who were, and still are, striving for a complete consciousness of their own mission.

PART IV

THE FUTURE OF CAPITALISM

CHAPTER XII

IMPERIALISM

The first three parts of this book have consisted of a survey of the present difficulties of carrying on the capitalist system. It has been submitted that these difficulties are insuperable.

The rest of the book is devoted to a discussion of what the future has in store for us. We should be forced to leave, to some extent at any rate, the firmer ground of fact and to enter the territory of speculation. But just in so far as our subject matter necessarily becomes more abstract and debatable, we shall strive to make our treatment of it more concrete and realistic. Thus, it is not by any means intended to embark upon a series of academic and theoretical speculations as to what kind of social system would be a desirable successor to capitalism. On the contrary, we shall fix our attention on those forces in our present society which are obviously and visibly trying to remould it. We shall in practice find ourselves largely engaged in describing and estimating the main political trends of our time.

This chapter, and the two which follow it, discuss the question of the immediate future of capitalism. For capitalism, although dying, is not yet dead. True, with the establishment of the Soviet Union, the period of capitalism as an almost universal world system came to an end: and at any time another area of the world may be lost to the capitalists. At the same time, it is clear that in some parts of the world, capitalism will continue to exist for a short period. And it is the character of this ultimate period which we shall here discuss.

Now capitalism has for many years been in what is called its imperialist phase. It will be our task to show that this is its ultimate phase, and that its only future will consist in the working out of the last possibilities of imperialism. Let us first, then, establish a definition of imperialism. Lenin devoted a close study to the conditions which must arise in the closing stages of capitalism's existence. He described the efforts of the capitalists to perpetuate their domination of society during the period when their own characteristic system, with its dependence upon the mechanism of the market, is falling under them. Lenin described their reactions in a book written in 1916, which he called *Imperialism*. His conclusion is that the last phases of capitalism "to some extent cause the capitalists, whether they like it or not, to enter a new social order, which marks the transition from free competition to the socialization of production. Production becomes social, but appropriation remains private. The social means of production remain the private property of a few."

Lenin implies that the scale of capitalist production has become so enormous, the great monopolistic trusts so vast, that it is no longer possible to deny that production has become to a large extent a process carried on, not by any individuals, but by society as a whole. And yet, at the same time, the capitalist class, which is still in power, makes desperate efforts to maintain the legal system of private property. The contortions of the present policy of all the great capitalist states are nothing but the efforts of the capitalists to accomplish the impossible task of making private property fit social production. The only result which such efforts can have, is, of course, the creation of ever-extending monopolies. Hence, as Lenin puts it, the shortest, most epigrammatic, definition of imperialism is to say that it is "the monopoly stage of capitalism."

Such a definition does not accord with the ordinary popular conception of imperialism. We are apt to think of imperialism as consisting in the annexation of colonies. Or, again, more especially in the case of vast and long-established empires, such as the British, imperialism means for many people a sort of "Empire spirit." (For H. G. Wells' modern imperialism was, we saw, "a vague exaltation.") This "Empire spirit" is fermented not so much in order to acquire new territories, as to retain, and more intensively exploit, existing colonies. And, undoubtedly, the acquisition and retention of undeveloped territories, as their preserves for monopolistic exploitation, by the groups which control the great powers, is an important objective of the policy of all modern states. But then such annexations were undertaken by older forms of the state. Eighteenth-century France and Britain, which had not begun to be imperialist powers in the modern sense of the term, were avid enough for colonies. And, even in the nineteenth century, when the great "grab for Africa" was taking place, the full characteristics of modern imperialism did not appear. The annexations could go on without arousing such extreme and immediate collisions between the interests of the great powers as are occurring to-day. The period of imperialism proper, as we experience it to-day, had not arisen. It had not arisen because in the last century there were still a sufficient number of empty spaces into which the capitalist empires could expand, while in this century the world is almost full up: one empire can only expand at the expense of another. Every part of the undeveloped world is somebody's colony or protectorate, mandated territory or sphere of influence. Thus, on Lenin's definition, the epoch of imperialism does not begin until "the partition of all the territories of the earth amongst the great capitalist powers has been completed."

For, when Lenin said that imperialism was "the monopoly stage of capitalism," he was not thinking of monopoly in connection with the creation of trusts and combines alone: he was also thinking of monopoly in the annexation of colonies. His point is that imperialism, as a distinct régime, does not begin until the whole earth has become the monopoly of one or other of the capitalist empires. This is how he puts it:

"Such a definition [his short definition, that is] would include the essential feature; for, on the one hand, finance-capital is the banking capital of the few biggest monopolist banks, fused with the capital of the monopolist groups of manufacturers; and, on the other, the division of the world in a transition from a colonial policy, ceaselessly extended without encountering opposition in regions not as yet appropriated by any capitalist power, to a colonial policy of monopolized territorial possession—the sharing out of the world being completed." [1]

[1] For the reader's convenience, it may be well to give Lenin's long definition of imperialism in full:

"(i.) The concentration of production and capital developed so highly that it creates monopolies which play a decisive role in economic life.

"(ii.) The fusion of banking capital with industrial capital and the creation, on the basis of this financial capital, of a financial oligarchy.

"(iii.) The export of capital, which has become extremely important, as distinguished from the export of commodities.

Imperialism, then, is monopoly capitalism in a double sense. It is capitalism in a stage of development in which monopolies play a decisive part in production. And it is capitalism in a stage of development in which every part of the earth has become the monopoly of one or another capitalist empire.

Let us see how the drive towards monopoly is working itself out, both in actual fact, and in the heads of the capitalist theorists, who are busy rationalizing the process. Let us compare, and contrast, the way in which monopolies are actually achieved, and the way in which the process is described by the theorists of monopoly capitalism (of imperialism, that is).

Now we have already (in Chapter III) given some account of the rise of monopolies, which inevitably cut athwart the freedom of the market, just so soon as sufficient capital had been accumulated for large-scale production. We saw that the rise of monopoly was no smooth or automatic process. On the contrary, it was achieved by an incessant and intensive struggle among different capitalist organizations. The process was, typically, one of the swallowing of small firms by bigger ones, of the strangulation and subsequent buying up, at a very low price, of independent producers, by some great industrial or banking organization.

Such a perpetual war among rival capitalist interests is clearly of the very essence of the system. Here, however, we come to a seeming paradox. For the capitalist class as a whole has obviously, on occasion, a strong internal unity. It is clearly necessary to it that it should be able to present an effectively united front in at least two directions: it is necessary that it should be able to face and fight the demands of the wage-earners, of the working class; and it is necessary that it should be able to show the same unity against the capitalist class of another and rival state. And, as we

"(iv.) The formation of international capitalist monopolies which share out the world amongst themselves.

"(v.) The territorial division of the whole earth completed by the greatest capitalist powers.

"Imperialism is capitalism in that phase of its development in which the domination of monopolies and finance-capital has established itself; in which the export of capital has acquired very great importance; in which the division of the world among the big international trusts has begun; in which the partition of all territories of the earth amongst the great capitalist powers has been completed."

all know, it does in fact show a high degree of unity in both these directions.

But does this undeniable unity in face of the common enemy entirely suppress, even while the occasion for it persists, the continual struggle of group against group within the capitalist class itself? How does it, in particular, affect the ever-growing drive towards monopoly, towards the subordination and the suppression of weaker capitalist groupings by stronger and more vigorous rivals? With this question we come to the heart of the matter. Nor can there be any doubt as to the answer.

The necessity for preserving a united front against either the workers at home or against rival capitalists abroad is itself used by the dominant and successful groups within capitalism to further their own interests at the expense of their weaker brethren: is used by the great trusts, and the great trustified banks, first to weaken and then absorb this and then that category of independent producers. Nor do the dominant groups neglect to use for this purpose the machinery of the State itself. A classical example may be found in the measures of Government control which were applied to British industry during the last war. Now it is quite true that these measures, by which the whole of the affairs of almost every British producer were laid open to the Government (and the Government was at that time proud to announce that it was composed of "business men"—of the great capitalists, that is), were genuinely necessary for the conduct of the war. Unless the British capitalists had achieved this degree of internal unity, they would very probably have been destroyed by their German rivals. But this does not alter the fact that the information, and the measures of actual control, which were thus obtained, were used at the end of the war, by the great trusts and by the trustified banks to force through the first big drive for the consolidation and monopolization of British industry: to squeeze out the independent producers, and to gather together the threads of industrial power into a few hands.

Not that the process is even now complete. The independent producers, especially in Britain, have put up a stubborn fight. In Lancashire, for example, we have witnessed what one is tempted to describe as the Thermopylæ of the British cotton masters. It is astonishing to what lengths these men, the heirs of the greatest tradition of independent capitalist production in the world, have gone, in order to prevent themselves from being encircled by the Lancashire Cotton Corporation—that long groping tentacle of the Bank of England. The necessity for unity in war only began the process by which the great barons of British capitalism are seeking to aggrandize their power and wealth at the expense of the whole class of smaller capitalists. But what war began, crisis can continue. Just as in 1914-1918 the necessity of unity against the German capitalists could be used as a shepherd's crook with which to gather the independent producers into the pens provided for them by the trusts and the banks, so now the no less evident necessity for unity against the workers during the crisis can be used for the same purpose. And used it is. Slowly but surely the drive towards monopoly goes on. The competitive struggle is as sharp as ever within the British system. But it is becoming a struggle between ever bigger and ever fewer competitors. The trusts and banks are like great pike in a fishpond. And, in the British industrial fishpond, many of the choicest minnows have been eaten; the pike are turning angry eyes on each other—are apt to quarrel as to who shall get the best remaining morsels.

This is how capitalist monopolies are created. Let us now look at the descriptions of the process which are given us by the contemporary theorists of imperialism. For just as in the war period the independent producers were delivered over to the trusts in the name of national defence, so now the survivors are to be rounded up under the cover of the most scientific policies. The new watchwords of the ruling class are well worth attention from this point of view. "National Planning," "Empire Planning," "Organized Capitalism," are the phrases on the lips of their most-up-to-date theorists. Now it would be the greatest mistake in the world to take these phrases at their face value: to suppose that they represent disinterested suggestions for the solution of the crisis. But, at the same time, it would be equally erroneous to dismiss them as meaningless. They are, in fact, the expression of the latest phase of the struggle of the great British monopolists to extend their grip over the British economic system.

For, naturally, it is only the representatives of the monopolists, of the bank and trust directors, who hold these theories: for it is in their favor that the monopolies are to be created. There

exists a minority opinion expressing the interests of the old independent producers, which still heartily opposes monopoly. We
have already noticed, in Chapter VII, the existence of these two
views and analysed this latter view—that of the small producers—
in some detail. We called the former, or pro-monopoly view, that
of the national planners. We postponed its consideration until
we have done with the whole question of the possibility of the
restoration of a greater measure of freedom for the market.

The national planners, far from wishing to restore greater freedom to the market, propose to further its curtailment. They have
been struck, it seems, with the advantages of a planned system,
independent of the motives of the market. They propose, they tell
us, to establish a system of "organized capitalism." Quite a school
of these "national planners" has grown up in Great Britain.

At the present moment (1932), for example, a group of politicians, business men and administrators, including highly placed
civil servants, is engaged in working out "a national plan for
Great Britain," under the auspices of the weekly journal, *The
Week-End Review*. And as Sir Josiah Stamp, chairman of the
largest railway company in Great Britain, and Sir Basil Blackett,
chairman of Imperial Cables, Ltd. (both of them, also, directors
of the Bank of England), are engaged in the work of this group,
it is worthy of some attention. The reader will probably get a
good sense of the views and objectives of this school of thought
by some quotations from a recent speech by Sir Basil Blackett,
one of its keenest members. Incidentally, the very existence of
Sir Basil Blackett, who is both a big banker and a trust director,
refutes the idea entertaind by the "monetary reformers" that there
is a conflict of interest between the bankers and the industrialists.
On the contrary, the capital of the big bankers and the big industrialists is perfectly fused. The real conflict is between these
big monopolist groups, on the one hand, and the remaining
independent producers, on the other. It is noticeable how many
of the monetary reformers are themselves, like the father of all
of them, Mr. Arthur Kitson, ex-independent producers who have
been squeezed out by the monopolists.

Lecturing on January 11th, 1932, on "The World Economic
Crisis and the Way of Escape," Sir Basil Blackett devoted the
first half of his speech to destroying, quite effectively, the case of

the market restorers. Thus, he began by a defence of tariffs. According to *The Times* report of his speech, he said that:

"Fatal to human progress as were the high tariff walls of to-day, it had long been obvious that the philosophy of *laissez-faire* had no answer to the reasoned demand for wider opportunities and a balanced economic life for large new communities overseas and for highly self-conscious national units in old Europe."

So much for any hope of a reconstruction of the world market.

"The spread of the technique of trade union organization and side by side with it the increase of humanitarian and social conscience regarding problems of housing, health, sanitation and working conditions generally, had rendered impossible or inadmissible many of those brutal economic adjustments which our grandfathers were able to regard as due to the intervention of a wise Providence, which used enlightened self-interest and unregulated human competitiveness as its material means to perform wonders in the cause of moral and material progress."

So much for any possibility of the restoration of the free market in labour.

Now, however, Sir Basil Blackett passes on to his own alternative solution. He tells us that a whole new "philosophy" is needed.

"In the second sphere, then, the first necessity for the building up of the twentieth century was a new philosophy to take the place of the doctrine of *laissez-faire*. If tariffs at long last won the day against free trade in this country it was not because the nation had been converted to protectionism, but because tariffs might well be a useful instrument in a consciously controlled reconstruction of our economic life and because we had realized that the whole body of *laissez-faire* doctrine, the undiluted, individualistic philosophy of Bentham and his school, had broken down, was dead, and ought to be buried....

"A year ago planning was a new and startling idea in this country. To-day, it had become a *cliché,* and is correspondingly devoid of content to most of us, but he thought it was still true to say that rooted as we were in British traditions of personal and political freedom the average man and woman among us instinctively distrusted the idea of conscious planning, and we trembled for our cherished privileges and liberty when it was suggested that we had something to learn from Italy and Russia. The immediate task to which we should bend all our energies was to prove to ourselves and to the world that planning was consistent with freedom and freedom with planning. . . .

"First and foremost in the planning of national reconstruction came the necessity for a comprehensive insight into and a firm grasp of the inter-relationships between the various aspects of our political and economic and social life. The Cabinet Room in 10 Downing Street ought to have prominently emblazoned on its walls the Hegelian motto, 'The Altogetherness of Everything.' "

Now we can find, if we look closely enough, the programme of the dominant British capitalists, lying concealed in this little exordium on the theme of "from Bentham to Hegel." We might expect it to be followed, however, by some indication of the particular measures of "planning" which, the speaker considers, should be introduced. But here the speaker becomes increasingly vague. He turns aside from "the planned twentieth century" to give us a few remarks upon the desirability of stable money. It is clear that he will give us no blue prints of an "organized capitalism." In this, Sir Basil Blackett shows his prudence. For the only reality of the whole programme would turn out to be, if it were expanded in concrete detail, the further squeezing out of the smaller independent capitalists. It is when its advocates attempt to bring down their descriptions of "organized capitalism" from the abstract and general to the concrete and specific, that its contradictory nature becomes apparent. We may give as an example of an attempt to carry the conception somewhat further some proposals contained in a memorandum, entitled *The State and Industry in 1932,* which was submitted to his parliamentary colleagues by Captain Harold Macmillan in that year. Captain Macmillan is a conservative member of Parliament and is evidently a keen "national planner." He summarizes his proposals as follows:

"A. Representative National Councils for each industry and/or group of industries whose function would be to en-

courage and assist the efficient co-ordination of purchasing, production, marketing, and research, on lines which would enable
the industry concerned to evolve towards the highest possible
unity of policy and the necessary degree of centralization of
control.

"B. The Councils to be given status by Government recognition of them as the authority with which it would deal on
all matters affecting the interests which they represented.

"C. Provision to be made for the association of Labour with
the discussions of these Councils in all matters affecting the welfare of the workers, with a view to avoiding strikes or lockouts.

"D. In the ten groups listed by the Board of Trade Journal
for purposes of the Index of Production in manufacturing industries, it would be easy to transform existing national associations
into the proposed industrial councils. By extending the scheme
to the 24 groups listed by the Ministry of Labour Gazette the
whole field of industry, commerce, and finance would be covered.

"E. A sub-parliament of industry elected from these Councils each sending two or three representatives. These representatives would be available for consultation by the Import Duties
Advisory Committee in its efforts to reconcile the interests of
producing and consuming industries where protective measures
were under discussion."

These proposals contain, the reader will observe, all those elements which we have mentioned as essentially characteristic of
the drive for monopoly. "The necessary degree of centralization
of control" is to be achieved; in other words, each industry is to
be consolidated by the great banks and trusts; the independent
producers are to be squeezed out; trade union officials, whose role
in the whole tendency we shall consider below, are to be "associated" with the councils controlling these increasingly monopolistic industries; and, finally, the apparatus of the State is to meet
and fuse with the apparatus of consolidated industry at the desig-
nated point, at the point of the imposition of tariffs by which external competition is to be progressively eliminated.

Such measures will excite the strongest opposition in old-fashioned
capitalist circles. For, however orderly and admirable they may
sound to persons whose interests they do not affect, the smaller

independent producers know from personal and painful experience that they mean death to them. They know too that the
absorption of the smaller firms by the big monopolists is in reality
the whole purpose of such schemes: that the talk of order and
planning is little more than an elegant intellectual disguise.

The apparent intellectual confusion of many of the national
planners is, we can now appreciate, well calculated. They do not
want the real nature of national planning to be realized, either
by others, or even to some extent, by themselves. If only national
planning is left as a more or less academic question of the re-
arrangement of the structure of industry and finance, and no
awkward questions of method, conditions or consequences are
raised, national planning can form a useful basis on which men
of every type, men belonging to every political party, can, and
do, join. There seems nothing in the idea of social order, planning, pre-arrangement, which cannot be accepted by conservatives,
liberals and socialists alike. Indeed, the very term "organized capitalism" was invented by a man who refers to himself as a socialist
—Herr Hilferding. And this is natural, for what could be more
comforting to men who have ceased to desire a socialist society,
than to dream that capitalism will soon settle down, solve its difficulties, cease its struggles, and afford us all the stability of socialism
without the necessity of fighting for it?

We now turn to the other aspect of imperialism, to the question of the growth of monopoly in the possession and exploitation
of colonial territories.

The national planners have thrown a mantle of intellectual
respectability over the appetites of the British trusts. (Leibknecht
called the Reichstag "the fig leaf of autocracy." We might call
the national planners the fig leaf of monopoly.) In the same way,
another theory has been elaborated to cover, albeit with considerably less intellectual pretensions, the turn towards the intensified
exploitation of colonial peoples, which the British imperialists
have executed. This theory, or policy, is called, quaintly enough,
"Empire Free Trade." It is the policy of the Right wing of the
Conservative party, which is of great power, and which is waging
a desperate struggle, which may yet succeed, to capture the whole
party machine. "Empire Free Trade" is the name given by the
British capitalists to the most clear and explicit policy for main-

taining themselves by increased overseas exploitation which they have yet formulated. Indeed the objection to it of such wise and cautious statesmen as Mr. Baldwin is just precisely that it is much *too* clear and explicit. For men who are in the real tradition of British statecraft know without even having to take the trouble to remember the reason, that everything which is over-precise and explicit, is also naive, amateurish and undesirable.[1] The object of Empire Free Trade is a simple one: it is to reserve the vast natural resources and the vast markets of the British Empire for the exclusive exploitation of Empire entrepreneurs. The difficulties which such a policy must face are, however, enormous. As these lines are being written, the first major effort to make some sort of a beginning at an application of the policy are being made at the Ottawa Conference (August 1932). And already the "difficulties"—the fact, that is, that the interests of the British capitalists and the Dominion capitalists are flatly contradictory—are found to be daunting. (So daunting, indeed, that a certain ex-Liberal statesman is reported as saying that "if the British Empire can stand Ottawa it can stand anything.") It is proving almost impossible to secure agreement between the British and the Dominion entrepreneurs as to a division of the spoils. For the Dominion entrepreneurs have already erected high tariff walls not only against the rest of the world but against Great Britain herself. Hence, some of the problems of free trade in the real, as opposed to the Beaverbrookian, sense of the word are actually involved in making the Empire a great preserved area, protected against the rest of the world by tariffs. In order even to approach toward Empire Free Trade, existing tariffs would actually have to be taken down as well as built up. And that is always, as we have seen, a very difficult business. This difficulty does not arise, it will be said, in the case of non-self-governing, or coloured, parts of the Empire. Prohibitive tariffs, Lord Beaverbrook used to tell us, should simply be imposed by the fiat of the Colonial Office on foreign imports into these colonies while British goods were to be let in free, and the trade of these nations compelled to come to this country. Since

---

[1] The transatlantic directness of Lord Beaverbrook will never be able to understand this. Lord Beaverbrook is perhaps destined to remain the Daisy Miller of British imperialism. The comparison may seem far-fetched but there really is a resemblance between Henry James's heroine, bewildered by the subtleties of the old world, and our vigorous but perpetually thwarted newspaper millionaire.

he first proposed this plan, someone seems to have informed Lord Beaverbrook that the docility of coloured peoples is not what it was. The moment is not propitious, say the more cautious British statesmen, for a wholesale intensification of the exploitation of the Indian and Burman peasants. For these peasants, and those in several other parts of the Empire too, have already been driven to simmering revolt by their increasing misery and starvation.[1] To make their few necessaries, their yard or so of cotton cloth, or their cooking utensils, dearer by a tariff might well prove the last straw.

And yet an intensification of the exploitation of the workers and peasants of the Empire is the whole reality of the policy of Empire Free Trade. In the case of the self-governing Dominions, it can only be achieved as the result of a bargain struck with the Dominion capitalists. And this, as we have seen, is very difficult. The Canadian, Australian, South African and New Zealand capitalists feel, probably quite justifiably, that they are competent to do their own exploitation for themselves, without assistance. On the other hand, intensified exploitation can only be imposed upon the already half-starved peoples of the non-self-governing Empire at the risk of formidable revolts. Hence, the elaborate cover of words, the amazing rigmarole of Empire Free Trade, the unmatched claptrap of the Empire Crusade, were considered necessary in order to hide a purpose fraught with such grave hazards.

This is not to say that determined attempts to apply measures of Imperial Protection will not be made. For an increase in the exploitation of the peoples of Great Britain and of the Empire, by one means or another, is the only way out for British capitalism. Moreover there is another and perhaps decisive reason why

[1] Starvation is not in the least an exaggerated term. For example, Mr. Hesketh Bell wrote to the London *Times* on August 12th, 1932, as follows:

"SIR,—The following somewhat startling figures are taken from the statistics published in the Official Gazette of the colony of Mauritius:

	Births	Deaths
1930	12,793	14,341
1931	11,890	15,467

"These figures show that, during the last two years, in a British colony with a population of about 400,000 souls, the deaths exceeded the births by more than 5,000! A perusal of the annual reports of the Medical and Health Department shows that this deplorable situation has not been due to any definite epidemic, but that it is chiefly the result of poverty and malnutrition among the labouring classes of the colony."

imperial consolidation must be attempted almost at any risk. For, even though Imperial Protection is, as opposed to direct wage-cutting at home for example, a round-about way of increasing exploitation, it has, as well as its greater demagogic possibilities, an important additional advantage. If the Dominions are given important concessions in the British market, the real *quid pro quo* for Britain is likely to be, not so much corresponding concessions in the Dominion markets, but confidential military and naval understanding—an attempt to stay the disruption of the Empire, in view of the ever-growing menace of war. There will be a last attempt to mobilize the united force of the Empire for the preservation of its world power against the menace of America, on the one hand, and of the Soviet Union, on the other.

We have seen that the policies of the theorists of imperialism are quite as much a cover for, as an expression of, the true purposes of the dominant capitalist groups. These purposes are the progressive destruction of the independent producers and the intensified exploitation of the workers at home and of the peasants abroad. For those who are ultimately responsible for the propaganda of both national planning and Empire Free Trade are quite aware of the unreality of the dream of a great "organized" monopolistic empire, to which these policies and phrases seem to point. They know perfectly that the competitive struggle of capitalism is to-day ten times as ruthless and violent as it has ever been before: that talk of "organizing" or "planning" such a struggle is, and always must be, nothing but talk.

But this is not to say that the whole character of the competitive struggle of capitalism is not changing. On the contrary, it is changing radically. For now that it is carried on, not between petty producers, but between mighty antagonists each of whom can enlist the power of whole states, these struggles are becoming nothing less than the grappling of great empires for the partition of the world. In the course of this vast, and final, expression of the competitive principle, the whole character of states and empires is being remodelled. Moreover, when capitalism has taken on its last and most monstrous form, when commercial competition has evolved into inter-imperial war, at this very moment the conflict between the two classes in society, the workers and the capitalists, is reaching its final stage. Thus when capitalism is torn by the most violent and unappeasable rivalries, it is faced with its ultimate opponent. Menaced from within and from without, it must become incomparably more violent. The democratic forms, Liberal ideas, and subtle methods of the rule of the capitalist class have to be scrapped. Direct, open terror against the workers, violent aggression against its rivals, can alone enable a modern empire to maintain itself. A name for such a policy has been found: it is fascism.

CHAPTER XIII

THE GOAL OF MONOPOLY

It may be that the reader, while finding the last Chapter a sufficiently lifelike picture of what is actually happening in the world to-day, will consider that the *inevitability* of these events has not been established. He may admit that the growing concentration of production, the squeezing out of small firms by big, the formation of monopolistic organizations, are only producing a more violent phase of the internecine struggles of capitalist producers. But is it inevitable that this should always be so?

"You have poured scorn," we may be told, "on the conception of 'organized capitalism.' But may not the eventual goal of this very struggle of the big producers toward monopoly, which you stress so much, be the creation of one single and complete monopoly? May not competition be thus entirely eliminated and the market totally abolished? Even though the process may be carried on exclusively by the violent methods you indicate, by the expropriation of the small independent producers by the trusts, may not the end be one single all-embracing trust, undertaking itself the whole of production?"

This question is really analogous to the question of ultra-imperialism which we discussed in Chapter IV. And in this case also it is perfectly easy to see that as a question of formal logic the end of a process of monopolization is complete monopoly. But it is equally easy to see that such formal logic has only the slightest reference to anything which is happening or can happen in the real world. It is quite true, we may concede, that if the process of monopolization were going on in a sort of social vacuum, its ultimate, logical, end would be unified monopoly. But this ultimate monopoly would not be capitalism. A non-competitive, "organized capitalism" is, indeed, a contradiction in terms. We saw in our original analysis that the mechanism of the market is at the very heart of the system. For the whole possibility of the existence of capitalism is dependent upon the possibility of there being some objective process for the determination of prices. And prices can only be determined by competition on the market. If there were no objective factor to settle prices, capitalism would lose its only "governor," and the whole machine would run amuck.

Consider, for example, the effect of even creating complete monopolies in each important branch of production. The result of such a process would be to transform, not to abolish, the principle of competition. For it is clear that if, to take three examples, the coal industry, the oil industry, and the hydro-electric industry, were each made into complete monopolies, the fiercest competition must immediately break out *between* these industries. For each provides an alternative source of power. The coal monopoly and the oil monopoly must fight each other for the market provided by the steel monopoly. But this would be only the beginning of the war of the industries which must ensue. Not only must the industrial monopolies producing interchangeable products struggle with each other, an equally fierce struggle must break out between monopolies producing quite different types of commodities. For the raw material of one monopoly would be the finished product of another. Thus, the engineering monopoly must struggle with the steel monopoly over the price of steel. For the lower the price of steel, the bigger the share in the wealth of society of the owners of the engineering monopoly, and the smaller the share of the owners of the steel monopoly and vice versa. This illustrates the fact, which we hinted at in Chapter III, that the super-profits of monopoly are only obtainable so long as considerable parts of the productive system are still subject to the laws of competition. If, for example, the steel industry has become a monopoly and both the mining industry and the engineering industry are still conducted competitively, then clearly the steel monopoly is "on velvet." It can buy its coal cheap from the unorganized mine owners, and sell its steel dear to the unorganized engineering firms. It can suck up to itself both the profits which are being made by the mine owners out of the exploitation of the miners and the profits being made out of the engineers by the engineering firms.

But if both the mining industry and the engineering industry have become monopolies also, the position is quite different. How in this event are the prices of coal and of steel to be fixed? Only by a direct struggle between the mining, the steel and the engineering monopolies. For the objective factor in the determination of prices will have been destroyed by the monopolization of the three branches of production. True, a competitive struggle is still available to fix prices—the struggle between the industries concerned as wholes. What would be the methods of such a struggle? They could not be the comparatively peaceful methods of price cutting: they could only be the methods of direct struggle by menace, by intrigue, and, in the last resort, by armed force. For there would remain no objective element in the process. The conflicting desires for profit of the respective trust owners would come into direct collision. And wherever the principle of monopoly has actually been pushed almost to this point, the trusts have begun to hire private armies of thugs, with which to enforce their will. (The classical example is the use of armed force by Mr. Rockefeller in building up and maintaining the monopoly of the Standard Oil Company over the trans-continental pipe lines.) Such would be the consequences of the destruction of the competitive method of determining prices within each branch of production, such the consequences of the first approximation towards "organized capitalism."

"But," we may be told, "you must not stop here. Not only must each industry be monopolized, but also there must be one single national monopoly of industry. One group of capitalists must absorb all the others, must become the owners of the whole of the means of production. Then, at any rate, organized capitalism would come into existence."

This conception is, perhaps, too fantastic to merit discussion. Undoubtedly, however, certain people are to-day playing with such ideas. Hence, it may be worth while to examine the consequences which must ensue from such an ultimate monopoly. What we are asked to envisage is a perfectly monopolized, non-competitive, planned economy, combined with the present class hierarchy. The inherent contradictions of such a conception may not be at once apparent. And yet it ignores at least two of the basic features of capitalism, features which it would be impossible to change while maintaining the present ruling class in power. The first of these features is, of course, the private ownership of the means of production. A planned, monopolistic, "organized" economy is quite impossible so long as the means of production are owned by a class of private individuals. Indeed, as we have seen, the appropriation of the entire means of production by a single capitalist group is a prerequisite to the whole conception. The whole of the rest of the capitalist class would have to become the passive pensioners of this one group. This consideration alone removes the idea of an "organized capitalism" to a distance very far from reality.

Let us assume, however, that somehow or other this task had been accomplished. There must immediately arise the question of how this perfect centralization of the means of production is to be maintained. We have to envisage, let us remember, a society in which a single capitalist group possesses the effective ownership and control of the entire apparatus of production, and yet, at the same time, the present numerically considerable capitalist class still exists, and still enjoys its present standards of income. They must presumably be paid this income by way of dividends, probably of a fixed character, on holdings of bonds in the giant unified concern—Great Britain Ltd.—which is undertaking all production. But what are they to do with their dividends? Spend part of them and save the rest, we shall no doubt be told. And certainly the instinct to accumulate is the deepest instinct in the whole of capitalist psychology. But it is surely clear that in our monopolist nightmare, saving by individual capitalists must be sternly forbidden. For saving, as we have defined it in Chapter VI, means buying a part of the instruments of production. And the instruments of production would be, in our imaginary society, the exclusive monopoly of a single capitalist group. Hence the outside capitalists, now become pensioners, could not possibly be allowed to buy them back. Some method of ensuring that the entire incomes of the capitalist class (now become pensioners) should be spent, would have to be devised. The magnitude of this task would be very great. It would be necessary for the capitalist pensioners to turn whole vast areas of the world into places comparable to the French Riviera to-day: whole coast-lines would have to be remodelled in order to find a use for incomes which must at all costs be spent. But let us suppose that a new race of capitalists, bereft of the instinct to accumulate, and highly skilled in the arts of super-spending, could be evolved. Even so, we are only at the beginning of the difficulties of our "perfect monopoly." What of the armies of skilled technicians and administrators, who would be necessary to such a régime—the present salariat? Are they to be forced to spend their entire incomes—or, are they to be allowed to acquire part of the instruments of production and so gradually to undermine the monopoly? Moreover, are they, and the whole of the lower middle class, to be prevented from engaging in trade, from starting "little businesses of their own"; and, if so, how? How, for example, are the scientific technicians to be prohibited from developing new inventions for their own profit? Certainly nothing short of a law prohibiting all technical changes will suffice for this purpose. And yet, if private individuals are allowed to start businesses, and if these businesses succeed, they will re-introduce the whole process of private accumulation, and this, in turn, must undermine the monopoly of the means of production, and so re-introduce competition, the market, the anarchy of production, and all the other features of present-day capitalism.

These objections to the possibility of a perfect monopoly of all the means of production could be studied in great detail. And there is no doubt that the conclusion which we should come to would be that what a capitalist group which had obtained the monopoly of all the means of production would have to do, if it wished to retain power, would be to abolish money. Only in a moneyless economy, in which goods and services were distributed by a rationing system, could the power by such a monopoly be maintained. For only so could the possibility of private accumulation be removed. But can any of us possibly conceive of the existence of a moneyless capitalism? To such contradictions are we led by the dreams of the national planners. In spite of this, it may be useful to examine what the character of such a society would be. In doing so, however, it must be clearly understood that such a future for capitalism is quite impossible. We discuss it simply and solely because there may be readers of this book who, while they will not admit the inherent impossibility of such a future, may yet be made to realize the full horror of the goal at which they are aiming. It is well to draw the attention of those in many cases well-intentioned persons, who talk of "national planning," "organized capitalism" and the like, to the consequence which would inevitably follow if their aim could be realized. We shall, it is hoped, be able to demonstrate irrefutably that the realization of their dream would, if it were possible, involve

THE GOAL OF MONOPOLY

the re-enslavement of nine-tenths of humanity and the ruin of human civilization.

We have not yet spoken about the position of the workers in our imaginary nightmare of monopoly. There is no doubt, however, that the re-introduction of serfdom for the workers must be one of its first consequences. It is clear that if we can conceive at all of one single monopolist, or group of monopolists, having secured the possession of the entire means of production of the community, that monopolist would have become, *ipso facto,* the State. He and his fellow directors would be omnipotent dictators. Now, as we have said, certain capitalist theorists have juggled with such ideas. We have already noticed Mr. Aldous Huxley's self-revealing sketch, placed far into the future, in his book *Brave New World*. A far less fantastic prediction of a similar future was made some years ago by the well-known Roman Catholic apologist, Mr. Hilaire Belloc. In his curious little book *The Servile State,* Mr. Belloc shows that he understands quite well the inherent instability of capitalism. He tells us that:

"This book is written to maintain and prove the following truth:

"That our free modern society in which the means of production are owned by a few being necessarily in unstable equilibrium, it is tending to reach a condition of stable equilibrium BY THE ESTABLISHMENT OF COMPULSORY LABOUR LEGALLY ENFORCEABLE UPON THOSE WHO DO NOT OWN THE MEANS OF PRODUCTION FOR THE ADVANTAGE OF THOSE WHO DO. With this principle of compulsion applied against the non-owners there must also come a difference in their status; and in the eyes of society and of its positive law men will be divided into two sets: the first economically free and politically free, possessed of the means of production, and securely confirmed in that possession; the second economically unfree and politically unfree, but at first secured by their very lack of freedom in certain necessaries of life and in a minimum of well-being beneath which they shall not fall.

"Society having reached such a condition would be released from its present internal strains and would have taken on a form which would be stable: that is, capable of being indefinitely prolonged without change. In it would be resolved the various

factors of instability which increasingly disturb that form of
society called *Capitalist,* and men would be satisfied to accept,
and to continue in, such a settlement.

"To such a stable society I shall give, for reasons which will
be described in the next section, the title of THE SERVILE STATE."

It may not, at first sight, be apparent why the abolition of competition, and the mechanism of the market, should necessitate the
legal imposition of compulsory labour. And yet, of course, the
reason is clear. A non-competitive society may be defined as a
society, in which the crucial questions of (i.) what work is to be
done, (ii.) who is to do it, and (iii.) who is to receive its fruits,
are not left to the motives of the market, but are consciously predetermined by some person or persons. It is clear that in such a
society an obligation to work (since men are not universally or
equally industrious by nature) must be placed on the members of
society, if, and this is the critical point, all are also to be guaranteed
a share in the product of this social work. If, however, as we shall
show in Chapter XIX, all men in such a society share approximately
equally in the product of social labour, there is no element of slavery
or serfdom in the universal obligation to work; for in that case it is
an obligation self-imposed upon society. (Mr. Belloc, than whom no
man could be more anti-communist, concurs, as we also show below,
in this view.) If, however, the share of the social product received
by individuals is grossly and systematically unequal, if, in particular,
some persons receive their incomes not in virtue of work done but
by virtue of the ownership of the means of production; and if the
legal obligation to work does not, either in practice, or in theory,
apply to them, then we have a system of serfdom for the workers.

Capitalism avoids an open and legal status of servility for the
workers because, and only because, it neither legally compels the
members of the community to work, nor guarantees them any share
of the social product. It relies on the motives of the market both
to induce men to work and to ensure that they shall provide each
other with sustenance. Now the argument of the first half of this
book has been that to-day the motives of the market are incapable
of performing either of these functions. On the contrary, they actually prevent millions of men from working, and ensure that other
millions shall not have sustenance. That is why we speak of the

breakdown of the capitalist system. But if the capitalists ceased to rely upon the motives of the market in order to induce the workers to work for them, they would have to rely upon legal compulsion. And if they imposed compulsory labour, they would re-introduce, unless they both imposed it universally and shared its fruits approximately equally, open serfdom for the workers. We reach the unavoidable conclusion that the serfdom of the workers must be the result of a system of universal monopoly.

As we have already noticed, however, such a perfect monopoly must be, in fact, if not in form, the State itself. The final trust, after absorbing all its rivals, must absorb the State as well. But just as we discovered that the monopolization of each particular industry served only to reintroduce competition between industries, so also the monopolization of all industries, and their fusion with the State, would only re-introduce competition at yet another point. And this new point would be the point of competition between the different State trusts (or "Trust States," it matters not at all which they are called). And the form taken by competitive struggle between states is war.

We have already seen that the degree of monopoly which has already been achieved within the principal capitalist states has immensely exacerbated the relationship between them. Capitalism, after the formation of these monopolies, has become imperialism. It has taken on a far more violent and bellicose form. What, then, should we say of the consequences of the establishment of our hypothetical, perfect monopoly, in a number of the great capitalist states? For clearly we cannot suppose that a perfect monopoly of the means of production could be formed on any other basis than a national or imperial one. Apart altogether from the fact that monopoly capital *is* imperialism, we find that in the field of ideas also the connection between the propaganda of extreme nationalism and the attempt to subject the workers to the domination of the great trusts is as necessary in theory as it is obvious in practice. For if the attention of the workers is to be distracted from the blatant inequalities of capitalism, so that they will not rebel too vigorously even against the attempt to impose the open, frank and rigid inequalities which, as we have seen, would have to be the first consequence of a perfect monopoly, they would have to be given some kind of ideal consolation. What is, in fact, done, even at the present stage of monopoly, is to excite ferociously nationalistic and patriotic feelings by every possible device. The propagandists of the capitalist class feel that it is vital that the workers should be made to forget as much as possible that they are workers and to remember every minute of the day that they are Britishers, Frenchmen, Germans, Americans, or Japanese. Their natural hatred of an employer who is cutting their wages must be drowned in an artificially evoked and stimulated hatred of all foreigners: their natural sense of fraternity with their fellow workers, suffering under the same wage cuts, must be drowned in a synthetic frenzy of unity with every class and kind of their countrymen. Thus, it is no accident, but an absolutely necessary, and logically correct, policy, which dictates the intense nationalism and bellicosity of all the propaganda of the capitalist class.[1] How much more violently nationalistic and bellicose therefore would have to be a State trust, or Trust State, of the kind we have postulated?

What would be the consequences of six or seven or more of them existing in this narrow planet at the same moment? Yet it is, as we have seen, inconceivable that one single international system of monopoly could be created. For each attempt to approach monopoly conditions necessarily involves the most extreme nationalism and imperialism on the part of the particular capitalist group which is making the attempt. Thus, the only prospect held out by the ideal of "organized capitalism," even if all its inherent contradictions are discounted, is a world system of internally monopolistic, ferociously bellicose, slave-empires. Needless to say, a whole series of wars, the smallest of which would dwarf anything which the world has hitherto known, as the recent war dwarfed a Roman border skirmish against the Picts and Scots, would inevitably result. For Mr. Hawtrey's "continuous conflict of national force" must time after time break out in open war, as the only conceivable way of deciding the issue of flatly conflicting imperial wills. There is, it is true, one

[1] Lord Beaverbrook, for example, recently issued the slogan "Thou Shalt not Steal." He told the readers of his newspaper that the livelihoods of British workers and farmers were being stolen from them by wicked foreigners who sold goods on the British market. The remedy lay to hand. Exclude the foreigners from the British market and take from him all those markets over which Britain has political control. The same idea has, curiously enough, occurred to the French, German, Italian, Dutch, American, Japanese, Polish, Spanish, Argentine and Czecho-Slovakian Lord Beaverbrooks.

way in which this series of wars between rival slave-empires might end. Sooner or later, some one empire might emerge the surviving victor in this immeasureable world tournament. And then at last the peace of a world monopoly might reign. Over what kind of world, however, would it reign?

We have now quite frankly entered the realm of the imagination. But let us follow our nightmare to the bitter end. Now it is usual to talk loosely of another war "destroying civilization." This is probably an exaggeration. The destructive power of the methods of modern war are, of course, terrific: the losses and suffering of the next war would be—or, rather, one must write, will be—incomparably greater than those of the last war. It may well be that civilization will be extinguished over whole areas of the earth's surface. Some defeated nations may well be exterminated *en bloc* in the concluding phases of the contest. It is quite true that this is the future prospect which capitalist imperialism holds out to us. This will certainly be our fate if we leave the capitalists in power. All the same, the next war will probably not destroy civilization. It is often forgotten that science is almost equally applicable to the tasks of reconstruction as to those of destruction. The world to-day has almost as great a power of recuperating as of destroying itself. Hence a single war, at any rate, would be hardly likely to destroy civilization all over the world.

We have envisaged, however, a whole series of wars, and these on the most gigantic scale, as the only conceivable way by which, even on our hypotheses, a world monopolistic slave-empire could be established. And it is certainly difficult to see how human civilization could stand such an epoch of wars. The level of the world's culture would at the very least deteriorate sharply. Each outbreak of war between the slave-empires would offer the workers the opportunity of emancipation. Every such war would be complicated, as were the wars of the Greek states, by revolts of the helots. And it is impossible to believe that some of these revolts would not succeed, and communistic communities be established. Let us, however, suppose that this new and appalling kind of inter-imperial tournament was fought out to a finish and that some victor empire came to possess the whole earth as its fief. Over what sort of a world, we may ask again, would such an empire reign?

If all the revolts of the workers during the earlier wars had been so thoroughly crushed that during the later ones the governing class would have become secure, it would necessarily mean that the workers had been debased into barbarians—incapable of turning their masters' instruments of war against them. Hence, as it would be necessary to reduce the workers to barbarism in order that they should find that their perpetual servitude was natural and appropriate, civilization for the immense majority of mankind would in any case have perished.

It is curious to speculate, however, on the culture of the governing class in such a community. For it would be naive to suppose that the characteristics of the culture of the heyday of capitalism could be retained under a system of universal monopoly. Such a society would be static. There could be no technical progress. For the most stringent (and as we have seen, in practice, quite unworkable) laws against any advance in technics would be necessary, lest opportunities for private accumulation might be given. Hence, scientific knowledge would inevitably cease to grow, and would soon begin to decay. Great efforts would no doubt be made to maintain it at a level adequate to the existing technique of production, and such efforts might well be successful for a century or so. Sooner or later, however, the fact that science had become, not a living and developing attitude of mind, but a body of dead rule of thumb formulæ for obtaining certain results—the fact that the reasons behind the rules of science were increasingly being forgotten—would make it impossible even to maintain the existing level of scientific knowledge. And so in the end the technique of production must begin to decline.

Again, as we have seen, it would be disastrous to the stability of the community that there should be any private savings or accumulations. The whole of the vast amount of wealth, beyond their own subsistence, created by the workers could and would have to be utilized for the pleasure of the governing class. The sheer horror of perpetual pleasure, however, would turn many of the governing class back to the consolations of religon. At first, no doubt, the incorrigible intellectuals would create a new stoicism.[1]

---

[1] Cf. the doctrine of "the great year" held by the Stoics of antiquity. This was a doctrine of the eternal return of all things, dated by the calculations of the astrologers. The Stoics believed that since the movements of the planets determined all human affairs, it must follow that when a moment came at which all

(And here begins to appear the parallel with the declining stage of the Roman Empire which is inevitable in any fantasy of this kind.) A far greater number, however, would no doubt turn to a religion rich in emotional content. And why not to a well-adapted version of Roman Catholicism itself? Roman Catholicism was the religion of agricultural monopoly. Why should not a new version of the same faith prove the dominant religion of an industrial monopoly? Would it not be reasonable to suppose that in such a society, the Church would, as the centuries went by, assume greater and greater importance? And would it be reasonable to suppose that that importance would be confined to things spiritual: would it not inevitably extend to things temporal? Would not a point be reached at which the Church would become of equal authority to the State? And would not the problems of this diarchy be solved, as they were once before, by the union of Church and State? May we not, then, envisage a new Constantine—approaching down the avenue of the future, as the Roman Emperor recedes from us into the past?

And, if this be the logical line of development, do we not know whither the assumption of temporal power by the Catholic Church would lead? We have already postulated that scientific knowledge and the technique of production would be in decline. Has not the race been once before at that point in history when, in a period of economic decline, the Catholic Church assumes control over the destinies of man? Is it not clear, then, that the new world empire would decline by the same road as the old one? True, the barbarians, who would in the end destroy it, would come this time from within rather than from without. For as the scientific knowledge of the governing class waned, and their religious preoccupation waxed, the workers, slaves for some centuries, would raise their heads again and the new world empire would dissolve as did the old, into a warring chaos. A new dark age of ecclesiasticism, in which the knowledge and skill, the culture and civilization of the world would temporarily disappear, must follow. Then the great monasteries would reappear, and, since by one of the paradoxes of

the planets had returned simultaneously to positions which they had occupied before, human affairs too would have completed their cycle and have returned to their starting point. This was the cycle of the planetary, or "great" year. Such a planetary cycle does exist and modern astronomers have calculated that its duration is of some 50 million solar years.

history, the Church is both the slayer of civilizations and the faithful preserver of their traditions, these monasteries would become the sole repositories of learning. The Europe of the Middle Ages would be re-enacted, but this time upon a world scale. And the civilization of such a new middle age might bear the same relationship to our civilization as did the civilization of, say, A.D. 1000 to the civilization of the zenith of the Roman system. The eternal return of all things—Nietzsche's "abysmal thought"—would have come to pass.

And yet even so, if a series of monopolistic slave-empires were to be achieved; if the stable monopoly of a victor empire were to be set up after a series of wars which reduced the workers of the world to helotry; if this victorious world empire were itself to decline over long centuries into a new dark age; if the great monasteries, the ignorance, the premature death, disease, want, and superstition of the Europe of A.D. 1000 were to come back; if it was seen that mankind had indeed trodden a ghastly circle of predetermined cause and effect, yet still we should not have the right to despair. If we were to have a new dark age, we should have a new mediævalism: if a new mediævalism, then a new renaissance. There is no more reason to suppose that mankind would stay at the nadir of the circle than at the zenith. Nor need we believe that the figure of history is a circle: it is a spiral. The new mediævalism would not be the old mediævalism. Its priests would mutter misunderstood fragments of Marx and Darwin, not of Aristotle. And when the renaissance came, we, and not the Romans, should be antiquity. A new Shakespeare might spread the glory of his young fancy over Lenin instead of Cæsar: a new Copernicus take up the work of Einstein and of Dirac, not of Ptolemy. For why should the achievements of our age be wholly and permanently lost when those of the Greeks and Romans were in part preserved? And since the new renaissance would start one turn further up the spiral than we did, the new capitalism which must follow would achieve a higher culture than did ours. And then, without doubt, men would come to the critical turning point of history which we have reached, adequately equipped to take without doubt or hesitation the road to communism.

But these are fantastic speculations. One hundred and sixty millions of men and women have already taken the road to communism. They have leapt out of the kingdom of necessity towards the kingdom of freedom: they have decided for themselves that it was from this turn of the spiral of history that men achieved communism. Who can doubt but that their example will serve to save the race from the necessity of repeating the pilgrimage of its last 2,000 years? [1]

We have only indulged in the foregoing piece of somewhat fanciful speculation in order to show those who cannot be convinced of the impossibility of complete monopoly, of "organized capitalism," that in any case, its consequence could only be the re-enslavement of man and the ruin of his cultural heritage.

The real business of these pages, however, is not with such nightmares: it is with the quite sufficiently grim realities of the existing situation.

---

[1] Naturally the repetition at a new level of development of this historical cycle of the last 2,000 years is only an arbitrarily selected example of one of the cyclical movements of history. Thus, the achievement of communism to-day could also be thought of as the return to a previous state of society, but on a new level of development. For the race has passed through a communistic stage once before in its tribal youth. But in this case the radius of the spiral would be a wider one. On the other hand, if civilization collapsed altogether and culture dropped to a semi-human or pre-human point, that too may be thought of as signifying merely that life has had to go rather a long way round.

CHAPTER XIV

FASCISM

At the end of our analysis of imperialism, we came to the conclusion that new methods, both at home and abroad had become necessary for the capitalist class. Capitalism was so hard-pressed alike by the rivalries of the competing empires, and by the disaffection of the working class, that new and far more violent methods than any which the capitalists had hitherto employed would alone suffice to maintain the system. We arrived at this conclusion theoretically. But, if we look round the world, we see at once that it is fully justified by direct observation. Everywhere the capitalist states are actually adopting methods of unparalleled violence both against the workers and against each other. We noticed that a name for the most characteristic expression of these new methods of capitalism has been found. They are called fascism.

Now fascism is a deceptive phenomena and needs some analysis before its real nature becomes apparent. Not so long ago, it was thought of as a purely Italian movement, incapable of export. In the last few years, however, unmistakable fascist movements have appeared in several European countries; notably in Germany. It has become clear that there is nothing peculiarly Italian about fascism: that it is a political phenomenon which appears wherever certain economic and social conditions prevail. Specifically fascist parties have appeared in countries such as Germany, Poland and Austria, which are in the grip of violent economic crises, and where the workers acutely threaten the stability of the capitalist state. Moreover, methods and catchwords which resemble those of the specifically fascist parties begin to appear almost everywhere.

Let us, therefore, attempt a definition of fascism, wide enough to cover these phenomena. We may say that fascism is one of the methods which may be adopted by the capitalist class when the threat of the working class to the stability of monopoly capitalism becomes acute. We say "one of the methods" because it is by no means certain the fascist method will be everywhere used by the capitalist class during periods of crisis in their conflict with the forces of the workers. For the fascist method essentially implies the attempt to create a popular mass movement for the protection of monopoly capitalism. Its adoption means that the directing capitalist groups consider that the regular State forces at their disposal are inadequate or unsuitable for repressing the workers. Thus, an attempt is made to create, by the employment of skilled demagogues, the expenditure of large sums of money, and the reckless dissemination of propaganda designed to play on every prejudice, a mass party composed of a petty bourgeois nucleus, combined with such backward workers and peasants as can be successfully deceived. This party is then used for the destruction by terror of working-class organizations of struggle, the workers' defence organizations, clubs, trade unions, newspapers and party "machines."

Now this method of defending capitalism has its disadvantages as well as its advantages. For example, it is impossible that a party recruited by the methods enumerated above should prove a reliable instrument in the hands of the capitalists. It is always liable to get out of control. For it is almost always impossible to get the fascist party together without using some anti-capitalist slogans, in the early stages at any rate, of the necessary propaganda. And this type of propaganda may have so coloured the minds of the rank and file of the fascist party as to make them difficult adequately to control. Again, the retention of power by the capitalist class by means of the success of a fascist party necessarily implies the scrapping of all democratic institutions. It involves the revelation, without any attempt at a democratic disguise, of capitalist dictatorship. And a wise capitalist class will certainly not dispense with the serviceable mask of democracy, which has stood it in good stead, until no other course is open to it.

The creation of a fascist party is, then, a desperate expedient only resorted to by a capitalist class in the face of the most urgent danger from the workers. And, even then, the capitalists may, in some states at least, adopt violently repressive methods by means of the use of the ordinary State apparatus, rather than attempt to create a mass party of their own. Indeed, we can all see that such methods of violent repression are being more and more adopted by even the most sedate capitalist classes. It is only if the ordinary official capitalist parties adopt these methods too slowly, if the march of events towards crises is too rapid for their power of adaptation, that overtly fascist, and nominally "revolutionary," mass parties are organized. For fascism is a "revolutionary"—actually counter-revolutionary, of course—force in but a very limited sense of the word. It does not seek to substitute the rule of one class for that of another, which is the only genuinely revolutionary act: on the contrary, its whole purpose is to preserve the rule of the capitalist class. But in certain circumstances fascism may become in a sense revolutionary. It becomes revolutionary in the sense in which the French politician Clemenceau was revolutionary when he preached and practised that, even though the Germans were hammering at the gates of Paris, it was the duty of good Frenchmen to oppose the weak French Government then in power à l'outrance. For he saw that the only way in which the French capitalist class could be saved was by the overthrow of their own Government. In the same way the fascists became "revolutionary," not in order to destroy the rule of the capitalist class, but in order to destroy weak capitalist governments which supinely allow the strength of the workers to grow to unmanageable proportions. If, however, an existing capitalist government is neither weak nor supine, and is quite ready to fight the workers itself, there is no need for the organization of a special fascist mass movement. This does not mean that in this case violent methods will not be used. It means that the capitalist class in question has shown sufficient flexibility to transform its existing political parties, to fuse them, into an instrument for the withdrawal of democracy and the forcible suppression of working-class organizations, thus avoiding the necessity of creating a new specifically fascist party. The question arises whether, in this case, these new and violent methods should be called fascist. The name is often applied to them, but it should be borne in mind that they are only fascist by analogy.

If a capitalist class can succeed in transforming and fusing its existing political parties—into a "National Government," for instance—the institutions of democracy will be gradually and, if possible, imperceptibly withdrawn. The Press will become a better and better directed and drilled servant of the capitalist class. All other methods of disseminating information, notably the cinema and the wireless, will be more and more consciously monopolized.

Power may be gradually withdrawn from a democratically elected Chamber (cf. Reform of the House of Lords in Britain) or alternatively the franchise may be gradually curtailed (cf. the proposals of the British Conservative party for withholding the franchise from persons in receipt of poor relief). At the same time, the habitual régime of police violence will be increased (cf. the present heavy sentences on working-class militants in Britain passed almost openly, not for any specific offense but because the accused *were* working class militants, as notably in the case of Arthur Horner; the increasing use of terror in all American wage disputes; the police régime in France, etc., etc.). This method applies the principle of "the inevitability of gradualness" to the introduction of an open capitalist dictatorship. And if the breakdown of the system and the revolt of the workers will await the convenience of the capitalists, then no doubt it is for them the preferable method. At any time, and in any capitalist state, however, things may begin to move too fast for this method to be successful. And in this event, it will be necessary to resort to the attempt to create a mass fascist party.

We have characterized the fascist parties as an attempt on the part of the directing capitalist groups to organize a mass party for their defence. But, as we saw, this task is a difficult and somewhat delicate one. For the rank and file of the fascist parties cannot possibly be allowed to realize that this is the only purpose for which they are to be used. A continual stream of the wildest appeals to all sorts of contradictory prejudices must be kept up. The German fascists have developed this technique to the greatest extent. Every emotion, which the hearts of backward members of the ruined middle class of Germany may cherish, is played upon. The fact that these emotions are of a confusedly anti-capitalist character does not worry the paymasters of the German fascists. On the contrary, such anti-capitalist emotions are carefully catered for. The fascist party is actually called a "National Socialist Party": "Loan Capital," a convenient term which need not be too closely defined, is denounced: above all, anti-Semitism, which in Germany has long been called "the socialism of fools," is fostered. (All the same the dissemination of this type of propaganda, which has proved very effective in Germany, may turn out to have been a very rash act on the part of the German capitalists who have paid for it.)

The Italian movement was, it is now conveniently forgotten,

built up on propaganda of a no less extravagant, and of a no less anti-capitalist, sort. Now, however, that fascism has become the official and permanent method of rule of Italian capitalism, other and more presentable theories have to be invented for it. Signor Mussolini and his lieutenants now talk the language of the "national planners." We hear a great deal about the "Corporative State"; about "paradisial" organizations and what not. And, in fact, since Italian capitalism has now more or less completed its evolution into monopoly capitalism or imperialism, these phrases do correspond, in a sense, to some economic reality. But it is an economic reality which has nothing specifically fascist about it. It is now nearly ten years since the fascist *coup d'état,* and yet Italian capitalism has developed along just the same lines as capitalism in the so-called democratic countries. The Corporative State has remained on paper. Some spectacular public works have been executed (but public works are after all a very old story even for such comparatively *laissez-faire* countries as Great Britain), some amalgamations, notably of shipping lines, have been promoted, the workers have been "compulsorily arbitrated" a good deal, and each industry has been made to establish a "council." But, after all, the coal owners, the steel masters, the textile mill owners, and so on, of even the most individualistic countries have had trade associations for decades. (And from what one reads in Press reports, the fascist councils of industry engage in just the sort of work which such trade associations specialize in. For example, a recent meeting of one of the fascist councils passed a strong resolution protesting against the unequal balance of trade between Italy and Jugo-Slavia, just the sort of simple-minded protectionist resolution which the Birmingham Chamber of Commerce has been passing for years and years.) The London *Times* is, no doubt, in the right when it gives the following instance as typical of the real workings of the "corporative system." The extract is from the issue of February 29th, 1932.

"A further instance of the collaboration policy in the industrial field, which is being carried out in Italy through the corporative system, is the special agreement reached at the Fiat Works in Turin.

"A further reduction of 10% in wages and salaries, which had been decided upon some time ago and then postponed, will be enforced from to-morrow."

The old-fashioned British employer might perhaps be tempted to retort that he had long known how to cut his workers' wages without calling it "a collaboration policy through the corporative system."

Thus, the more elegant Italian theories of fascism, the Corporative State and all the rest of them, prove on examination to be just as much a set of catch-phrases as are the crude herd cries of the Nazis. The only difference is that the "national planning," "Corporative State," phrases are designed to catch intellectuals, and the "kill the Jew," "Nordic brotherhood" phrases are designed to catch shopkeepers.

Thus, fascism has no theory, and needs no theory. For fascism is simply the bludgeon of the capitalist class, hard-pressed by the workers. Undoubtedly, however, fascism has a technique. Nor is it difficult to see where that technique has come from. The chief characteristic of fascism was, we saw, the creation of a mass party. And the parties which the fascists create are parties in the new and not the old sense of that term. They are not polite organizations of voters, such as the Conservative or Liberal parties in Britain used to be, for example. They are rigidly and elaborately constructed organizations, which attempt to capture the whole lives of their members. And when they obtain power, they utilize the State apparatus quite frankly as their instrument. There is no doubt that the fascists borrowed this technique from the communists. And, unquestionably, this borrowed technique has given them a great advantage over the older capitalist parties.

What estimate should be made of the utility of the fascist method as a last resort for hard-pressed monopoly capitalism? It would be absurd to deny that this weapon has proved very effective in Italy and represents a formidable menace to the German working class. And yet the dangers and difficulties involved in its employment by the directing capitalist groups are no less apparent. These difficulties all arise from the fact that monopoly capitalism seeks to enlist into its service, when it creates a fascist party, classes and elements whose interests it cannot possibly serve. The whole propaganda of every fascist party must be equivocal and contradictory from the start.

Hence, the necessity, for example, for the fantastic contradictions of Nazi declarations. For the Nazis, from Hitler downwards, are recruited from the lower middle class in the towns and the richer peasants—the German "Kulaks"—in the villages. Now these are precisely the classes of the remaining independent producers for the market. They are classes which are to-day trapped between the better organized sections of the community, between the great integrated, capitalist monopolies, on the one hand, and the solidly built German trade unions, on the other. It is to tickle the ears of these followers that Hitler makes his passionate denunciations of "loan capital," on the one hand, and hints at the breaking up of the trade unions, on the other.

All this seems to make the Nazis but strange instruments for monopoly capitalism; for Hitler, of course, has derived most of his funds from just those monopoly capitalists whom he denounces. His chief paymasters are the coal and iron monopolists of the Ruhr. For the Ruhr coal and iron masters are quite willing to put up with a few hard words—which damp no blast furnaces—in order to hire an army of thugs to break down the resistance to still more gigantic wage cuts of the German working class. But it is clear that if and when the Nazis obtain power, they can make not the slightest attempt to serve the interests of their supporters. They could only do so by attempting to restore some of the lost freedom of the market. And this would involve attacking just those great monopolists who are the true authors of the Nazi movement. It would involve deflation carried to a point hitherto regarded as utterly impracticable. If this could be done, the large monopolies would no doubt be forced to break up, production on the present large-scale basis would be paralyzed and would have to start again on a smaller, less-mechanized, more decentralized, basis. This is the only road to the economic paradise of the richer peasant and the petty shopkeeper.

But the hands of the clock of economic events cannot thus be put back. A Nazi Government, far from imposing unparalleled deflation —always the most unpopular measure any Government can take— would be much more likely, at the bidding of its paymasters, to inflate, and so produce, if it is still possible, another hectic epoch of German big-business monopoly, another "Stinnes era." In this way, an assumption of power by the Nazis could do much to promote the interests of German monopoly, at the expense of all re-

maining free producers. The most probable economic effects of a
Nazi régime in Germany would be, therefore, the final destruction
of just those elements which form the basis of the Nazi party. It
does not necessarily follow that this would immediately destroy the
hold of the Nazi leaders upon their supporters. But yet, in the long
run, and more especially in a country such as Germany, where the
opposition of the workers is very difficult to crush, so crass a contradiction must always prove a grave danger to the stability of the
Fascist party.

To sum up: we conclude that fascist parties represent a formidable weapon in the hands of the monopoly capitalists. But this
weapon has a flaw in it. For it is constructed of elements the interests of which it must flatly betray. Hence, fascist parties must do
their job—the destruction of the organization of the workers—
quickly. If an obstinate, gallant and successful struggle against them
can be maintained they will sooner or later reveal their inherent
weakness. And the immediate future may well reveal that a fascist
party may in this case prove a menace to those who created it.

It may be, therefore, that the most determined efforts of the
capitalist class to hold power will be made, not by specially created
fascist movements, but by the adoption of methods analogous to
those of fascism, by the old official capitalist parties. A preliminary
to such a manœuvre is for the old parties to tend to fuse; to form
a single governing organization of the capitalist class—and this
tendency is already well developed in Great Britain. Then at some
appropriate moment, the forms of democracy can be quietly dis-
pensed with, and the whole power of the State used to crush working-class organizations.[1]

[1] A classic working model of how constitutional democracy can be slipped off
was afforded by the Brüning Government in Germany. As the London *Times*
Berlin correspondent wrote on May 30th, 1932, when the Brüning Government
went into power the establishment of an open dictatorship would have caused a
severe struggle: by the time that Brüning had completed his work a dictatorship
could "slip into the saddle," without anyone noticing any difference. But such
successful manœuvring requires the active collaboration of the workers' own leaders
with the capitalists. We consider this question fully below.

PART V

THE POLITICAL STRUGGLE IN BRITAIN

CHAPTER XV

AN EMPIRE ON THE DEFENSIVE:
THE ROLE OF MR. BALDWIN

THE creation of fascist parties is, then, by no means the only expedient of the ruling class for maintaining their power in the final imperialist phase of capitalism.

The alternative policy of the capitalists is to meet "the crisis," to meet, that is to say, the growing chaos of their system of production, and the growing challenge of the working class, by fusing the old capitalist parties, and transforming their character and methods. This policy has some important advantages for any ruling class which has the skill to use it. It enables many more of the deceptive forms of democracy to be maintained: above all, it facilitates the transformation of the leaders of the workers' own parties into invaluable allies of the ruling class.

If Germany and Italy have given us examples of the creation of fascist parties, the present policy of the British governing class is the leading example of this important alternative. This does not mean that the British capitalists may not be forced at a later stage to create a fascist party: but at the moment they are giving the "National Government" policy a full trial. It will be natural for us, therefore, in dealing with this alternative to discuss the course of the contemporary political struggle in Britain. It will be necessary to appraise the effects of the crisis in capitalist production upon the world position of the British Empire, and to attempt some estimate of the strength and weakness of that position. For it is only as seen against the background of a world empire, fighting an obstinate defensive struggle for existence, that contemporary British politics can be understood. We must also pay particular attention to the character and leadership of the British workers' movement, for only so shall we discover why the workers, apparently both strongly organized and increasingly exploited, have not already made the existence of British capitalism impossible.

In entering upon such a discussion, we must effect a sharp change in the focus of our eye. Hitherto, we have been looking at the long-term consequences of the basic economic factors of the present world situation. We have been establishing such propositions as that the concentration of production within every capitalist state has now reached the point when capitalism must be said to have entered a new phase—the phase of monopoly capitalism, or imperialism. Such questions are, as it were, qualitative questions. We now come to the discussion of quantitative factors. Instead of trying to find answers, as we have been doing, to the question of "How does history work?" we shall be trying to answer the question, "How *long* does it take history to work?" We must try to qualify every "how" with a "how long." And this is an infinitely more complicated business. The time factor is always at once the most important, and the most indeterminate of all factors.

For example, the time factor is all important when we come to consider the present position of the British Empire. Now there is little doubt that in principle the power of the British Empire is in decline. Great Britain is the Austria of the twentieth century. The stage of the nineteenth century was, it is true, the narrower stage of Europe: the stage upon which the complex tragedy of the twentieth century is being enacted, is the whole world. But, with this qualification, the parallel is obvious. The Austrian Empire was, and the British Empire is, a conglomeration of extremely dissimilar parts: no ties of blood, religion, race, or tradition being common to these parts. Both have been the result of long processes of historical accretion, in which pieces and bits of territory have been slowly brought together.[1] Both have been continually disturbed by nationalist movements, and at intervals by open revolts, in one or more of their parts. Both, from time to time, though reluctantly, have granted a greater measure of local autonomy, first to this part, then to that.

It is not, however, in these actual resemblances, striking as they are, that the essence of the analogy is to be found. It is rather that both empires have passed through the same relative positions, the one to Europe, the other to the world as a whole. Just as Austria in,

[1] The British Empire, however, has been formed by much more violent methods than was the Austrian. It used to be said that Austria had grown by successful dynastic marriages, rather than by war. "Bello gerunt alii, tu felix Austria nube." Nobody ever said that about Britain.

say, 1900, though still indisputably a great power, was equally indisputably waning and not waxing, relatively to the other great powers
of Europe; so to-day the British Empire, though still possessed of
immense reserves of strength, is indubitably a waning and not a
waxing influence in world affairs. There cannot be any serious
doubt about the direction of this long-term trend. British power,
even though it were to increase *absolutely* (and this is not out of
the question) would certainly decrease *relatively* to the power of,
for example, America and Russia. These, however, are but plati-
tudinous considerations. Anyone (outside Great Britain) can see
this obvious general trend. What is really of interest and importance,
however, is the question of the *rate* of this decline. How *long* will
the British Empire last? How *far* has its decline gone? (And on
this, the relevant question, non-British opinion probably makes as
grave an error in one direction as does British opinion in the other.)
Will, for example, the British ruling class succeed in effecting a
marked temporary revival? Will it, in the hope of effecting such a
revival, pursue a policy of intensified imperial exploitation? The
successful application of such a policy as Empire Free Trade, for
example, might well cause a temporary revival in British power.
In so doing, however, it would immensely intensify the rivalry
between Britain and younger rival empires—and thus almost certainly provoke war. Or, to put the question the other way round,
will the British capitalist class suffer the slow and peaceful decline
of British power without putting up a fight for their old position?
These are the sort of questions which are at once the most interesting and the most difficult to answer. We shall perhaps find the
best indications of both the strength and the weakness of the British
position by a consideration of the various policies represented by
various groups within the British ruling class.

The manœuvres and intertwinings of British governing class
politics are to-day somewhat complex. And this is itself a sign of
the difficulties of the British position. These somewhat laughably
sudden re-alignments, the adoption of social democratic Prime
Ministers by Conservative parties, the decline to impotence of one
of the great capitalist parties, the fusion, whether temporary or
permanent, of all sections, however relatively antagonistic, of the
capitalist class into a National Government, these violent, and perhaps rash, attacks on that very friendly enemy, the faithful Labour

party, are not done for nothing: they are the storm signals of an Empire facing heavy weather. But all this at first somewhat baffling maze of splits, fusions, resignations, reconstructions, feuds and reconciliations, is not so labyrinthine after all if we begin our inspection of it at the right place.

Let us begin with the central block of British governing-class opinion: let us begin with the Conservative party, and with that central core of the Conservative party which Mr. Stanley Baldwin both leads so wisely and personifies so perfectly. For then all the other sections, the raging, tearing, Empire Free Traders with Lord Beaverbrook; the various shades of ex-liberals, even the remaining liberals; the patriotic social democrats under Mr. MacDonald, the abandoned and excluded social democrats under Mr. Henderson, will all fall into their places relatively to the main Baldwinite mass. What policy, then, have Mr. Baldwin and the great party which he controls? Whither is he leading the Empire which he rules? When we have found the answer to these questions, we shall have discovered the basis of British policy.

For it should now be apparent to even the most superficial observer that Mr. Baldwin is the dominating figure upon the British political stage. He is surely the one man of to-day who, in the perspective of history, will be found to have attained the stature of the statesmen of the heyday of British capitalism. And if his methods are more hidden, his effects less obvious, his triumphs less spectacular than those of a Peel, a Gladstone or a Salisbury, that is precisely because the problems with which he has to deal are more baffling and more menacing than any which faced his predecessors. His career has been extremely spectacular, because he has acted only once or twice during the whole course of it. And an analysis of it might be instructive. Here, however, our task is rather to discuss what Mr. Baldwin, and his followers, stand for to-day. We have already indicated that two main alternatives confront the leaders of the British Empire. In the first place, they can adopt a "forward" policy; they can attempt to consolidate the British Empire as a great, preserved market for British entrepreneurs; to reserve its raw materials for British producers. Nor is there any need to deny the strength which the successful achievement of such a policy would lend to British capitalism. Even to-day its Empire connections are of the greatest importance. The measure of Empire preference already achieved, not so much by means of preferential duties, as by administration methods in granting concessions, etc., such as Mr. Hawtrey describes, is a highly valuable asset to British entrepreneurs. This asset, and the direct tribute, representing interest on former loans to the Empire, are the factors which enable British industry, which is not more efficient, to pay considerably higher wages than are paid by most of its competitors. Thus it is quite obvious that if the products of foreign industry really could be excluded more or less completely from Empire markets, an immense reinforcement for British industry would have been secured. But, alas for the British capitalist, all good things in this world have a price. And the price and the risks of a forward Empire policy are high and serious. In the first place, the exclusion by high tariffs of foreign foodstuffs and raw materials from Great Britain, which alone can bring in the Dominions, must mean a sharply increased cost of living. It will, therefore, be certain to increase the severity of the internal class struggle, already serious. Again, as we have already suggested, the coercion of the Crown Colonies would be a grave business. For example, Great Britain's best hope of retaining India at a not too prohibitive cost in blood and treasure, is, no doubt, to make a bargain with the growing Indian capitalist class. But it is precisely these Indian capitalists whose interests would be most adversely affected by an "Empire economic plan." For such a plan would necessarily have to assign to India the role of a producer of raw materials. In every considerable Crown Colony, too, a forward policy of imperial exploitation must create trouble. In Africa, for example, an effort rapidly to develop natural resources must lead to tribal revolts from natives, whose primitive ways of life would be suddenly disturbed.

But if such a forward policy would cause trouble within the Empire, it would have much more serious consequences in the rest of the world. In order to envisage such consequences, one has only to imagine for a moment the reaction of America to a serious attempt to keep American goods out of the British Empire—out of Great Britain, Canada and Australasia, for example. Nor would such a policy affect America alone. The most violent reactions must occur in Japan, for example, if her cotton goods were to be shut out of the markets of the British Empire. Again, the closing of the British home market would complete the ruin of Europe. Nor do powerful nations accept their ruin, or even their perceptible injury, without action. Their first actions would be in the nature of economic reprisals—a "tariff war" would ensue. Great Britain could, of course, refer to the fact that tariffs had always been erected against her: that she was now merely adopting the policy of her rivals. But such unanswerable debating points, when used in international controversy, usually exacerbate the dispute in exact proportion to their own excellence. Hence, it would be a most serious matter to attempt to apply a forward Empire policy with any vigour. It would, in a word, bring the British Empire into the double and acute danger of disruption from within and of attack from without.

Naturally no one, outside the office of the London *Daily Express*, envisages the application of such a policy with the pristine crudity with which it was first announced. But it is often overlooked, even by the most "scientific" imperialists, that the penalties and dangers of a "forward" policy are exactly proportional to the benefits to be achieved. Strain on the cohesion of the Empire, internal class friction in Britain, and hostility from the rest of the world, will inevitably be incurred to exactly the extent to which benefits for British industry are secured. It will be quite possible to go so slow that, for example, the situation will not be materially worsened in India; serious trouble with the workers at home may be avoided, and the resentment of foreign powers kept below the point at which very grave economic reprisals are taken, certainly below the boiling-point of war: but, in that case, the benefits to British industry will also be inconsiderable. So much benefit, so much risk: the ratio is a direct one.

What then is the alternative to a forward policy of intensified imperialist exploitation? It is the policy of cautious inaction, which successive British Governments have pursued since the war. British post-war Governments, while getting every ounce of benefit which the Empire already gives—and it is a very important benefit—have attempted at the same time a policy of international collaboration; have attempted to reconstruct the world free market. They have pursued a policy of waiting; of hoping for better times; of contemplating the remaining but solid advantages of the British position; of unwillingness to jeopardise them for risky and problematical gains, however brilliant.

To which of these policies does Mr. Baldwin adhere? It is perfectly characteristic of the man that we cannot give an unqualified answer to that question. He has hitherto followed the second and more cautious policy. But now it is clear that the National Government, which he, of course, really controls, is moving towards the forward policy. A tariff has been adopted in Great Britain. Agreements for mutual tariff preferences have been made with the Dominions at the Ottawa Conference. Thus Mr. Baldwin is showing himself too cautious even to be quite consistently cautious. He realizes that the situation demands some action. Reluctantly we may be sure, for he has a deeply rooted instinct that all action is prejudicial on the long view to British interests, he is moving towards an intensification of imperial exploitation. But we may be sure that such a forward policy will be conducted by the present Baldwinite National Government with far greater tact, deliberation and skill than it would be by the Empire Free Traders.

And this was one of the principal reasons for the formation of the National Government. When the Labour Government broke up in the summer of 1931, it would have been perfectly easy for Mr. Baldwin to have taken office as the Prime Minister of a purely Conservative Government and to have secured a conservative majority. Such a prospect did not, we may be sure, invite him in the least. To have embraced it would have given him no real power; on the contrary, it would have put him at the mercy of Lord Beaverbrook and his own uninstructed rank and file. The prospect of presiding for five years over a purely Conservative Government, with a mandate to carry through any tariffist Empire scheme, clearly appalled him. He knew that he would be no more than the crowned prisoner of men infinitely less wise than himself. He may have doubted whether he could have got through the five years without war itself.

Mr. Baldwin, dreading impulsion from the right, stretched out his hand for counter-weights on the left. Nor were such counter-weights hard to come by. If Mr. Baldwin cared nothing for the appurtenances and appearances of power, and everything for the reality, Mr. MacDonald took a different view. He was entranced by the sudden suggestion from Buckingham Palace—had not Mr. Baldwin seen the King just previously?—that he should lead a National Government. Several other competent liberal and social democrat politicians were readily, most readily, available. They

were enraptured at the idea of serving as ballast (not that this was
how it was put to them) in the Cabinet which Mr. Baldwin, with
characteristic indirectness, was constructing. The National Government, both in its original and its reconstructed forms, beautifully
served Mr. Baldwin's purpose. Instead of facing at the head of the
Cabinet table, as their alarmed Prime Minister, two long rows of
imperial Tory faces, woodenly bent on Empire Free Trade, Mr.
Baldwin found himself quietly seated as one member of a nicely
balanced Cabinet. A good sprinkling of the Empire Free Trade
Tories were there, as they had to be, but they were nicely offset by
the much greater abilities of Sir John Simon, Mr. Runciman, Sir
Herbert Samuel, Lord Snowden, and the other moderating influ-
ences which Mr. Baldwin had recruited. (Almost the first act of
the National Government was to pass an "Abnormal Importations
Bill." And the conservative rank and file were so delighted at being
able to exclude foreign greengrocery from Britain that they never
noticed that Mr. Baldwin had quietly introduced into the Tory
party the largest "abnormal importations" in history.)

And how well Mr. Baldwin's new recruits are serving him!
Instead of being obliged himself to wage a desperate battle in order
to keep his imperial champions within bounds, he can sit back and
see the debating powers of his liberal and social democrat recruits
doing the work for him. If pressed into a corner himself, he can
always say that he would adopt the most extreme Empire measures
with all his heart if it were not for the necessity of "preserving the
national unity during the crisis." If the balance seems to tip a little
more towards liberalism than he can expect his followers to stand,
or a little more towards intensified imperial exploitation than he
can expect the world to stand, he can redress it by a movement,
almost imperceptible and quite unnoticed. By the wonderful device
of a National Government, he finds himself comfortably seated at
the exact centre of a nicely balanced seesaw. If he had been Prime
Minister of a purely Conservative Government, he would have
found himself desperately trying to hold down one end of the
seesaw whilst the other was weighted with almost the whole of the
rest of his party. For it is their own supporters alone whom statesmen fear.

There is something decidedly first rate about this manœuvre of
Mr. Baldwin's. To have seen that the only possible way to retain

power was to appear to resign it; to have hired Mr. MacDonald as the most suitable person to engage when one happened to want a Prime Minister at short notice; to have thrown some of the highest offices of the State to one or two hungry and efficient liberals, and then to have sat back knowing that Lord Beaverbrook's ace had been trumped once more, must have been a satisfying experience. Not that Mr. Baldwin does these things in a mood of personal emulation. He is deeply concerned for his class, or, as he thinks of it, his nation, and he is rightly conscious that he, almost alone, stands between the British Empire and the adoption of a policy the risks of which are too dreadful for him to contemplate. Nor, of course, does he formulate his policy in the theoretical and conscious way with which we have had to formulate it in order to discuss it. With him, it is all a question of instincts, traditions, inherent tendencies. These are, no doubt, so strong in him that he never exerts himself much in thinking of the reasons for his actions. There is nothing, however, in the least unconscious about the subtle, and yet violent, methods by which he ensures that it is his will, once he has semi-consciously made it up, which prevails.

One of his supporters once said that Mr. Baldwin's achievements were always negative; that he had spent his political life almost exclusively in *stopping* things from being done. It is true; for Mr. Baldwin knows that the limits of profitable action in Britain are becoming narrower and narrower. The strength of the British Empire is still enormous, but it is an almost wholly defensive strength. He realizes instinctively that almost anything that any-one *does* will only make matters worse. He is the perfect statesman for an empire in decline; he is for ever stopping things. He, in effect, attempts to stop the decline, and if he does not wholly deceive himself into believing that he can do that, he can at any rate, he knows, prevent it being immeasurably accelerated by the foolish actions of others.

When Confucius was asked to describe the activities of the per-fect ruler he replied that such a ruler "would sit gravely upon his throne, and that is all." He was, of course, prescribing for an empire in a completely stable condition; a condition towards which the Chinese Empire has hitherto approximated the most closely. The period of decline during which Mr. Baldwin finds himself in charge of the destinies of the British Empire, does not allow of such perfect immobility in its ruler. But Mr. Baldwin moves as little as he can, and when he does move, it is always to prevent something from being done.

Even caution, however, has its limits. Even after his superb manœuvre in political counter-weighting, Mr. Baldwin finds himself compelled, if not by the pressure of his supporters, then by the real exigencies of the economic situation, to move towards a forward policy. For Mr. Baldwin is no pacifist. He does not suppose that war can be indefinitely averted. He knows, however, that war would be wholly disastrous to the British Empire now, and, that at all costs a respite must be obtained. Mr. J. L. Garvin, on the whole the most far-sighted of the theorists of British imperialism, probably expressed Mr. Baldwin's real views on the matter in a recent article. He was dealing with the Sino-Japanese conflict of 1932 and arguing vehemently against any proposals for interfering with Japan. His headlines explained very vividly why he considered that any active or interventionalist policy on the part of Britain would be disastrous. They were "Keep out of War," "An Issue of Life and Death," "Britain and Sanity." He finished his article with a paragraph, noteworthy for its clarity rather than its discretion. For he made it clear that, although he considered that Britain was in no condition to fight now, yet war must be her "future purpose."

"Meanwhile," he wrote, "and at all costs, the British people must and will keep out of war. Lasting and universal peace is their moral desire. Twenty years' peace is their practical necessity. Carrying one-sided disarmament honestly to a hazardous degree; reducing the Navy to a nucleus; cutting down the Army to a minimum; accepting mildly a preposterous inferiority in air-power; and with a democratic financial system paralysing the old 'sinews of war'—Britain before engaging again in the hideous gamble with human life and blood, must at least take some years to reorganize her whole national system if war is indeed to be the future purpose."

Behind Mr. Garvin's pacific phraseology lies his passionately conceived design for a recovery of British world power. Behind the talk of British "moral desire" for lasting peace, is revealed the British "practical necessity" for twenty years' peace (later reduced to "some years" of peace). Behind the talk of disarmament, ludicrously untrue in the case of the British Navy, which has been "reduced to a nucleus" which costs over £50 million a year and has still the largest fighting force of any Navy in the world, is revealed "the paralysis of the old 'sinews of war.'" And the reason for this paralysis is given: it is because of the heavy price ("the democratic financial system") which has had to be paid to keep the workers quiet. And, at last, we are given almost nakedly the proposal that Britain must take some years to "reorganize her whole national system" (to get the workers well under control) "before engaging again" in the war gamble, "if war is indeed to be the future purpose." Really, Mr. Garvin, these things are thought but not said. Even if Mr. Baldwin was on the point of declaring war upon the whole world, he would not permit himself to talk like that.

At any moment, however, the economic situation of Britain may become so acute that a more rapid drive towards a forward policy than Mr. Baldwin would be willing to lead, may become inevitable. A point of crisis may be reached when wisdom itself may become too costly a luxury for the nation to afford. Statesmanship and caution themselves may come under the economy axe. If this point is reached, Mr. Baldwin's day will be over and the advocates of action will suddenly reappear upon the political stage. Mr. Churchill, Lord Beaverbrook, Mr. Amery, Sir Oswald Mosley, or perhaps other leaders who cannot as yet be discerned, will take over the helm.

Of the leaders whom we have mentioned, the last is something in the nature of a special case. Sir Oswald Mosley has both the advantages and the disadvantages of having become a fully conscious and avowed fascist. He offers to the British capitalist class the reorganization of their dictatorship by way of the creation of a specifically fascist party, as against the method of gradually "fascising" (if we may use such a term) their existing parties. This means, no doubt, that he must await his opportunity until the safer and more congenial method has been tried and failed. Such an opportunity may well sooner or later occur, however, unless the working class has in the meantime succeeded in freeing itself from the helplessness of social democratic illusions. We shall discuss this whole question below. Suffice it here to say that the leaders of the Labour party are at present using all their powers to ensure that the workers should be so powerless, so castrated, that a fascist dictatorship would be the inevitable result of the crisis of the class struggle in Britain. And there would certainly be a fateful justice if the ex-Ministers of the 1929 Labour Government should live to be proscribed by the man whom they so despised when he was their colleague. Sir Oswald Mosley has come to stand for fascism naked and unashamed. But, in this, he differs from the other leaders of the British ruling class by the frankness of his statements, and the extreme brutality of the methods which he already advocates, alone.

We must not, however, forget the real purpose behind the whole drive towards intensified imperial exploitation. Its object is to enable the British capitalists to avoid adopting the advice of their foreign "well-wishers" to reduce the standard of life of every class: to avoid resorting to smaller-scale, less capitalistic, methods of production. The reduction in the national wealth which must at once result from a resort to such a policy, would immediately reduce British power: and a reduction in their power would in turn, immediately reduce the British capitalists' opportunities for acquiring future wealth. A vicious circle would be set up, the operation of which would very quickly transform Britain's position, and reduce her to an unimportant and impoverished state. It is to avoid so dire a consequence that the policy of intensified imperial exploitation will be in the end wholeheartedly adopted. It will be adopted just as soon as it is clear that there is no other way in which the world position of Great Britain can be preserved.

It would be idle to speculate as to the leadership which the British capitalist class will find for their ultimate adventure. But the policy of action when once it has been adopted, will, no doubt, be vigorously pursued. Nor, and here is perhaps the most fateful aspect of the whole situation, will it lack initial success. Just as there is very little realization in Great Britain of the fundamental gravity of the position of British capitalism, so amongst the ruling classes of the other great powers there is an immense exaggeration of the extent of British decline. (Each national capitalist class is as sharp-eyed as any revolutionary to detect the weak spots in any capitalism but its own.)

The immediate position of Great Britain is indeed in one sense very strong. For all that has so far happened is that her difficulties have compelled her to resort for the first time to courses, such as currency depreciation, tariffs, and intensified imperial exploitation, which other states have adopted years ago. It is admittedly a sign of *growing* weakness that Britain has had to adopt these courses. But the fact that she has only now adopted them: that she can still utilize them to the full, is a sign of great *remaining* strength. For these policies are like drugs: their application really does relieve the condition of the patient; but if they are taken for too long a period, or in excessive doses, they themselves begin to produce symptoms worse than the original disease. Thus it is an important immediate advantage to Great Britain that she has only just begun to need them. In the case of tariffs, for example, most other nations must be compared to insomniacs who are so dosed with opiates that their doctors dare give them no more; and if Britain too has now lost the power of natural sleep, she can still safely be given the drug. At the moment of writing, Britain is showing distinct signs of the extent of these reserves of strength. They are all in the last resort, of course, the result of her very long predominance. Britain has unparalleled reserves of fat which she can live on for very much longer than many observers suppose. Her Empire, so long as she can hold it together, will repeatedly give her sudden and remarkable assets. (For example, at the moment of writing, the release of India's hoards of gold is benefiting Great Britain, because of her hold over India.)

All these measures are, however, strange drugs in one respect. For they only do the patient good by harming everyone else. Hence they will—and we are now thinking of their wholehearted application by the advocates of action—both increase Great Britain's strength and exacerbate her relations with the rest of the world. And that is the danger-point. There will arise precisely one of those situations when a country's prestige, when its reputation for strength, that is, deviates from its real strength. And Mr. Hawtrey discovered that this situation was the immediate cause of the outbreak of war. The undeniable fact of Britain's long-term decline over the decades will have blinded the eyes of, say, the French or the American or the Japanese ruling classes to the possibility of a sharp rally in British strength over the years. Such a rally (there are some signs of one at the moment) will have emboldened the British imperialists to seek to attempt some policy—the still more rigorous exclusion of foreign goods from the Empire market, let us say, which would enable them to carry the recovery a step further. The vision of reversing the whole process of decline, of reasserting the old British predominance, will float before their eyes. The same vision—and it will be to them a menace—will occur to Britain's rivals. The application of the new British policy will become a test issue. The estimates of the true relative strength of Britain and her rivals will vary wildly: there will be no objective way of measuring them. Is India to be considered as an asset or a liability? Are the British workers infected with anti-patriotic, communistic ideas or not? Is the American (for America is, of course, the most likely antagonist) fleet really inefficient? Will Japan take the opportunity to attack from the Pacific? A dozen such questions will be answered confidently and with a perfect disregard of the facts (which cannot in any case be ascertained) according to the wishes of the conflicting parties. Solemn British memoranda will prove American impotence: equally solemn American memoranda will prove British decadence. Each side will feel that to yield now will make it incomparably harder to avoid the necessity of yielding on future occasions. Yet to yield on a series of occasions will quickly reduce the party which does so to impotence and poverty. What alternative will there be to war? [1]

We may conclude that, when the advocates of action get power in Britain and begin to apply a policy of intensified imperial exploitation, war either with America, or with a coalition of other powers, or with Russia (which is a special case which we shall notice later) will not be indefinitely postponed.

The reader will have observed that the assumption has been made that the only form of remedial action which is open to the British ruling class is an intensification of imperial exploitation. The British choice, it has been assumed, lies between a forward empire policy and inaction leading to an acquiescence in decline. Now this as-

---

[1] Sir Arthur Salter has no illusions as to the inevitable consequences of an aggressive British policy, although he sees that Britain may well be forced to adopt it. He writes:

"As the world closed against her Great Britain might be forced to supplement such preferential trade with the Dominions and India as may be practicable with a policy of exploiting and closing in her own Self-Governing Empire from the rest of the world.... This line of development would mean an organization of the world into separate units and groups which would soon be dangerous and ultimately fatal to world peace!"

sumption may seem at first sight arbitrary. It will be objected that there are all sorts of "economic reforms" which could benefit the British position. Some of these reforms have already been mentioned, e.g. the introductions of tariffs, "industrial reorganization" (i.e. the formation of monopolies) and the like. And, it will be said, it has already been admitted that these reforms are efficacious, at any rate in the short run. For our purposes we have included such measures under the heading of imperialism, as in fact we are bound to do if we accept the view expressed throughout these pages, that imperialism is monopoly capitalism. Thus these measures must be regarded as indissolubly associated with the imperialist drive. And there really are no other measures of any substantial value in which the British governing class can itself take the initiative.

All other reforms, the suggestions of Mr. Keynes, the elaborate "policies" of the Liberal and Social Democratic parties, fall into one or other of two categories. Those which could theoretically improve the position, depend upon international co-operation; they are, in effect, proposals designed to restore the world free market. We have already suggested the final impracticability of such a policy.[1] Those reforms, on the other hand, which could be undertaken by Great Britain alone, are all based on fallacies (such as those of the currency cranks) as to the nature of capitalism: their effect would either be nil, or they would result in an ordinary inflation of the currency with exchange depreciation, which is a special, and particularly dangerous and drastic, form of protection. Therefore the alternatives which face the British ruling class are intensified aggression abroad combined, of course, with intensified exploitation of the worker at home, and doing nothing.

This conclusion was implied in a speech delivered in the spring of 1932 by Mr. Lloyd George on his return to public life after an illness. Mr. Lloyd George is by far the most vigorous and lively minded, if by no means the wisest, remaining British statesman. He like Mr. Baldwin feels the fearful risks, both of internal class

---

[1] This does not mean that the world market may not recover to some extent from the state of utter disorganization which it has got into at the time of writing (summer 1932). For if it did not, a general collapse of capitalism during this particular slump would ensue: and this we do not, as we have already argued, anticipate. What is suggested, however, is that the world market will be more injured in each slump than it is reconstructed in each boom. There can be nothing more than temporary recovery.

conflict and of external attack, which Britain is incurring by her turn towards intensified imperial exploitation. He shows that he understands perfectly the indissoluble connection between tariffs and war.

"Free trade is not merely a fiscal issue," he said. "Free trade is not merely an economic issue. It is a great human issue. It is the issue of peace on earth and good will among men. Tariffs and armaments grow together side by side. You build one up and the other goes up and up and up until the world is encircled, and within those walls armed men are pacing ready for the destruction of their fellow-creatures. Free trade is a great issue of peace on earth." (The London *Times* report.)

This is all in a sense true. But it is also quite academic. For when Mr. Lloyd George proves that tariffs inevitably bring war, he is not proving that capitalism must avoid tariffs, for that is no longer possible. He is merely proving, what the avowed protectionist Mr. Garvin sees so well, that capitalism must bring war. For Mr. Lloyd George has absolutely no suggestions to make for an alternative form of action to save the position of the British capitalist class. Must we not doubt, then, whether Mr. Lloyd George is fair in accusing British conservative statesmen of thinking too much of revolution?

"Statesmen," he said, "in my judgment to-day have their minds too exclusively fixed upon the dangers of revolution. What they don't understand is that reaction is the surest way round to revolution."

But can the capitalist statesmen of to-day think too often of revolution? For reaction has become absolutely inevitable; and, on Mr. Lloyd George's own showing, reaction can have only one end. Naturally, therefore, the statesmen of to-day must think far more of revolution than did the men of Mr. Lloyd George's generation. The utterances of Mr. Lloyd George have great interest; but they have a wholly historical interest. They serve merely to remind us of what liberalism was like when capitalism could still afford to be liberal.

There is, however, one other type of measure, besides intensified imperial exploitation, which British capitalism can resort to; and this is a direct attack on the standard of life of the workers at home. It goes without saying that such measures are being resorted to, and will be resorted to, to an ever-increasing degree. But such measures of direct attack upon the workers at home can hardly be regarded as efforts to improve the position of British capitalism; they are rather the obvious symptoms of its decline. (And they suffer from the further defect that they are difficult to enforce in a state still nominally democratic.) Thus, we come back to the conclusion that a choice weighted with the destiny of the world faces the British ruling class. Shall they tamely acquiesce in decline for an indefinite period? Or shall they mobilize their still vast resources in order to attempt to retrieve and consolidate their position at the expense of the rest of the world? In the last resort, no doubt, they will have no choice. However much they may try to keep to the path of caution, however tightly Mr. Baldwin may cling to the reality of power, sooner or later they will have to fight. For the moment will come when it will be inescapably clear that they will lose all if they do not; and that every year of postponement prejudices their chances of success.

Capitalism, then, if left undisturbed, must certainly produce the next round of that clash of empires which we saw to be its next stage of development. It would be idle to speculate overmuch on the combatants in the next imperialist war, or on its result. But we cannot but feel fairly clear that the result must be unfavourable to Great Britain.

Moreover, it would be wholly misleading to suggest that capitalism will be allowed to fight out its next imperialist war undisturbed. Already capitalism faces at least four acute and closely interrelated menaces, which are certain to grow, and which will result in a conflict between capitalism, on the one hand, and the workers, on the other, long before capitalism has had time to fight out its hideous inter-imperial tournament for the domination of the world. These factors will surely cause a conflict between classes to break out simultaneously with the next large-scale inter-imperialistic war. Indeed, their growth may easily be the occasion for that outbreak. We may perhaps list these factors, somewhat arbitrarily, as follows:

In the first place, there exist in the world to-day certain acute capitalist "weak spots." There are areas in which for various reasons capitalism has never been able to get a firm hold since the war. One such weak spot consists in the clutter of petty states which now make up Eastern and Central Europe. In these states, the present political settlement, although vital to the dominating European power, France, forbids successful capitalist recovery. A second related but distinct weak spot is Germany. Here again the interests of a particular capitalist power conflict sharply with the interests of capitalism as a whole. And it has been the interest of the particular power, France, in Germany's permanent weakness which has on the whole prevailed over the general interests of the world capitalist class in Germany's recovery. Another type of weak spot is typified by Spain, a country in which capitalism has only now just completed its struggle against feudalism. (Spanish capitalism is certainly coming in towards the end of the third act of the play!)

A second and distinguishable menace is the failure of the great empires to continue to exploit their colonies without causing strong nationalist movements of liberation in which the colonial capitalist class itself leads the revolt. On this question, also, the capitalist classes of the world cannot secure a united front amongst themselves. India affords the stock example of this difficulty. The case of China is somewhat different. China, though to-day definitely a subject nation, is not the colony of any one particular power. She is a colony of capitalism in general. Hence, "a grab for China" is clearly developing in this century just as "the grab for Africa" developed fifty years ago. But conditions in the China of to-day are very different from those of Africa in the nineteenth century. Not only is China to a certain extent a united nation, with the greatest tradition of civilization in the world behind her; not only has she a strong national capitalist movement which does not intend to allow foreign capital to do all the exploiting of the Chinese workers and peasants, but she has, in whole areas of the interior, strongly entrenched Soviets of these workers and peasants who do not intend to let anyone exploit them. The exploitation of China presents a problem which capitalism has not yet been able to solve. For some imperialist power has always been pursuing a policy of conciliation and common interest with the Chinese capitalist class, just when another has decided on a policy of repression.

The third menace is the existence for the first time in modern history of a non-capitalist power. The growing economic strength of the Soviet Union is becoming every day a more serious challenge to capitalism. And in this case, also, it has been impossible to secure sufficient inter-capitalist unity to pursue any common policy towards Russia. One empire has been all for armed intervention, just when another has been out for trade and vice versa. The particular interest has as yet always taken precedence of the general.

Lastly, there is the fact that at the centre of every great capitalist empire there is an increasingly exploited, dissatisfied, insecure and unemployed working class, which is becoming ever more rebelliously inclined. This is the fundamental factor in the whole situation. Indeed, when one envisages the standards on which the workers of the weaker capitalisms of Europe are forced to live, compared to the visible potentialities of production, and the terrifying insecurity of even the comparatively well circumstanced workers of the great dominant empires; when the high standard of working-class education, and the intensity and long duration of working-class self-consciousness, reflected in numerically powerful working-class movements, are all taken into consideration, we are astonished that capitalism has not been decisively challenged already. We shall not, however, be in a position to assess the actual weight of this last menace to capitalism until we have given some consideration to the nature of existing working-class organizations. This we do in the following chapters.

CHAPTER XVI

THE NATURE OF SOCIAL DEMOCRACY

WHAT, then, is the character of existing working-class organizations? What part do the political parties and the trade unions, which the workers have built up, play in the life of the world to-day?

Now there is not the slightest doubt that the political parties, and the trade unions, which are to-day typical of the labour movements of all European countries, grew up as the direct expression of a working-class revolt against capitalism. Nor is there any doubt as to the strength and persistence of that revolt. When the difficulties and perils of working-class organization in the last century are remembered; when the immense and unshaken prestige, enjoyed by the apparently triumphant capitalist class of seventy years ago and their rigorous domination of every aspect of life, religious, educational, economic and social, are envisaged, we cannot fail to realize that it required the strongest determination to build up the organizations comprising the labour movements of the different capitalist states as we know them to-day. The very existence of these extensive organizations proves that during the last seventy years the working class of all Europe has made unnamed sacrifices and unchronicled efforts to create effective instruments for its struggle against capitalism. If, therefore, these instruments of working-class struggle, the Labour or Social Democratic parties, and the official trade unions, have now been perverted in the most astounding way, their creation nevertheless represented a stubborn and unquenched revolt of the workers, which has persisted during the last three-quarters of a century and has affected every state in Europe.

This fact must never be forgotten. Even if these organizations have now become, as we shall show immediately, the principal and essential bulwarks of capitalism; if the machinery of the trade unions and Labour parties has become an apparatus used, not by the workers to oppose the capitalists, but by the capitalists to control the workers; if the leaders of the workers have become the trusted, and petted, servants of all capitalist Governments, yet that does not mean that the workers' revolt against capitalism, which originally created these organizations, was not, and is not, formidable and unappeased.

The history of the words "social democracy" which, on the continent of Europe is the most general term used to describe these long-established workers' organizations, epitomizes the transformation which they have undergone. Until the year 1914 the word meant, to friend and enemy alike, the revolutionary movement of the working class. We find it used in this sense in the earlier works of Lenin, for instance. With the break-up of the Second International, comprising all of the Social Democratic parties of Europe, and the entrance of the most prominent leaders of those parties into the war governments of their respective capitalisms, this sense of the term became obsolete. And Lenin, in 1917, formally repudiated it, recognizing that a new term with which to denote revolutionary working-class parties was necessary. He naturally chose the term communist, since by so doing, he was but returning to the terminology used by Marx and Engels in the 1848 period of intense working-class activity.[1] Hence, social democratic has become an epithet reserved for the official, non-revolutionary, Labour parties into which the old revolutionary working-class movement developed after the war. Needless to say, the term is here used in this new, post-war, sense.

It is only by means of an analysis of the present condition of social democracy that we shall find the solution of the problem which we raised at the end of the last chapter; the problem of how it was that the workers, apparently at once extremely discontented and well organized, did not offer an immediately decisive challenge to the existence of capitalism. This problem becomes all the more striking when we realize that powerful working-class movements, all ostensibly anti-capitalist, have held political power in many of the states of Europe during the past decade. And that all of them have exercised, everywhere, and during the whole period, a very great measure of power.

Indeed, it is not too much to say that Western European politics

[1] It is now being forgotten that the term social democracy ever had a revolutionary meaning. Yet, in 1914, when Lenin heard that the German social democrats had voted war credits, he refused to believe the news for several days.

are to-day dominated by Social Democratic parties. This is the epoch, the heyday of social democracy—at least for Europe. (Russia is beyond this stage of development. America has not reached it.) Now in every country the characteristics of this epoch are the same. Briefly, it may be said that in the epoch of social democracy the workers are in office everywhere and in power nowhere.

Social democracy is the same everywhere because it is the typ_ of working-class organization consistent with a particular phase of economic development. For example, in comparison with the extreme diversity of economic conditions in the rest of the world, the nations of Western Europe are in the same stage of development. Accordingly, we find that to-day the working-class movements, in each of them, are of a very similar character. The social democrats of Germany, the Labour party in Great Britain, the Socialist party in France, the socialists or social democrats of Holland, Sweden, Czecho-Slovakia, and the smaller nations, are each the national expression of an identical political movement. These national movements are linked together by the Labour and Socialist International. This, indeed, is the feeblest of bodies; it hardly pretends to unite its constituent parties. Indeed, these parties make a great virtue of the fact that they are good, patriotic national parties free of all "foreign domination." Hence, their undoubted similarity is not the product of any conscious unity but is the automatic result of their similar origins.

For identical characteristics brand, and an identical destiny awaits, all these movements. Even the minor differences which these national Social Democratic parties do display correspond very closely to the comparatively minor differences in the economies of the national capitalism, with which they co-exist. Thus post-war social democracy could, and did, come to its full flowering in Britain and in Germany alone, for a flexible, large-scale capitalism has, in Britain and in Germany alone, arrived at, and passed, its maturity. The French socialists, on the other hand, bear all the marks of the comparatively small-scale methods of their capitalism: and their days of influence and office will probably be shorter. While in the still more primitive economy of Italy, a young Social Democratic party was hustled off untimely to its grave before ever its hands touched the sweets of office. The character, then, of Social Democratic parties seems to be closely dependent upon the character of the particular national capitalism under which they exist. They do not fully flourish unless their capitalism has come to full maturity.

Thus, even at first sight, Social Democratic parties do not to-day seem to be mainly or altogether the expression of a working-class revolt against capitalism. For if they were, they might be expected to flourish in an inverse ratio to their capitalism. Yet we find in practice that their success appears to vary in direct ratio to that of the capitalism on which they depend.

Admittedly, however, a Social Democratic party needs for its growth something more than a still functioning capitalist system. (America has that, and yet knows no social democracy.) It needs for its growth a capitalism, sufficiently old for the vast majority of its possibilities of development to have been already exhausted: with its arteries so hardened that a working class has developed which has already seen that there is very little hope of any significant number of its members climbing out of their class: a working class, which has begun to *look* outside and beyond capitalism for its possibilities of development. For a long time, however (and in this fact lies the first secret of social democratic power), for just so long indeed, as the national capitalism in question continues to function without sharp, intolerable crises, such a working class will only *look* outside of capitalism. It will never *go* outside of capitalism. Its "fantasy life" alone will become socialistic. Such a working class, living in an old, slowly declining, but still rich capitalism, may for a long time, and to a very complete degree, separate its words and thoughts from its actions. In these conditions the workers may become intolerant of anyone who does not use socialistic phraseology when addressing them. The whole terminology of their politics may become socialist. The affirmation of socialism may become a prerequisite for the politicians who lead them. (Our old friend "the nationalization of the means of production, distribution and exchange" will appear on all party programmes and trade union rule books.) The mildest trade union officials will often be required to breathe ferocities from the platform. A thousand times will the workers' enemies be slain with words. And all the while the real life of such a working class may go on quite as usual, very tamely and quietly, within the limits set for it by capitalism. As the national capitalism in question declines those limits will grow narrower. If only, however, the process is reasonably gradual, nothing will happen. The oratorical socialism of the labour politicians will become more pronounced in nice proportion as they are driven by the exigencies of capitalist decline to make their actions more reactionary. A kind of verbal socialism—a socialism of the hereafter—will be established amongst wide circles of the workers. And such a verbal socialism may actually make them support the more easily the hard, and ever more hard, conditions of capitalism. For verbal socialism, like religion, can in these conditions become the opium of the people. Nor will those workers who have been effectively drugged with the socialism of the hereafter thank anyone (so long as these conditions last) who attempts to dispel the fantasy. (How could it be otherwise? Do we ever thank the man who seeks to wake us from warm dreams to cold reality?)

It is in these economic and psychological circumstances alone that Social Democratic parties flourish. And such have been the condition of Great Britain and the other nations of Western Europe since the war. Accordingly we have had the high noon of the Labour parties —the period of the MacDonalds, the Snowdens, the Hendersons, and, on the trade union side, the Ernest Bevins, the Thomases, the Clyneses, and their precise Continental equivalents. In the post-war decades these men have been dressed in their little brief authority: and undoubtedly they have succeeded in making the capitalists laugh.

Thus, the Social Democratic parties, although they were created to express the workers' revolt against capitalism, have to-day another purpose and character. They have, indeed, many functions, which we shall consider, but their psychological function is to cater to a subjective need of the workers in the developed capitalist countries. They satisfy the workers' need to dream of socialism, whilst remaining tied to capitalism. And they do this with great skill.

Indeed, all things considered, the factor that needs explanation is the brevity and insecurity of the social democrats' periods of office. It was suggested that our period was one which found the representatives of the workers everywhere in office, but nowhere in power. Such a statement is truer to reality than to form. For instance, the period in which the social democrats have held office in Germany since the war is only three or four years out of thirteen. For the whole of the post-war period, however, Germany has been, in fact, dominated by the Social Democratic party. No Government has been able to secure a majority in the Reichstag without its support. And in a far deeper sense, Government, Capitalist Government, that is, would have been quite impossible in Germany, but for the control which the massive social democratic machine has exercised, both industrially and politically, upon the German workers. Only the truly marvellous grip of that machine, based on its close knowledge of the psychological needs of the upper sections of German workers, and its ability to satisfy those needs to perfection, *in fantasy,* could possibly have induced the advanced German masses to suffer *in reality* the unparalleled sacrifices and humiliations which a hard-pressed German capitalism has had to demand of them. Certainly we may say that in the real and deepest sense, German social democracy has been in power ever since the war.

In Britain, the Labour party—social democracy, that is, expressed with an appropriately anglicized accent—has actually held office only for about thirty-five months since 1918. (And that short day is very likely over.) Yet here again it would be a great mistake to underestimate the part which the Labour party has played in post-war politics—to estimate it by the length of its periods of office, or, worse still, by its legislative achievements. For in Britain, too, it is the Labour party which has been the main and necessary support of the existing system—the essential party of the State without which "the King's Government could not have been carried on." And certainly the stupider kind of capitalists have recently shown the Labour party a gross ingratitude to deal it such a blow as they dealt it at the general election of 1931. Such backward representatives of the British ruling class still deplore the existence of the Labour party because they remember the halcyon days of British capitalism, when, even after the granting of the franchise to a large proportion of the workers, no even nominally separate or independent workers' party arose. Certainly they are right in believing that such a state of things, when the two great capitalist parties could themselves command the alternating support of the masses, was, for them, a preferable state of affairs. For it meant that the British workers were so dominated, and so satisfied, by capitalism that they did not look even in fantasy outside and beyond it.

Those were, indeed, the good old days. What, however, these duller elements of the ruling class fail to realize, is that this golden

age can never be regained: that this is not the alternative to the
Labour party. The abler capitalists know perfectly well that the
psychological grip of capitalism upon the majority of the British
workers has in one sense irrevocably slipped. They know that some
separate working-class party must inevitably have arisen as a response to the urgent need of the British workers to dream, at any
rate, of some alleviation of their lot. How altogether felicitous,
therefore, was it that the working-class party which did emerge
turned out to be of the most innocuous character conceivable! Its
socialist phraseology was strongly counterbalanced by the sturdy,
the rigid, conservatism of its actions. What more marvellous mechanism could conceivably have been devised for drawing off into
channels, which led nowhere, those waters of working-class dissatisfaction which, dammed back, might have broken the social
dyke? For consider the result. A very extensive political machine
has been created. Hundreds of competent orators tour the country
with unexampled frequency, expressing, liberating, and thus very
largely dispersing, the anti-capitalist impulses of the workers. Many
thousands of trained trade union officials follow in their footsteps,
gathering the workers into industrial organizations which work in
the very closest touch and co-operation with the employers.

For a Social Democratic party really is a class party, however
much some of its own leaders, in a frenzy of conservatism, may deny
it. If it were not, it could never have arisen, for it is nothing but
the expression of the first independent political activity of the workers breaking loose from liberalism. Moreover, it is a working-class
party because it is predominantly financed, not as all capitalist
parties must be, by the capitalists, but by the trade unions. And,
however reactionary the trade unions may become, however great
an obstacle they are, under corrupt leadership, to the possibility of
working-class advance, they are in their very essence working-class
institutions. Indeed, unless the whole social democratic machine was
in quite a real sense working-class, it would be unable to fulfil its
function. It would be unable, any better than an ordinary Liberal
party, to cater for the increasingly anti-capitalist mood of the workers. The essence of a Social Democratic party is that it does cater
for just these impulses: that its orators use socialist phraseology: that
its street agitators thunder against capitalism as fiercely as any
revolutionary: that its trade union officials preach the opposition of

the interests of employers and employed like so many Marxian scholars.

A strong force of working-class opposition to capitalism is thus collected: a force quite sufficient to make the continuance of the senile capitalisms of Western Europe impossible, if the leaders of social democracy dreamt of using it for such a purpose. But have no fears, Ladies and Gentlemen! It was for very different ends that all this sound and fury was developed. When a Social Democratic Government is returned by the efforts and sacrifices of the workers, the legislative programme which it introduces, turns out to be the most weary, stale, flat and unprofitable liberalism: turns out to have nothing whatever to do with the socialism of the street corner: turns out to be simply an attempt to bluster or cajole a few more concessions from capitalism. It is the same story in the case of the trade unions. For example, after nearly a century of tireless effort, the mass of the British workers were, by the second decade of the twentieth century, mobilized into trade unions. Their power was very great. And at the same moment, the decline of the rate of profits drove the British capitalists to attempt to lower the whole standard of life of the British workers. And then it was seen that the British trade union machine, the creation of which was perhaps the greatest achievement of any working class under capitalism, was being used, not to prevent the attack upon the workers by the only method which it could now be prevented, namely, by the overthrow of capitalism, but to minimize, to deflect and, in 1926, definitely to betray the workers' resistance.

Thus, the secret of political social democracy is to use the appeal and dynamic of revolutionary socialism, but to use it in order to implement a programme of most mediocre liberalism. And the secret of industrial social democracy is to mobilize the industrial strength of the workers, but to mobilize it for trivial and in the end reactionary purposes.

Two very important difficulties arise in the carrying out of the political side of this policy. And it is these difficulties which account for the comparative brevity of the time which Social Democratic parties have actually held office. The first difficulty is the very obvious one that the workers, whose votes have been won, whose enthusiasm has been roused, whose pennies have been collected, by socialist agitation, will surely be bitterly dissatisfied with mildly liberal measures as the only result. And indeed this is a delicate matter. Almost the whole of social democratic "statesmanship" is, in fact, concerned with the turning of this somewhat awkward corner. It is with this question that innumerable "confidential talks" in all the admirably appointed "smoke-rooms" of the legislative assemblies of modern Europe are concerned. You may be sure, for instance, if you see the heads of two or three labour members bowed together over the glasses in the "Members' smoking-room" of the British House of Commons, or still more, perhaps, in the company of a trade union official or two, downstairs in the "Strangers' smoking-room," that the conversation is on this topic. In one form or another the technique of social democracy, either in the political or in the industrial field, is being discussed. In essence, the question is always the same. How is the workers' strong and simple desire for an alleviation of their lot—and this alone is the motive force which has hoisted the social democrats into place—to be transformed, once the social democrats have "arrived," into a dull acceptance of the narrow limits which capitalism imposes on the worker? For, even though the workers may be only slowly awakening to the necessity of revolutionary action, if they wish ever to actualize their dreams of socialism, yet they have always a sound and vigorous impulse towards struggle for immediate improvements, without waiting to consider one way or the other whether these improvements are compatible with the existence of capitalism. The subtle task of the social democratic office holder is to encourage this impulse: for this he must do, for he lives by it. Yet, at the same time, this gold of instinctive working-class revolt must be somehow transmuted into the lead of working-class passivity and subservience. The social democrat is, in fact, a kind of inverted alchemist—for ever labouring at this task.

We must admit, however, that the technique which has been evolved for this delicate and difficult task is marvellously efficient. Thus, in the industrial field, a simple and effective procedure has been invented. For example, a course of events approximating more or less closely to the following procedure is noticeable in nearly all current wage disputes. Let us say that the employers in a given industry come to the conclusion that a certain reduction in wages—say, 10%, is necessary. This decision may or may not be privately conveyed to the leading trade union officials. The employers then demand publicly a 30% reduction. The trade union officials indignantly reject the demand. A campaign of protest is organized. The employers seem inexorable. Lockout notices are posted. Conference after conference is called between "owners" and "men." Each breaks down before the firm refusal of the men's leaders to give way. At the eleventh hour, an outside arbitrator is consulted. Strangely enough, he proposes a 10% reduction. The employers, protesting that it is quite insufficient, accept it "as a patriotic gesture." The men's leaders, equally reluctantly, but "to avoid the suffering of a stoppage," also accept. Mass meetings are summoned in which the trade union officials "courageously" defend their acceptance of the terms, and point out that they have succeeded in avoiding at least two-thirds of the threatened reduction. So long as it is not repeated too often the whole well-staged and exciting drama effectively serves its purpose.

The corresponding device in the political sphere is, no doubt, the heaven-sent possibility of Minority Government. It is doubtful whether without this device a Social Democratic party could ever take office. As soon as it secured a majority, the blank contradiction between its programme and its performance, above all between the whole strain and tenor of its propaganda and the actions it invariably finds itself performing when in office, would be too brutal. Even the simplest voter would be undeceived. And the menace of obtaining a majority has hung oppressively over the heads of Social Democratic parties. The Germans and the French, indeed, have guarded against it almost perfectly by so arranging their electoral systems that it is almost impossible for any one party ever to obtain a clear majority over the others.

The British Labour party is most exposed to this grave risk. And, indeed, in 1929 a clear majority was perilously near. (I recollect the great anxiety which Mr. MacDonald showed just before election day. He kept reassuring himself by saying that he was sure the liberals would do well. He remarked several times that it would be much better *not* to have a majority than to be at the mercy of those labour supporters whom he described as "some of our easy-oozy asses.") However, the "majority danger," as in 1923, was averted. A triumphant minority was secured: the great alibi— "we have never had a majority"— still stood. Nor should the real strength of this alibi be underestimated. For the worker has no

easy means of judging the good faith of his leaders. To anyone
who has had personal contact with labour leaders, the idea that if
another thirty or forty labour members had been elected in 1929,
thus securing a majority, the whole conduct of the Labour Government would have been transformed, is grotesque. It is laughable
to suppose that in that event Mr. MacDonald would have sprung
forward, a British Lenin, and begun the gigantic and hazardous
task of destroying British capitalism and replacing it with a socialist
economy. As a matter of fact, of course, the actions of the 1929
Labour Government were determined, not in the least by the
precise number of Labour supporters who sat in the House of
Commons, but by the objective difficulties of British capitalism:
by the economic crisis with which the Government was confronted, and which finally wrecked it in August, 1931. And this
crisis would not have been charmed away by the presence of another forty trade union officials at Westminster.

None of this, however, was visible to the average British worker
who voted labour. All he knew of Mr. MacDonald was that he
was an imposing gentleman who came down to great Town Hall
meetings and declared that he was in favour of socialism. "So
that's all right," said the worker, "he shall have my vote." True,
there were no signs at all of socialism when Mr. MacDonald,
having got the votes, became Prime Minister. "But, then, he didn't
have a majority. And he always said that you had got to have a
majority before you could begin to bring in socialism. True, the
local 'Reds' say that Mr. MacDonald never meant 'all that about
socialism,' anyhow. But how can one tell that? Anyhow, he never
had a majority, had he?"

The force of this argument for the workers, who, in the nature of things, cannot know the real intentions of their leaders,
cannot be overestimated. Communist propaganda has hurled itself
for these ten years past upon the hitherto impregnable rock of
that great excuse—"Well, they never did have a majority, did
they?" If, therefore, the election of another forty trade union officials
to Parliament would have made no difference at all to the economic
situation with which the Labour Government had to deal, it would
have transformed the political situation. It would have destroyed
the great excuse. The masses, and what is still more important the
rank and file of the organized Labour movement—the N.C.O.s of

the working class—would really have expected a steady advance towards socialism—and when they got "economy" instead, the Labour movement would have been irretrievably damaged within a year. Thus, in the case of a politically advanced nation like Great Britain, it can perhaps be laid down as one of the conditions for the existence of a Social Democratic party that it should never obtain a Parliamentary majority.

Now, the British Labour party has never obtained a majority. Another difficulty has, however, confronted it. It is consequential upon the first. With the aid of a good minority, the workers can often be induced to take liberal performance for socialist promise. But by the time that a Social Democratic party reaches office, the achievement of anything comparable to an ordinary liberal legislative record (a record comparable to that of the Asquith Government before the war, for example) is found to be utterly impossible. We have seen that social democracy never arises till a comparatively late stage in the development of a national-capitalistic system. During the heyday and early afternoon of capitalism, the political stage is inevitably occupied by a Liberal party. During its later phases, such a liberalism does usually grant the main concessions possible under capitalism. Various social insurances—health insurance, workmen's compensation, old age pensions, Trade Boards in sweated industries, and, most important of all, some system of unemployment insurance, are established. Capitalism, while still comparatively vigorous and resilient, can carry these burdens with only verbal protests. At a certain stage in its development, however, the inevitable ossification of capitalism will begin to disillusion the workers and so turn them from liberalism towards the establishment of an, at any rate ostensibly, socialist party. By the time that this new Social Democratic party has grown up and has won its way to office, the decadence of the capitalism in question will have gone a considerable distance.

How inevitably unfortunate, therefore, will be the economic situation which will confront the social democratic ministers when they enter their Government offices. They will be pledged to introduce socialism. Not very many people, however, are really expecting very much of them in that direction. Well sheltered behind a comfortable Parliamentary minority, they feel pretty safe there. But what the workers really are expecting from them are some good substantial social reforms, pensions, insurances, housing subsidies, etc., etc. And no doubt some of the social democratic Ministers genuinely meant to give them such things. But what do they find is the real position? All the really valuable, and easily practicable, concessions have already been granted by previous Liberal Governments. This, in itself, would not perhaps matter very much. Rates of benefit could all, at any rate, be increased. Far worse, however, is to follow. The social democrat Ministers soon discover that the economic basis which alone made possible these social services has been eaten away. There is no question at all, their well-informed permanent officials will conclusively prove to them, of extending and so increasing the cost of these services. Already it is certain they will demonstrate that the chronic unemployment, which is by this time an aging capitalism's chief and intractable disease, is aggravated by the weight of taxation upon entrepreneurs which these insurances, etc., impose. To increase them, and consequently to increase taxation, would be, they teach a socialist Chancellor of the Exchequer to say, "the last straw for industry." On the contrary, the alarmed Ministers will realize, the *real* question with which inexorable economic fact confronts them, is by how much these social services must be cut down. And these iron economic facts, not their previous intentions, nor their possibly sincere benevolence, nor their realization of the urgency of cashing some part of that vast promissory note which they signed at the previous election, must of necessity control their actions once they are in office. This, then, is the second, and by far the graver of the difficulties which confront a Social Democratic party. Pledged to introduce socialism, such a party actually intends to extend liberalism. Yet the very nature of the eonomic circumstances which alone have placed it in power, utterly forbid a programme of even liberal social reform. The decline of capitalism, which is itself the only begetter of social democracy, is thus its grave-digger also. For it hoists the social democrats into office only to impose upon them the repulsive task of taking back from the workers those concessions which had been won under liberalism. The same dilemma always confronts the social democrats. The workers, having been promised socialism, would, no doubt, accept the tangible benefits of liberal social reform as a substitute. They might even, perhaps, be persuaded for a time, at any rate, to accept nothing at all. But how are they to be persuaded to accept, at the hands of their own leaders, the withdrawal of all that they have won by their previous efforts? How can they be persuaded to tolerate, not only the non-fulfilment of every promise, but the loss of nearly every privilege which they have won from previous capitalist Governments? Is this to be the reward for all their efforts in putting the social democrats into office? Here, indeed, is a situation that taxes to the full all the arts of social democratic oratory. And yet, unless they are willing to undertake just this task of "economy," the social democratic Ministers must quit the stage—the very pleasant political stage. For an old capitalism cannot exist without "economy" (that is, the enforced economy of the workers). There is, of course, a third course of action—an alternative either to doing capitalism's dirty work for it, or of quietly quitting the stage: and that is to join in the revolutionary struggle of the workers to overthrow capitalism and to begin to build socialism. That alternative, however, has never been known to occur to a social democratic leader.

CHAPTER XVII

MR. MACDONALD AND THE 1931 CRISIS IN BRITAIN

It is now time to exemplify these general conclusions about the present character of Social Democratic parties. Great Britain has just had an opportunity of observing the practice as well as the theory of social democracy. For the economic crisis which confronted the capitalist world in general, and Great Britain in particular, in the late summer of 1931 found a Social Democratic Government in Whitehall.

During the whole of the two years (June 1929 to August 1931) during which the British social democrats were in office the two difficulties which we have distinguished in the last chapter confronted them. As we anticipated, they were able to guard against the first difficulty—that of reconciling their supporters to the non-introduction of socialistic measures, by an appeal to their minority position. Within six months of their accession to office, however, the second difficulty, namely, that of applying a programme of liberal social reform to a declining capitalism, became apparent. In the autumn of 1929, when the period of relative capitalist stabilization (1924-1929) was at its height, the Labour Cabinet was able to make a move towards the extension of that body of social legislation which Mr. Asquith's pre-war Government had created, and which successive Liberal and Conservative Governments had ever since extended. The Labour Cabinet extended, quite materially, their conservative predecessor's widows' pensions scheme. But this was their final achievement; for this was the very last sop which British capitalism was able to throw to the workers.

By January 1930, the economic crisis was already deepening with every week. From that moment until the last panic-stricken meetings of the Labour Cabinet in August, 1931, there was no further question of giving the workers anything. On the contrary, the question of how much had to be taken away from them began to be asked with ever-growing insistence. And when it was no longer possible to delay giving the answer for even another week, the Labour Government simply broke up. For a majority of its members took the view that while it was easy to give the workers social reforms instead of socialism; while it was even possible to arrest the progress in social reform achieved by all previous capitalist Governments, and to give the workers nothing at all, yet it was not possible for a Labour Government to take back from the workers what the capitalists had already given them.

A special circumstance makes the fall of the British Labour Government particularly apposite for the purposes of our enquiry. For different social democratic leaders chose different alternatives. Mr. MacDonald, Mr. Snowden (as he then was) and Mr. Thomas preferred to remain upon the stage of action and to carry through the attack upon the workers. Mr. Henderson and the rest of the Labour party preferred to leave the stage, handing over the Government of the country to the liberals and conservatives. We had the instructive spectacle of both the possible alternatives open to a strictly non-revolutionary Social Democratic party, in office in a period of capitalist decline (as it always must be), being taken simultaneously. Connoisseurs in political ignominy may estimate the relative merits of the two courses.

We may content ourselves with observing certain of the characteristics which the leaders of British social democracy have exhibited, both in the 1931 crisis and in the earlier history of the Labour party. For there is nothing accidental about the way in which these men have behaved. Just as the strong hands of economic necessity have moulded the Labour party itself, so that party has gradually, by a process of political natural selection, produced the types necessary to play the parts that had to be played. To suppose that things could have been otherwise, "if only MacDonald had been firmer, if Snowden had read an economist later than Jevons, if Henderson had ever guessed that there were worlds undreamt of in annual conference resolutions," is vulgarly to misread history. If Mr. MacDonald, Mr. Snowden, Mr. Henderson and the other Ministers had been different in character, then they would not have come to the leadership of the British labour movement, and the men who would have played their parts would have borne other names. That is all. This very element of inevitability is, however, the one factor which lends interest to the characters and actions of these men. For as these were the men which the Labour party had to produce as its leaders, we can throw light on the character of the party from the character of the men.

Mr. MacDonald is certainly the most interesting of them. Originally he must have been a gifted man: even to-day Mr. MacDonald has, within certain strict limits, within, in fact, Parliamentary limits, qualities which make him a very valuable servant of British capitalism. It was submitted above that the main task of social democracy is to undertake a kind of pernicious alchemy, whereby the gold of the workers' revolt against their conditions of life under capitalism is changed into the lead of a timid and unprofitable liberalism. It is appropriate, therefore, that the first leader of British social democracy should have, both in his appearance, and in his utterances, more than a little of the alchemist or wizard about him. When Mr. MacDonald rises to his feet he does not so much speak as weave a spell. No doubt, some of his female biographers have already noted this. They may not, however, have defined the nature of the incantation. Yet of recent years, at any rate, there can be no doubt about it: the spell has had one undeniable purpose, and that is to bemuse its hearers so that they shall have no idea whatever of the nature of the issues under discussion. And for that purpose the spell is unrivalled. Here, for example, is how Mr. MacDonald recently enchanted his miner constituents on the subject of the 1930 Coal Mines Act. He spoke at Seaham Harbour on January 8th, 1931 (*The Times report*). He is complaining that the coal owners are not working the Act in a proper manner.

"I say that if they continue in that attitude, they are setting an example which, if you should follow it when it suits you, knocks them completely out of court, if they object to that action in your power."

There indeed is a clarion call to democracy! Later on in the same speech, Mr. MacDonald makes a defence of the whole "gradualistic" position. He is still complaining of the owners' refusal to work the Coal Mines Act.

"Supposing it had been the miners; supposing the Tory party had passed an Act, a reactionary class Bill, which you did not like and which you objected to, at any rate in some of its details."

How perfectly characteristic is that last qualifying clause—"at any rate in some of its details"! The orator was becoming quite warm about a hypothetical "reactionary class Bill"; and then the caution of the statesman intervened. The miners, it seems, would only object—since they were good social democrats—to a "reactionary class Bill," *"in some of its details."* To do more would surely be unwise, impolitic, extreme, savouring of Moscow and direct action. Mr. MacDonald, moreover, goes on to tell the workers why they must always obey the laws.

> "I believe that if laws are passed they ought to be worked. I believe that when a law is passed, if it is bad and unjust, by its very working, it will kill itself, and by being killed in that way it contrives more to the side of enlightened intelligence from which future laws that are good will come."

Here, then, is the key to progress discovered at last. Simply remain quiet. Do not fuss, do not fume, above all, do not agitate. If laws are good—well then, what more do you ask? If they are bad, then you have it on the Prime Minister's authority that they will "kill themselves" and so "contrive more to the side of enlightened intelligence from which future laws that are good will come." So really, you see, bad laws are even better than good, because they "contrive," phœnix-like from their ashes, still better ones.

Mr. MacDonald goes on to contrast this correct attitude to the State and its laws with that other attitude of which the Durham miners may, he fears, have heard.

> "By that attitude to the State and to the authority of the State" (i.e. an attitude of passive obedience) "enlightened men and an enlightened community will gain far more progress than by a fussy challenging of the law, which upsets the whole conception of ordered evolution and creates a condition of mind which will accept nothing and imagines that the will of a few individuals is of more importance than public opinion itself."

Surely of all the innumerable indictments of the revolutionary case, which every social democratic leader is eternally making, this is the strangest? We are very familiar with hearing Lenin's methods called "brutal," "barbaric," "infamous," "hellish," or even, worst crime of all, "un-British." But to hear them stigmatized as "fussy"—that, indeed, was unexpected!

What are we to make of this extraordinary verbiage—verbiage absolutely typical of Mr. MacDonald's speeches whenever he touches general conceptions at all? It would be a complete mistake to think that his incomprehensibility is accidental: to suppose that Mr. MacDonald cannot speak with normal clarity. The truth is that Mr. MacDonald has grasped, probably instinctively, that the real purpose of social democracy is obfuscation: that its essential act of political alchemy cannot be performed except behind the most opaque smoke-screen. Hence the function of its leader is to blur and confuse everything to the utmost possible extent. The real issues involved, the hard facts of every question, the actual play of interests, must be hidden in every possible way. Perhaps Mr. MacDonald himself could hardly tell you why he is so determined not to be understood. And yet the reason is obvious. When Mr. MacDonald tries to conceal everything behind his great fog of words, he is really trying to conceal one thing alone, and that one thing is the steadily growing and inescapable clash of class interest. That is the ruinous truth which must be hidden at all costs. For, if it is not hidden, will it not one day "upset the whole conception of ordered evolution"? And one must not upset Mr. MacDonald's conceptions.

And so the whole art of statesmanship is seen by Mr. MacDonald to consist, for the social democrat, in postponement, in evasion, and, above all, in obfuscation. One would not even like to say without qualification (for Mr. MacDonald's methods are infectious) that he has abandoned socialism. It is rather that he has emptied the concept of every shred of meaning. It is quite possible that Mr. MacDonald still thinks that capitalism will slowly consolidate into great corporations, over which the authority of the State may slowly extend; that the League of Nations will gradually assume beneficent regulative functions between such great national and international corporations; that taxation will tend towards a perceptible levelling out of the very great fortunes, etc., etc., etc. He probably has little time or inclination to think of the future of society at all; but if he does occasionally give it a thought, he probably supposes that it will develop along some such lines as these. And this, no doubt, is precisely what Mr.

Baldwin hopes for too: it is to make this possible that he trips and traps Lord Beaverbrook. All but the most blind of the capitalist leaders realise the necessity for development along these lines if capitalism is to survive. (And even the most far-sighted of them try to blind themselves to the fact that it is developing in a very different direction.) There is not the slightest difference of opinion here. The only dividing line in modern politics is between those who believe that capitalism can solve its problems and develop along these lines, and those who believe that its difficulties are insurmountable without demanding of the workers the sacrifice of their liberties, their livelihoods, and, sooner or later, their lives in war. And, of course, Mr. MacDonald is ten miles on the capitalist side of this line. Indeed, the British social democrats in general show a quite touching faith in the infallibility of capitalism—a faith not shared at all by the more shrewd and clear-sighted capitalists themselves. These younger capitalists are quite able to see the extreme difficulty of their position; but they are determined to make one more attempt to save the system which has done so much for them. And they realise that they have at least one great asset: and that is the childlike and untroubled faith in capitalism of the British socialists.

During the period of office of the Labour Government, Mr. MacDonald and his friends had almost daily to do things which violated the most elementary of those socialist principles which they had spent their lives in advocating. Naturally, the subjective effect on their own personalities was not beneficial. No great damage to the "psyche" was done in the case of a really crude type such as Mr. Thomas. Mr. Thomas has probably never been insincere in his life—for how can one be insincere when one has absolutely no beliefs of any kinds? But on a considerably more developed organism such as Mr. MacDonald, the constant violation of every principle must have—and, indeed, obviously has had—a gradually disintegrating effect. It is true that Mr. MacDonald's socialism was never of a very powerful or, as one would expect, of a very clearly defined type. A perusal of one of his chief theoretical works, *Socialism, Critical and Constructive,* will show that.[1] Still there is no particular reason to suppose that Mr.

[1] Mr. MacDonald tells us that British socialism derives from Godwin rather than from Marx. So far as his own views are concerned he is no doubt quite right.

MacDonald did not quite sincerely believe in the pleasant and, unfortunately, quite fallacious set of maxims which constituted his political philosophy. At any rate, they were all he had, and until the cold touch of reality ·shattered them for ever, they served him very well for the purposes of the platform.

Now, however, that he has had to abandon them all, since he violates every one of them every day, he is left utterly naked of any principle, of any sense of values at all. The social democrat who has found that real life compels him to do the exact opposite of all he has ever thought or said, is in much the same position as the Christian who has lost his faith. Neither has any touchstone been left with which to try whether one thing is better or worse than another; neither has any sense of purpose or direction by which to guide his actions. Both become completely opportunist, in the fullest sense of the word, carrying on from day to day along the line of least resistance, mere corks bobbing on the stormy seas of politics, responsive to every wave and current. The ordinary capitalist politician often has some more or less vague set of general principles to guide him, principles which in practice all boil down to maxims for the better preservation of the system of society which has done him so well, but which are well disguised by religious or patriotic formulæ. He is scarcely ever quite so psychologically naked as is the evolutionary socialist who has allowed himself to be stripped by the ruthless fingers of reality. It is this terrible lack of any vestige of social purpose—this lack of any sense of direction at all—which has at length produced in Mr. MacDonald those ultimate and least estimable signs of decay.

The pathos of his surrender to London Society; his meandering reminiscences of visits to "the great"; his feeble little attempts to play the role of "the gentleman connoisseur"; his visits to Christie's; his Jacobean bedsteads; his interminable little gossipings over the tea-cups with the hostesses, whom he considers to be the great ladies whom he had so often dreamt of in the days of his poverty—all this makes but a gloomy, trivial, and, above all, philistine end to the career of a once gifted man.

And naturally, if insensibly, Mr. MacDonald's opinions have accommodated themselves to his life. The "dole" and all the other *bêtes noires* of the drawing-room have become his *bêtes noires* also. After all, as he himself has discovered that his socialism is but a dream, is it not natural for him to deplore what in truth are the chief burdens upon capitalism? As for his political life—well, "the King's Government must be carried on"—and who is so unquestionably cast for the role of first Minister as this leonine, white-haired, superbly handsome man? How clearly every moment of his Downing Street days does Mr. MacDonald see himself as Prime Minister. He never misses a moment of his own performance: "He sits attentive to his own applause." Sometimes, perhaps, he is inclined to doubt if the whole nation is equally attentive. At such moments the anxious look of an actor, when he asks you whether you have seen his new play, crosses Mr. MacDonald's face. Mr. MacDonald has become, since, having no social purpose left, he had nothing better to do, an actor—and that type of actor which the cruel French call a *"m'as tu vu?"* "Have you seen me as the Prime Minister?—My greatest role, I assure you," Mr. MacDonald is anxiously asking the nation. Yes, we have seen him.[1]

And very likely we shall see a great deal more of him. For Mr. MacDonald has got into the habit of saving the country. He has saved it from the Labour party's extravagance. If Mr. Baldwin fails in the end to restrain the advocates of action, Mr. MacDonald will very likely feel constrained to save it again. He may yet emerge as the leader of a "great centre party, sane yet progressive, including all that is best in the traditions of liberalism and labour, appealing to all sections of the community, to rich and to poor alike: to the duke in his palace and to the crofter in his cot, seeking once more to build a new Jerusalem in England's green and pleasant land"—why, his future speeches simply write themselves!

The crisis of August 1931, which so exposed British social democracy, did Mr. MacDonald a very great service. It relieved him, for example, of the necessity of making statements so preposterously at variance with all his opinions as this one, which

---

[1] Leading actors and actresses when they appear under the management of one theatrical entrepreneur, while under contract with another, often have printed after their names on the programme: "Presented by C. B. Cochran, by arrangement with Basil Dean"—or whoever they have contracts with. It would express some of the realities of the situation if there appeared after Mr. MacDonald's name on the order paper of the House of Commons, "Presented by Stanley Baldwin, by arrangement with the Labour party."

he made in the Scottish journal *Forward* no longer ago than October 8th, 1930. "...the capitalist system has crashed in England, Europe and America. This system has crashed because it was inevitable. There is only one means of saving humanity and that is socialism." The crisis has made him in fact, as well as in fancy, an ordinary capitalist politician. At long last he has been freed from what must have become, at any rate, an arduous, if not a distasteful, life of pretence. He is now able to stop pretending to be anything but a sensible-minded, moderate conservative. His speeches and writings have improved: they have become quite comprehensible. He now tells us what he really thinks. And we discover that he thinks exactly what the average occupant of, say, a first-class carriage in a suburban train, travelling up to business, thinks too.

The crisis did the same service to Mr. Thomas and Mr. Snowden. It was evident from their speeches that all three of them had shaken off a very considerable burden. After all, few men—few politicians even—enjoy perpetual dissimulation for its own sake. Besides, there was a very considerable felicity in sitting in a Cabinet composed of such undeniably genuine English gentlemen and conservatives as Mr. Baldwin, Sir Samuel Hoare, or Sir Philip Cunliffe-Lister. Surely, however, Mr. Baldwin was a little cruel in telling the House of Commons, on the very first day that the new National Government appeared in public, that the situation reminded him of an old illustration from *Punch,* drawn by the famous artist Leach. Leach drew a picture of fox-hunting in which the little hairdresser rides up to the duke at the meet and says, "What I like about 'unting, your grace, is that it brings together people who might never 'ave met hin any other way." It was not, however, any of the promoted social democrats, but Sir Herbert Samuel who noticed the remark and, looking a little sharply at Mr. Baldwin, his neighbour on the Treasury bench, told the House that in the interests of the nation he was quite willing to play hairdresser to Mr. Baldwin's duke.

To the other social democratic leaders, Mr. Henderson, Mr. Clynes, the late Mr. William Graham, and the rest, the August 1931 crisis was in one sense less kind. Far from being able to drop their burden of conscious, or unconscious, dissimulation, they had to redouble their efforts. Having consented to nine-tenths of the attacks on the workers effected by the National Government, they had to appear as stern and unbending class-warriors over the remaining tenth. Having for two years taken not a single step towards introducing socialism, and having done for that matter very little towards salvaging capitalism, they now had to step forth as wizards of finance who could have solved the crisis (had they not inadvertently resigned) in a twinkling, without the slightest sacrifice, or, indeed, inconvenience, to any-one, whether worker or capitalist. All these tasks, however, were very cheerfully undertaken by the social democratic leaders. Indeed, they found them not in the least embarrassing. For they were conscious of being once more in the classic social democratic position. They were verbally opposing the unpalatable necessities of capitalism, without having to suggest any alternative of their own. Indeed, they never felt more optimistic: there was only one cloud in the sky—and that was one which they were used to: there was the menace of a majority. It was possible that they might win the ensuing election—and then! However, that was only a possibility, so why worry about it? (As it turned out, there was not the slightest reason to worry about it.) Sufficient unto the moment was the fact that they were once more free from the horror of actually facing the real economic facts of 1931, free to talk, to bluster, to deceive—to lead the workers to another Labour Government and to another resignation.

Besides, as the late Mr. Graham, with commendable frank-ness, pointed out in the *Daily Herald,* the workers were free to forget their leaders' record during the two years of office. Above all, they were themselves free to forget both the Labour Gov-ernment and the crisis which had ended it: free to ignore every lesson to be learnt from the farce of their office and the ignominy of their fall: free to go back exactly as if nothing had happened, to the repetition of the old herd-cries, to the old pretences, and the old deceptions. They were determined to show that they had learnt absolutely nothing from what had happened to them. (Mr. Clynes, for example, was at pains to point out that he would not oppose the National Government from "a narrow manual worker's point of view.") For the only lesson which they could have learnt was the lesson that social democratic gradualism was bankrupt. And where would they have been then?

The most gifted of their younger supporters did, it is true, achieve a brilliant analysis of the situation. He showed that, whether the crisis was regarded as a "bankers' plot" or as a genuine crisis in capitalism, in either case it entirely destroyed the philosophy of gradualism upon which the Labour Party was based. His argument cannot be better put, and deserves quotation. Writing immediately after the August 1931 crisis, he said:

"In the first place, of course, it is necessary to agree upon what has occurred. The view appears to be held that the Labour Government was destroyed by a 'Bankers' Ramp.' In the language of a member of the late Administration, 'The 1924 Labour Government was destroyed by a Red Letter; the last was ended by a Bankers' Order.' It is an astonishing charge to find in the mouths of those committed to gradualism. If a weak and comparatively innocuous Minority Government can be broken by a conspiracy of finance capitalists, what hope is there for a Majority Government, which really threatens the bankers' privileges? If capitalism is in such a state of organized self-consciousness that it can conspire against a Government and bring it down by moving its international financial forces against it, what hope is there for a gradual and peaceful expropriation of the bankers?

"But, it may be urged, they would then have to deal with a strong Government backed by a majority in the House of Commons, which would be a different proposition. What would the 'strong' Government do, committed, as it would be, to peacefulness and gradualism? Let us remember that the conspiracy takes the form of an acute economic crisis induced by certain financial steps, taken in the ordinary course of business, by persons, most of them beyond the reach and control of the Government. In addition, it must be remembered that the new crisis would be superimposed upon an already existing one, for it is reasonably certain that there will never be another Labour Government in England except in conditions of economic crisis and consequent mass unrest. The ascension of the Labour Government, charged with menace to the whole capitalist interest, will augment this condition, and the Minority Government will find itself faced with another 'National Emergency.'

"What will it do? Drop its gradualism and tackle the emer-

gency on socialist lines? Or drop its socialism in the hope of reassuring private enterprise in order to get a breathing-space? It
will find itself hesitating between these two opposite courses.
On the one hand, the state of the country will demand prompt,
vigorous, and revolutionary measures. On the other hand, it will
bring to the emergency a mandate for conventional Parliamentary
legislation, a working class fed on pap, and a Parliamentary party
totally unprepared either theoretically or practically to deal with
the crisis. A Majority Labour Government in such a situation
would do nothing effective, but would pause irresolutely between
the two alternatives, until either fascist power would accomplish
a *coup d'état* or a new National Government would be formed
on the ruins of the old, something on the lines of what we have
just seen.

"Therefore, it would seem that, even if one takes the view that
the end of the Labour Government was not necessitated by the
needs of private enterprise, but was destroyed by finance seeking to
profit itself, the policy of the party needs to be drastically over-
hauled.

"Having stated its charge against the banking interest, the
Labour party goes on to say that the crisis could have been met
without resorting to the measures which resulted in the end of
the Labour Government. They assert that the Budget should be
balanced, but that this could be done without attacking wage
standards, or the social services. And yet at the same time, they
claim, they could still have stopped the run on sterling.

"In short, they hold that capitalism could have saved itself
without attacking the workers. This involves the assumption that
capitalism can be carried on more efficiently by socialists than by
capitalists: that the sacrifices demanded of the workers are the
result, not of the needs of private enterprise, but of its stupidity.
This, of course, is quite consistent with gradualism, which requires that private enterprise shall continue reasonably successful
whilst it is being slowly and painlessly eliminated.

"The difficulty about accepting this pleasant and convenient
view is that there does not appear to be the slightest evidence to
justify it. Apart from the growing mechanistic friction of private
enterprise, there are profound psychological reasons why the Labour
party will never be allowed to rationalize capitalism. It must never

be forgotten that the mainspring of capitalist production is the individual investor. Whatever tends to make him nervous and apprehensive of the fate of a possible investment causes him to hold tight to that liquid capital, the release of which is essential to the maintenance and expansion of fixed capital. We may rail against him, but whilst we allow him to be the prime motivator of the productive process the sensitiveness of his psychology is always a factor to be reckoned with. It is just this psychology that a Labour party, climbing to power in circumstances of economic difficulty, not only cannot reassure, but must of necessity offend. In opposition, the Labour party is compelled, by the nature of the class struggle, to take up an alignment which hamstrings it when in office. A party climbing to power by articulating the demands of the dispossessed must always wear a predatory visage to the property-owning class. Thus in a society involved in the throes of an ever more heavily waged class struggle, the Labour party must wear the face of the implacable revolutionary, although all the time its heart is tender with the promise of peaceful gradualism. It knows that the limited vision of the workers will behold only its outward appearance, but it hopes that the gods of private enterprise will look upon its heart.

"In either case one must be deceived. To satisfy the workers, the Labour party must fulfil the threat of its face, and so destroy the political conditions necessary to economic gradualism. To calm the fears of private enterprise, it must betray its promise to the workers, and so lose their support. Once again the only result will be political vacillation and economic catastrophe. There will be another crisis in the party. Some of its leaders will take the heroic course, and in obedience to the call of a lofty patriotism will rally to the help of the nation. More in sorrow than in anger with this democracy, which cannot wait the far-off interest of tears, they will cut themselves off from the sumptuous ease and lotus-eating of the workers and condemn themselves to the deserts of London society, and the company of Spartan, ascetic bankers.

"Others of the leaders, thus made powerless, will cry with a loud voice, inviting all men to behold them, to bear witness to their self-abnegation in refusing office and their heroism in coming to the help of the workers in this time of need. The political arena will be thick with heroes. The poor, bewildered worker will be asked to regard as heroes those leaders who have left him and those who remain. Both, he will be told, obeyed some lofty and austere sense of duty, far beyond the limited region of class loyalties. The position was put with commendable, if unconscious, clarity by a member of the recent Labour Government. 'In refusing to join the National Government,' he said, 'Mr. Henderson had saved the soul of the Labour party, and Mr. MacDonald, in forming the National Government, had saved the nation.'

"Thus is the fundamental and fatal contradiction of the Labour party exemplified in the mouth of one of its most illustrious leaders."

Unfortunately, however, the writer of this analysis had to present it, since he remained one of their supporters, in the form of an appeal for reformation to his old leaders. It fell on deaf ears. How could it have been otherwise? To have accepted it would have meant a complete retreat from the position which they had held for their whole political lives. And social democratic leaders never make retreats of this sort. For it is an interesting fact that your MacDonalds, Snowdens, and Hendersons wear two very different faces, the one presented towards the capitalists, the other towards the workers. Their whole bearing, their attitude of mind, and, above all, their actions when they are dealing with the capitalists are most pliable: nothing could be softer, more mobile, more accommodating. But when they come to deal with the workers it is a very different story. Mr. Henderson has shown genuine determination and vigour in expelling and excluding all revolutionary elements from the Labour party. Mr. Clynes, Mr. Bevin, and the other trade union leaders have been implacable in purging their organizations of members who might give them trouble. Nor could (or did) the most rigorous advocate of economy complain that the burdens which Mr. Snowden placed upon the workers and the unemployed, both in direct "cuts" and in taxation, were inadequate. On the contrary, his measures brought the whole Tory party to its feet cheering in the House of Commons, and won the unanimous praise of the Press. (As the political correspondent of the *Evening Standard* admiringly put it: "It required courage to tax the beer, the tobacco, and the entertainments of the poor. But the Chancellor never faltered.") Nor will any of the leaders of the Labour party, on whichever side of the House they may find it convenient to sit, ever falter before the expostulations of their supporters, however cogent, so long as they know that in the end the expostulator will remain a supporter. "The war and fortune's sons," they will "march indefatigably on," so long as life is in them, to ever new defeats, surrenders, deceptions and betrayals.

CHAPTER XVIII

THE FUTURE OF SOCIAL DEMOCRACY

THE preceding chapters may be thought to have taken a somewhat unfavourable view of social democracy. It must be admitted, however, that if the criterion of judgment be the carrying on of a society upon the capitalist basis, then there is a great deal to be said in favour of social democracy.

It was suggested in Chapter XIII, that the workers inevitably appear, at a certain stage in capitalist development, as an independent force upon the political scene. They do so in order to fulfil two purposes. First, they wish to satisfy in fantasy their dream of something better than capitalism: to burn, but only in effigy, those class enemies who prevent their dream from coming true. This is the psychological basis of social democracy. Secondly, and this is a far more important consideration, the workers quite realistically desire, not to end capitalism, but to modify it; to pad it in the hope that it can be made more tolerable to live with; to establish breakwaters and dams against the flood tides of uncontrollable private profit-making, to set downward limits to wages, upward limits to hours, to establish insurances against accident, ill health, unemployment, and old age. And this is the practical trade union basis of social democracy.

Now let no one be so foolish as to deny that so long as capitalism continues, such trade union politics are of great importance. The capitalist leaders are often very ignorant of the workers' needs, and stupidly unwilling to make even those concessions which can perfectly well be afforded. Indeed, in the heyday of capitalism, and up to a certain strict limit, such concessions, no doubt actually do, as the advanced liberals allege, benefit capitalism. For it does not really pay the capitalists, while they are still genuinely prosperous, to pay, house, and work their employees as disgustingly as they usually do, if they are not subjected to strong trade union pressure. Hence, the concessions that will be won by such trade union politics, suitably ornamented with social democratic trimmings, will be real and substantial enough to occupy the gradually awakening political consciousness of the workers for some years. The rise of social democracy does draw the workers into politics. By erecting the umbrella of the social services over their heads, it does do something for them. This, however, is a strictly conservative function. By making capitalism comparatively tolerable for the workers, by occupying their energies in so doing, social democracy and "reformist" trade unionism can sometimes prevent a head-on class conflict for several decades. Are we to regard this as to the credit or debit of the social democratic account? We must do neither: we must rather recognize that in the determinism of history it was inevitable that such parties should arise and flourish in the countries of the comparatively successful and flexible capitalisms of Western Europe. For in Western Europe very considerable sections of the population did undoubtedly obtain some of the crumbs of capitalist civilization. The whole lower middle class, and, in the richest countries such as Great Britain, a definite category of skilled workers—"the Labour aristocracy"—arose, the members of which were quite unwilling to admit that capitalism was something alien to them, from which they received nothing. The limits which capitalism, even in its heyday, set to their lives were indeed narrow enough. Men, however, are as yet content with very little.

For these classes, social democracy and trade unionism did, no doubt, obtain something. That something was very small compared to what contemporary technique could have given them in a socialist society. But to them it seemed much, for they compared it with the frightful destitution and insecurity which they had known before. Moreover, their trade unions and their "Labour" parties gave them, besides these material advantages, the feeling that they possessed some voice and weight in national life. Western European civilization, even in its best decades, was certainly no fairy godmother to the workers. Yet they did not feel wholly excluded from the national life in the way in which, for example, the Russian workers and peasants were excluded from everything desirable in Russia. And that they were not so excluded was very largely the work of social democracy. It would be vulgar to attempt to evaluate this work as either good or bad; it was a work which, owing to the automatic development of capitalism, it was inevitable that a body of men and women should arise to undertake. But it is a work which has no relevance to the present situation of the working class.

It is easy, in retrospect, to see what were the limits of this function of social democracy. We said that social democratic and trade union politics held an umbrella over the heads of the workers, both by setting limits to their wages and hours, and by obtaining social insurances for them. But it was a watertight umbrella only for so long as two conditions were fulfilled: for so long as capitalism was prosperous; and for so long as the social democrats did not get too much, did not succeed in raising wages very much, in greatly shortening hours, or in obtaining very extensive social services. For the instant that capitalism ceased to be prosperous, the instant that the economic burdens on it of minimum wages, maximum hours, and expensive social services, passed a certain point, an enormous rent appeared in the umbrella. And that rent was unemployment.

In other words, it became clear that capitalism sets a very strict limit above which it is economically impossible to raise the workers' standard of life. If wages and social services are pushed up beyond this limit, chronic unemployment is created and the workers as a whole secure no gain. A moment's consideration shows why this must be so. The first effect is, of course, to increase costs of production in the particular country in which social democratic pressure is at a maximum. Thus, the competitive power of the industry of such a country in the world market is diminished, new capital investment is discouraged at home, and encouraged abroad. Consequently in the country affected savings exceed home investment and unemployment results, for the reasons which we analysed in some detail in Chapter VI. Moreover, even if we neglect such disequilibria as between state and state, the attempt indefinitely to raise working-class standards within capitalism must fail. For the social democrats do nothing to remedy the chaos and anarchy of economic life under capitalism. They take no steps to replace the will of the private investor and entrepreneur, to continue old enterprises and to start new ones. Yet this "will to invest" is the motive force which alone makes the wheels of capitalism to turn. The burden of the concessions to the workers, and the fear of further burdens, sensibly decreases that expectation of profit which alone under capitalism makes the entrepreneur *entreprendre*. Thus, other things being equal, each social democratic advance in social services is bound to slow down the revolutions of the whole capitalist machine, by weakening the force of its mainspring: since that mainspring is nothing else than the expectation of profit in the mind of the investor.[1]

The specifically socialist side of a social democrat's creed always remains, as we have seen, purely verbal. For the reduction of the existing economic anarchy to method and order, and the replacement of the private expectation of profit, by a social will to produce, expressed by a Government which itself establishes agencies of production and distribution, all involve the overthrow of the ruling class. They involve also some form of working-class dictatorship during the years of transition. And these things are not dreamt of in a social democratic philosophy. Since they will not face these hard implications of struggle, the social democrats can take no steps in the direction of the organization of social production. They merely oppose (though not very vigorously) the chaos of capitalism with demands for concessions for the working class. In the case of a national capitalism, with as vast an accumulation of fat to live on as has the British, they may have quite a long innings during which real concessions are won. But by just so much as their pressure on capitalism grows, the whole economic machine will begin to run more and more slowly.

As we saw in Chapter VII, the interferences of trade unionism and of the social services (above all, of unemployment insurance) with the freedom of the labour market, now make it impossible for capitalism to recover from its periodic crises. An extraordinary position of Class Stalemate may be sometimes reached. On the one hand social democratic propaganda has taught the workers to demand concessions from the capitalists: on the other

---

[1] It would be interesting if an estimate could be made of the absolute minimum rate of average profit—independent of the factor of competition between the industries of different states—which would suffice to maintain accumulation and so the output of fixed capital goods. For it is surely the case that if the average rates of profit and interest (which depend, of course, in the last resort on the rate of exploitation) sank below a certain minimum, a process of disaccumulation would set in. Property-owners instead of exchanging lump-sums for claims to annual payments would exchange claims for annual payments for lump-sums.

hand, social democratic practice demonstrates to them that they must never attempt to overthrow the capitalists. The result is the condition of stalemate which, for example, tended to immobilize British political and economic life from 1921 to 1931. In such a period the actual physical consequences of the even balance of class forces can be seen. In such places as the Lancashire cotton towns, capitalism had been just about brought to a dead stop: in some towns every single mill was shut. They stood like grim, tremendous, and inexplicable monuments of some other age. At the same time, no effort at all had been made to overthrow capitalism and begin any other system of production.

Meanwhile, the very factors which were largely responsible for the paralysis of capitalist production were maintaining the workers sufficiently well to take any desperation out of their politics. But such a situation can never last. It is always, in fact, ended in the same way: the social democrats are hurriedly bundled out of office and the capitalists take up again the initiative of government. They begin the task of throwing back on to the workers the burdens which are causing the paralysis of capitalism.

As then capitalist decline becomes pronounced, retirement to opposition becomes more and more the lot of the social democrats. The capitalist cannot well afford to delegate to any subordinates, however reliable, the tasks of government during a crisis; moreover, the tasks which must now be performed by Ministers become so flagrantly anti-working-class in character that the social democrats would risk the loss of their influence if they stayed to perform them. And so the future of social democracy will probably lie in opposition rather than in office. But this is by no means to say that its day is done. On the contrary, social democracy has a role to play in the acute stages of capitalist crisis which lie ahead, more important if possible than any which it has played hitherto.

It is true that its new role will be in essence the same as the old one: the role of the saviour of capitalism. But as the need for a saviour increases, so does his importance. Hitherto, we have considered only the present and the immediate past of social democracy. The social democratic parties of Europe are, however, at least thirty years old. In the chief countries of Europe they were already of great importance by the outbreak of the war. Their actions after the war have been so remarkable that we tend to forget how great a part they played in the war itself. Yet it is certainly not too much to say that the war could not have been fought without them. Now all the major parties of the Second International, except the British Labour party, were avowedly Marxian parties accepting, indeed reiterating in innumerable resolutions, the whole of the Marxian view of society. They were the creation of the working class of Europe: to them were confided the hopes and aspirations of many millions of Europeans: their leaders were trusted by the workers always to tell them where their true interests lay. In 1914, these parties supported the declarations of war of their respective Governments with the greatest possible vigour. The remarkable fact that in the early years of the war the workers created practically no trouble to their rulers is well accounted for, since the workers' leaders themselves had joined the rulers' Governments. The pacifists of yesterday had had the honour to become the members of inner war Cabinets: the fiery orators of pre-war labour insurgence now used all their talents to induce their countrymen to believe that if only they would fight and die for their respective masters, a new era of peace, prosperity, democracy and equality would dawn, after their respective masters' victories. Nor could any other influence have been as effective as theirs in justifying the war to the workers of all the combatant nations. For were not these the men who had themselves taught the workers that war was the supreme evil of capitalism; that the inevitability of war under capitalism was the ultimate justification of its overthrow? And yet, now that capitalist war had duly arrived, these very men were preaching that it must be accepted enthusiastically; that so much as to annoy the capitalists—far worse to dream of attempting their overthrow—was now criminal. Thus, instructed by their own leaders, how could the workers but suppose that this was some special kind of war to which all previous teaching did not apply?

Nor can we doubt that it was the apostasy of almost every social democratic leader alone which prevented the workers from turning against the ruling classes under the hideous and ever-growing strain to which they were subjected in the later stages of the war. For after all, even alone, leaderless, abandoned as they were, the workers of half the states of Europe were in open rebellion by the end of the war. In the opening stages of the war, however, the majority of the workers had undoubtedly been swept away by the terrific propaganda of the ruling class. Thus to have remained socialists in 1914, would have meant for the social democratic leaders facing a period of unpopularity. To have preached against the war in 1914-1915 would have meant persecution. And that was not to be thought of.[1] Thus, in the event, it was the workers' own leaders who taught them to fight and die for their masters. This was the first time that social democracy saved capitalism.

The second occasion was even more critical. As we have said, even as it was, the workers had become exceedingly revolutionary by the end of the war. And, in the state of extreme demoralization and disorder in which capitalism found itself during the first years of the peace, it seemed certain that in more countries than one a successful revolution would take place. But here again social democracy came to the rescue. The social democrats leapt from their seats in Government offices and successfully assumed the leadership of the working-class revolt. After that, of course, there could be only one result to the struggle. And yet it is evidence of the strength of working-class pressure at that time, and of the weakness of capitalism, that even when the forces of the workers were led by men whose whole object, for which they worked night and day, was to bring the revolt to nothing—that, even so, capitalism had to use in many places very violent and even desperate measures to preserve itself.

Capitalism to-day, however, needs constant support, and the social democrat may not weary in well doing. No sooner had the fierce onset of the workers in the immediate post-war years been overcome, than it became necessary to direct the still formidable forces of the working-class revolt into harmless channels. This object also the social democrats accomplished in the period from 1922 to 1929, by occupying the workers with the task of securing a Parliamentary majority and electing a social democratic Government, whilst praying, and so far as possible arranging, that they should achieve the latter and fall short of the former. This phase of social democratic activity, which is just concluding, we

---

[1] There were of course instances of individual social democratic leaders who opposed the war. The present Lord Snowden, it is curious to remember, did so. So did Mr. MacDonald, but much less vigorously. These pacifist individuals within social democracy opposed the war from a liberal position, however. They opposed the war because they thought that it might be the ruin of capitalism: the war they felt must at all costs be stopped lest it bring revolution.

have already considered in some detail. But capitalism is once again in need of a saviour. Once again its difficulties are so considerable that at first sight it seems inevitable that the workers' power should destroy it. It is not, of course, that the workers may be expected in the immediate future, or at any time, to rise in conscious revolt. Nor is any such action necessary for the destruction of the existing order of society. The problems of capitalism are such that what is necessary to its salvation is not that the workers should refrain from spontaneous revolution; what is necessary is that the workers should submit, and should submit without considerable resistance, to immense deprivations; that they should submit to vastly increased insecurity, poverty, and misery; and that sooner or later they should be willing to give their lives to capitalism in war.

And the workers will not suffer all these things again, at any rate without considerable persuasion. Fortunately for capitalism, the most powerful of all its advocates, the workers' own leaders, are once more available. And it is clear that this is to be the chief future function of the social democrats. In the industrial field it will be necessary to secure reductions in wages without causing dislocating strikes. In every contemporary instance the efforts of the trade union officials are being devoted to the difficult task of inducing the workers tamely to accept unheard-of cuts. For these officials are as keenly alive to capitalism's necessity for sweeping wage reductions, as they seem blind and deaf to the workers' necessity to resist these reductions, if they are to find food, clothing and shelter for themselves and their families. Politically, it will be necessary to induce the workers to occupy themselves with the harmless pastime of trying to elect a new Social Democratic Government: or, if this seems an ideal equally difficult of attainment and uninspiring when attained, then at any rate to prevent by their votes the accession to power of some Government, which may be represented as being particularly unwelcome to them. For if the new tasks of social democracy are fully as important as the old, yet they are, it must be admitted, a good deal more difficult and arduous. Always hitherto the social democrats have been able at any rate to speak about advances and improvements in working-class conditions. Thus, in the post-war crisis of capitalism, the function of the workers' leaders was to moderate, to tone down, demands for higher wages and shorter hours. And capitalism, only too thankful to buy off such formidable opponents so cheaply, did often make small, but to the workers valuable, concessions. Thus the influence of the social democrats was actually increased by their activities. On the political side, during the period of increasing electoral success, the party theorists could weave the most elaborate schemes of socialization, and the party orators call for extensive measures of nationalization, to be put into effect by future Social Democratic Governments.

The present tasks of social democracy are more delicate. Industrially, the trade union leaders have not now the comparatively simple task of obtaining some, if not all, of the concessions demanded by the workers. On the contrary, their job is to secure the acceptance of the greater part of drastic cuts demanded by the employers. The politicians cannot now be much concerned with promises of what they will give the workers in return for their vote. They are increasingly reduced to threatening that still worse will befall the workers if they vote for someone else.

Moreover, it becomes necessary for the social democrats at the same time to reassure the capitalists and to maintain their hold over the workers. In Great Britain, traditionally the motherland of political invention, the defeated social democrats solved their difficulties after the 1931 election by flatly contradicting each other. It was a sort of political division of labour. Some of the ex-Ministers undertook the task of assuring the capitalists that the Labour party was even more innocuous than it looked: that the murderous kick which the capitalists had given it was wholly undeserved. At the same time, other ex-Ministers undertook the work of assuring the workers that if the Labour party had in the past failed to achieve very much, yet in the future a far more vigorous and militant policy would bring untold benefits. Thus, some leaders went to the Left, some to the Right. One may contrast, for example, the following four statements of policy, all made during the early months of 1932 by prominent Labour leaders. Mr. Herbert Morrison, the defeated Minister of Transport, remarked at Bristol that "Socialism in our time is all romanticism." Meanwhile his colleague, Sir Stafford Cripps, was saying, "Gradualism is gone from the Labour programme for ever." (It is of course open to Sir Stafford to reconcile his views with Mr. Morrison's by saying that he meant that in future the Labour party would not attempt even the most gradual approach to socialism. But I hardly think that he will take that line.) Mr. Greenwood, the defeated Minister of Health, was also bent on denying, to the members of the Cambridge University Socialist Society, any tendency to timidity on the part of his party. "I know," he said, "the Communists are always saying that the Labour party suppresses the militancy of the working class. This is absolutely untrue; the working class in this country is not militant, and if it were the Labour party would welcome it." Mr. Walter Citrine, the Secretary of the Trade Union Congress, took another view, however. Speaking in the more mixed atmosphere of the Union Debating Society, he argued that it was essential to maintain a close connection between the Trade Unions and the Parliamentary Labour Party. "For," he said, "the Trade Union movement may convert itself into a revolutionary body, and I ask you not to dismiss that proposition very lightly."

In Great Britain the social democrats are still in this stage of the division of Labour. In Germany, they all speak with one voice, but they speak, not to cajole but to threaten. For in Germany, the crisis of capitalism is far more severe. Thus, in the presidential elections of March 1932, the German social democrats could not run a candidate of their own at all and had to set themselves the task of inducing the workers to vote for Field Marshal von Hindenburg, in order, not to achieve anything, but to *prevent* the election of Hitler. (The difficulty of the task may be seen from the fact that even this most formidably organized of all social democratic parties could not prevent five million workers from voting communist.) Nor is this an isolated example. The whole policy of German social democracy in supporting the Brüning Government, which imposed enormous sacrifices upon the workers, had to be defended as a policy of supporting the "lesser evil." The menace of fascism as the greatest abstract evil had to be continually conjured up before the eyes of the German workers in order to induce them to accept any concrete "cut" at the hands of the ordinary official capitalist parties. Nor will this state of affairs be long confined to Germany, Austria, and the other capitalist states which are worst hit by the crisis. Already the official policy of the Second International is to place the menace of fascism above every other consideration. For this is the sole way by which the workers can be induced to accept the ever more desperate sacrifices imposed upon them by existing capitalist Governments.

It might well be imagined that these new tasks are so heavy that the backs of even the trusted bearers of the burdens of capitalism, those bent social democratic backs, would break under it. And break in the end they will. In the meanwhile, however, social democracy, like the British Empire, has very great defensive strength. And, indeed, for very similar reasons. For both the British Empire and the social democratic machine are parts of capitalism. And so long as capitalism exists, so will they. We are certainly justified in saying that the extensive apparatus of modern social democracy, the huge trade union machine and the nation-wide political party, have become in fact a part of the machinery of capitalism.[1] The trade unions and the Labour parties were created as instruments by which the workers might oppose capitalism. And, no doubt, this is what some even of the party officials (especially in the lower ranks) *think* that they are still doing. But the pleasant ideas which people may quite sincerely entertain about their own functions do not alter in the least the actual facts of the situation—the fact, for example, that objectively all social democrats are being used as a means of controlling the workers in the interest of capitalism.

And what an incomparable instrument they are! The more unconscious of their real function, the more naively and sincerely anti-capitalist, the "non-commissioned officers"—the part-time trade union organizers, branch secretaries, local party agents and the like —may be, the better will they perform their task of binding the workers to the social democratic machine, and consequently to capitalism. For when the worker is told that "Old Joe"—the secretary, let us say, of the local branch of the National Union of Railwaymen—is a capitalist agent in their midst, he simply will not believe it. He knows that it is untrue. But that does not prevent "Old Joe,"

[1] For practical purposes, however, the case of the trade unions and the social democratic political parties is dissimilar. No one can imagine the political parties being won back by the workers, hence they should be abandoned by all revolutionaries. It is perfectly possible, however, to utilize the trade unions, against the wishes of their present leaders, for the purposes of the workers' struggle. For the trade unions are by their very nature so intimately connected with the workers' daily struggle for existence that they are susceptible to the mass pressure of their members, in times of crisis at any rate. Hence, all revolutionaries should be inside the trade unions.

however sincere that individual may be, from being joined by an unbroken chain of trade union officials, each link of which is a little more conscious of the real task which he is performing than is the link below him, to a national leader of the type of Mr. J. H. Thomas. And Mr. Thomas used half the time hardly even to trouble to pretend that he was much more than a sort of special officer of the railway companies, charged with dealing with "labour problems." Moreover, just as the task of social democracy is becoming more onerous, just as its propaganda has to concern itself more with playing on fears and less on hopes, more with threats and less with promises, than ever before, so its methods also are changing.

The relationship, for example, of the trade union machine to its membership is in some cases beginning to lose its voluntary character. Just in so far as the trade unions become a part of the structure of capitalist industry—and this is now one of their conscious aims—they become part of the apparatus of capitalist coercion. And in many British and German industries in which powerful but reactionary unions exist, this is what is visibly taking place. It does not mean, of course, that all friction between the trade unions and the employers will cease. Even if a union were actually to become a department of the big trust or corporation which is running the industry in which its members worked (and things never go as far as that) it would not mean that a conflict of interest might not occur. On the contrary, bitter disputes notoriously occur between the departments of big organizations. Thus, even the most reactionary union does not simply carry out the wishes of the employers without question. To suggest this would be greatly to over-simplify the position. On the contrary, the union will always put up the case against, say, wage reductions, just in the way in which a "Personnel Department," as the Americans call it, would do. But when once the employers are finally determined on "cuts," then the role of the union is always to minimize their amount sufficiently to make it possible to persuade the men to accept them without resistance; or, if this is impossible, to minimize the intensity and duration of the men's resistance, and to induce acceptance of the slightest concession from the employers.

Once again, objectively, and quite without reference to anyone's ideas about what he is doing, the trade unions more and more act as the instruments by means of which the capitalists make wage contracts with the workers. Inevitably therefore the same methods of extra-legal (not illegal but merely economic) coercion, which the employers have always used to secure workers for their factories are now used by the trade unions to secure that the workers remain "organized." For example, in some "well-organized" trades, the possibility of employment is largely confined to trade unionists. Thus, a member who is giving trouble, who is suspected of communist leanings for example, can have the terrible threat of unemployment suspended over his head by the mere mention of his expulsion from the union. (The expulsion of a group of prominent members of the Amalgamated Engineering Union, for no other crime than that they held political opinions obnoxious to the paid officials of the union, is a recent and notorious example of this procedure.) Again, the administration of a complicated system of social insurances is becoming to some extent bound up with the trade union machine. In Great Britain, for example, an unemployed worker can in certain important cases appeal against a disallowance of unemployment benefit only if he is a member of a trade union and if he makes his appeal through his trade union officials.

Nevertheless, in some cases, old-fashioned employers are still fighting the trade unions. They dream of the days when no apparatus for the control of the workers was necessary, and their simple fiat settled everything. They still resent the degree of complication, argument, and sometimes expense (by way of payment to officials, etc.) which dealing with even the most reactionary union entails. All the more modern employers realize, however, the inevitability of trade union organization. Like Mr. Citrine, they know that the alternative to the present reactionary unions is not no unions, but revolutionary unions. Accordingly, they do all in their power to strengthen the hands of the existing unions. They see that their officials are received at the manager's office: that small concessions are made after their representations: that the union officials are able to claim that so many cases of accident insurance, old age pensions, and the like, have been successfully negotiated by them. Above all, they allow the union officials to have a say in the all-important matter of who is discharged, and who given employment.

Perhaps the most complete example of the tendency of modern big business to incorporate the trade union apparatus, and thus make it a part of its own system of labour controls, was represented by the well-known "Mond-Turner" conference in Great Britain in the period of extreme reaction after the General Strike. These negotiations, though of the greatest psychological significance, did not end in any overt agreement. And, from the point of view of both parties, this was wise. For any written bargain between the employers and the trade union officials would have been far too open to attack. A tacit understanding served their purposes far better. The sign of the real success of the negotiations was the receipt of honours by both parties. Sir Alfred Mond became Lord Melchett, and Mr. Ben Turner became Sir Benjamin.

The trade unions, since they are the organ of social democracy which is dealing with actual everyday life, exert the most important part of the social democrats' hold over the workers. But at election times, the Social Democratic party, as we have seen, plays the same role. And, already in countries such as Germany, the whole strength of the social democratic propaganda machine has been put at the disposal of a capitalist Government, in order to enable that Government to direct the workers' votes towards an agreed candidate. In general, therefore, we may prophesy that the social democratic system will, more and more, become the mechanism by which the capitalists control the workers. And while in the end this will break its hold over the workers' minds, yet it immediately increases its hold over their bodies. Social democracy, by selling itself to the ruling class, receives in return some of those formidable weapons of coercion which the employers have always used against the workers. The trade unions, from being outlaw organizations, become "valued collaborators in industry": the Social Democratic parties become the trusted electoral allies of the capitalist parties, privileged even to support field marshals! And the social democratic Press is suddenly equipped with all the resources of capital. The *Daily Herald,* the newspaper of the British Labour party, for example, from being a struggling party sheet became overnight the lavishly equipped organ of Messrs. Odhams, a large and rising newspaper trust. The social democrats, even if their new masters do occasionally treat them a little roughly, as in the British 1931 election, are not on the whole ill recompensed.

The way is now clear for the final development. For social democracy has become the instrument of the capitalist class just when that class itself is moving strongly towards the employment of new methods. Fascist methods, we have seen, are becoming more and more necessary to the capitalists. How excellently the social democratic machine, the new instrument of policy which the capitalist class is acquiring from the workers, is suited to this tendency. For a capitalist class, using fascist methods, will not dare to allow the workers to remain unorganized. In order to prevent the workers from being organized *against* them, the capitalists must organize the workers themselves. What better instrument would there be for this purpose than those original working-class organizations, whose leaders can very easily be brought to see a resemblance between the socialism they used once to preach and the fascism which they are now required to practise? Thus social democracy, while passing its furious resolutions against "the menace of fascism," while sacrificing every present working-class interest to the plea that only so can this menace be avoided, is all the while itself laying down the working-class organization necessary to a fascist system. Social democracy becomes in fact "Social Fascism."

We have now made some attempt to comprehend the nature of social democracy: to understand the question of why it was that the workers, apparently well organized, and certainly suffering most acutely from the growing disorders of capitalism, did not present an immediate and conclusive challenge to the existing system. The truth is that those very organizations of working-class revolt, which the workers have gradually and painfully created over nearly half a century, have now passed over almost completely to the side of capitalism. Far from being an assistance to the workers in their life-and-death struggle, they are to-day by far the most formidable obstacle in the way of an early victory. They force upon the workers the immediate task of recapturing these organizations, or of freeing themselves from them and developing new and reliable organs of struggle.

PART VI
COMMUNISM

CHAPTER XIX

THE NATURE OF COMMUNISM

THE first half of this book was devoted to a discussion of the nature of capitalism. We came to the conclusion that capitalism was a method of organizing production by means of the concentration of the ownership of the means of production in the hands of a class, and the adjustment of the economic life of the community by a reliance upon the motives of the market. We traced in some detail the present difficulties of this system and came to the conclusion that they were insuperable.

The last seven chapters have consisted in an analysis of the nature of imperialism, the present and ultimate phase of capitalism, and of a description of social democracy. The last part of the book is devoted to a discussion of communism.

Communism is a principle of social organization antithetical to capitalism. It solves the problem of organizing production by entirely different methods. It does not attempt to secure the concentration of the means of production by vesting their ownership in the hands of a class, nor does it leave the adjustment of the life of the community to the motives of the market. Indeed, communist methods of organizing production cannot be even attempted until the class ownership of the means of production has been ended, and until the economic adjustments of society have been freed from the influence of the motives of the market.

Now, communism proper, namely, that system of society in which the principles of social organization which we shall describe immediately have been fully developed, can only start to come into existence with the overthrow of capitalism. Hence, a very considerable period must elapse after that event before a full communist society can appear. All that we can do to-day is to envisage the general principles upon which a society of full communism will be based. We can say that such a society will be based upon the principle of need: that the goods and services created will be sufficient to allow of their distribution upon the principle that everyone can have as much of them as he needs: that their production will be so little toilsome that it can be organized upon the principle that each citizen shall contribute that quota of service which he is able to contribute, and that these citizens shall be of such a kind as to make such principles of distribution and production workable. Such a society would, of course, be moneyless as well as classless.

Marx long ago distinguished (in his criticism of the Gotha programme of the German Social Democratic party) between such a fully communist society and the type of society which the working class would establish on the morrow of capitalism. He showed that what it would be possible to abolish on the morrow of the revolution would be the gross inequality of capitalism, namely, the inequality between the workers who receive a subsistence wage for performing the work of society, and those owners of property who receive extremely large incomes for doing nothing. Society could immediately be organized upon the basis of payment for work done, and for nothing else. But to suppose that a working-class community could immediately leap forward to an application of the principles of distribution suitable for a fully communist community, and give all its members an equal claim to the stock of social wealth, was utterly Utopian.[1]

Marx, then, distinguishes clearly a primary, transitional stage of communism, which must follow the revolution. In this stage, payments are made to the members of society in respect of the duration and the intensity of work done. It is this stage of communism which we shall consider in this chapter. For, the most interesting question to us is the question of how the working class will organize production after the revolution. It must, therefore, be clearly understood that when we use the word communism we use it to denote not ultimate, fully developed, communism, but the primary transitional stage of communism which must follow the overthrow of capitalism.

A distinguishing feature of communism, we have said, is that it does not seek to use the motives of the market, the motives, that is to say, of private profit, as the prime mover of the productive

---

[1] How much ink and paper the Riga correspondent of the London *Times* would have been saved if he had ever read this passage from Marx. He need never have given us these almost daily reports of how the Russian Government has abandoned every principle of Marxism and communism, and has established a system of "payment by results."

machine of society. It substitutes for this motive force a pre-arranged plan under which the multitudinous tasks necessary to the life of the community are consciously and regularly allotted to its members. Now we saw that reliance upon the mechanism of the market, alone, enables capitalism to avoid an open and avowed slavery for the working class. Communism, however, is able to abolish the mechanism and the motives of the market, without reducing any part of the population to serfdom. For under a sys-tem of communism, the instruments of production are taken out of the hands of their present owners and are vested in the hands of the working class. And as the consequence of that act, the working class becomes coterminous with the community as a whole. For a member of the capitalist class shorn of his possession of the instruments of production becomes, objectively though not sub-jectively, a member of the working class.

Lest this very simple proposition be questioned, as it is, of course, continually questioned, and it be suggested that a communist society involves industrial serfdom, "state-slavery" and the like, it may perhaps be useful to quote the testimony of one of the most strongly anti-communist thinkers of to-day. We have already referred to *The Servile State,* one of the earlier works of the Roman Catholic writer, Mr. Hilaire Belloc.

Mr. Belloc agrees that the communist solution avoids what he calls "the servile state," that is, serfdom for the workers. He states this very clearly on page 18 of the new edition of his book.

> "Similarly, that State is not servile in which *all* citizens are liable to submit their energies to the compulsion of positive law, and must labour at the discretion of State officials. By loose meta-phor and for rhetorical purposes men who dislike collectivism (for instance) or the discipline of a regiment will talk of the 'servile' conditions of such organizations. But for the purposes of strict definition and clear thinking it is essential to remember that a servile condition only exists by contrast with a free con-dition. The servile condition is present in society only when there is also present the free citizen for whose benefit the slave works under the compulsion of positive law."

Mr. Belloc's last sentence is the important one. Serfdom and free-dom are, in other words, what Hegel called "reflex categories."

The one cannot exist without the other. Hence, in a communist society, which has actually succeeded in abolishing social classes, in which there no longer exists a category of persons living on income drawn in respect of their ownership of the means of production, there is literally no meaning in such expressions as serfdom, slavery, "the servile state" and the like.

We are in a position to attempt a definition. A communist society (in its primary transitional stages) is one in which the mechanism of the market has been superseded by a planned direction of production; in which this change has been effected by taking the instruments of production from their present owners and vesting them in the hands of the working class. In consequence of this act, the working class gradually becomes identical with the community. Thus, a community without social classes comes into existence, a community in which all its members live upon incomes derived from the same source. For these incomes consist of payments made, by way of wages, social services or the like, from the flow of use-values maintained by the operation of the available means of production.

We may observe that it is this identity in the source from which all incomes are derived, rather than any precise similarity in their amounts, which characterizes a communist society. Naturally the amounts of incomes will vary much less in a communist society than in a capitalist society.[1] But this is not the distinguishing factor. The distinguishing factor is that in a communist society no incomes shall be derived by virtue of the possession of the instruments of production: that all shall be derived by virtue of services rendered, either now, in the past, or in the future. And it is only in so far as this state of affairs comes into existence in any community that it can claim to have abolished social classes and to be, in fact, a classless communist community.

We shall also observe that a communist society does not distribute everything which it produces to the individuals who compose it. Each worker as an individual receives less than he creates by his

---

[1] Thus, even in the Soviet Union to-day, which, as we shall see, lays no claim to being as yet a communist community, the maximum "spread" of the variation of incomes seems to be from about fifty roubles a month to a thousand roubles a month. In Great Britain, the maximum spread must be from under £4 a month to say, £120,000 a month. In Russia, then, the variation is as 1 to 20: in Britain, as 1 to 30,000.

labour. For a part of the productive energies of society are devoted to producing capital goods instead of consumable goods. These new capital goods are retained by the working class, which has become the community, and are used as the workers decide. In any given communist community, such and such a proportion of these new capital goods may be devoted to the production of further means of production, and such and such a proportion to the production and upkeep of objects of utility, which are by their nature only enjoyable by the workers in common, for example, the production and upkeep of public buildings, theatres, museums, sports stadia, parks, playgrounds, rest-houses and the like. Again the workers, the community as a whole that is, will decide what proportions of its energies shall be devoted to the production of capital and consumable goods, respectively. A communist community might, for example, in theory at any rate, decide to create only enough capital goods to enable the existing instruments of production, and such objects of utility as were held in common, to be kept in repair, and to distribute all other products to individuals in the form of consumable goods. Conversely a communist community might choose to apply a very high proportion of its resources to the production of capital goods. In either case, the distinguishing factor between a communist community and a capitalist community is the fact that under communism both the amount of capital goods annually produced, and the uses to which they shall be put, are under conscious control, while under capitalism these factors are left to the adjustment of the motives of the market.

Communism is, in one aspect, a new solution to the original problem of the collective labourer. Large-scale methods of production involve, we saw in Chapter II, some methods of mobilizing large numbers of labourers and of either compelling or inducing them to work at a common task. This problem has been solved in the past in two ways. In classical antiquity, comparatively large-scale production was conducted by means of direct forcible compulsion by the class of freemen exercised upon the class of slaves. Under capitalism it was, and is, conducted by means of the indirect economic compulsion of the class of the owners of the means of production, exercised upon the class of the workers, or non-owners of the means of production. The establishment of a communist system marks the substitution of a third and new method. For the assumption by society, by the working class that is, which in the very act becomes society, of the ownership of all the means of production makes it possible to solve the problem of the collective labourer by the method of the voluntary association of the workers for large-scale production. An immense scepticism exists in regard to this conclusion. Such scepticism is partly the result of the "mental climate" of capitalism in which we all live; and it is partly the result of a misunderstanding of what is meant by voluntary association. Now nobody is suggesting that in a communist society everybody will perform the arduous and unpleasant work which, for a good many decades, will still be necessary, for the sheer love of the thing, and without control and supervision. What is suggested, however, and what is already beginning to be indicated in practice, is that in a classless society, the necessity and obligation to work will be universally felt. In fact, of course, the realization that only by labour can man induce his environment to yield him a livelihood, is an immemorial and by now innate constituent of the consciousness of the race. Only amongst some of the oldest aristocratic and capitalist families in long-settled communities, which have for several generations lived exclusively from incomes derived from the ownership of the means of production, has this realization decayed. For the overwhelming mass of mankind, the necessity, albeit the unpleasant necessity, to work, is an assumption which is not questioned. In the old decaying capitalisms of the West, the natural position has, indeed, been inverted, and one of the principal claims of the wage earners is now "the right to work." This does not mean that the wage earners have a passion for spending eight hours a day in factory or mine. It means that the association of receiving an income and of working has become so fixed that the tacit assumption is made that only by working will an income be forthcoming. Hence, in a communist society, in which no citizen derives income from rights of ownership, there is not the slightest doubt that the population as a whole will appreciate perfectly the necessity to work. And this is what is meant by the principle of voluntary association, as the solution of the problem of the collective labourers.

What in practice happens in a communist society is simple. Society, through the institutions (councils, committees, call them what you will) which it sets up for the purpose, frames a body of rules for the duration, conditions, and remuneration, of the work which different categories of its members must perform. And these rules the members of society impose upon themselves. They see the necessity of going each day to factory, mine or field, and utilizing the means of production to satisfy their needs. Naturally, this does not mean that individuals here and there will see any such necessity: that particular individuals will not seek to enjoy the social fruits, without undergoing the social labour necessary to their production. And it will certainly be necessary to enforce compulsorily upon such individuals the rules of work which society has laid down. And all the other members of society will be strongly in favour of such an enforcement. For no one likes to have the maintenance of his neighbour imposed upon him by that neighbour's idleness. Hence, the obligation to work which in a communist society is binding upon all its members, is not in the least a contradiction of the principle of voluntary association upon which the productive activity of such a society is based. For the obligation is self-imposed.

No community, however, can pass overnight even to the primary transitional stage of communism. In the early stages of a working-class dictatorship, it may even be true to say that the obligation to labour is a compulsion imposed by the conscious and reflecting members of society both on themselves and on those members who, if left to themselves, would not realize the desirability of more labour than would just maintain themselves on the most primitive standards. Even at this stage, however, the labour performed in a classless society will be far more voluntary in character than the labour which the iron, if invisible, compulsions of capitalism extort from the workers. And, with every year that passes, a greater proportion of the population will emerge from the category of persons on whom regularity, and a minimum of intensity, of work have to be imposed, into the category of persons who realize fully the universal benefits of such labour, and who themselves take a conscious part in carrying it out. Moreover, with each advance in the level of technique, the character of necessary labour will change; it will become less irksome and arduous, more interesting and less exhausting. The barrier between mental and physical labour will be broken down. This will be done, partly by the actual interchange of personnel between manual and administrative tasks which becomes possible when a classless society reaches a certain level of culture, partly by the growing importance of labour which, like so much modern scientific labour, is mental and manual at the same time. With these changes the remaining elements of compulsion will slowly disappear. The process will be neither short nor simple but the direction is clear.

In order to hasten this process, communism requires, and requires urgently, the very maximum possible application and extension of scientific knowledge. The ruling class, which must rapidly become coterminous with society as a whole, will have a direct and personal interest in minimizing the amount of human toil necessary to a given standard of life. Since under communism there is no longer an antagonism of opposite status—freeman and serf, property owner and proletarian—man will be at last in a position to turn his entire energies to the subjugation of his oldest antagonist, nature. Indeed, just as communism only becomes possible when previous social systems have raised the level of man's comprehensive-command over nature to a certain point, so the maintenance of communism is closely associated with a continued development of scientific knowledge and skill. After all, it is only natural that when the men and women who do the work of society also control society, they will eagerly pursue every possibility of lightening the burden of toil which humanity has hitherto had to carry. Rapid scientific development will everywhere follow, as it followed in Russia, the establishment of working-class power. For there will be no ruling class to fear that any change in society will be for them a change for the worse. No one will fear to make those continual readjustments of the social structure, which are necessitated by developments of scientific technique.

This brings us to a wider consideration. Since there are, by definition, no classes in a communist society, there can be no class friction: there can be no necessity for those immense expenditures of social effort which are to-day necessary in order forcibly to adjust the relationship of inherently antagonistic classes. How immense a gain this is can be realized only when we appreciate the fact that the State itself is such an organization of forcible class adjustment. No honest observer of the modern State can possibly deny that it is, in fact, an apparatus, the primary purpose of which is to uphold the present social hierarchy. Remove class conflict in the only way in which it can be removed, namely, by the abolition of classes, and nine-tenths of the present activities of the State become redundant. What are left are not really State activities at all; they are rather economic functions of regulation and distribution which are not part of the original work of the capitalist State at all: they are functions which it has assumed during the period of the growing chaos of capitalist production. Such functions can easily be distinguished by the fact that they involve essentially the administration and manipulation of things: while the proper and traditional functions of the capitalist State consist in the coercion of men. (For example, the classical function of the capitalist State is to enforce contracts to which one of the parties was not a free agent; to uphold the labour contracts which the workers are driven to accept since they are faced with the alternative of starvation.)

This, then, is the distinguishing factor: in a communist society those functions of the State which consist in the regulation and planning of things, of the control of nature, will long persist and at first increase; but those functions of the State which consist in the coercion of persons will disappear just in so far as social classes disappear.

Thus a communist society, and a communist society alone, will be able to dispense with that immense apparatus of coercion which all societies divided into antagonistic classes must for ever maintain. For this apparatus of coercion, the police, the present judicial system, the armed forces of the State, in one of their aspects, are simply the methods which a class society must take in order to overcome the huge amount of social friction which it sets up.

We now come to the most striking of all the contrasts between communism and the present, imperialist, phase of capitalism. Communism is, in its very essence, internationalist. Just as communism provides the only possible solution of the problem of the class conflict by abolishing classes, it also provides the only solution of the problem of the international conflict, by abolishing national sovereignties. It is non-national, both in its economic basis and the system of ideas which it builds upon that basis. A communist economy cannot possibly admit of national boundaries.[1] A single

---

[1] The abolition of nations as political and economic units is, however, perfectly compatible with the development and flowering of national cultures. The point is developed in Chapter XXI.

planned economy must extend throughout the area which has become communist. Thus there cannot ever be (unless very temporarily and because of the *force majeure* of an intervening capitalism) two communist nations in the world at the same time. So soon as the working class obtains power in any state it will, as well for the most urgent practical reasons as for theoretical considerations, fuse with all other areas within which the workers have either previously or simultaneously taken power. For example, when the German working class obtains power, the world will not see a communist Germany and a communist Russia. There will still be one Union of Socialist Soviet Republics, but now it will extend westwards to the Rhine. And in the case of so large and advanced a state as Germany being captured by the working class, the centre of gravity of world communism may tend in some respects to shift westwards towards Berlin. (Lenin has an interesting passage on this possibility. He writes: "It would be likewise erroneous not to keep in mind that, after the proletarian revolution in at least one of the advanced countries, things will in all probability take a sharp turn; Russia will cease to be the model, and will become again the backward (in the 'soviet' and socialist sense) country."—*Left Wing Communism*.) Now it will hardly be disputed that new areas in which working-class dictatorships are set up will in fact, for the most urgent purposes of self-defence, coalesce with the existing communist communities, just as the various republics of the present Union coalesced for defence during 1918 to 1921. But how, it may be asked, will such larger coalitions of communist communities adjust their economic life? Will it be as easy to adjust the economic claims of a great historic area such as Germany, with those of Russia, when constructing future Five Year Plans, as it has been to adjust the respective claims of, say, the Ukraine and the North Caucasus? The answer must be that although in the early stages such an adjustment may not be *easy* yet it will be intrinsically *possible* in a sense in which it is intrinsically *impossible* to adjust the conflicting claims of two separate capitalist states. For confirmation of this fact we may again appeal to Mr. Hawtrey. The reader may recall (Chapter IV, page 81) the passage from his book *Economic Aspects of Sovereignty,* in which he contrasted the objective of "welfare" with the objective of "power" as "economic ends." It may be well to reproduce the passage here.

"We are accustomed to think of economic ends in terms of welfare, but in matters of public policy that is never the whole story. To each country power appears as the indispensable means to every end. It comes to be exalted into an end itself.

"So long as welfare is the end, different communities may cooperate happily together. Jealousy there may be, and disputes as to how the material means of welfare should be shared. But there is no inherent divergence of aim in the pursuit of welfare. Power, on the other hand, is relative. The gain of one country is necessarily loss to others; its loss is gain to them. Conflict is of the essence of the pursuit of power."

If we admit, as Mr. Hawtrey may or may not admit, that the ultimate end of capitalist states, for which they seek power as the inevitable means, is not the welfare of all their citizens, but the wealth of their property-owning citizens, we may accept this analysis. The immediate object of all capitalist states is, as Mr. Hawtrey shows, the pursuit of power; and the pursuit of power must engender armed conflict because power, like slavery, is a reflex and not an absolute category. One empire's power, that is to say, is necessarily and always the weakness of another empire. Hence, the simultaneous pursuit of power by several empires is the pursuit of an end unobtainable for more than one of them. And a finally victorious empire can only obtain its end and make power at last an absolute category, by irrevocably reducing all its rivals to impotence. The pursuit of welfare is obviously, however, the only economic end which a communist community will propose to itself. For welfare, their own welfare, that is, is clearly the only end which the workers are interested in. Nor will power, the power, that is, of their nation appear to the workers as the prerequisite of their welfare. For separate sovereignties, and the international anarchy which they entail, will have disappeared. The wealth of the capitalists of Britain, for example, is dependent upon their power, relative to the power of the capitalists of the United States. But the welfare of the workers of a Soviet Britain will in no way depend upon their power relative to some other constituent part of the worldwide Union of Soviet Republics. Hence, it will be possible for such communities, and for such communities alone, "to cooperate happily together." For welfare, the end which they pursue, is an absolute category and its attainment by one is not in the least exclusive of its attainment by the other. "Jealousy there may be," we shall agree with Mr. Hawtrey, "and disputes as to how the material means of welfare should be shared. But there is no inherent divergence of aim in the pursuit of welfare."

Thus we arrive at the crucial contrast between communism and present-day capitalist imperialism. Communism does provide a basis upon which the world can be progressively unified. For it provides a ruling class (gradually to become identical with society as a whole) whose end can be welfare, not power. And the attainment of welfare by one area of the world is complementary to the attainment of welfare by another, while the attainment of power by one area is contradictory to the attainment of power by another area.

Again, of course, in the field of ideas, communism is necessarily and notoriously internationalist. For just as the capitalist class is driven, in order to maintain itself in power, to seek to divide the workers into mutually odious national groups, so the conscious elements in the working class, in order to achieve working-class power, must necessarily urge the basic identity of interest, the basic solidarity, of all workers; must urge the unreality in the modern world of national divisions, and the reality of class divisions. Hence, all communist propaganda necessarily seeks to bind the workers of the world together, to unify and not to divide, and thus prepares the way for that close collaboration of communist communities for which their economic characteristics provide the objective basis.

There is little doubt that this final distinction between communism and any system of society involving the existence of antagonistic social classes, is the decisive factor when we come to consider the further question of whether communism is likely to conquer the world during this century. Communism is inherently capable of world unity; capitalist imperialism is inherently incapable of world unity. This advantage of communism will out-weigh in the long run all the factors in which it is so glaringly at a disadvantage. Communism is to-day extremely weak in material power as compared to world capitalism. World capitalism has resources of violence which united could, it would seem, crush the forces of communism without difficulty. But it is, we have shown in some detail, of the inmost essence of world capitalism that these resources can never be united. Thus, a wholly misleading picture of the world situation is painted if we add, say, the American, British, French and Japanese armed forces together and compare them to the armed forces of the Soviet Union, plus the assistance which the resistance of the workers in the capitalist countries would lend to the communist side. For the armed forces of, say, Britain and America must be rather subtracted the one from the other. They are pointed quite as much against each other as against the Soviet Union. They may, it is true, at any given moment come together—for the express purpose of an attack on the Soviets. But that moment of unity must, by the very nature of capitalist imperialism, be transitory. For Mr. Hawtrey's "continuous struggle of national force" must at once reassert itself. Even if the imperialist powers attacked Russia, as indeed they sooner or later must do, and even if their attack for a time succeeded, they would certainly quarrel again over the booty. They cannot possibly avoid the necessity of fighting out amongst themselves the battle for world supremacy. And it is inconceivable that they can avoid their own self-destruction in such a struggle.

We have now sketched the basic outlines of the primary stage of communism. And that is all that can be done. For it is no part of the purpose of these pages to paint the portrait of another facile Utopia.

But it would be absurd to consider the nature of communism without alluding to the Soviet Union. The first thing, however, which we must observe is that never has a single Soviet leader claimed that the Union is to-day a communist community. The Soviet Union cannot be considered to be as yet a community in even the primary stage of communism, which we have defined. Many capitalist remnants are still present. It is hoped, however, that by the end of the Second Five Year Plan, in 1937, that is, it will be possible to speak of a communist society in Russia. Both Lenin and Stalin, for example, have been scrupulous to point out that it would be childishly and ridiculously un-Marxian to suppose that the Russian republics could leap in a year or so from the conditions of 1917 into communism. The most historically minded men who have ever ruled, the leaders of the Russian Revolution, were not likely to make so elementary an error. Not only was Russia in 1914 only beginning to assume the aspects of a modern capitalist state, beginning to push aside the gigantic lumber of a semi-Asiatic feudalism, but in the war years between 1914 and 1917, and above all in the civil war years from 1917 to 1921, she necessarily regressed, in material assets, to a point much below even the humble level of 1914. The communist leaders would have been foolish visionaries if they had supposed that by some magical process a communist society could suddenly emerge from the flooded mines of the Don Basin or the dark and forsaken villages of central Russia. But they showed themselves to be men of incomparable resolution and marvellous historical insight when they determined that the smoking ruins which were bequeathed to them by the Russian imperialists did offer the possibility of a firmly established working-class dictatorship; and that such a dictatorship alone could rebuild Russia. With what dazzling audacity did Lenin conceive his project: with what colossal tenacity has Stalin clung to its execution. The little group of Marxists who helped the Russian worker to build that indispensable instrument for the execution of their class will, the Russian Communist party, are now passing one by one into history. And it is certain that history will record no parallel to the task which they attempted, and which their survivors and successors are now carrying forward, stage by stage, towards its completion. For they conceived the extraordinary project of laying the basis upon which a communist society would gradually grow up, by the same act with which they finally destroyed both the substantial remains of Russian feudalism and nascent Russian capitalism.

There was an almost mad heroism in such a decision. For Lenin and his associates knew perfectly well the terrible handicap which the inadequate development of Russian capitalism imposed upon them. They had no illusion that Russia could painlessly leap over the fully developed capitalist stage. On the other hand, they were free of the preposterous, and in effect disingenuous, pedantry of Kautsky and the German Marxists who supposed that every country must pass through precisely the same stages of development: that it must tread the capitalist path to some exactly determined point at which, and not a moment sooner or later, it would be correct for the working class to seize power. Lenin knew that history is not so accommodating: that the working class must seize power when and where it can: that a combination of favourable circumstances

such as took place in Russia in 1917 might not occur again anywhere for decades. Thus, he determined that it would be criminal
to neglect such an opportunity, though he knew perfectly well that
the maintenance of working-class power and the progressive establishment of communism in Russia presented problems of extreme
difficulty. That Lenin was perfectly aware of this is certain. For
example, we find him writing, in 1920, that "it was easy for Russia,
in the concrete, historically quite unique, situation of 1917, to begin
a Social Revolution; whereas to continue it and complete it will
be more difficult for Russia than for other European countries." It is
the tremendous achievement of the Communist party of the Soviet
Union that the Russian Revolution has been continued and is, it
is hardly too much to say, almost within sight of completion.

For revolutions are not, as is sometimes erroneously supposed,
events which occur on a particular day of a particular month of a
particular year. It may be possible to fix, as in 1789, though always
with some arbitrariness, a particular point in time at which they
begin. But they take decades to complete. Thus it will not be
.possible to say that the Russian Revolution has been completed
till a genuinely classless society has been achieved. Then and then
only will it be possible for communism to begin to appear.

What does exist in the Soviet Union to-day is a working-class
dictatorship, solidly and powerfully engaged upon transforming
the basis of society. The process is continuous. But there have
been two decisive periods. The first was from 1917 to 1920 in
which the working class seized power, destroyed the old State
apparatus and created a new one of its own. The second critical
period was from 1929 to 1931 when the last substantial class of
persons who derived their income from the possession of the means
of production, the class of rich peasants, was dispossessed. Hence,
the history of the Soviet Union affords an example of the power
and achievements of a working-class dictatorship in transforming,
in the face of the most adverse circumstances, the basis of the life
of a community, rather than an example of communism in existence. But the Soviet Union does of course give us by far the best
indications—indeed the only concrete indications which we have—
of what communism will be like when it does come into existence.

Communism is best regarded as a method by which human
civilization can be maintained and developed. Communism is

indeed the only method by which it can be maintained at all. For capitalist imperialism is in an evident and acute stage of disintegration, and would sooner or later, if left unchallenged, physically overwhelm civilization in a tornado of high explosives. It is this consideration which makes so pathetically irrelevant the protests of well-circumstanced intellectuals against the very real difficulties and ardours which must for many decades characterize a communist system. Western intellectuals are continually proving that communism would be unlikely to provide them with the economic advantages, the leisure, the physical and mental comforts, which, in one or two of the most favoured empires of the world, they enjoy to-day. They are quite right. But to deduce from this fact that their interest (even on the most rigidly personal grounds) is to prevent the coming of communism, is as ill advised as it would have been for a passenger on the sinking *Lusitania* to have pointed out to a ship's officer, who offered him a place in a boat, that the deck-chair in which he was seated was much more comfortable. Communism offers no one of this generation a ticket to Utopia. But it does offer to intellectual workers of every kind the one road of escape out of a paralysing atmosphere of capitalist decay, into a social environment which will give a limitless stimulus to the achievements of the mind of man.

But communism does not offer itself to mankind as a sort of painless and patent cure for all the ills of the universe. The essential argument in its favour is rather that it is the one method by which human civilization can be maintained at all. It is true that some members of the Western ruling class are so accustomed to the automatic benefits of a, for them, very perfectly functioning civilization that they cannot even conceive of what barbarism is like. Hence they do not feel the necessity of maintaining civilization despite all its burdens. But for the workers, who are nearer to reality, the absolute necessity of maintaining civilization itself, even though they rightly feel that there is no necessity whatsoever for maintaining the present form of civilization, is manifest. And it is upon the foundation of working-class support that all future civilization must rest. The workers and they alone have untapped reserves of strength and vitality which can carry the race, through the crisis of the breakdown of capitalism, on to the new basis of a planned economy and a classless society.

The coming of communism can alone render our problems soluble. A working-class dictatorship can alone open the way to communism. A working-class dictatorship can only be successful if the workers as a whole achieve a clear understanding of the historic destiny of their class. And this understanding, in turn, cannot be developed unless the working class succeeds in organizing its most conscious and clear-sighted members into that indispensable instrument of the workers' will, a Communist party. The assumption of power by the workers can occur by means of revolution alone; by means, that is, of an event which takes place over a limited number of years, and of which there may be a critical moment, such as the conquest of the existing State apparatus in a capital city, which can be "dated" to a given week of a given month of a given year. The coming of communism itself, however, after the achievement of working-class power, must be a gradual process. And it is only gradually, with the emergence of communism, with the creation—and that, we may be sure, only by Herculean labours and painful sacrifices—of the essential economic basis for a classless society, that the problems which to-day threaten civilization with eclipse will actually be solved.

Nor, of course, will the coming of fully developed communism itself, solve *all* our problems. For example, the supreme enemy of man's complacency; his knowledge of his own proximate annihilation by death, must long remain with him under any system of society. It would be foolish to deny, however, that communism by allowing of the maintenance and development of civilization, would progressively postpone the menace of death. As a matter of fact, even our present poor apology for civilization does now, and will do until it enters on its final holocaust of wars, push forward perceptibly the boundaries of life. For that small proportion of the population for whom capitalism does secure all the benefits of man's power over nature, for the ruling class, human life has already been much prolonged. In a society which was so organized as to give full possibilities to the development of science, a century or so of biological and medical research might enormously extend the average span of life. Nor, although our minds rebel against the conception to-day, is there any scientific necessity to suppose that in the end death could not be indefinitely postponed.

One of the reasons, no doubt, why the conception of the in-

definite postponement of death seems remote to us to-day is because, in the degenerating and hope-forsaken condition of the capitalist world, we are unable to imagine that men will need or desire
a great extension of their lives. In the great cities of the capitalist
world, in London, in Berlin, in Chicago, in Shanghai, capitalism
both kills the workers' will to live and withholds the possibility of
any but a short and disease-ridden life. We need not doubt, however,
that the achievement of a classless society will produce possibilities
of life—a level both of physical and psychological vitality—such as
to induce the workers systematically to seek for the extension of
their life's span. Even to-day in the Soviet Union, during the very
brunt of the initial struggles of a working-class dictatorship, before
a classless society has fully emerged, there is perceptible an exhilaration of living which finds no parallel in the world. To travel
from the capitalist world into Soviet territory is to pass from death
to birth. Certainly death, until the final agony ensues, is the more
peaceful, quieter and tidier process. "One must have all chaos
within one to give birth to a dancing star," and, for those who
cannot support the sight of a continent in labour, of the vast,
baffling, contradictory stirrings of a young giant still half-cabined
in the womb, the Soviet Union is an alarming place. We may leave
such people to enjoy their tiny pleasures and comforts: for these
will not long remain to them. They will find that in shrinking
from the agony of birth they have chosen the agony of death.

CHAPTER XX

THE FUTURE OF GREAT BRITAIN

In this chapter, an attempt is made to exemplify the foregoing discussion of the nature of communism, by a sketch of the problems involved in the struggle of the workers to overthrow capitalism and establish communism in one particular state. The state selected must perforce be Great Britain, for lack of adequate first-hand knowledge of any other. The British position is of such crucial world importance, however, that our particular instance throws a good deal of light on the general rule.

It is not proposed to attempt a discussion of the tactics appropriate for a Communist party working in an old-established democracy such as Great Britain. The steady growth of the Communist parties of the West is clearly dependent upon the continued development of a tactic exactly appropriate to the conditions of those capitalist states in which the forms of democracy have been, hitherto, preserved. But such a tactic cannot, we may be sure, be worked out in paper propositions, however ingenious. It can only be evolved, and it is now being evolved, gradually and painfully as the result of the experiences of the Communist parties of the West, gathered in the course of long and obstinate struggles. Nor does the undoubted fact that the tactics of the class struggle must differ from place to place, indicate in the least that the fundamental antagonism of class interest is not everywhere the same. Moreover, nothing is more disgusting than to sneer or jeer at the efforts of the men and women who are engaged in finding the correct tactics for each particular set of conditions, at heavy cost to themselves and by the only possible method, the painful and laborious method of trial and error.[1]

[1] Lenin wrote:
"The problem, here" (in Britain that is) "as everywhere, consists in the ability to apply the general and fundamental principles of communism to the specific relations between classes and parties, to the specific conditions in the objective development towards communism—conditions which are peculiar to every separate country, and which one must be able to study, understand, and point out...."

All that is attempted here is a summary of the general position of Great Britain in respect of the need for, and prospects of, the communist movement. It may be worth while first of all to enumerate those, in themselves quite obvious, factors which make Great Britain a particularly favourable ground for communism. For these factors are, naturally, ignored whenever possible by British capitalist opinion. We will then come to a discussion of those objections to the possibility of communist success in Great Britain of which we already hear so much, and of which we shall hear to an ever-increasing extent.

The principal factors which give a revolutionary working-class movement in Great Britain a basis of strength, unequalled anywhere else in the world are as follows:

First: in actual numbers, the British working class is immensely strong. The proportion of the population of Great Britain which consists in industrial workers is higher than the corresponding proportion in any other important state. Britain is by far the oldest and is still the most heavily industrialized of all the great states.

"The main thing now is that the communists of each country should, in full consciousness, study both the fundamental problems of the struggle with opportunism and 'Left' doctrinairism, and the specific peculiarities, which this struggle inevitably assumes in each separate country, according to the idiosyncrasies of its politics, economics, culture, national composition (e.g., Ireland), its colonies, religious divisions, etc. Everywhere is felt an ever-widening and increasing dissatisfaction with the Second International, a dissatisfaction due to its opportunism and its incapacity to create a real leading centre, able to direct the international tactics of the revolutionary proletariat in the struggle for the world Soviet Republic. One must clearly realize that such a leading centre can, under no circumstances, be built after a single model, by a mechanical adjustment and equalization of the tactical rules of the struggle. The national and state differences, now existing between peoples and countries, will continue to exist for a very long time, even after the realization of the proletarian dictatorship on a world scale. Unity of international tactics in the communist labour movement everywhere demands, not the elimination of variety, not the abolition of the national peculiarities (this at the present moment is a foolish dream), but such an application of the fundamental principles of communism—Soviet power and the Dictatorship of the Proletariat—as will admit of the right modification of these principles, in their adaptation and application to national and national-State differences. The principal problem of this historical moment in which all advanced (and not only the advanced) countries now find themselves lies here; that specific national peculiarities must be studied, ascertained, and grasped before concrete attempts are made in any country to solve the aspects of the single international problem, to overcome opportunism and Left doctrinairism within the working-class movement, to overthrow the bourgeoisie, and to institute a Soviet Republic and proletarian dictatorship." (*Left Wing Communism.*)

In America, for example, about a third of the population is still directly or indirectly on the land. Of the British population, something like four-fifths is industrial and commercial, hardly one-fifth agricultural. Even Germany, which is also heavily industrialized can show no nearly corresponding proportion. Nor is it necessary to emphasize the cardinal importance of this fact in estimating the possibility of the working class being able to establish their dictatorship in Britain. For it is always upon the urban industrial workers that the whole body of wage-earners must rely. The industrial workers alone can play the leading part in the revolt of all non-property-owning sections of the population.

Second: the level of technical and educational development of this enormous British industrial working class is very high, relatively to that of the working class of other capitalist states. The British workers, as they have shown, by their unparalleled practical achievements in building trade unions and a Social Democratic party, have unrivalled powers of organization. And there is no reason to suppose that they will not exhibit those powers in the building of a Communist party.

Third: the converse of the extreme industrialization of Britain is, of course, the smallness and unimportance of her agricultural population. Now the comparative insignificance of British agriculture is usually quoted as one of the greatest objections to the maintenance of a communist régime in Britain. We shall consider this objection in a moment. It is obvious, however, that the absence of any large class of agriculturists, owning their means of production, and living by operating them themselves, is an enormous initial advantage to the British communist movement. For such a class is necessarily conservative, and will almost always ally itself to the big capitalists. We may recall the part which the farmers and richer peasants have played in Europe, and which they have sought to play in Russia. They have proved everywhere the readiest instruments of the big capitalists, when these determined that the time had come to resort to methods of open violence in order to smash all working-class organizations. How great then is the advantage of the British workers in the fact that this agricultural class is in Britain comparatively insignificant in numbers.

Fourth: what agricultural interests do exist are sharply divided into two antagonistic classes. For it is the unique characteristic of

British agriculture that it has not developed a system of small holdings, and consequently a peasant class. On the contrary, British agriculture at an early stage in its development created units of production, farms, that is, too big to be worked by a single family. Hence, there grew up a relatively large class of wage-earning agricultural labourers, landless workers, as bereft as any urban proletarian of the means of production. And the agricultural workers, to the number of some 800,000 are a genuine rural working class. It is true that they are to-day on the whole backward, intimidated by the farmers and landlords and an easy prey for the old capitalist parties. British social democracy has never been able to secure their votes. (Not that this is necessarily a sign of their backwardness.) But everyone who knows anything of the British agricultural workers agrees that, ill paid, and still suffering all those petty oppressions characteristic of the exploitation of small masters, they have intense, if latent, class antagonisms. Nor must all, at any rate, of the smaller tenant farmers be placed on the side of reaction. The "direct action" which the British farmers have lately taken by the refusal of many of them to pay tithes for the upkeep of the State Church shows that under the pressure of economic circumstances they can become a force hostile to the capitalist State. Hence, even that rural population which does exist in Britain is by no means a unitedly anti-working-class force. The agricultural workers in a time of crisis could certainly be relied upon by the urban workers, at least to neutralize the efforts on behalf of the capitalists of the farmers and landlords.

Thus, the intrinsic balance of class forces is certainly more favourable to the workers in Great Britain than in any other major capitalist state. Nor is this truth ignored by the leaders of the British ruling class. Behind all their endless talk of the impossibility of communism in England, of the special immunity of the good, honest, British workers from the communism microbe, there lurks the "anxiety neurosis" of men who know that their position is especially insecure. And just occasionally, in moments of special tension, the anxiety of the most intelligent and best-informed leaders of the British capitalist class secures conscious expression. There is, for example, that well-known passage in one of Mr. Lloyd George's speeches in 1920, a passage which drew from Lenin the comment that Mr. Lloyd George was "not only a very clever man, but that he has learnt much from the Marxists." Mr. Lloyd George was arguing in favour of the necessity of his coalition of all the forces of the capitalist class into the then existing "National Government." Such a coalition was necessary, he told his audience, in order to combat the communist menace.

"If you go to the agricultural areas," he said, "I agree that you have the old party divisions as strong as ever; they are far removed from the danger. It does not walk in their lanes. But when they see it they will be as strong as some of these industrial constituencies now are. Four-fifths of this country is industrial and commercial; hardly one-fifth is agricultural. It is one of the things I have constantly in my mind when I think of the dangers of the future here. In France the population is agricultural, and you have a solid body of opinion which does not move very rapidly, and which is not easily excited by revolutionary movements. That is not the case here. This country is more top-heavy than any country in the world, and if it begins to rock, the crash here, for that reason, will be greater than in any other land."

We have already discussed the intrinsic assets and liabilities of the British capitalist position. (For, of course, the British workers are not either absolutely weak or strong; they are weak or strong relatively to the strength or weakness of the British capitalist class.) We concluded that while immediately the British capitalists had very great—in some respects unrivalled—remaining strength, yet their world position was foredoomed to decline. We saw that the wisest and most successful of their leaders realized this, and that all their efforts were directed to mitigating Britain's decline: that they realized, whether consciously or unconsciously, that any strong action taken with a view to a permanent and decisive restoration of the British position necessarily involved war with some other empire; and that such a war held but the darkest prospects for Britain. But such considerations, although they are themselves decisive in the long run, do not necessarily help us much in estimating the balance of class forces which may be expected to arise in Britain in the near future.

Let us next attempt to estimate the assets possessed by the British workers during that critical period which must supervene immediately after the establishment of their dictatorship. The factors which we have hitherto considered are assets only from the point of view of the possibility of the attainment of working-class power. It is one thing, however, for the workers to take power and another for them to be able permanently to maintain it. Nevertheless it will, on examination, become apparent that the British workers have important assets for this second period. We may summarize these assets as follows:

First: that same generally high level of technical skill, educational standards, and political experience which we noticed as forming an important asset for the building up of a communist movement in Britain, as objective circumstances become more and more favourable, is an asset of even greater importance for the maintenance of working-class power, once it has been achieved. No one who has seen the immense difficulties which the Soviet Union has faced in consequence of the backward state of development which Tsardom had imposed upon the Russian workers, can doubt that the task of laying the foundations of a communist economy in Great Britain would be immeasurably simpler, chiefly on account of this particular factor. The British workers are probably the most generally capable in the world: they will be far less dependent than are the Russians upon middle-class technicians, some of whom may be unreliable, for the maintenance and development of their economic system. (It may well be expected, however, that a much larger proportion of British technicians, with the example of the scope for technical ability which the Soviet system gives, will rally to a working-class régime.) It is probably not too much to say that the British workers are capable themselves of running the British productive system. Nor is it merely a question of technical skill. Several generations of industrial experience undoubtedly give a reliability, a sense of order, a power of co-operation for large-scale production which the Russian workers, outside Leningrad and one or two other exceptional places, necessarily lacked.

Second: the geographical nature of Great Britain makes her an ideal country to which to apply the principles of a planned centralized economy. Her geographical area is so small, and her system of communications so complete that the problems of centralized control will be greatly simplified. Britain is the most compact large-scale productive unit in the world. Her industries have been brought by capitalism to the point where they simply cry out for unified control. Nor will there be in Britain anything like the difficulty in generalizing the organizing committee or council of each industry into a nation-wide planning commission, which existed in Russia.

Third: moreover, the actual quality and quantity of the technical equipment of Great Britain (though some of it is now beginning physically to deteriorate) is perhaps unparalleled anywhere in the world. Think for a moment of the transport facilities of Great Britain—perhaps the most important single factor in the economic life of a nation. Great Britain has a double system of inland transport, by rail, and road, each of which is perhaps comparable to the very best of the systems of any other country. Her railway system throws a close mesh over the country, and is still on the whole better maintained than are the railways of any other area (though the Ruhr area of Germany and parts of Belgium and Luxemburg have an even closer mesh of railway lines). Her roads, though not nearly so well designed as those of France, are better maintained and, again, have a closer mesh. Moreover, they are equipped not only with an immense fleet of lorries for the transport of all kinds of goods, but with a very large number of passenger coaches or omnibuses. It is true that some parts of Britain's inland canal system, once one of the finest in the world, have been allowed to fall into decay. But the system would be restored very easily and cheaply if it were not considered redundant. It is probably not too much to say that either the road or the railways system of Great Britain could independently, and in the impossible event of the other being totally destroyed, carry on quite effectively the entire transport services of the community. The roads could certainly do so if they were supplemented by the extremely cheap transport of heavy raw materials, which is possible by canal. In addition, however, to these incomparable forms of inland transport, probably the best method of all for British bulk transport is by coastal steamer. For it is an important and often neglected economic fact that something like two-thirds of the population of Britain lives in seaport towns—in areas which can be reached by ocean-going ships.[1] It is only necessary to compare these transport facilities, now so squandered by capitalism, with the meagre resources inherited by the

---

[1] Manchester and the neighbouring Lancastrian towns fall into this category since the building of the Manchester ship canal.

Russian workers, to understand the advantages which a British workers' dictatorship would possess. And the remarkably high development of the British transport system is only an instance of the general development of British capital equipment. For example, another source of immense strength to a workers' dictatorship in Britain will be the unequalled development of the British machine-building industries. Britain can produce machinery of all sorts, and above all machine tools, the machines for making machines, better than any country in the world. Thus, damage to existing plant, or its obsolescence, are factors which can be eliminated with unexampled ease in Britain.

In some respects certain British industries, it is true, lag behind the best German, French, American, and now Russian, practice. For example, British blast furnaces are mostly of small capacity; the surface equipment of her coal mines is inadequate; her motor-car industry is largely carried on by firms too small to apply all the advantages of mass production. A good deal of the equipment of the Lancashire cotton industry needs replacement. But on the whole British industrial equipment is probably as good as any in the world. For if it has many defects, so have the equipment of all other capitalist states. Certainly it represents a productive power which, if operated steadily, and at full capacity, as it would be operated by a working-class dictatorship, could, even without extension, produce a standard of life for the British population at present unrivalled in the whole world. For it is not any lack of the technical ability to produce which is to-day progressively bringing British industry to a standstill. It is that the existing social relationships, the impasse which British capitalism has reached, make it impossible to utilize her admirable productive equipment.

The fourth factor which would facilitate the task of maintaining and consolidating a working-class dictatorship in Britain (for a period sufficiently long, firmly to lay the foundations of communism) is the unrivalled inheritance of what one may call "cultural" and "amenity" equipment which will accrue to the British workers. For example, Britain has, on the whole, an extensive system of school buildings and general educational equipment:[1] her public utility services are well developed: she has the nucleus of a

---

[1] Compared to what they might and ought to be, British schools are pitiable; compared to what the Russians inherited in 1917, they are superb.

comprehensive system of free lending libraries: a network of cine-
mas: a large number of wireless receiving sets and excellent transmitting stations. Again, there exist in London the largest and finest
plants in the world for the production and distribution of daily
newspapers on a vast scale. (It is sometimes forgotten that the big
London dailies, because of their national distribution, have much
larger circulations than any American newspapers. This is another
instance of the advantages of the compactness of Britain.) It is, of
course, quite impossible for the British working class to make use
of these assets to even 1% of their possible value in existing conditions.

It is true that in another respect a British working-class dictatorship will be seriously handicapped. The housing conditions which
it will inherit are abominable. It is not too much to say that one of
the most urgent tasks of a working-class dictatorship in Britain will
be the rebuilding of whole areas of every city in the land. On the
whole, however, the British workers will find themselves, once they
have attained power, in an incomparably better material position
than did the Russian workers. They will be able at once to devote
a much higher proportion of their energies to the production of
consumable goods, as distinct from capital goods, than could the
Russians. They will be able to satisfy all the basic wants of the
population at a much earlier stage. It is not too much to say that
while the primary problem in Russia has been to construct the basic
equipment necessary to a communist civilization, in Great Britain
the workers' first task will be the adaptation of a rich inheritance
to new uses.

All the foregoing considerations, however, apply to the situation
of a workers' dictatorship in Great Britain regarded in isolation.
Such a view is highly abstract. A workers' dictatorship in Great
Britain could, in fact, only be, as we show below, a part of a wide-
spread working-class assumption of power extending to considerable areas of Europe at least. It may be best, however, to discuss
this subject, which raises the real prospects of communism in
Britain, by coming to a discussion of the principal objections to the
possibility of communist success which are always raised in British
capitalist and social democratic circles.

The first of these objections represents the other aspect of the undoubted fact, which we have already discussed, that Britain is a highly industrial country in which agricultural production plays a relatively small part in the national economy. This fact is expressed by the oft-repeated cry of the spokesmen of British capitalism, a cry which, as the power of communism grows, will rise into an almost deafening shriek, that "Britain cannot feed herself." From deter, mined fascists, bewildered liberals, and socialists finding excuses for the abandonment of socialism, this cry already resounds. It is impossible, unthinkable, mad, outrageous, we are told, for the British workers even to dream of taking power. For if they did so, Britain would starve in a few weeks. The capitalist countries would boycott us. We could not buy our food. We should all perish miserably. Every shade of opinion within British capitalism, from the Churchills on the Right to the disaffiliated pacifists of the I.L.P. on the Left, feel that with these magic words they have laid the communist spectre. What further need have we of witnesses? "Britain cannot feed herself" and—oh, what a relief—that settles the matter.[1]

What importance have we to attach to this question? On examination, the whole thing boils down to one simple proposition: viz. that a working-class régime in Britain must be part of an international movement. And whoever dreamt of it being anything else? Is it not precisely because communism is in its very essence international: because it is a movement which can recognize no frontiers of race, of colour, or of territory, that all the Communist parties of the world are tightly bound together into the Third International? It might be impossible to maintain a workers' dictatorship in Britain against a united capitalist world. Already, however, such a world does not exist. Capitalism has lost control of Russia. Moreover, the remaining capitalist powers are at daggers drawn with each other, so that they have never yet been able to combine even against the Soviet Union. This does not mean that the problem of securing regular and uninterrupted supplies of raw materials and foodstuffs

[1] Thus Professor Harold Laski, in his well-known little book entitled *Communism*, tells us that "the rupture of Anglo-American trade would be fatal to an English revolution." But still Professor Laski's fears and anxieties lead him to stranger statements still. We are told, for instance, that "an American communist revolution would have to cope with problems of distance which would probably render it abortive at a very early stage." What luck for Lenin that he had to deal with a handy little pocket handkerchief of a country like Russia!

to a Britain in which the workers had taken power would not be an important one. (Incidentally a tremendous lot of nonsense is talked about the actual quantity of food produced in Britain. Taking one type of foodstuff with another, Britain produces about a five months' supply annually. And she habitually carries a stock of food adequate to last from two to three months.) But it would not be an impossible task, even in the case of Russia and Britain being the only two communist areas in an otherwise capital world. But is such a case likely to arise? It is improbable that Britain will be the next place in which, after Russia, the conflict of class comes to the point of decision. As a matter of fact, history will probably record that the Kwangsi province of China was the first area of the world after Russia, in which a stable workers' Government was set up. For already (March 1931) some sixty million Chinese, according to the Shanghai correspondent of the London *Times* (who is not a communist sympathizer) are living under the rule of Soviets. Again, there are half a dozen points in Europe in which the capitalist crisis is more acute, and, naturally therefore, the communist movement is more developed, than it is in Britain. The workers will probably obtain power in Poland or Roumania or Spain or Hungary or Austria or Germany, for example, before they do so in Britain. And the overthrow of capitalism in one or more of these countries would immediately transform the international balance of power. Thus the whole picture of a communist Britain surrounded by a ring of hostile capitalist powers is a preposterously unreal one. It is a picture which could only be found convincing by people whose desires and fears combined to allow them to cherish any illusion which helped them to believe that communism in Britain was impossible.

One other form of this objection is sometimes raised. It is suggested that even though it is extremely probable that a communist Britain will not arise until most of the rest of Europe is also in the hands of the workers, and is thus in a position to form, with Russia, a self-supporting unit, the British Navy would be used by the British capitalists to blockade the coasts of Britain, prevent food supplies from reaching her, and so either starve to death the population of her great cities, or, if necessary, bombard them into submission. It is probable that less will be heard of this objection after the revelation of the true spirit of the British sailors at Invergordon in the autumn of 1931. It is quite clear that it would be utterly impossible to order British seamen to intercept food ships bound for British ports and so starve to death their own countrymen, including their own wives and children. Still less could they be induced to lay waste British coastal cities by bombardment.[1]

As a matter of fact, the real and urgent task which faces the revolutionary movement in Britain is to keep up with the forward surge of development which Communist parties the world over are experiencing as a result of the present crisis (1932) in capitalism. There is visible no danger of the British workers making such rapid progress as to become, materially or psychologically, ready to take power before the workers elsewhere are able to give them such assistance as will secure for them supplies essential to the maintenance of their power. This is not in any way to reflect on the intelligence and courage of the British workers, which will, we may be confident, in the end prove to be second to none. It is not to subscribe by implication to any absurd doctrine of there being an inherent incompatibility between communism and the psychology of Britons. It is merely another way of repeating that the crisis in capitalism is as yet less grave in Britain than it is in many other parts of the world. When the British workers find themselves at last face to face with the same inescapable realities which, for example, the German workers are beginning to face to-day, they will, it is safe to prophesy, show themselves not less, but (because of their high level of development) more ready and active to take the road of their salvation. In the meanwhile, during the period when the

---

[1] The theorists of the British Independent Labour Party now use simple and direct appeals to funk as their chief anti-revolutionary propaganda. They tell us that revolution is now utterly impossible because of the nature of modern armaments. Thus a speaker at a 1932 I.L.P. Summer School told his audience that revolution was for ever impossible in Great Britain because power was now concentrated in the hands of the air force. And the air force could easily bomb "camps of the unemployed" out of existence. Why, in a revolutionary situation, the unemployed should go camping was not explained. And in the case of the bombing of cities, it may be asked how the pilots of the air force are to pick out revolutionaries as their targets from a height of ten thousand feet.

Actually modern developments in the technique of warfare have probably not affected the balance of class forces one way or the other. It is quite true that to-day no workers' revolution can hope to succeed unless it receives the aid of the workers in the armed forces of the State. But then this has been true for the last two hundred years, at least. The most cursory examination of all previous revolutions will show that their success has always been due to the disaffection of the workers in the ranks of the armed forces of the established order.

vast remaining resources of British imperialism still make Britain one of the strongest links in the capitalist chain, the task of British workers is not to worry as to what would happen in the quite impossible event of their getting power before the workers of Europe were in a position to prevent their destruction by a vengeful world capitalism. Their task is to see to it, by every means in their power, that they are strong enough to prevent British capitalism from destroying those workers' dictatorships which will certainly be established elsewhere in the coming years. Nor indeed is this a question of the future. It is an urgently necessary task of to-day for which it is essential to mobilize the whole strength of the British working class. At the present moment, British capitalism is helping, as actively as its jealousy of Japan, its bickerings with France, and its fear of America will allow it, to suppress the Chinese Soviets, and to egg on Japan to attack the Soviet Union. To hamper and if possible to prevent action of this sort is an immediate task for the British workers. They must see to it by their present efforts that when the time for them to take power does come, there will be workers' Governments puissant to aid them both in Asia and in Europe.

The second great objection to the possibility of communist success, and this objection is raised not only by the British capitalist class, but by the capitalist classes of all the Western powers, is that in contradistinction to Russia, the capitalist classes of the West are so overwhelmingly strong in numbers, wealth, intelligence, skill, and power of organization, that the workers have no chance against them. Let us consider these supposed qualities of our capitalist classes. They are said to be, compared to the Russian capitalist class, extremely numerous. This is undeniable. But then the working class of the Western powers is also, compared to the Russian working class in 1917, extremely numerous. As a matter of fact, the proportion between the two classes is probably just about the same in the two areas. And, needless to say, it is the proportion alone which is relevant to the argument.

Again, we are told that the Western capitalist classes are far richer than was the Russian. Hence, they can command vastly greater resources both of propaganda and of intimidation; moreover, they can make expensive concessions to the workers if they ever find themselves temporarily in a tight place. In the first place, this difference of the greater wealth, and therefore power, of the capitalist classes of the West compared to the same classes in pre-1917 Russia, applies to their respective working classes to an equal degree. The Western workers, also, can command resources—by reason of their universal literacy for example—which were totally closed to the Russians. It may be objected with some force, however, that this factor at any rate is not merely a question of the relative strength and wealth of the two classes. For while the wealth of the capitalist classes of the Western states increases their strength for the purposes of class conflict in direct ratio, the higher standards of the Western working classes, as compared to the Russian workers in 1917, may weaken, if not their strength, at any rate their will for the same purpose. Hence, while it is quite unreal to suggest that the higher standards of both of the opposed classes in the West is an absolute gain to the capitalist class yet it may be agreed that it has on this account some net gain. And, in fact, the workers have usually been able to take power at times and places where the material strength of both sides has been low: while capitalism has been strongest where the standard of life both of the workers and capitalist class has been high. An important qualification immediately arises, however. The worker's urge to struggle is not so much a question of any absolute standard of life, as of sudden changes in his standard. A sudden drop in the worker's standard of life is naturally always accompanied by a sharp increase of class antagonism: interestingly enough, however, a sudden increase of standards—more especially in the case of the increase being due, not to a rise in wage-rates, but to a temporary absorption of the unemployed into industry (owing to a war, let us say)—may also increase class antagonism. And this latter case, which can be easily substantiated historically (cf. conditions in the last stages of the war in Great Britain and for that matter in Russia) shows clearly the limited character of the advantage to the capitalist class of a high standard of life for the working class.

But the main criticism of the claim that the Western capitalist class is unassailably strong, even if we discount the foregoing qualifications altogether, is that its strength and wealth is visibly, obviously, and now rapidly, declining. Again, of course, this process has not gone anything like so far in Great Britain as in Germany or Central Europe, for example. But one has only to compare either the income or the capital possessed to-day by the capitalist class of all the capitalist states, with what it possessed as lately as 1929, to realize the magnitude of the fall. We shall be told no doubt that this is only temporary: that the slump will soon be over and that then everything will be normal again. Well, that may, or may not, be true. It is quite possible that the present conditions of acute crisis will pass: for if they do not, then in the opinion of leading capitalist authorities, from the Governor of the Bank of England downwards, world capitalism will cause such appalling misery to the workers as to produce immediate and decisive revolt.[1] Let us suppose for a moment that the best hopes of the capitalist world are realized, and that the present crisis is overcome. Even in that event, it seems most unlikely that any boom comparable in magnitude, duration or stability to the period 1924-1929 will recur. The 1924-1929 boom itself was far less general, secure and vigorous than were the great pre-war booms of the heyday of capitalism. (In fact, in Great Britain, it was considered to be merely the mitigation of permanent depression.) In the same way it seems clear, from the amount of permanent and irreparable damage that this slump has already done to world capitalism, from the extent to which it has forced all the great states to disrupt the world free market, and from the degree to which it has sharpened imperialist antagonisms, that the next boom period, if it comes, will be comparatively short, patchy, hectic and unstable. In general, one may venture to prophesy that with the progressive break up of a unified world market, possessing a unified currency based on gold, or any other objective standard, the quality of "patchiness" in capitalist booms will become especially pronounced. Thus, we are probably entering a period in which, say, Great Britain will be enjoying a boom and, say, America will be in deep depression (or vice versa), while, in a third country, capitalism will have so disintegrated as to have driven the workers to take power. And not only will future booms, if any, be patchy as between country and country: they will be patchy as between industry and industry in the same country. To demonstrate the gross intensification of the political instability of world capitalism which

[1] Mr. Montagu Norman, the Governor of the Bank of England, in one of his more dramatic moments, prophesied that this would happen. His remark, however, was probably only made in an effort to impress the Americans and the French, in order to induce them to do what he told them.

such conditions will produce would be to recapitulate the main argument of preceding chapters. It is clear that such conditions will create, on the one hand, the greatest possible disproportions between different branches of production, leading to world-wide economic catastrophes which will make the present (1931-193?) slump look like a period of stable prosperity: and, on the other hand, will vastly exacerbate every imperialist antagonism and so speed up the coming of war. Moreover, the efforts at readjustment which capitalism will be forced to attempt in order to overcome these more violent crises must themselves become more and more violent. Unheard-of wage-cuts, the wholesale abolition of social services, the iron repression of mass agitation, desperate attempts to crush the resistance of colonial peoples to intensified exploitation, will become the order of the day. In general, then, we may say that while there may be further periods of capitalist boom, they will have the characteristics which the philosopher Hobbes attributed to the life of primitive man—they will be nasty, brutish and short.

There does not seem to be room for doubt that, neglecting the periodic ups and downs of the trade cycle, the whole trend of the wealth, and consequently of the strength, of the capitalist classes of the West is steeply downwards. Although it may be true that they are, in certain exceptionally favoured spots, such as Great Britain, still too strong to be overthrown by the workers, they will not long remain so. For the ruling classes of the West to pin their hopes of defeating the workers upon the fact that their wealth is incomparably greater than that of the Russian ruling class in 1917, is to rely on a wasting asset. Truly, the workers are not likely to achieve power in those places where the capitalist class is still very rich and strong: but then in one country after another the capitalist class is becoming progressively poorer and weaker.

There is one further factor which qualifies the power of the capitalist classes of the West. Their internal unity is by no means complete. What these classes now need for their self-preservation is an iron conservatism. But some sections of these classes, the intelligentsia and salariat in particular, have long traditions of liberalism. These sections of the capitalist class are unfitted to enter upon the policy of repressive violence, which their class interest now urgently requires. It is true that up to a point these individuals unconsciously play a part very useful to the main mass of capitalist conservatism. For the propaganda of liberal, pacifist and equalitarian ideas, which they maintain, serves to cover up the otherwise naked reaction of the policy of all capitalist Governments to-day.

As, however, the situation grows more desperate, such a smoke-screen of liberalism may well become more of an embarrassment than an assistance to the governing class. For it hampers that freedom of swift and ruthless action which a hard-pressed class requires. Then dawns the day of what we have called the advocates of action—the Mussolinis, the Churchills and the Hitlers. The "liberal-minded statesmen," the "enlightened intellectuals," the whole paraphernalia of constitutionalism, are bundled off the stage. It is at this point, when the final struggle approaches, when the economic situation has become desperate beyond anything which we in Great Britain have guessed at, that the Western capitalist class will begin seriously to lose its cohesion. Some of those sections which possess long liberal traditions will simply oppose the new fascistic methods, without facing the fact that the only alternative to their employment is a surrender of power to a working class dictatorship. Such liberal opposition may to a significant extent, hamper the forces of the capitalist class. Another and much smaller section of the ruling class, faced at last with inescapable choice, will break away entirely and throw in its lot with the working class. Marx defined this process very clearly, as early as 1848.

"Finally," he wrote, "when the class war is about to be fought to a finish, disintegration of the ruling class and the old order of society becomes so active, so acute, that a small part of the ruling class breaks away to make common cause with the revolutionary class, the class which holds the future in its hands. Just as in former days, part of the nobility went over to the bourgeoisie, so now part of the bourgeoisie goes over to the proletariat. Especially does this happen in the case of some of the bourgeois ideologues, who have achieved a theoretical understanding of the historical movement as a whole." [1]

(Incidentally, the last sentence of Marx sums up almost the whole duty of the honest intellectual of to-day. His duty is to master "the historical movement as a whole." If he does so he can have no pos-

[1] *The Communist Manifesto.*

sible doubt as to the necessity of throwing in his lot with the workers.)

The third "fatal" objection to the success of communism in Britain is, we are told, the "psychology" of the British workers. Stripped of a mass of quite meaningless nonsense about "the national psychology," this objection is an appeal to the fact—and it is a fact—that sections of the British workers have been strongly infected with a capitalist point of view. (There is nothing in the least peculiar to Britain about this phenomenon: it has occurred in America, in Holland, in Sweden, wherever, in fact, capitalism has been until quite recently fairly successful and prosperous. And the capitalist classes of such countries have solemnly assured themselves that "their" workers—their good-hearted British, Dutch, Swedish or American workers—have a heaven-sent immunity from the communist bacillus.) Now this third objection is obviously consequential upon the second. The permeation of strata of the British workers by a capitalist point of view is simply an expression of the wealth and strength which the British capitalists have hitherto enjoyed. And it is clear that if this wealth declines, so also will its former owners' hold upon the workers' minds. It is worth while, however, to examine the basis of the present degree of capitalist control over the workers' psychology. The permeation of the workers by capitalist ideas is effected in several ways. The essential basis is an ability to give some sections of the workers a taste of middle-class economic security and sufficiency. American capitalism probably did this in the years between 1923 and 1929 to the greatest extent. A locomotive engineer (or as we in Britain would say an engine driver) on, say the Pennsylvania Railroad, a plumber, or any building trade craftsman in New York City, really did in those years enjoy the standard of living of a distinctly successful retail tradesman in Great Britain.

Moreover, at an earlier stage, American capitalism was unrivalled at providing the second instrument for promoting a capitalist point of view amongst the workers: it actually did offer a certain significant number of opportunities for the workers to make money, leave their class and become fully fledged American property-owners, living by virtue of their ownership of the means of production. But although American capitalism exhibited both these characteristics to an unrivalled degree, it never exhibited them for so long a period or so consistently as did British capitalism. The British railway engine driver may never have owned a motor-car; but he may have been in the apparently secure possession of the basic necessities of middle-class comfort—a satisfactory house, ample food, good clothes, some pocket-money—for the whole of his life—and he may remember that his father, who was also an engine driver before him, had the same good fortune. In other words, British capitalism by reason of the immense super-profits of its empire was able to maintain in comparative comfort a "labour aristocracy" of skilled workers for several generations. And in its earlier period, it provided enough examples of workers rising into the ranks of the property-owning class seriously to affect the minds of the whole working class. Moreover, British capitalism kept up until very recently yet another method by which the most active and intelligent workers were systematically "declassed." It possessed a comparatively well-developed educational ladder, by which the cleverest sons of workers could climb to a higher education by means of scholarships, and then be absorbed into administrative posts (the Civil Service) or become teachers or technicians. The rungs of this ladder are now being cut away, however, by the educational axe. Moreover, the number of administrative and technical posts open to this class of candidate is now rapidly decreasing, with the contraction of British industry and the difficulties of British imperialism, involving the surrender of administrative posts to the native middle class. These characteristics of a given capitalism are the indispensable basis for a capitalist point of view amongst sections of the workers: but upon this basis the ruling class seeks to build a whole variety of institutions designed to confirm and spread its ideas. The same wealth which allows the capitalists to maintain a labour aristocracy in comfort enables them to organize all sorts of institutions for controlling the minds of the rest of the working class. Thus a whole section of the Press grows up, the function of which is to cater for the tastes and aspirations of the slum workers, tastes which capitalism itself has so brutally restricted. Every form of gambling—in Britain predominantly betting on horse-racing—is organized on the scale of a national industry: or, for unfortunate workers of more earnest tastes, "missions" of all sorts, religious, educational, and charitable are sent down to the slums: and now the great twin weapons of the cinema and the wireless are unsparingly used.

In general, we may conclude that these efforts at the permeation of the workers will not lack some success, so long as the capitalist class which is using them remains rich and powerful. But so soon as its wealth declines, so must its ability to maintain these mental controls over its workers. In the end, therefore, this third "fatal objection" to the success of communism in Britain, or in any of the Western capitalist States, boils down to a repetition of the fact that Western capitalism will not be overthrown so long as it remains rich, strong and successful. Let us admit this most readily. For the whole point at issue is the question of whether it is in fact possible for these national capitalisms to remain rich, strong and successful. The first half of this book was devoted to a demonstration which (it is submitted) drove us to the conclusion that the national capitalisms of the West could not in the nature of things permanently arrest their present decline. Hence, the capitalist point of view which is held by, for example, some sections of the British workers, and which at first sight does appear a formidable obstacle to the success of communism in Britain, will disappear, is indeed now disappearing, with great rapidity. For the economic basis of imperial super-profits by which it has alone been possible for the British ruling class to maintain it, is now also in progressive disintegration. (One factor which tends to maintain the hold of the capitalists over the workers' brains, is the efforts of the social democratic functionaries, whose role it is to perform just this service to the governing class. Even they, however, will not indefinitely be able to make the bricks of a capitalist point of view in the workers' minds, without the straw of a share of capitalist super-profits in the workers' pockets.)

We can now attempt a general estimate of the weight which should be attached to these three "fatal objections" to the success of communism in Great Britain. For while we have, it is submitted, shown the relative and temporary character of these objections, which the British capitalists naturally delude themselves into supposing are absolute and eternal, we are not for a moment denying that they exist. What has been shown, it is suggested, is that all three objections, the objection that "Britain cannot feed herself," the objection of the overwhelming power of the British capitalist class compared to the Russian capitalist class, and finally the objection of the capitalist psychology of the British workers, are all objections based on conditions which are more or less rapidly disappearing. A thing, however, must exist in order for it to be possible to disappear. Hence, these conditions certainly do to some extent exist to-day. We must ask, therefore, that most crucial and most difficult question, which we posed earlier in these pages—the quantitative question of "How long?" How long for example will these objections to the success of communism in Britain persist to a significant degree?

He would be no better than a charlatan who would pretend to give any precise answer to such a question. It has been one of the arguments of these pages that the general trend of human development has at last come within the range of human cognition: that we are at last beginning to know enough about the past to be able to produce the historic curve of events for a little distance into the future, with a margin of error not too great to make it useless to come to certain conclusions of a general character. (And there is no room for doubt that the refusal of all the theorists of the capitalist class to do so, has nothing whatever to do with the scientific caution which they profess, but is dependent upon the painful nature of the conclusions to which any serious appraisal of the facts would drive them.) But this does not mean that our knowledge is yet adequate for any but broad and general conclusions about the future.

Let us first give the fullest possible weight to the factors of strength in the capitalist position. There exists in Britain, no doubt, a certain tradition of social intercourse between the classes which, while it is in many respects markedly inferior to that of France or America, is very different from anything which was known in pre-war Russia or Germany. The long-continued expansion and the incomparable stability of British capitalism ever since 1850 have undoubtedly established traditions of class collaboration which are only gradually being broken down by the repeated shocks of the present governing class offensive against the workers. Such transitory, but still noticeable, social phenomena as these allow the members of the British capitalist class, fixing their eyes resolutely on these purely local British conditions, to convince themselves that the communist position, while perhaps strong in theory, has no application to Britain. Conditions such as these allow those trusted allies of the British capitalists, the members of the British Labour party, to convince themselves that communist methods are useless for the purpose of appealing to British workers. And, in truth, if we concentrated our attention on the internal situation of Great Britain, on the balance of class forces within her shores; on the present psychology of her workers; on the abilities of her ruling class; on the obstructive strength of her social democracy; on the shifts and devices still open to all those who desire to maintain the rule of the capitalist class, we might be disposed to agree that the task before the British communist movement was very formidable, and that success must be long postponed.

But to confine our appraisal to the internal situation, though it is a common error even amongst genuine sympathizers with the workers' cause, leads to an estimate of the prospects of British communism totally at variance with reality. For we must never forget for one moment that British communism is part of a world-wide movement, the successes, or failures, of any part of which quickly react upon the prospect of all its other parts: and that British capitalism is, to a degree unparalleled by any other national capitalism, intertwined at a thousand vital points with the capitalism of the whole world. Thus, when we raise our eyes from our island, the shores of which have too often marked the limits of vision for British social theorists, the scene changes. If the British people were an independent isolated community inhabiting a little planet of their own (and yet, by some magical process, able to draw their present imperial tribute), then the rule of the British capitalists might not have reached by many years its inevitable term: by a mixture of class collaboration where that was possible, and of the unflinching repression of the workers (which British rulers have always known very well how to use when they had to) their days of privilege might have continued for some time yet.

How different is the real situation. Britain is but an island in a sea which encompasses the whole world. No special providence reserves for her a peculiar destiny. On the contrary, her immense imperial possessions, scattered in every quarter of the globe, make it certain that her fate will be especially dependent upon that of the rest of the world. And when we shift our appraisal to the prospects of communism and of capitalism on the world stage, a different picture presents itself to our eyes. Only in a few exceptional areas do we find anything at all comparable to the economic conditions which have allowed of the comparatively pacific class relationships which we discover in Britain. On the contrary, we find in area after area of the earth's surface a political situation dissimilar to that of Britain. We find that in such areas the capitalist class has not now, nor ever has had, sufficient wealth to impose its outlook upon considerable sections of the workers; that it has had neither the skill in collaboration nor the decision in repression, which has characterized the social policy of the British ruling class; that a dozen different political complications have forbidden the capitalist classes of such areas to devote themselves to the task of controlling their workers; that in many areas, as in the colonies of the great empires, the capitalist class is largely of another race and colour from the workers.

Those possibilities of subtle and imperceptible social re-adjustments which seem so real in Britain are utterly out of the question in most of the rest of the world, and consequently communist theory and communist methods are the only ones which apply to the social conditions of nine-tenths of the inhabited globe. And if this is the case, then we may be assured that in a very short while they will apply also to such countries as Great Britain. Britain has her own history and consequently her own peculiar characteristics: but if we suppose that she will be allowed to work out her destiny in isolation, unaffected by the events which are unfolding themselves in the rest of the world, then we delude ourselves. The truth is rather that Britain is quite peculiarly vulnerable to the reactions of events which may take place at the other side of the globe. Her whole economy is based to an unparalleled degree upon profits drawn from the exploitation of her Empire. Colonial revolts already menace essential parts of her system. The social reactions which are bound to follow the crash of the high-piled pyramid of her super-profits, may well be especially violent and sudden. If communist theory and practice is the only possible policy for the working class of the world as a whole, then it is the only possible policy for the workers of Great Britain also.

CHAPTER XXI

THE SALVATION OF THE BRITISH PEOPLE

IF British governing class opinion, in its restless search for reasurance, enormously overestimates the difference between the social conditions of Britain and those of the rest of the world, there is no need for us, on that account, to deny the individual and proper characteristics which Great Britain does possess. Nothing is more foolish than to deny the importance of such national characteristics. Lenin realized this truth very clearly, for he wrote that "the national and state differences now existing between peoples and countries, will continue to exist for a very long time, even after the realization of the proletarian dictatorship on a world scale." "The abolition of national peculiarities is," he added, "at the present moment a foolish dream."

And certainly the British, if only because they live in an island, have their full share of national peculiarities. Nor would it be natural if some of their own peculiar characteristics were not charged for them with a deep emotional content. For men form profound emotional ties with familiar surroundings; with, above all, the surroundings which were theirs in childhood. And this is the drop of truth which lies at the bottom of that most horribly polluted of all wells: the well of patriotic emotion.

Now it is often said, and more often felt, that communism necessarily flouts and outrages those deep emotions of personal identification with their nation which most men feel. It would indeed be a heavy handicap to communism if this were to be the case. Fortunately for the cause of the working class, the truth is very different. The truth, which, as the crisis in capitalism deepens will become inescapably apparent to everyone; which will break through the most passionate efforts at suppression by the ruling class, is that it is capitalist imperialism which outrages, ravages and despoils the motherland of every race of men in turn; and that it is communism alone which can bring national liberation to the peoples of the earth. We have but to glance either at the history of the last few decades, or at the present world situation, to substantiate both halves of this statement. Who can deny, for example, that capitalism is to-day trampling upon the patriotism of a dozen peoples? It is true that at the same time it seeks to excite for its own purposes a horrible parody of patriotism, a repulsive spirit of jingoistic aggression, in the peoples of the great predatory empires. These empires, however, have no relation whatever to nationality. The Hindu is asked to fight and to die for the Petition of Right, and is assisted to do so by the Bengal Ordinances; the Filipino must swear loyalty to the Declaration of Independence, lest he dream of separation from the United States; and the Senegalee stands sentinel upon the ramparts of Metz, the better to enforce the immortal principles of 1789. But if capitalism attempts to whip up a jingo fervour in the nameless, shapeless conglomerations of nations and races which have been herded together to form the great empires of to-day, it has no answer but the bomb, the tank and the bayonet for the patriotism of subject peoples. If the children of Confucius show signs of succeeding in their hard task of recreating a united China, the imperialists of the world are quick to show them that the love of country is a characteristic to be stamped out by wholesale massacre, if it happens to interfere with capitalism's search for markets.[1] Nor is patriotism always permissible even to white races. If Germany, for example, aspires ever again to be anything but a subject people her only hope of success, every French statesman of the last ten years has made it clear, is to resort to arms. And capitalism can never hope for respite from this desperate struggle with the forces of subject nationalism. For the very basis of modern capitalism, without which great empires, such as the British, could not exist for a single day,

[1] "Wholesale massacre" is the actual phrase used by the Shanghai correspondent of the London *Times* (who is warmly sympathetic to Japan) to describe what happened in Shanghai in January 1932. This journalist has a particularly clear view of the function which workers should perform in capitalist wars. Thus in his message of February 17th, 1932, he tells us that "intelligent elements" in China (i.e., Chinese capitalists) consider "that China has nothing to lose and much to gain by a policy of military resistance.... For this reason the Chinese are prepared to go on fighting and retiring indefinitely, losing little that matters much in this agricultural and over-populated country." Or again we can take the description of their own action by the Japanese capitalists themselves. Thus Admiral Shiozawa told the *New York Times* in an interview of Japan's "merciful intent" and promised "only two more days of indiscriminate bombing of civilians."

is super-profits derived from the exploitation of colonial and subject peoples.

Let us never forget, moreover, the part played by love of country in the first great victory of communism: in the freeing of the soil of Russia from the invading expeditions of half the world. For it is hardly too much to say that it was the spectacle of the Russian courtiers, generals, landowners, capitalists and merchants, of the very men who had made patriotism their special monopoly, invading Russia in a desperate attempt to recover their profits, often at the head of foreign troops, and always using foreign bullets with which to shoot down their fellow countrymen, that finally rallied the overwhelming mass of the Russian people to fight for a communism which had become the cause of their national liberation.

To-day we find the same process repeating itself in Germany. Side by side with the ever-growing revolt of the German workers against the German ruling class, there exists a mighty, if as yet deluded, revolt of all exploited Germans against the subjection of their fatherland to alien domination. This natural and just indignation has been canalized by the German fascists. But the very success of the Nazis is already on the point of exposing the hollowness of the claim of Hitler and his lieutenants to be able to deliver Germany from her foreign exploiters. For Hitler's paymasters are, in fact, that group of German capitalists who demand a bigger compensation for themselves as the price of their co-operation with France and England in an anti-Soviet *bloc*. The Nazi movement is intended by them as an immense piece of *chantage* by means of which German capital may be re-admitted to participation in the markets of the world on equal terms. But they have no real intention of pushing matters to the point of a war of national liberation. (This, though, is not to deny the possibility of the Nazi rank and file getting out of hand.) Accordingly, as the time of Hitler's participation in the Government of Germany draws near, all his thundering menaces to the foreigners die away, as they needs must, at the sight of a French bayonet. They are replaced by the most banal appeals— far less dignified, far more grovelling, than those of previous German Governments—for a little respite from the stranglehold of Versailles. Sooner or later, this fact must become apparent to the German people: sooner rather than later they will learn the lesson that there is no possibility of German liberation from the foreign yoke so long as capitalism exists in the Reich. Then they will be shown by the undeniable evidence of events themselves that it is the German communists, and the German communists alone, who can effect the national liberation of Germany. For they alone dare to invoke the only force which can shatter the Treaty of Versailles, the force of the workers united in struggle against international capitalism.

Nor are these lessons, which Russia has taught, and Germany is teaching, without interest to us all. They seem to show that communism has often conquered, when it becomes apparent that the workers of any nation are the sole remaining force which can deliver their fatherland from the intolerable servitude which foreign capital imposes upon all subject peoples. By one of the most profound of those paradoxes with which the history of humanity abounds, communism, which is in essence international, finds a natural and powerful ally in the spirit of national liberation. Capitalism, still mouthing its jingo sentiments, sees itself wrecked at last by the love of country of simple men and women.

Nor is the paradox difficult to understand. For capitalism in its early stage of development pushed the principle of political nationalism to its very limits. The cause of the self-determination of all nations became, since this was the best method of destroying the semi-feudal empires, the cause of the capitalist class. The process reached its apogee with the Balkanization of Europe in 1919. Yet all the time that capitalism was politically splitting up the world into fragments, the economic necessities of large-scale mechanized production more and more required the welding of the world into vast economic units. Thus capitalism involves hypernationalist politics combined with supernational economics. Capitalism is now carving the world up into great monopolistic empires, each with a ring of satellite petty States. And in doing so it must trample without so much as a thought on the national sentiments and loyalties of a hundred peoples. Communism, however, goes to work in an opposite manner. Just because communism recognizes the technical necessity of a complete internationalization of the economic life of the world: because it rejects utterly the capitalist attempt to cut up the world into warring imperial zones, because it leads the workers to the only possible solution, namely, a comprehensive world union of Soviet Republics: just because of this, communism can, and does, dare to allow and indeed foster the most complete cultural, and educational nationalism. Communism is able to do so, because it can achieve the welfare of the workers of the industrial areas of the world, by their own productive power and not by the exploitation of the peoples of undeveloped areas. Here, again, we see that the welfare of different peoples is mutually compatible, while their power is not. Communism, thus, provides an objective basis for co-operation instead of conflict between the peoples of the world.

Nor is this a mere theoretical claim. Even the most bitter enemies of the Soviet Union do not deny that its "national policies," the treatment, that is, of the former subject peoples of the Russian Empire, are one of its incontestable successes. Where the Tzarist empire had to repress, and that violently, a score of subject peoples, the Soviet Union has been able actually to encourage the national self-consciousness of every ethnic group within its borders. The culturally advanced Ukrainian, and the nomadic illiterate Uzbek are alike free to develop their national heritage, both of culture and of national resources, to the utmost possible limit. Nor has this been a matter of the mere freeing of these peoples from a burden of exploitation. Positive action of the most energetic kind has been taken to assist these peoples to make good their lack of economic development. Huge sums of money have been invested in providing the basis of local industries in these national republics. For it would be little use to talk of the liberation of national cultures, if the material basis for any kind of culture was not provided. It would be sheer hypocrisy to suggest that the Ukrainian or the Uzbek was "free" to develop his culture, if, in fact, a lack of industrial equipment meant that he had to toil sixteen hours a day. The liberation of Ukrainian culture, for example, will be effected quite as much by the power which is just beginning to flow from Dnieperstroy dam, as by the right to teach Ukrainian in the schools of Kiev.

What has been possible over a sixth of the world's surface will certainly be possible wherever the workers take power. A Soviet Germany, and a Soviet Central Europe, can alone solve the problems of nationalism which are to-day dragging these ancient centres of civilization back into barbarism. Western capitalism will founder on its inability to produce any solution for the national problems of Europe. Considerable elements from classes usually hostile to communism will be driven at the hour of crisis to support it, as the only hope of salvation for their fatherland.[1]

We see plainly this conjunction of the forces of communism and of nationalism in the case of colonial peoples such as the Chinese and the Bengalese; or in the case of despoiled peoples such as the Germans. In these instances there is a conjunction of the revolt of the workers against the capitalist class and the revolt of subject nations, as a whole, against the predatory empires. And it is clear, that this conjunction of forces is first taking place, in these instances. But how, it may be asked, can such a coalition of the revolt of the workers, and of a movement of national salvation, take place in one of the great dominant empires of the world? How can such a thing occur in Great Britain, for example? There is no foreign capitalist class holding down the British people. No intolerable load of foreign debt hangs around their necks. Their capitalists are still on balance creditors, who can afford to dole out to them a pittance from their imperial tribute, not debtors compelled to demand that the British workers should starve in order to help them to meet their liabilities to foreign capital. All this has been hitherto of substantial truth: and it is another factor which accounts for the slowly developing consciousness of the working class in Britain. But in this case also we must put the question, how long will it remain true? For error itself is often a dying truth; and the truth of Britain's dominant position in the world is already sick unto death. The prospect of the conquest of Britain by a rival capitalist empire, of her reduction to the status of a subject people, and the extortion from her of a Reparations tribute may seem remote. Yet there undeniably exists an immediate prospect of British imperialism being compelled to engage in a struggle, growing ever more desperate, at first with the forces of colonial revolt, and then with a rival empire, or with a coalition of rival empires, who will see their own growing strength mirrored in her growing weakness.

---

[1] It must not be supposed that communists consider that the existence of separate national cultures, separate languages and the like, will be a feature of fully developed world communism. Such phenomena belong to the present, not to the ultimate, stage of human development. It is clear that man will in the end tire of the inconvenient idiosyncrasies of locality, and will wish to pool the cultural heritage of the human race in a world synthesis. Communism, however, recognizes that the path to such a world synthesis lies through the encouragement of the fullest development of those national cultures which capitalist imperialism seeks to repress.

390 THE COMING STRUGGLE FOR POWER

The struggle of the British Empire against colonial revolt has indeed long ago begun. In India the effort at compromise, even with those not very uncompromising patriots the Indian capitalists, has, for the moment at any rate, broken down. Britain is now relying upon two things alone in India: the high-explosive bomb and an alliance with extreme reactionary feudalists. Every Indian prince and rajah is now, it is clear, to be propped upon his throne by very little else than British bayonets and bombs. And that this is a conscious and well-thought-out policy is made evident by the address of the British Viceroy, Lord Willingdon, to the Chamber of Indian Princes on March 28th, 1932. Lord Willingdon defined his "duty as representing the Crown" to the Indian Princes, as follows:

"The Viceroy," he said, "has the duty of maintaining to the States the absolute security of their rights and privileges which have been assured to them under their treaties, *sanads,* and engagements, and, if necessity arises, to give protection to any ruler."

This then is the new and frank definition of Britain's role in India. British high-explosives are to protect against their starving subjects the privileges and persons of some of the most decadent and extravagant tyrants left anywhere in the world. She is to maintain by the terror of the death-dealing inventions of the year 1932, the squalor, want, dirt, disease and injustice of the Europe of the year 1000, over areas almost as large. She is to support and encourage everything corrupt, rotten and outworn; to stifle, to extirpate with bomb and tank, everything young, growing, vital and progressive which shows itself anywhere on the soil of India.

For only so can be maintained that exploitation of the Indian workers and peasants which forms the greatest part of the imperial tribute upon which British capitalism is to-day entirely dependent. We saw in previous chapters that British capitalism was turning towards an attempt to intensify its colonial exploitations at whatever risk. Hence, it must fight to the death against the growth of any forces in India, or in its other colonies, which might become capable of resisting exploitation. Moreover, since British capitalism is now wholly dependent upon the exploitation of colonial peoples, the cause of the liberation of these peoples is identical with the cause of the British workers in their struggle for the overthrow of capitalism. Their enslavement is maintained principally by means of the proceeds of the exploitation of the peasants and workers of India. Their liberation is dependent upon the liberation of the colonial peoples. Again, the only possible solution for the problem of the relations between Britain and her subject peoples lies through the overthrow of British capitalism. Then, and not till then, the workers of Britain will be able genuinely to co-operate with the workers and peasants of India and Africa. A British Soviet régime, as one of the most advanced and industrialized units in a growing federation of Soviet republics, will take its share, in economic co-operation with the workers and peasants of India and Africa in the same way in which the comparatively advanced districts of Russia proper are now co-operating with the former subject races of the Tzarist empire. Britain will be able to devote some of her immense productive resources to the export of capital goods of every kind to India and other undeveloped parts of the world, in return for imports which she needs. To-day, British capitalists draw their wealth from the exploitation of these areas. To-morrow, the British workers will find continuous employment, at the occupations at which they have unrivalled skill, in co-operating with the former subject peoples of all the capitalist empires, in the development of their own industries.

British support for the Indian Princes is perhaps the most extreme case of the manner in which the British Empire is driven, by its need to screw up the process of exploitation, to rely solely upon the forces of reaction, and to fight desperately against all the forces of progress, everywhere in the world. (The British role in China has been and is exactly similar.) If the analysis of the world situation which we have submitted in earlier chapters has any validity, this process must grow more and more pronounced. An empire on the defensive must always find its allies amongst the friends of what is, or of what has been, all over the world. This is the immediate prospect which British imperialism holds out as a field for the exhibition of British patriotism. If we wish our country to become the universal agent of the force of black reaction, of superstition, of prejudice, of every old, possessing, frightened and reactionary class on earth, then we can feel that we are serving our country by serving her present rulers: but not otherwise.

The repression of incipient colonial revolt is, as yet, a fairly simple matter. As yet, it is true, all that is asked of the British armed forces is to disperse a few frontier tribesmen round Peshawar with well-aimed bombing attacks:[1] to shoot down a few of the more determined of the Congress supporters in Bombay: to send a few battalions to prevent that gentleman whom we knew in London as "Mr. A" and who is now the Maharajah of Kashmir, from being deposed by his subjects; to round up a few helpless and starving savages in Burma; or to provide a base, well protected by British cruisers and battalions, for Japan's "errand of mercy" by means of "only two days of indiscriminate bombing of civilians," in Shanghai. Such deeds as these will call forth in old-fashioned English men and women, whose patriotism has not adapted itself to the needs of imperialism, a feeling of nausea rather than of pride. But admittedly they entail very little danger or risk to the British nation. Sooner or later, however, our imperialists will have to call on the British people to fight against very different enemies. Sooner rather than later, as we have sought to show, British imperialism, forced by its economic necessities to drive forward ever more strongly along the path of an exclusive, aggressive and violent policy, must come into collision with one of the other great empires of the world. Britain is at once the richest empire and the most vulnerable to attack. She is a huge treasure-ship, carrying an increasingly obsolete armament, sailing through an impoverished world. Such voyages have seldom ended well.

[1] The Peshawar correspondent of the London *Observer* gives us an account of the routine adopted by the British Air Force in India. In his message of April 10th, 1932, he writes: "An account of how the R.A.F. carry out these bombing operations is of interest. The pilots of the bombers each carry an aerial photograph of the country with the specified targets clearly marked on them. These photographs are about eight inches square, are very clear, and the target is marked with a circle. The bombing machines carry 230-lb. and 112-lb. bombs, and the fuses are arranged according to the nature of the target so that they penetrate before bursting. Twenty-pound bombs are also carried, and are used as 'sighters.'

"Raids are carried out by Squadrons in a series of flights. These flights, which consist of three planes each, leave the base at half-hour intervals, so that not only is the bombing continuous, but the enemy cannot tell from which direction to expect the bombing nor the particular planes which are going to bomb next. During one day (the 11th) the R.A.F. from Kohat carried out more than two complete squadron raids, and the planes from Risalpur completed three squadron raids, obtaining over seven tons of direct hits. It is interesting to note that some of these planes are the Hawker-Hart type, with which some of the squadrons of the R.A.F. are now being equipped.

"The aeroplanes carrying out these raids bombed their targets from a height of 3,000 ft., and the very good results obtained have once again proved the value of this arm of the Service."

The one alternative open to the British imperialists is to forestall the outbreak of war with a rival empire by leading a joint attack upon the Soviet Union. And it is certain that they will make a determined effort to palliate inter-imperial rivalries sufficiently to make possible such a combined attack. It is impossible to believe, however, that these rivalries can be sufficiently appeased to secure a whole-hearted united front, even against Russia. The outbreak of war between, for example, Great Britain and Russia would certainly be used by other imperialist powers to encroach on British preserves. For the revolutionary action of the British workers which would certainly challenge a British attack upon Russia from the outset, would reveal a condition of internal weakness, which would be extremely tempting to her enemies. In general, we may say that although the next world war will very probably begin by an attack on Russia, this attack will certainly be the signal for the outbreak of violence both within and between the other imperialist powers.

In any event, there will then be no question of the bombing of helpless Indian tribesmen. If British imperialism is allowed to run its course, a war, the horror of which we know nothing, except that it will almost certainly exceed our wildest imaginings, will fall upon the British people. It would be a war in which, for the reasons which we have already discussed, the chances of victory for Britain would be small and remote. In any case, whatever the fortunes of war might be, it would be very improbable that at all a high percentage of the population of these islands would survive such a conflict. However formidable were the armed forces of Britain by sea, land and air (and they might well be very formidable), the position of the British civil population would be vulnerable in the extreme. They would be exposed to the double menace of repeated aerial bombardment with gas and incendiary bombs from bases upon the European continent, and to the still worse menace of the interruption of their food supplies, for it is most improbable that Britain would again be able to clear the seas of hostile warships and submarines, or the air above the sea of seaplanes. Even if resounding victories were being won by British admirals and generals, British men and women would certainly be perishing wholesale, some by fire, some by gas, some by starvation.

Moreover, is there much chance that the British governing class, marvellously adroit and intelligent as it still is for the purposes of politics, could produce leaders who would be successful in the extremely technical business of modern war? Even in the last war, when the degree of mechanization was incomparably lower, the anti-scientific, anti-theoretical type of mind which is produced by the British public schools began to show grave defects. British officers had muddled through so often before that they supposed that they could muddle through the entrenchments on either bank of the Somme. Instead, they hung up the bodies of whole army corps —of a whole generation—of their fellow countrymen to rot on the German wire. In some respects, Britain has never yet recovered from the effects of that slaughter. How can there be any hope that she would survive the infinitely greater carnage towards which her imperialists are infallibly leading her? There is only one thing which can possibly save her: there exists only one force which can draw her back from the abyss into which she seems foredoomed to plunge. And that is the organized force of her workers, awakened to the necessity of overthrowing once and for all the rule of the capitalist class and taking power into their own hands.

And so after all the question of national liberation and salvation is raised no less acutely by the workers' struggle for power in Britain, than it is elsewhere. For which will exhibit a true love of his country, the Englishman who follows blindly where his present rulers are leading; who follows them till they have taken his country to certain destruction, or he who joins with that advance guard of the British working class which has already realized that the only possible future for Britain is as a free Republic of an at first European, and later world-wide, Union of Soviet Republics? Such a future cannot indeed be assured without a struggle. In their struggle for communism, however, the workers of Britain will find trusty allies in the workers of all the world. Moreover, the amount of violence involved by even the greatest social upheavals, by the seizure of power by the French middle class in 1789, or by the Russian workers in 1917, has always been infinitesimal compared to the devastations of the wars of capitalism.

It would be false to pretend that there was any path forward which could relieve the British workers of efforts and sacrifices. Their choice is not between violence and peace. History has not even raised the possibility of universal harmony. And if the workers, misled by the disingenuous pacifism of social democracy, were to deny themselves the right to fight for their existence, they would find that all they had accomplished was to give free rein to the imperialists who will inevitably plunge the world into universal war. For if men hesitate before the task of achieving a new civilization; if they draw back because no new order of society can be born without violent conflict, they will not achieve an epoch of peaceful stability. The alternative to the violence entailed by the lifting of human life to a new level is the violence entailed by the decline of human society, the break-up of such world civilization as exists, the dawn of a new dark age of perpetual conflict. It is not given to men to stand still upon the path of history. Forward or back is their only alternative. Nor will either road be smooth. The road forward, however, is infinitely the less beset by violence and suffering.

The sufferings, for example, which the workers will have to undergo in order to establish and maintain their rule in Britain, will be incomparably smaller than those which face them as the inevitable consequence of deciding once again to fight their masters' battles for them. And these are the sole alternatives before them. Instead of fighting, and that vainly, as they must if they remain under the leadership of their imperialists, to preserve all that is worst in the world, they will fight, if they fight for themselves, to secure a new epoch in the history of mankind. Their struggles will ensure that Britain takes a leading part, as befits her workers' high degree of development, in the establishment of communism, instead of playing the shameful role of the protectress of universal reaction. And the struggle for communism can surely be won by the workers of Britain, unshakably allied to the workers of all the world. There is no force on earth which can long prevent the workers of the world from building a new and stable civilization for themselves upon the basis of the common ownership of the means of production. Nor is there anything in the geographical, industrial, cultural, or economic position of Great Britain which forbids the British workers from taking a decisive part in the establishment of world communism. The realization of this new stage in the history of mankind is not in doubt. But the immediate future of all humanity rests in no small degree in the hands of the workers of Great Britain.

A NOTE

ON AMERICAN EVENTS SINCE THE FIRST
PUBLICATION OF THIS BOOK

OF the reviews which the American Press gave to this book, when it appeared in February 1933, the shortest, and one of the most critical, was in many respects the most striking. This notice appeared in June 1933 in a journal called "The Chicagoan." Its author informed us that he was "a little out of step with the writers on economics, social trends and class interests." Nor, he added playfully, was he sorry for this, for the writers had themselves got out of step with events. "The bookish boys were getting pretty hopeless about everything. It's too bad, though, that a book so soundly conceived and ably written as the present volume should break upon the rock of unforeseeable good fortune."

The reviewer, in spite of his somewhat idiosyncratic methods of expression, raises an important issue. Is it true that the prospect of an inevitable and oncoming struggle for power has been averted? Now it should be fairly generally agreed that the prospect of both social and international struggle could only have been averted if a way had been found by which the present economic system (i.e., Capitalism) could have been made to work with comparative harmony and stability. And it was, no doubt, the belief that a way to achieve just this had been found in America by President Roosevelt which inspired the strictures of "The Chicagoan's" reviewer. I, for one, could bear those strictures very easily, if indeed it could be shown that Mr. Roosevelt, or anyone else, had found the gateway to a new era of harmonious social progress. Who would not willingly see his book "break" if what broke it was "the rock of unforeseeable good fortune"?

When, therefore, we attempt, as we must, to assess the events of the year 1933, we shall all feel the strongest temptation to believe that they have unexpectedly revealed the possibility of a new period of expanding civilization, social harmony, and international peace upon the basis of a readjusted capitalism.

It is this hope which makes the whole world follow Mr. Roosevelt's New Deal with almost breathless attention.

For the present condition of by far the larger part of the population of the world is so desperate that if their ills cannot be relieved within the capitalist system then certainly, and whatever may be the cost, they must be relieved by the overthrow of that system.

That vast numbers of earnest men and women will make up their minds on this overwhelmingly important issue according to their experience of the results of the New Deal, is evidently realized by those who pin their faith to the reform of Capitalism. Mr. John Maynard Keynes, who may be regarded as the leading world theorist of the reform of Capitalism, begins his survey of the New Deal with these words:

"Mr. Roosevelt has made himself the trustee of those in every country who seek to mend the evils of our condition by reasoned experiment within the frame-work of the existing social system. If he fails, rational change will be gravely prejudiced throughout the world, leaving orthodoxy and revolution to fight it out."

(*London Times,* Jan. 2nd, 1934.)

Nothing less than this hangs upon the success or failure of the policies of the American Administration.

It would, however, be naive to suppose that it will be possible at some spectacular moment of the future suddenly to assess the New Deal as a completed whole and declare it either a triumph or a catastrophe. History is seldom as simple or as clear cut as that. The present policies of the American Government are still unfolding and, no doubt, will continue to unfold. Nor are they by any means so completely discontinuous with the policies of previous administrations as is often supposed. Again, many other factors, mainly without the control of the President, such as the international situation, will profoundly affect the question of recovery, and so complicate any final assessment of the effect of the New Deal itself. Above all, an extensive governmental policy such as Mr. Roosevelt's has differing reactions upon the different groups or classes which make up the modern social structure. The New Deal may prove itself a purgatory for one class and a paradise for another.

The crucial question of success or failure *for whom* will insist on presenting itself.

Hence we must not suppose that the New Deal offers to us the prospect of an automatic answer to our social doubts. We cannot sit back in complacent agnosticism, quiescent in the belief that in a little while it will be irrevocably and undeniably clear that this decisive attempt to reform and reconstruct the Capitalist system has either failed or succeeded. On the contrary, the success or failure of the New Deal will itself be as hotly debated an issue as was ever the original proposition of the possibility or impossibility of reforming Capitalism. For even if, as I believe it must, the New Deal "fails," in the sense that it will never give to the vast majority of the American people tolerable conditions of life, it may well for a time at any rate, succeed in giving a very great deal to particular interests and persons. Moreover, as these interests and persons are likely to be amongst the most influential and vocal in the community, success—for them—may be vigorously hailed as success—in itself.

It is necessary to attempt to restate briefly why those who subscribe to that analysis of human society which is known as Dialectical Materialism consider it certain that this admittedly decisive attempt to reform Capitalism cannot succeed: cannot avert, that is, that period of international and social struggle which unreformed world capitalism is so visibly precipitating.

At the same time, I am conscious that for many American and English readers the mere mention of a theory will have prejudiced their minds. Nothing is more striking in all the eulogies of Mr. Roosevelt, in the apologetics of the New Deal, than the triumphant repudiation of the view that the President or his advisers are guided by any consistent body of knowledge or reasoning. His undoubted and unbounded empiricism and experimentalism are hailed as his greatest claim to support. These qualities are scathingly contrasted with both the "hide-bound" theories of the orthodox Capitalist economists and, above all, with the "pedantry," "rigid dogmatism," and "absurd theorizing" of the Marxists.

This is a remarkable situation. For what, after all, is a theory? Is it not an attempt to summarize in some applicable form such knowledge of the past as men have hitherto been able to gather? The theory, or "law," of supply and demand, for example, attempts to formulate the observed fact that the price of a commodity tends to rise with a fall of supply and an increase of demand, and conversely. But what, we may ask, is the value of such a theory to "the practical man" engaged in the art of government? Simply that a knowledge of it will enable him to foretell, *without going through the laborious and costly process of trial and error,* that the price of a commodity will, for example, fall if he increases the supply and leaves the demand constant. The example is absurdly simplified. But is there not an analogy in it which is applicable to the present situation? May it not prove that Mr. Roosevelt's scornful rejection of the theories—the accumulated and organized experience, that is —of both the capitalist and working-class economists, and his jubilant reliance on empiricism, will result, merely, in compelling him to go through an unparalleled process of trial and error? At the end of the process, the doctors of the "New Deal" may have rediscovered some of the simpler theories of economics: but the American people will have paid a stupendous price for their education.

Let us first summarize the reasons which lead the soundest school of Capitalist economists to express their lack of confidence in the New Deal: The essential feature of the whole New Deal is the attempt at a general stabilization of the economic system. In turn the essential feature of a policy of general stabilization is the attempt to create a permanently stable price level: the attempt, as Mr. Roosevelt puts it, to create a dollar which shall have a permanently stable purchasing power over the years, the decades, and even the centuries. Beside this overwhelmingly important objective, the other features of the New Deal are but secondary. Indeed, the codification of industry, the attempt to regulate agricultural production, the attempt at the revival of loan expenditure, through both public and private agencies, are clearly but additional efforts to secure the great aim of stable prosperity. And the sign and condition of a stable economy is taken to be a stable price level.

The most penetrating school of Capitalist economists themselves deny, however, that a permanently stable price level is possible. They assert that to attempt to obtain it can only result in gravely accentuating the violence of boom and slump. The argument is in essence simple. The attempt to issue sufficient money and credit to balance the production of goods and services, the attempt "to gear money to production," as Professor Irving Fisher, the spiritual father of the New Deal economists, puts it, and thus maintain a permanently stable price level, ignores a vital element in the situation. It ignores the fact that in modern conditions, the real costs of production are continually dropping, owing to unceasing technical improvements in the methods of production. Hence, if you keep prices stable by monetary means, while costs are steadily dropping, you will create an ever-widening gap between costs and prices. What can fill this gap? Profits. Profits are precisely the gap between costs and prices. Hence a policy of stabilizing the general price level will produce an ever-augmenting volume of general profits throughout industry.

But the appearance of ever-growing and general profits, far from stabilizing your economic system, will create all the conditions for a new boom of unprecedented dimensions. Anybody who can borrow enough money to start production will be assured of a profit: a wild, anarchic rush to produce anything and everything will result. Soon all the conditions which produced the last crash will have reappeared, though in an aggravated form. The new crash will follow. Hence, say the Capitalist economists, the only possible way of preserving stability in modern conditions of technical progress is to allow the price level to fall in proportion as the costs of production fall. For only so will the force of competition between producers be allowed to operate, will profits be made by the more efficient producers alone, proportion between the different branches of production be preserved, and a stable economic system, though not a stable price level, be achieved. (This is only the first point of the criticism of the Capitalist economists. The rest of their argument is concerned with the relationship between industries producing goods for the consumer and industries producing goods for other producers. See Chapters IV and V of this book.) For a convenient summary of these views the reader is referred to *"Purchasing Power and the Price Level"* by E. F. M. Durbin.

If this argument is accepted, we can begin to understand the horror with which the soundest Capitalist economists look upon the present policies of the American Administration. For if a stable price level is what Mr. Roosevelt and his advisers want in theory, what they are at present trying to achieve in practice is a rapidly rising price level. It is clear that in so far as they do achieve it they will create unprecedented general profits in industry which will rapidly throw the whole economic system out of gear again. They are heading *via* a new, much more hectic, much shorter boom to a much more severe crisis.

What view do the Marxists take of these predictions of the Capitalist economists? They do not deny their accuracy as far as they go. But they do not consider that as a contribution to an analysis of the crisis they go very far.

In the first place, it is worth while to observe that the Capitalist economists' alternative of allowing the deflation of prices to continue almost unchecked had been tried, and tried exhaustively, by Mr. Hoover and had led straight to the collapse of March 1933. Hence it does not look as if all that was wrong with Capitalism was that misguided persons such as Mr. Roosevelt interfered with the system's otherwise harmonious working. Indeed, however much we may agree that any revival achieved by the monetary means which Mr. Roosevelt had adopted will be short-lived and must be achieved at the cost of increasing the instability of the system, yet we cannot agree that he had any alternative open to him. In the condition to which American Capitalism had reduced itself by March 1933 the application of the monetary drug was inevitable and essential to survival. We may, therefore, comprehend the impatience with which Mr. Roosevelt has brushed aside those of his advisers (such as Professor Sprague) who warned him that his drug would have a permanently bad effect on his patient's constitution. "Maybe," the President must have been tempted to reply, "but at present the patient is *in articulo mortis:* if we do not give him the inflationary pick-me-up he will soon have no constitution which we can either damage or preserve: he will be dead."

The truth is that Capitalism has now reached a situation in which no "sound" policies are open to it. In order to keep going at all, it must adopt expedients which intensify its most fatal characteristics. In particular, in order to survive at all, it must try to create new booms. It is useless for Capitalist economists to point out that these booms will be followed by new and far worse slumps. *Carpe diem* must needs be the motto of the latter day statesmen of Capitalism. Their lives will certainly be short, so they may as well try to make them merry.

For in reality the symptoms of crisis which the Capitalist economists observe are but secondary effects of the deep-rooted disease from which the system suffers to-day. All the complicated "disequilibria" which these economists so painstakingly, and, so far as they go, accurately, describe, those "distortions of the structure of production," those maladjustments between the rate of savings and the rate of investment, those divergencies between the "natural" and the actual rate of interest, those "sticky" or "specific" factors of production, those social "rigidities," are all but the effects of one fundamental "distortion" in the system. And that fatal distortion is in the last analysis the simple and undeniable fact that Capitalism is ever more powerfully piling up wealth at one end of the social scale and poverty at the other. This is the palpable, visible fact, and no "proofs" by the "equilibrium" economists that this need not be so, and no statistics from the hack politicians about the "distribution of property" can alter it.

It may be possible by this device or that, by redistributory taxation and doles as in Britain, or by attempts to set wage minima as in America, to offset this overwhelming drive towards the concentration of wealth, to a certain limited extent and for a certain limited period. But these are but little delaying dams set against a flood tide. Through boom and through slump the process goes on. One mighty monopolist eats a hundred puny competitors, a vast wave of unemployment devours the petty investments of the artisans, one new process of production brings limitless profits to a handful of shareholders, and ruin to a whole category of workers and technicians.

Is it to be wondered at that the system jams? The remorseless law of the concentration of capital is everywhere at work. It seizes the very policies, such as the New Deal, which were intended to remedy the devastation it had wrought, and makes use of them to accelerate its march. Uncounted billions of capital, the counterpart of the uncounted millions of the unemployed, pile up in the hands of the capitalist class. How are these billions to be used? How are they, that is to say, to be invested, and invested at a profit? How are they to be turned into new factories, fields and mines which shall produce and sell at a profit new streams of commodities? For the millions of the unemployed can only be set to work building the new factories, etc., if it is profitable to build them. But how can it be profitable to build new factories when the goods produced by the existing factories cannot be sold except at a loss? This problem may sometimes be solved temporarily by so raising the price level by inflation that paper profits reappear upon that portion of the products of the existing factories as are still being sold. But who can doubt that if the Capitalists are thus tempted into investment again, into building new factories, that is to say, by these delusive paper profits, they will soon find that they have once more choked the market and made it unprofitable again by the new stream of commodities which will issue from the new factories as soon as they are finished?

What escape can there be from this dilemma? Does it not lead to the conclusion that, while Capitalism is an effective system for the process of industrializing a continent, for creating the fundamental means of production, the mines, the railways, and the power stations, it is not a workable system for the purpose of distributing the products of those means of production once they have been created?

But does this conclusion exhaust the last possibility before the system? Clearly it does not—or rather, it only does so if we think of Capitalism as what the economists call "a closed system," as a system which cannot reach out into other and as yet non-capitalist or semi-capitalist areas. Such an assumption would still be, of course, unreal. There is an evident possibility for the profitable investment of the vast hoarded surpluses of the American Capitalists, for example: but that possibility does not lie in America. It lies in China, in South America, in Africa, in all the undeveloped parts of the world which still lack industrialization.

There, and there alone, can adequate profits still be won. But if this is true of American Capitalism, it is also true of every other Capitalism—of British, of French, of German, of Japanese Capitalism. And the simple question of the hour is the question—which of the Capitalist groups shall win the right to invest their surpluses at a profit in the few remaining undeveloped areas of the world? This question is answered by the sword alone.

These, very briefly, are the reasons which compel the conclusion that, alas, no "unforeseeable good fortune" has intervened to avert the prospects of that struggle which stood before the world a year and a half ago.

The New Deal, this decisive attempt to reform and stabilize the Capitalist system, will fail completely and absolutely if it is judged by the criterion of whether it makes the system either more equitable or more stable. On the contrary, if its inflationary side is pushed hard enough to produce all-round profits in industry again, it will create first an extreme boom and then an extreme slump. If monetary expansion is "soft pedalled," it will slowly re-create (as it is already doing) good profits for the great corporations, a speeding up of the concentration of wealth, and some temporary increase in general industrial production, but will utterly fail to deal with the ever-growing nightmare of mass unemployment. In either event, its permanent effect will be to make the system more inequitable and unstable than it has ever been before. The New Deal, in fact, formally marks the passing of American Capitalism into what is called the monopoly or imperialist phase.

What, then, is our prospect, if it is not one of unforeseeable good fortune? It is not possible for any rational man to see anything to comfort him in the prospect which Capitalist Imperialism offers to the human race to-day.

The social consequences of the unparalleled inequity and instability of latter-day Capitalism are already apparent. In order to maintain the fantastic injustice of the distribution of wealth which obtains in all modern Capitalist communities, in order to preserve the unexampled luxury of the few from the devouring want of the rest of the population, a new system of oppression has to be organized. Similarly, in order to snatch the ever-dwindling opportunities of profitable investment in undeveloped areas from equally hard-pressed rivals, a state of permanent semi-mobilization for war must be increasingly enforced. Gigantic armed forces must be maintained and, above all, the whole population must be psychologically prepared to fight in their masters' battles in the name of patriotism.

The name of the political régime which fulfils these two requirements of Capitalism in its present-day monopoly-imperialist form is, of course, fascism. And already the Capitalist world is predominately a fascist world. For once several important Capitalist powers have assumed this new and ultra-aggressive form their rivals cannot afford to lag behind. Already three important powers, Italy, Germany, and Japan, are organized under one form or another of fascism.

A fascist world is the true prospect which Capitalism holds out
to us. If we maintain the Capitalist system, there is no other possibility. What, then, would a fascist world be like? There is little
difficulty, at any rate for a European, in answering that question.
For Europe is to-day predominantly a fascist continent. Nor should
there be much need to remind the American reader of what Europe
is like to-day. This motherland of modern civilization is split up
into over twenty sovereign states, the great majority of them maintaining the power of the Capitalist class by an open and ruthless
dictatorship. Trade is stifled by an almost incredible system of
tariffs, quotas, licences, and controls: Censorships are maintained
over every form of human thought and expression. Some fascist
states impose heavy penalties on those who doubt the superstitions
of the Middle Ages; some compel conformity to the new, far more
barbarous, and far less beautiful "racial" myths of the twentieth
century. Science, art, and letters must necessarily and are visibly
languishing; spiritual despair and material want are alike seizing
the intellectual classes. Each and every one of these fascist states
suffers from incurable and violent economic disorders; its workers
are decimated by unemployment, its peasantry is crushed by taxation and by debt. In each the state finances are in disorder, the
budget is unbalanced, the public debt is growing greater and
greater. But this does not prevent each state from piling ever higher
and higher a fantastic mountain of armaments, of conscripting more
millions of its young men, of imposing yet heavier taxation to
build more and more warships, tanks, gas containers, and bombers.
For each can see that a new war is very close.

Such is the reality of fascist Europe. It is a reality which is
already nothing less than the first stage in the break-up of Western
civilization into a new dark age of barbarism. Nor would a fascist
world be anything other than a fascist Europe on a gigantic scale.

This is the bitter world in which we live: this is the character of
our epoch. This, and no cosy dream of a reformed, organized, stable
system presided over by a smiling and democratic President, is the
sole prospect of Capitalist Imperialism.

If we look at the world as a whole, and at the decades, and not
at the years, we shall not be able to delude ourselves any longer.
Western civilization, the civilization built up upon the system of
the private ownership of the means of production, the civilization

of Europe and America, is in full decline. Unless we can free ourselves from the embrace of dying Capitalism there is no help or
hope for our generation.

Unquestionably the American people are destined to play an
historic part in the vast issues of our century. The very fact that
the definitive attempt to reform Capitalism has been undertaken in
America is of good augury. Just as in the nineteenth century social
issues found their clearest and sharpest expression in France, so
to-day they are most directly presented in America. America is the
land of the highest development of Capitalism, and so of the
highest development of the contradictions of Capitalism. Here,
above all, the issues are inescapable.

The American people are, of course, bound to exhaust all the possibilities of the system before they overthrow it. They are doing so
with unparalleled rapidity. Only one more possibility remains after
the inflation of the New Deal has run its course: and that last possibility is extreme imperialism.

This bloody road, too, must no doubt be travelled. But as each of
the concluding scenes of the last act of the tragedy of Capitalism
is played out, more and more millions of the American people will
grasp the purport of the whole play. More and more millions of
Americans, with their characteristically direct approach to reality,
will see that they have only to take back the mighty instruments of
production, which they themselves have built, in order to break
for ever the chain of destiny which now imprisons them. They
have only to take the fields, the factories, the railroads, and the
mines from the tiny gang of millionaires which now controls them,
and apply them to their own use. They have ready to hand incomparable technical skill. They lack nothing on earth for the building
up of an incomparable civilization upon the American continent.
For them there is no question of undertaking the desperate, if
heroic, process of laying the foundations of the industrialization of
a continent—the task which the Russian workers are accomplishing.

Not the most embittered Capitalist can deny that there is literally
nothing to prevent the American people from producing and distributing *from to-morrow* sufficient goods and services to secure for
every single one of them an ample and secure standard of life: or
rather there is nothing except the vile tangle of worn-out social

relations in which their feet and hands—and alas, their heads also—
are enmeshed.

They have only to free themselves from the net of the private
profit-making ownership of the means of production, and to
organize production for use on the basis of communally owned
industry, agriculture, and transportation to realize their wealth.

Thus, and thus alone, may they leap from the kingdom of necessity into the kingdom of freedom.

April 1934.

36 Regent Square
   London.

INDEX